Fuel and Power

This is a very timely study of Russia's development into a global energy power from the Russian Revolution to the present day. Beginning in the late nineteenth century, Russia emerged not only as a key producer but also as one of the world's leading exporters of oil. Russia's transformation into a modern global power was connected to its ability to make use of its vast natural resources and produce energy in increasing quantities. While the development of Russia's energy industry went hand in hand with a profound socio-political and economic transformation, the book also tells the story of international cooperation and competition, transnational exchanges, and transborder interdependencies. Through energy exports, Russia shaped global energy flows and connections; at the same time, the growth of international trade impacted the views and decisions of Russian leaders, affecting the fabric of the country's foreign relations and, ultimately, the course of Russian history.

Jeronim Perović is Professor of Eastern European History in the University of Zurich's Department of History. He specialises in the history of Russia and the Soviet Union, as well as the history of the Balkans. He has previously held visiting scholarships at the Davis Center for Russian and Eurasian Studies at Harvard University, the Woodrow Wilson International Center for Scholars, and the Center for Russian, East European and Eurasian Studies at Stanford University. He is the author of several monographs, including *From Conquest to Deportation: The North Caucasus under Russian Rule* (2018), and the editor of several collected volumes, including *Cold War Energy: A Transnational History of Soviet Oil and Gas* (2017).

Fuel and Power

Energy, Trade, and Russian Foreign Relations from Lenin to Putin

Jeronim Perović
University of Zurich

CAMBRIDGE
UNIVERSITY PRESS

CAMBRIDGE
UNIVERSITY PRESS

Shaftesbury Road, Cambridge CB2 8EA, United Kingdom

One Liberty Plaza, 20th Floor, New York, NY 10006, USA

477 Williamstown Road, Port Melbourne, VIC 3207, Australia

314–321, 3rd Floor, Plot 3, Splendor Forum, Jasola District Centre, New Delhi – 110025, India

103 Penang Road, #05-06/07, Visioncrest Commercial, Singapore 238467

Cambridge University Press is part of Cambridge University Press & Assessment, a department of the University of Cambridge.

We share the University's mission to contribute to society through the pursuit of education, learning and research at the highest international levels of excellence.

www.cambridge.org
Information on this title: www.cambridge.org/9781009449106

DOI: 10.1017/9781009449090

First published 2024

A catalogue record for this publication is available from the British Library

A Cataloging-in-Publication data record for this book is available from the Library of Congress

ISBN 978-1-009-44910-6 Hardback
ISBN 978-1-009-44914-4 Paperback

Contents

Maps

Preface

This is a history of Russia told through the prism of energy, trade, and international relations. While this study takes a longitudinal view – from Lenin to Putin – the focus is on the later period of the Cold War, as it was from the late 1960s and throughout the 1970s that the Soviet Union and Western Europe became increasingly interdependent in the oil and gas trade. The reason such a relationship came about despite differing ideological and political positions is not immediately apparent. Countries such as West Germany, Italy, and France were eager to diversify their energy imports away from the Persian Gulf to enhance the security of their energy supplies. By importing ever-larger quantities of Soviet oil and gas, however, these countries made their economies dependent in a strategically important sector on a neighbour whose nuclear weapons were still pointed westwards.

Equally in need of explanation is the Soviet leadership's choice to allow this massive increase in trade and the consequent increase in interdependence. By concluding long-term economic agreements and creating an ever-expanding international energy transportation system, Moscow retreated from its long-standing principle of modernising and developing its economy, if not in isolation, then preferably without the risk of becoming too reliant on the capitalist-dominated world economy. In deciding to establish energy trade relations with countries beyond the Iron Curtain, the Soviet Union opted for close economic cooperation with Western European states that endured well beyond the end of the Cold War. At the same time, growing addiction to oil and gas rents led to the kind of structural distortions that have affected the Russian economy also after the collapse of the Soviet Union.

This book is mainly concerned with the Soviet perspective, seeking to understand the meanings that political leaders and decision-makers in Moscow have attached to natural resources and international trade, particularly in oil and gas, and why and how these meanings have changed over time. In so doing, it brings to the fore a history of energy and trade that has been treated as peripheral in the general literature.

Although the focus of this study is on the Soviet era and developments during the Cold War, this book traces Russia's trajectory from the early twentieth century up to Putin's war of aggression against Ukraine in 2022. With this war, the entire system of Russian–European economic relations as it has evolved over decades is undergoing profound changes, with geopolitical interests dominating the Russian leadership's agenda. In fact, this book evolved from a history of how Russia became Europe's key supplier of fossil fuels into a history of the rise and decline of Russian–European energy relations. Moreover, since Europe was Russia's most important trading partner and investor until the war, the disruption of economic ties will also impact the geographical parameters of Russia's external trade relations and contest Russia's future role as an international energy power.

Historians explore the past. But they are also subjects of their own time and place. Given Russia's aggressive behaviour and its use of energy as a political 'weapon' against those European states that support sanctions against Russia, the history of Russian–European economic relations is currently being viewed in a more critical light. 'Change through rapprochement' – the slogan that inspired Willy Brandt's *Ostpolitik* more than half a century ago, leading to a massive expansion of West German–Soviet trade relations – is now seen by some as naïve. But each period of history must be judged on its own merits. Oil and gas have repeatedly been the subject of economic conflicts and political tensions. At the same time, energy trade became the lubricant that fostered mutual trust across the Iron Curtain. It facilitated exchanges among politicians, trade representatives, and engineers and had an overall stabilising effect on political relations.

My interest in energy history was sparked in the early 2000s, when the global oil market experienced a massive price spike, helping Russia's beleaguered economy begin to recover from the deep slump of the crisis years of the 1990s. Studying these developments revealed to me not only how important it is to understand the history that underpins them but also how under-researched the field of Russian energy history was at the time. This research desideratum was the focus of my project 'Energy and Power: A Cultural History from the Early Soviet Era to Contemporary Russia', conducted at the University of Zurich in 2011–2017 and supported by the Swiss National Science Foundation.

During this project, I benefitted greatly from exchanges of views with Dunja Krempin, Felix Rehschuh, and Felix Frey. They all wrote pioneering studies on different aspects of the history of Soviet energy and technology as part of their dissertations, which I had the privilege of supervising. I would like to express my sincere thanks to all of them for reading and commenting on earlier drafts of the manuscript or individual chapters thereof. I would like to thank my colleague Viacheslav Nekrasov, with whom I have exchanged views on questions related to oil, gas, and pipelines in the late Soviet period. His assessments have enriched the content of this book. I would also like to thank Ellen Powell for editing and commenting on a first English version of the book manuscript and Trent Hancock for his careful copyediting of the final text.

The international conference 'Oil, Gas and Pipelines: New Perspectives on the Role of Soviet Energy During the Cold War', which we held at the University of Zurich in 2015, provided important impulses for my book project. This conference resulted in the edited volume *Cold War Energy: A Transnational History of Soviet Oil and Gas* (Cham: Palgrave Macmillan, 2017). I benefitted greatly from exchanges with participants during and after the conference. For this, I thank Margarita Balmaceda, Alain Beltran, Elisabetta Bini, Nada Boškovska, Roberto Cantoni, Nataliia Egorova, Falk Flade, Rüdiger Graf, Jussi Hanhimäki, Per Högselius, Niklas Jensen-Eriksen, Suvi Kansikas, Galina Koleva, Tom Koritschan, Dunja Krempin, Giacomo Luciani, Lorenz Lüthi, Viacheslav Nekrasov, David Painter, Tanja Penter, Felix Rehschuh, Oscar Sanchez-Sibony, Benjamin Schenk, Hans-Henning Schröder, Andreas Wenger, and Jean-Pierre Williot.

I was able to present early ideas and book excerpts on various occasions, including at a conference on the energy crisis of 1973–74 at the University of Potsdam (26–28 September 2013), at a conference on the energy history of Eastern Europe during the Cold War at the University of Tübingen (10 January 2014), at a research colloquium at the University of Regensburg (22 December 2016), at an event on energy history at the Università di Napoli (30 November 2017), as part of a lecture series on economic history at the University of Zurich (10 December 2018), and at a workshop at the European University Institute in Florence (27 September 2019). I would like to thank Elisabetta Bini, Frank Bösch, Alexander Etkind, Klaus Gestwa, Rüdiger Graf, Guido Hausmann, and Matthieu Leimgruber for inviting me to these events and for the fruitful discussions.

In writing the original manuscript, I drew on my previously published contributions on Russian energy history. I also made use of the lectures I gave at the University of Zurich in the autumn semesters of 2014 and 2020 and in the spring semester of 2023, as well as at the University of St Gallen in the autumn of 2017. The students' questions and comments encouraged me to rethink some of my ideas and to re-examine certain assertations, for which I am grateful.

This study represents a substantially revised and updated version of my German-language book *Rohstoffmacht Russland: Eine globale Energiegeschichte* (*Russia as a Natural Resource Power: A Global Energy History*, Vienna, Cologne: Böhlau, 2022). I have also added a short chapter ('Energy, Geopolitics, and War' [Chapter 6]) that looks at Russia's use of energy as a political 'weapon' in recent history and traces developments up to the start of Russia's war against Ukraine in 2022.

On the journey from the manuscript to the finished book, I received valuable assistance from the publisher. I would like to thank Michael Watson, Rosa Martin, and Anita Atkinson of Cambridge University Press for their excellent cooperation and the anonymous reviewers for their insightful feedback and constructive criticism, which helped to improve the quality of the final product.

This book would never have come about without the support of my wife, who has stood by me through this and many other projects. I dedicate this book to you, Franca, with love.

Abbreviations

ARCOS	All-Russian Co-operative Society Ltd.
BAM	Baikal-Amur Mainline (Russian: Baikalo-Amurskaia magistral')
BP	British Petroleum
CC	Central Committee (of the Communist Party of the Soviet Union)
CIA	Central Intelligence Agency
CIS	Commonwealth of Independent States
CMEA	Council for Mutual Economic Assistance
CNPC	China National Petroleum Corporation
CPSU	Communist Party of the Soviet Union
Cominform	Communist Information Bureau
ENI	Ente Nazionale Idrocarburi (English: National Hydrocarbons Board)
EU	European Union
FRG	Federal Republic of Germany
FSB	Federal Security Service (of the Russian Federation) (Russian: Federal'naia sluzhba bezopasnosti)
GDP	gross domestic product
GDR	German Democratic Republic
GOELRO	State Commission for the Electrification of Russia (Russian: Gosudarstvennaia komissiia po elektrifikatsii Rossii)
IEA	International Energy Agency
IMEMO	Institute for World Economy and International Relations (Russian: Institut mirovoi ekonomiki i mezhdunarodnykh otnoshenii)
LNG	liquefied natural gas
MFN	Most-Favoured-Nation
NATO	North Atlantic Treaty Organization

ÖMV	Österreichische Mineralölverwaltung Aktiengesellschaft (English: Austrian Mineral Oil Administration Stock Company)
OPEC	Organization of the Petroleum Exporting Countries
PSA	production sharing agreement
R.O.P.	Russian Oil Products Ltd.
RSFSR	Russian Soviet Federative Socialist Republic
SMEs	small and medium-sized enterprises
SMV	Sowjetische Mineralölverwaltung (English: Soviet Mineral Oil Administration)
SSR	Soviet Socialist Republic
USSR	Union of Soviet Socialist Republics

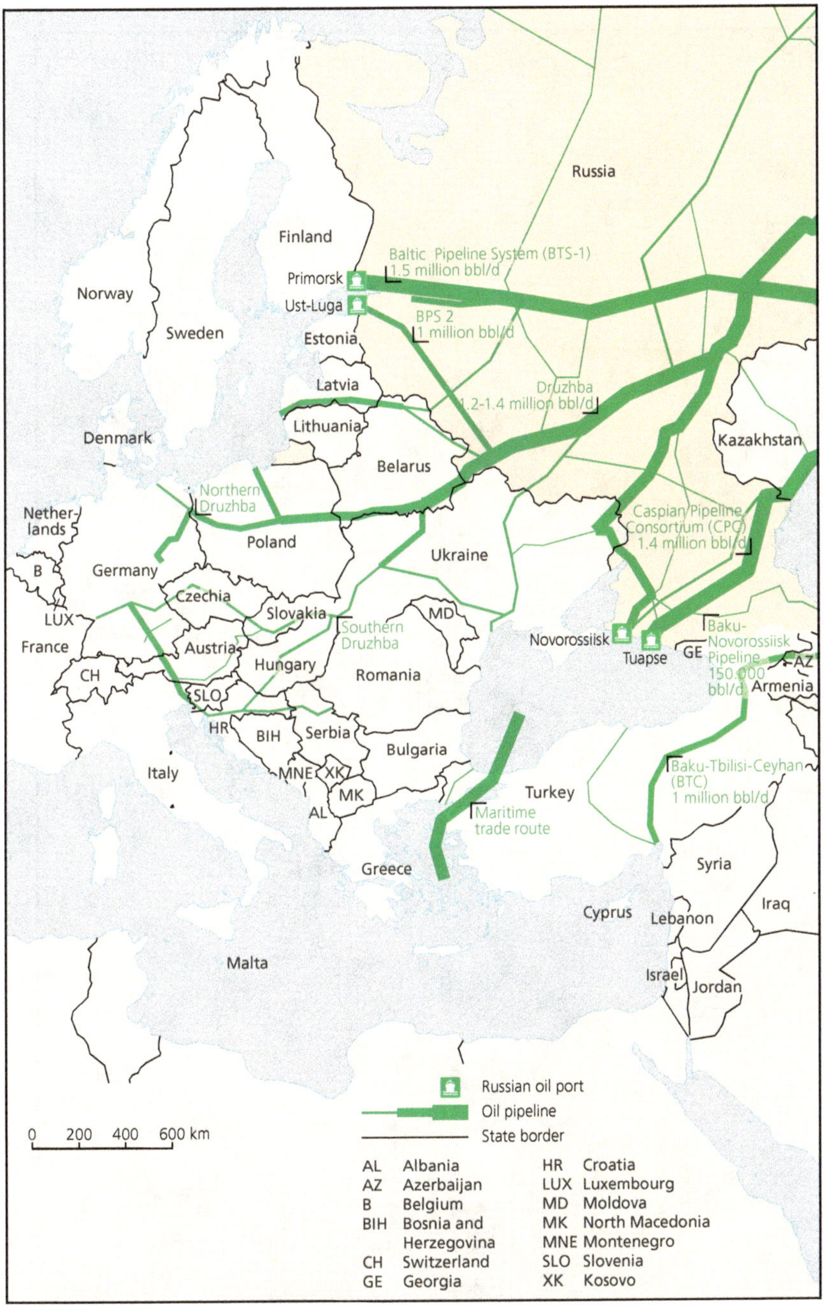

Map 1 Oil pipelines to Europe (as of February 2022)
Source: Cartography: S. Dutzmann Leipzig, 2023 © J. Perović

Map 2 Gas pipelines to Europe (as of February 2022)

Source: Gazprom (2021/2022) Cartography: S. Dutzmann Leipzig, 2023 © J. Perović

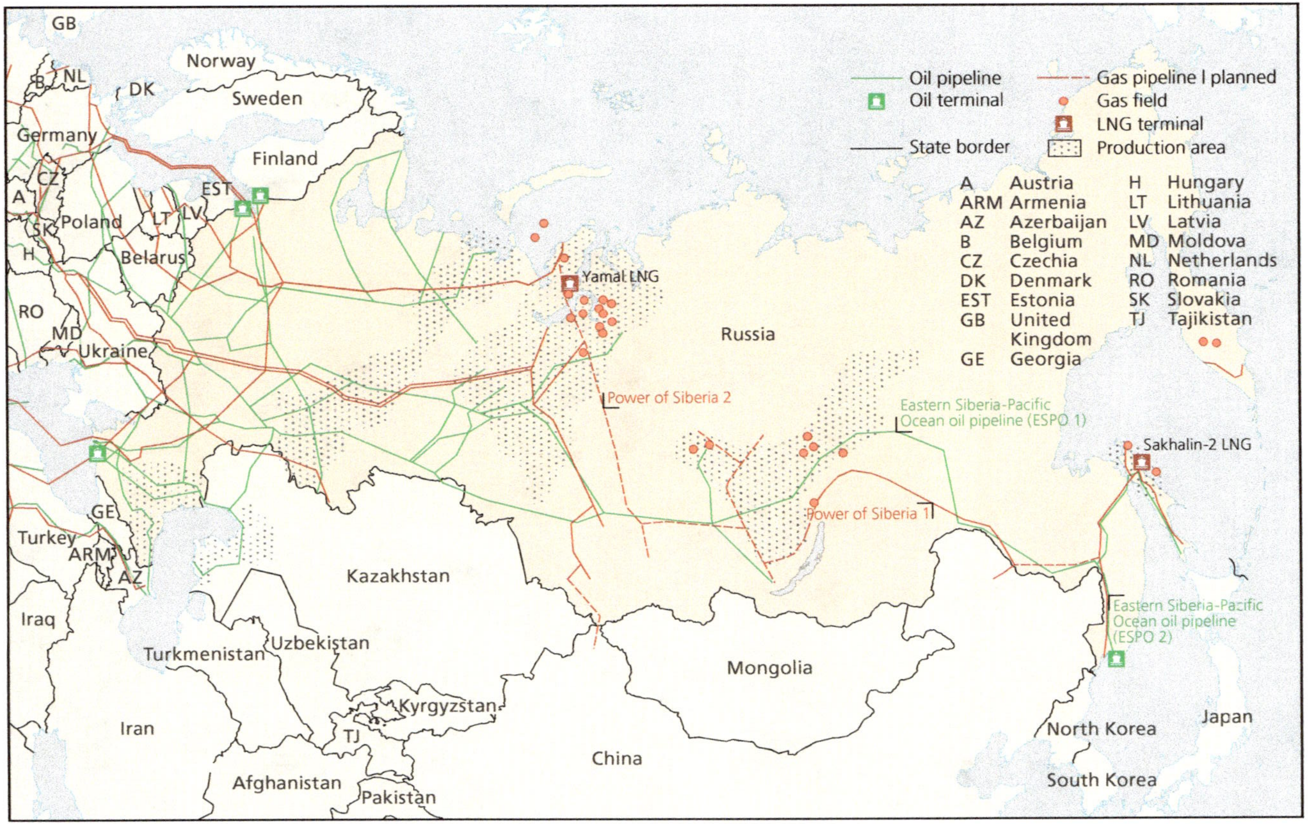

Map 3 Oil and gas transportation infrastructure (as of February 2022)
Source: Cartography: S. Dutzmann Leipzig, 2023 © J. Perović

Introduction

Energy is about flows. The availability of ever-larger quantities of energy has enabled civilisational progress, facilitating the transformation of rural communities into industrial and urban societies. Modernisation has gone hand in hand with the rise of energy networks: if rural communities are largely self-sufficient, relying on local energy sources, modern societies are dependent on increasingly complex production, transportation, and distribution networks that transcend local and national boundaries. During the twentieth century, it was oil that rose to become the elixir of modernity and mobility. Oil's strategic importance made it a key concern for governments around the world. Because oil reserves are unevenly distributed across the globe, securing sufficient supplies led to an unprecedented surge in trade and global connections as states and companies jockeyed for control over one of the world's most contested commodities.

This book is concerned with Russia's role in the global history of fossil fuels. As the world's largest storehouse for natural resources, Russia emerged not only as a major producer but also as one of the world's leading exporters of oil and other key commodities. Russia's transformation into a modern global power over the course of the twentieth century was connected to its ability to make use of its vast natural resources and produce energy in increasing quantities. While the development of Russia's energy industry went hand in hand with a profound socio-political and economic transformation, it also tells the story of international cooperation and competition, transnational exchanges, and transborder interdependencies. Through commodities' exports, Russia became part of global energy flows; at the same time, the growth of international trade impacted the views and decisions of Russian leaders, shaping the fabric of the country's foreign relations and, ultimately, the course of Russian history.

The precise form and intensity of Russia's outside economic engagement varied over time, but through all periods of its history, access to foreign capital, technology, and knowledge was key in harnessing the country's vast energy potential. Already Count Sergei Witte, finance minister and head of government under Russia's last tsar, Nicholas II, recognised that without foreign assistance, the country's enormous natural riches could not be exploited to the full. In his posthumously published memoirs, he aptly summarised Russia's core dilemma regarding the development of natural resources:

> The economic wealth and consequently the political strength of a country depend upon three factors: natural resources, capital and labour .... With regard to natural resources, Russia is extremely rich, although she is unfavourably situated because of the rigorous climate in many of her sections. In capital, that is, accumulated values, she is poor, for the reason that the history of the country is a continuous chain of wars, not to speak of other reasons. Considering her population, she is rich in physical labour and also in intellectual resources, for the Russians are a gifted, sensible, and God-fearing people.[1]

The three categories mentioned by Witte – natural resources, financial capital, and human capital – have been central to the country's economic development since the late nineteenth century. In the Caucasus, the engagement of Western companies such as the Nobel brothers (Branobel), Rothschild, and Shell helped to build a modern industry for the extraction and processing of oil but also an extensive infrastructure for its transportation via pipelines, a fleet of tankers, and a railway network. After the October Revolution of 1917, the Bolsheviks nationalised industry, expelled foreign entrepreneurs and banned private property. Yet the leaders of the Russian Revolution knew that the success of their great socialist transformation project would depend to a large extent on the pace of growth in the production of raw materials and the development of a modern energy industry. Lenin's famous 1920 slogan, 'Communism is Soviet power plus electrification of the whole country',[2] expressed a central social-utopian idea of Bolshevik imagined modernity, calling for backward Russia, its societies, and its landscapes to be transformed along the rational lines demanded by technology and the natural sciences.[3] The world's first socialist state could only be successful and powerful if it had a sufficiently large energy base.

[1] *The Memoirs of Count Witte: Translated from the Original Russian Manuscript and Edited by Abraham Yarmolinsky*, Garden City, NY, and Toronto: Doubleday, Page, and Company, 1921, p. 72.

[2] Lenin probably mentioned this exact sentence for the first time during a speech at the Moscow Governorates Conference of the Russian Communist Party on 21 November 1920: V. I. Lenin, *Collected Works*, vol. 31, Moscow: Progress, 1966, pp. 408–26, here p. 419.

[3] Dietrich Beyrau, 'Das bolschewistische Projekt als Utopie und soziale Praxis', in Wolfgang Hardtwig (ed.), *Utopie und politische Herrschaft im Europa der Zwischenkriegszeit*, Munich: Oldenburg, 2003, pp. 13–40, especially section 6 'Technikgläubigkeit und Standardisierung', pp. 33–36.

The Soviet leaders by no means wanted their country to become too intertwined with the capitalist-dominated world economy and thus dependent on it. But Lenin and his comrades-in-arms recognised already in the early 1920s that Soviet Russia would not be able to modernise and catch up without the support of the advanced Western capitalist powers. Therefore, the Bolshevik leadership sought to revive international trade, which had virtually ceased during the Russian Civil War, to generate foreign currency for the purchase of much-needed technology and equipment. The Bolsheviks granted concessions to foreign firms to help restore Russia's industry and were keen to continue the technical-economic cooperation with European and American companies that had begun under the tsars.

Oil occupied a special place in these modernisation efforts. Not only was it increasingly important for Russia's economic development, but it was also a commodity in growing demand on world markets. Although the Bolsheviks condemned the imperialists' greed for oil, they were aware of the economic importance of 'black gold': Oil burned more efficiently than coal, had a wider range of uses, and, because it was lighter than coal, it was also easier and cheaper to transport. During the First World War, it also became clear how important petroleum-derived fuel was in a mechanised war with mobile troops. In the 1920s, the Soviet Union's export of petroleum was still far from generating the returns it would in the late Soviet period. But oil was in such high demand worldwide that it could be sold to states hostile to the Bolsheviks and their communist ideology. Cheap oil from the East was simply too attractive to be kept off the world market, and not even the boycott attempts by Western oil companies could ultimately prevent the international triumph of Soviet oil.

In the 1930s, misguided investment policies left the Soviet Union with too little oil to meet foreign demand in the face of rapidly growing domestic consumption. Following Nazi Germany's attack on the Soviet Union and Hitler's efforts to seize the Caucasian oil fields, Soviet oil production plummeted. To fuel its tanks and aircraft during the war against Nazi Germany, the Soviet Union was therefore forced to import large quantities of American fuel under the US Lend-Lease programme. The wartime experience heightened the Soviet leadership's awareness of the importance of oil, and it was during the war that Stalin ordered the rapid development of a new oil-producing region – the so-called Second Baku – in the Volga-Urals.

In the 1950s, the Soviet Union again began to export oil to Europe in increasing quantities. But it was not until the 1970s, after the large natural gas fields of Western Siberia started to come on stream, that the country emerged as a major international energy power. Given the geographical remoteness and harsh climatic conditions, developing these new gas reserves posed a formidable technological and financial challenge. Indeed, much of Siberia's natural resources would probably have remained in the ground for several more decades had the Soviet Union not received billions of dollars in loans from Western European banking consortia to buy steel pipes and energy technology from abroad. Western companies entered into these big business deals because the Soviet Union held out the prospect of long-term supplies of raw materials in return.

The development of trade activities, encouraged by superpower détente in the late 1960s and early 1970s, was accompanied by the expansion of an ever-growing cross-border pipeline system. Notwithstanding US sanctions imposed under Reagan in 1981/1982, a first major export pipeline was completed in 1983, carrying gas from the enormous Urengoi field in northern Tyumen directly to West Germany and other Western European states. With the completion of this key energy infrastructure project, the Soviet Union became Europe's most important energy supplier – a position that Russia maintained and even expanded in the years following the break-up of the Soviet Union.

As the Soviet Union emerged as a major international energy power, it became increasingly dependent on global markets and prices. This meant that the country was exposed to price volatility and unpredictable fluctuations in supply and demand in the international energy market. With rising prices, trade with Western Europe appeared more and more attractive to the Soviet leadership. However, the foreign exchange earnings from the commodities business were used primarily to compensate for the inadequacies of a rigid and inefficient centrally planned economy. Moreover, despite the growing unsustainability of subsidised energy deliveries to the socialist states of Eastern Europe, Moscow continued to supply oil, gas, and other commodities to prop up the ailing economies of its communist allies. This often necessitated accepting inferior goods in exchange, all in the interest of maintaining the cohesion of the 'Eastern bloc'. But when world oil prices collapsed in the mid-1980s, the systemic deficiencies of the planned economy could no longer be compensated for in the short term. Indeed, the failings became so obvious that even Gorbachev's reform efforts came too late. By the end of the 1980s, the 'Eastern bloc' had virtually disintegrated, and the Soviet Union dissolved in 1991.

Unlike most of the extant literature, which focuses on how (Western) Europe became increasingly dependent on Soviet oil and gas imports, this book takes the Soviet perspective, asking why Moscow allowed international trade to expand to the point that it created long-term structural dependencies on the Western capitalist market. The early Bolsheviks saw Russia's enormous natural wealth as a tool for overcoming economic backwardness and eventually catching up with – or even overtaking – the industrialised capitalist world. However, the Soviet leaders did not want their country to become a mere supplier of raw materials to the West. But the expansion of the country's fossil trade, combined with rising world oil prices from the late 1960s, meant that the Soviet economy became increasingly dependent on the rents generated by a single export commodity. Moreover, the construction of a vast transnational pipeline system – largely financed by Western loans and supplied with Western European steel pipes and technology – linked Soviet oil and gas fields in the Volga-Urals and Western Siberia to markets in Western and Eastern Europe, thus integrating the Soviet Union into an ever-expanding cross-border energy transportation network. The Soviet Union thus became increasingly part of an international economy, and this affected the views and decisions of the country's leaders.

Compared to the amount of research on Soviet foreign and security policy and international relations, economic issues have not figured prominently in the general Cold War historiography.[4] While Western historians produced a number of studies on energy and trade during the Cold War period, these remain somewhat separate from general historical accounts.[5] Meanwhile, the existing global histories of oil (such as Daniel Yergin's seminal book *The Prize*) tend not to give Soviet energy the prominence it deserves.[6] Many of the overviews of Russian history, including those that take a global perspective,[7] do not consider energy

[4] Cf. John Lewis Gaddis, *The Cold War: A New History*, New York: Penguin Press, 2005; Odd Arne Westad, *The Global Cold War*, Cambridge: Cambridge University Press, 2007.

[5] Representative of this literature is Thane Gustafson's 1989 book *Crisis Amid Plenty*, one of the best studies on Soviet energy policy published before the opening of Russian archives: Thane Gustafson, *Crisis Amid Plenty: The Politics of Soviet Energy under Brezhnev and Gorbachev*, Princeton, NJ: Princeton University Press, 1989. Other important studies on Soviet oil, gas, and international trade published during the Cold War include: Arthur Jay Klinghoffer, *The Soviet Union & International Oil Politics*, New York: Columbia University Press, 1977; Marshall I. Goldman, *The Enigma of Soviet Petroleum: Half-Full or Half-Empty?*, London: George Allen & Unwin, 1980.

[6] Yergin's book was first published in 1990. In the following, I rely on Daniel Yergin, *The Prize: The Epic Quest for Oil, Money, and Power*, New York: Free Press, 2009.

[7] For some time now, there has been a tendency in Eastern European studies to read Russian and Soviet history as part of a global history. However, economic aspects have so far been rather neglected in these studies. This also applies to the anthology edited by Martin Aust: Martin Aust (ed.), *Globalisierung imperial und sozialistisch: Russland und die Sowjetunion in der Globalgeschichte 1851–1991*, Globalgeschichte 13, Frankfurt am Main: Campus Verlag, 2013.

and foreign trade issues.[8] Even in works that explicitly adopt a structural approach to history writing, there is often no serious discussion of the importance of international trade to Soviet economic policy and foreign relations because, in the eyes of these authors, trade accounted for too small a share of Soviet GDP to be worthy of consideration.[9]

Only recently have studies appeared that emphasise economic issues and stress the role of fossil fuels in shaping international relations.[10] These rely on declassified Soviet documents and holdings in other national archives (see the works of Falk Flade, Per Högselius, Dunja Krempin, Jeronim Perović, Felix Rehschuh, and Mariia Slavkina).[11] Drawing on new archival findings, some authors also question the long-held assumption that autarky was a guiding maxim of Soviet economic policy during the Khrushchev years of the 1950s and 1960s (see, for example, Oscar Sanchez-Sibony's *Red Globalization*).[12] In line with this, Western researchers have begun to scrutinise Soviet economic data more critically, demonstrating that foreign trade was far more important to the national economy than official Soviet statistics would suggest. But even if the statistics are disputed and the figures for trade as a proportion of the national economy are indeed low, the essential story remains the same. Throughout Soviet history, but especially during the latter part of the Cold War, the Soviet Union sought international business opportunities and its leaders became increasingly aware of global economic

8 Dietmar Neutatz, *Träume und Alpträume: Eine Geschichte Russlands im 20. Jahrhundert*, Munich: Beck, 2013.

9 Carsten Goehrke, *Russland: Eine Strukturgeschichte*, Paderborn: Schöningh, 2010, p. 138.

10 Bernd Greiner, Christian Th. Müller, and Claudia Weber (eds.), *Ökonomie im Kalten Krieg*, Studien zum Kalten Krieg 4, Hamburg: Hamburger Edition, 2010.

11 Falk Flade, *Energy Infrastructures in the Eastern Bloc: Poland and the Construction of Transnational Electricity, Oil, and Gas Systems*, Wiesbaden: Harrasowitz Verlag, 2017; Per Högselius, *Red Gas: Russia and the Origins of European Energy Dependence*, New York: Palgrave Macmillan, 2013; Dunja Krempin, *Die sibirische Wucht: Der Aufstieg der Sowjetunion zur globalen Gasmacht, 1964–1982*, Osteuropa in Geschichte und Gegenwart 7, Vienna, Cologne, Weimar: Böhlau, 2020; Jeronim Perović (ed.), *Cold War Energy: A Transnational History of Soviet Oil and Gas*, Cham: Palgrave Macmillan, 2017; Felix Rehschuh, *Aufstieg zur Energiemacht: Der sowjetische Weg ins Erdölzeitalter, 1930er bis 1950er Jahre*, Osteuropa in Geschichte und Gegenwart 1, Vienna, Cologne, Weimar: Böhlau, 2018. Russian-language historiography, on the other hand, has many studies dealing with the topic of energy, which I draw on in this book. Studies based on Soviet archival material, however, are also rather rare for Russian-language historiography, especially for the later Soviet period, because the corresponding archival holdings have not yet been released. One of the best Russian-language analyses of recent Soviet energy history, which also includes Soviet archival documents, is that of Russian historian Mariia Slavkina: M. V. Slavkina, *Neftegazovyi faktor otechestvennoi modernizatsii 1939–2008*, Moscow: Ves' mir, 2015.

12 Oscar Sanchez-Sibony, *Red Globalization: The Political Economy of the Soviet Cold War from Stalin to Khrushchev*, Cambridge: Cambridge University Press, 2014.

dynamics. As will be argued, this awareness had a significant impact on Moscow's foreign economic direction and its foreign policy choices.

Drawing on material from Russian archives, published document collections, memoirs, and new research in multiple languages, this study ties in with a growing body of literature that argues that international trade issues played a far more important role in the Soviet Union's economic development path and its foreign policy orientation than previously recognised. By looking at internal Soviet discussions on the use of natural resources and energy strategy, this book provides deep insights into Soviet thinking about oil, gas, trade, and external relations. In line with other recent scholarship, this book maintains that the fabric of energy relations between Western Europe and the Soviet Union that emerged in the late 1960s and 1970s did not develop because of such 'impersonal forces' as technological progress and economic globalisation. Rather, these relations resulted from the preferences and choices of concrete actors involved in economic and trade policy decisions.[13] In the late Soviet period, the Soviet leadership weighed various options for the future of its energy industry and considered several different international cooperation efforts, including major natural gas projects in Siberia with US and Japanese companies. The question is why some projects came to fruition while others did not. To answer this, we need to consider global, regional, and domestic dynamics and also the mindsets of the key actors involved in planning and policy-making at the time.

It is certainly true that, especially during the Cold War, political considerations played an important role for the Soviet Union in selecting foreign business partners and determining the geographical direction of trade. After all, for Soviet decision-makers, trade was always part of the systemic struggle between communism and capitalism. Contrary to the notion, widespread among Cold War–era Western observers and policymakers, and also reflected in parts of Western historiography, that the Soviet Union's foreign economic policy was mainly a function of its desire to expand its global political influence, geopolitics was not the main driver behind the Soviet leadership's eagerness to establish ever-closer energy ties with the capitalist West. From the late 1960s, when Moscow signed its first long-term contracts on natural gas supplies with Western European companies, the Soviet Union committed itself to international trade agreements motivated much more by sober cost-benefit calculations than by any geopolitical grand design.

[13] Per Högselius, et al., *Europe's Infrastructure Transition: Economy, War, Nature*, Basingstoke: Palgrave Macmillan, 2016, p. 9.

The rise of the Soviet Union as an international energy power went hand in hand with growing East–West economic ties and deepening of contacts between the socialist and capitalist markets. This process had a profound impact not only on the Soviet Union's self-perception as an energy power but also on Moscow's ideas about the nature of its relations with both the socialist states of Eastern Europe and the Western capitalist world. The history of Soviet foreign trade is important because the ever-closer economic interdependence of the late Cold War period stimulated debates within the Soviet Union on fundamental questions of trade policy, profitability, exchange rates, the international credit market, and the state monopoly on foreign trade – precisely those issues that would become relevant in the second half of the 1980s in the course of the gradual privatisation and liberalisation of the economy under Mikhail Gorbachev. The evolution of the relationship between oil, natural gas, trade, and international relations during the late Soviet period would have a major impact on Russia's development after the break-up of the Soviet Union, affecting its position and role in the post-Soviet space, in Europe, and in the global economy.

The fact that there are still relatively few studies addressing the connection between energy and the formation of Soviet foreign relations is surprising since the possession of large quantities of oil and other valuable natural resources had an important impact on how decision-makers in Moscow thought about economic development, international affairs, and the opportunities and risks of their country's participation in world trade. Whereas in the eighteenth and much of the nineteenth centuries, there was a widespread belief that it was Russia's almost infinite territorial expanse that made it superior to its neighbours, in the late nineteenth and twentieth centuries geography was increasingly supplemented by geology – the notion of an almost limitless wealth of natural resources.[14] The concept of virtually inexhaustible natural resources became more and more prominent, with these resources serving as a crucial element in the state's perception of its great power status and also as a kind of 'backup' in the event of an international crisis or even hostile attack.

The mere availability of natural resources does not necessarily explain why a country has followed a particular historical path. An abundance of natural resources can create opportunities for modernisation, transformation, and trade. But it can also be an obstacle or even a 'curse' if governments use the rents from hydrocarbon exports to postpone

[14] Sonja Margolina, 'Geographie und Herrschaft: Russland und das Öl – eine alte imperiale Strategie gelangt zu neuer Entfaltung', *Neue Zürcher Zeitung*, 13 July 2006, p. 25.

necessary economic reforms, buy the loyalty of elites, placate society with low taxes, and strengthen the military and security apparatus.[15] Given Russia's enormous wealth of natural resources, an account of Russian history through the lens of energy thus promises to reveal much about the workings of the political and economic system but also about notions of modernisation and development, great power identity, and how to engage with the outside world.

Russia's behaviour, both past and present, cannot be adequately understood without considering the energy factor, and the aim of this book is to uncover the manifold links between resource wealth and policy choices. It asks how Russian political leaders and decision-makers, at different points in time, viewed the role of energy – particularly oil and gas – and how they assessed the political and economic opportunities they believed would arise from international trade and exchange. While the primary focus of this book is on the Soviet Union during the later Cold War period, the analysis of energy policy and trade relations over a longer period helps to improve our understanding of Russia's changing self-image as part of an interconnected world.

[15] On the 'oil curse', see the seminal work by Michael L. Ross, *The Oil Curse: How Petroleum Wealth Shapes the Development of Nations*, Princeton, NJ: Princeton University Press, 2012.

1 Russia in the Global History of Oil

Energy is the lifeblood of modern economies. The provision of energy made possible the industrial revolution and the transition from an agrarian society to an industrialised world – and in the twentieth century, no source of energy has been as important as oil. Oil was a prerequisite for the emergence of mechanised warfare with mobile troops, tanks, and aircraft; it was no less important for the technological revolution in agriculture that saw the introduction of oil-powered tractors. Serving as fuel for the movement of goods and people, oil increased global trade and connectivity to an unprecedented degree. Thus the growing importance of oil was ultimately accompanied by the rise of multinational corporations, the spread of capitalism, and global economic interdependence. Due to its enormous strategic importance, oil has always been closely interwoven with international politics, great power ambitions, and conflict.

Over the twentieth century, the Western industrialised world became increasingly addicted to oil. Shortly after the Second World War, the United States began to consume more oil than coal, ending the latter's long reign as the 'king' among energy sources. Although no other country pumped more oil out of the ground than the United States, by the early 1950s national demand was outstripping domestic production. As a result, the country began to import ever larger quantities of the commodity, particularly from Venezuela and the Persian Gulf states. At the same time, Europe became increasingly dependent on oil imports. Even though it was not until the 1960s that oil gained a dominant position in the European energy mix, Europe's small reserves and the sharp decline in US exports meant that Europe soon became dependent on oil imports from other parts of the world, notably the Middle East and North Africa.

In the 1970s, the importance of the Soviet Union for European energy supplies increased markedly. In addition to oil, which Russia had been exporting since Tsarist times, the Soviet Union began supplying increasing amounts of natural gas to Europe from the late 1960s onwards. After the end of the Cold War and up to Russia's invasion of Ukraine in 2022,

Russia strengthened its position as the main supplier of energy sources to Europe and Turkey, including not only crude oil, oil products, and natural gas but also coal and uranium. During this period, Russia also expanded its supplies of fossil fuels to countries outside Europe, mainly China, Japan, South Korea, and increasingly also India.

Although the dominance of oil has declined over the past four decades from its peak of over 50 per cent in the early 1970s, it remains the world's most important energy source and the most traded commodity in the global economy.[1] Because oil is lighter than coal, it has proved more attractive to ship it around the world in barrels by tanker, giving it more flexibility than natural gas, which still relies largely on pipelines for transport. The fact that oil is easier to transport than natural gas affects relationships between producers, suppliers, and consumers: 'black gold' allows for spontaneous transactions and the short-term rerouting of flows of goods. This is likely to change in the future as globally traded but still relatively expensive liquefied natural gas (LNG) gains greater importance compared to pipeline gas.

Whatever becomes of fossil fuels in the future, the twentieth century will go down in history as the age of oil. The availability of ever-greater quantities of oil has not only influenced politics, the nature of warfare, and the global economy but has also shaped the lifestyles of societies and thus the emergence of industrial modernity as such. Modern history cannot be told in isolation from oil – and Russia, as a key storehouse, producer, consumer, and exporter of raw materials, is an integral part of that tale. This chapter provides a brief overview of the history of oil and explains how Russia fits into it.

A Brief History of Oil

Oil has long been known to mankind. In ancient times, it was mixed with sand as bitumen (pitch) to seal wooden ships. The Romans had already

[1] In 2021, oil accounted for 31 per cent of total primary energy consumption, followed by coal (27 per cent) and natural gas (25 per cent). In terms of world trade, about 1,829 million tons of crude oil were transported by sea around the world in 2021, representing approximately 44 percent of global crude oil production. A much smaller but still significant proportion is also transported via international pipelines. Data from Our World in Data, 'Primary Energy Consumption by Source, 2021', https://ourworldindata.org/grapher/primary-energy-source-bar?country=~OWID_WRL (last accessed 5 January 2022); BP, 'Statistical Review of World Energy 2021', www.bp.com/content/dam/bp/business-sites/en/global/corporate/pdfs/energy-economics/statistical-review/bp-stats-review-2021-oil.pdf (last accessed 5 January 2022); Statistica, 'Transport Volume of Crude Oil in Seaborne Trade Worldwide from 2010 to 2021', www.statista.com/statistics/264013/transport-volume-of-crude-oil-in-seaborne-trade/ (last accessed 5 January 2022).

discovered oil as a lubricant for chariot wheels, and it was also applied as a medicine against all kinds of ailments. Petroleum was probably also used as a fuel already in antiquity; Greeks are said to have employed it as a preliminary form of flamethrower.[2] However, because of its low luminosity, strong smell, and soot production, petroleum was only rarely used for lighting. While vegetable oils (olive oil, rapeseed oil, etc.) were also applied as lamp oil, high-quality oil from whales was added during the eighteen and ninetheenth centuries. However, the slaughter of these animals for the extraction of whale oil took on such vast proportions that whaling ships had to sail further and further out, causing some populations to plummet significantly and thus the price of whale oil to soar.[3]

A pivotal moment in the energy transition of the time occurred with groundbreaking discoveries such as that of the Canadian physician and geologist Abraham P. Gesner, who, in the middle of the nineteenth century, worked out how to produce petroleum (light petroleum distillate, kerosene in American English) from coal and crude oil by fractional distillation. This invention was the starting point for the modern petroleum industry.[4] From then on, petroleum was adopted as an inexpensive alternative to lamp oil and was produced in ever-greater quantities.

Initially, oil was only extracted from the earth's surface. It was not until commercialisation began that drilling techniques were developed that made it possible to search for oil in the earth's interior. In the process, a technique was used that had already been adopted by the Chinese for salt drilling some 2,000 years ago.[5] People had long suspected that oil might be present deep in the earth, as it repeatedly came to light when drilling for salt and water. Yet the idea that oil could lie in lakes under the earth's surface and be pumped out was initially considered absurd and had to be proven. The first successful wells were drilled in the 1850s in the United States, in Europe (for example in Galicia, which at the time belonged to Poland), and in the Russian Empire (especially near Baku). Of these, Colonel Edwin Drake's 1859 discovery of crude oil during deep drilling in Pennsylvania achieved the greatest fame, triggering the first commercial oil boom in the United States.[6]

[2] K. Krejci-Graf, *Erdöl: Naturgeschichte eines Rohstoffes*, 2nd rev. ed., Berlin, Göttingen, Heidelberg: Springer-Verlag, 1955, pp. 1–2.

[3] James L. Coleman, 'The American Whale Oil Industry: A Look Back to the Future of the American Petroleum Industry?', *Nonrenewable Resources*, 4 (1995), pp. 273–88.

[4] Rainer Hempel, 'Abraham Gesner: Father of the Petroleum Industry', *German Canadian Yearbook*, 17 (2002), pp. 129–38.

[5] Krejci-Graf, *Erdöl*, p. 139.

[6] Edgar Wesley Owen, *Trek of the Oil Finders: A History of Exploration for Petroleum*, Tulsa, OK: American Association of Petroleum Geologists, 1975. Cf., on the development of Europe's oil and gas industry, J. Craig, F. Gerali, F. MacAulay, and R. Sorkhabi (eds.),

Petroleum continued to be used as a means of illumination until the beginning of the twentieth century, becoming increasingly widespread, especially in the cities of North America and Europe. With the advent of the light bulb, it initially looked as if electric light would herald the end of the petroleum boom. At the same time as the light bulb was spreading, however, the automobile industry in the United States was also taking off, and by the outbreak of the First World War, it was clear that petroleum-derived fuel would play a central role in powering ships, tanks, locomotives, troop transport vehicles and aircraft. Thanks to its high efficiency, petroleum was an ideal means of propulsion – if only because the same heat effect as coal could be produced with far smaller quantities of fuel. Winston Churchill also noted that oil-powered warships sailed much faster than those running on coal. Then the head of the British navy, he, therefore, urged as early as 1911 that the entire war fleet be converted to oil to help Great Britain, a maritime empire, secure sea routes and bases around the world.[7] The US Navy likewise set about converting the operation of its warships, destroyers, and submarines to oil.[8] On land, too, gasoline and diesel power were used to make armies more mobile. Such vehicles could be moved anywhere in a short time and were no longer necessarily dependent on a railway network.

The growing military importance of oil meant that countries that could not supply themselves with sufficient oil from domestic production had to look for possible sources of imports. To gain access to this coveted commodity, Western energy companies began securing mining rights in oil-rich countries through concessions from the beginning of the twentieth century. A sufficient supply of crude oil also became increasingly important in larger economic terms with the advent and rapid growth of the automobile industry, not only in the United States but also in other parts of the industrialising world.

The global struggle for access to oil would intensify as oil was also increasingly used as a key heating fuel. Compared to coal, oil not only achieves a higher degree of efficiency but can also be burned more cleanly. Particularly in big cities, which suffered from dirty air and smoke, oil, therefore, presented itself as an alternative heating fuel to coal. Later, this logic would come to apply to an even greater degree to natural gas, which can be burned with even fewer residues. While most of

History of the European Oil and Gas Industry, London: Geological Society of London, 2018.

7 Erik J. Dahl, 'Naval Innovation: From Coal to Oil', *Joint Force Quarterly (JFQ)* (2000/2001), pp. 50–56.

8 Boverton Redwood, 'The Future of Oil Fuel', *Journal of the Royal Society of Arts*, 62, 3188 (1913), pp. 103–16, here p. 107.

the oil was used as fuel, crude oil also became the starting material for the manufacture of numerous products in the chemical industry, among them fertilizers, plastics, paints, medicines, and even foodstuffs. By the 1960s at the latest, oil had established itself as the most important raw material in the global industrial society.

Unlike oil, natural gas – which had likewise been known to mankind for centuries – was long traded primarily on a regional basis. Also, in contrast to oil, gas was hardly used for industrial purposes at first. Gas was usually discovered when drilling for oil. Natural gas can appear alongside oil ('associated gas') or be found in deposits where only natural gas is present; it can also occur mixed with rock or coal ('shale gas', 'tight gas', or 'coal seam gas'). Historically, however, the extraction of these so-called non-conventional energy carriers was seldom profitable if oil was available in large quantities. If the gas came to the surface with the oil in the form of associated gas, it was sometimes pumped back to be stored for later use. Often, however, the gas was simply burned off because it was not commercially viable to build a pipeline from the field to the end user. Even today, gas-rich countries like Russia, Iraq, Iran, and the United States flare billions of cubic metres of associated gas every year instead of using it commercially.

As with oil, a pioneering role in the industrial use of natural gas was played by the United States, where the first natural gas companies were founded already in the middle of the nineteenth century. Indeed, for a long time, only the United States had a significant natural gas industry. Nevertheless, the United States initially exported hardly any natural gas, shipping only small quantities via pipelines to Mexico and Canada. It was only with the expansion of production and the extension of the pipeline network that the United States began to drastically increase its international exports from the 2000s onwards. Exports of gas in liquefied form also began to play an increasingly important role in the global market. Although the liquefied natural gas industry emerged in the United States as early as the mid-1960s, it is only since 2015 that American companies have been supplying the global market with large quantities of LNG. Production has since grown rapidly: by 2020, American LNG was responsible for around 45 per cent of total US gas exports making the United States one of the world's top LNG exporters, along with Qatar, Australia, and Russia.[9]

[9] US Energy Information Administration (EIA), 'Natural Gas Explained: Natural Gas Imports and Exports', www.eia.gov/energyexplained/natural-gas/imports-and-exports.php (last accessed 16 September 2021); John Kemp, 'Column: U.S. Gas Industry Increasingly Relies on LNG

Compared to the United States, Russia was a late bloomer in terms of gas production. A modern gas industry only started to develop in the Soviet Union during the Second World War. In 1944, construction began on an 800 km pipeline from Saratov to Moscow, which was opened two years later.[10] After the Second World War, the most important production areas were in the western part of the Ukrainian Soviet Socialist Republic (SSR), which had developed a petroleum industry already in the late nineteenth century in the northern Carpathian Mountains (now part of Poland and Ukraine). But it was not until the development of the oil and gas fields of the Volga-Urals region in the 1950s and 1960s, and especially the huge Western Siberian deposits in the 1970s, that the Soviet Union became the world's largest gas producer and Europe's most important supplier of raw materials. As a continental power, the Soviet Union was able to transport its gas via pipelines far into Europe, provided that steel pipes of the appropriate quality were available in sufficient quantity.

In the early 1990s, after the break-up of the Soviet Union, coal was added to oil and natural gas as an important part of Russia's trade in fossil fuels, and Asia joined Europe as an increasingly important export destination for Russian energy. Liquefied natural gas also became more important, and Russia's share of global LNG production, which already stood at around 10 per cent in 2019, has the potential to increase.[11] All that being said, Russia has, up to the outbreak of war with Ukraine, exported most of its natural gas to Europe using its huge pipeline infrastructure. The advantage of transporting gas via pipeline is that it can be offered at more favourable terms than liquefied natural gas, which has traditionally given Russia an advantage over LNG competitors in the European market. This meant that Russia and Europe became far more interdependent in the natural gas sector than in the oil sector; apart from the Druzhba (Friendship) oil pipeline built already in the mid-1960s and connecting Russia with a number of former 'Eastern bloc' countries, Russia has been transporting most of its oil to its maritime ports, from whence it has been shipped not only to refineries in Europe but also (albeit in lesser quantities) to other parts of the world.

Exports', *Reuters*, 26 March 2021, www.reuters.com/article/us-column-global-gas-kemp-idUSKBN2BI2HV (last accessed 16 September 2021).

10 Högselius, *Red Gas*, p. 13.

11 Szymon Kardaś, *Great Ambitions: Russia Expands on the LNG Market*, OSW Commentary 394, Warsaw: Centre for Eastern Studies, 17 May 2021, p. 3; for further reading, see James Henderson and Arild Moe, *The Globalization of Russian Gas: Political and Commercial Catalysts*, Cheltenham: Edward Elgar, 2019.

Historically, energy flows have been subject to intermittent disruptions, but stopping them permanently has proven almost impossible. When the EU and other Western states imposed, among other things, restrictions on Russian oil exports in response to Russia's war of aggression against Ukraine, Russia was able to offset some of the impact by diverting a portion of its oil to other markets (notably Turkey, India, and China).[12] Even before the sanctions, around 20 per cent of Russia's oil exports went to Asian countries, a share that has increased significantly since Russia invaded Ukraine in 2022. China alone imported more than 8.4 million tonnes of Russian oil in May 2022, a 55 per cent increase from the previous year.[13]

In addition, Gazprom began exporting gas to China via a pipeline that opened in 2019.[14] Faced with significant disruptions in pipeline gas supplies to its traditional European customers due to the closure of major pipelines such as the Yamal-Europe pipeline through Poland and the destruction of the Nord Stream pipeline system, the company plans to further increase its gas export capacity to the Asian market, while expanding supplies to other countries that have not formally supported the EU sanctions regime against Russia. Notably, Turkey is to remain not only a key importer but also to become a major hub for further Russian gas distribution in south-eastern Europe.[15] Moreover, while overall pipeline gas supplies to Europe have declined, Russia during 2022 has increased its LNG exports also to the EU, overtaking Qatar to become Europe's second-largest LNG supplier after the United States.[16]

Capitalism, Geopolitics, and the 'Hydrocarbon Man'

The history of oil in the twentieth century is much more than the history of a commodity. From a global perspective, the history of oil is generally

[12] Jeronim Perović, *Russia's Future as an Energy Power*, CSS Analyses in Security Policy 316, Zurich: Center for Security Studies, ETH Zurich, December 2022, p. 2.

[13] 'China's Russian Oil Imports Spike, Surpassing Saudi Supplies', *Radio Free Europe/Radio Liberty*, 20 June 2022, www.rferl.org/a/china-oil-russia-imports/31906255.html (last accessed 26 January 2023).

[14] The contract runs for 30 years and the total value of the deal is estimated at around 400 billion US dollars. How profitable the agreement is for Gazprom, however, or at what price the Russian gas is sold to China, is unclear; information on this has so far been kept under wraps. Cf. Maxim Kireev, 'Mega-Deal: Russland nimmt Gasleitung von Sibirien nach China in Betrieb', *MDR*, 2 December 2019, www.mdr.de/nachrichten/welt/osteuropa/ostblogger/russlands-globale-gasprojekte-nord-stream-und-andere-pipelines100.html (last accessed 26 July 2021).

[15] 'Behind the Scenes of Russia's Gas Strategy', *Enerdata Executive Brief*, July 2023, pp. 8–9, https://d1owejb4br3l12.cloudfront.net/publications/executive-briefing/russia-gas-strategy.pdf (last accessed 30 August 2023).

[16] Ibid., p. 8.

associated with three major themes:[17] First, the rise of oil as the most important globally traded commodity was accompanied by the spread of capitalism, the emergence of multinational global corporations, and the development of modern management structures. In this context, the global oil boom can be linked particularly vividly to the American company Standard Oil, which towards the end of the nineteenth century dominated not so much US crude production but the refining and distribution of oil to domestic consumers, as well as exports abroad. The United States was the most significant exporter of petroleum in the late nineteenth century, and Standard Oil was responsible for about 90 per cent of total US petroleum exports. Thus, the company controlled an estimated 70 per cent of the global market at the time, propelling the company's founder, John D. Rockefeller, to the status of richest man in the world.[18]

Over time, Standard Oil increasingly found itself under pressure in the European and Asian markets from such competitors as Shell, Branobel, and the Rothschilds, who at that time were also involved in oil production in the Caucasus – which was then part of the Russian Empire – and were competing with the Americans for the European market with Russian-produced oil. In 1911, the American government sought to end Standard Oil's monopoly position on the American market by bringing a suit under the Sherman Antitrust Act of 1906. The company was subsequently broken up into thirty-four separate entities. Powerful companies nevertheless rose from its ashes; they would later go on to pursue their global business under such names as Chevron and Exxon. Nor was Rockefeller to be impoverished: he had previously secured shares in his company, the value of which rose massively thanks to the oil boom during the First World War and the rapid expansion of the US automobile industry.

Oil companies were among the richest multinationals in the twentieth century, with business operations spanning the globe. Well until the early 1970s, a little more than a handful of Western companies dominated the international oil market, securing extraction rights around the world through long-term contracts. This small group of companies based in the United States, the United Kingdom, and the Netherlands, commonly referred to as the 'Seven Sisters',[19] controlled the entire global supply chain – from rig to petrol pump – for decades. It was only with decolonisation

17 Adapted from Yergin, *The Prize*, pp. xiv–xvii.

18 Ibid., pp. 19–39; for further reading, see Ron Chernow, *Titan: The Life of John D. Rockefeller, Sr.*, 2nd ed., New York: Vintage Books, 2004.

19 Standard Oil of New Jersey (Esso; later Exxon), Royal Dutch Shell, Anglo-Persian Oil (later BP), Standard Oil of New York (Socony; later Mobil; now part of Exxon Mobil), Standard Oil of California (Socal; later Chevron), Gulf Oil, and Texaco (now part of Chevron).

and the rise in nationalisation tendencies in the producing states that these companies' monopoly positions came under pressure. Whereas the oil-rich Arab states that had emerged from the collapsed Ottoman Empire and the former British and French colonial territories in North Africa had previously sought simply to negotiate better conditions for the exploitation and sale of their natural resources, the 1970s saw a wave of nationalisation proper, as a result of which the 'Seven Sisters' lost their former dominance.[20] Their share of known oil reserves fell from well over 90 per cent in the 1950s to just 7 per cent by the end of the 1970s.[21]

The oil-producing countries also increased their influence on world market prices when the most important of them, including initially Saudi Arabia, Iran, Iraq, Kuwait, and Venezuela, joined forces in the Organization of the Petroleum Exporting Countries (OPEC), which was founded in 1960. At first hardly noticed, this growing cartel came to influence global supply – and thus prices – by means of agreements on price and production volumes. The effect of this became particularly pronounced in the 1970s as global demand rose and the market tightened.[22]

Energy companies have continued to play an important role in the global economy. According to the Fortune Global 500 ranking, five companies from the oil and gas sectors – Sinopec (China), China National Petroleum Corporation (CNPC), Royal Dutch Shell, Saudi Aramco, and British Petroleum (BP) – remained among the world's ten largest companies in 2020.[23] Unlike in the past, however, it is primarily national energy companies – from such countries as Saudi

[20] Wiebke Glässer, *Marktmacht und Politik: Das internationale Kartell der Ölgesellschaften 1960–1975*, Schriftenreihe zur Zeitschrift für Unternehmensgeschichte 32, Berlin, Boston: De Gruyter Oldenbourg, 2019, especially chapter 3 ('The Seven Sisters', pp. 41–106) and chapter 5 ('The Seven Sisters and OPEC', pp. 181–251).

[21] Steffen Bukold, *Öl im 21. Jahrhundert*, vol. 1, Munich: Oldenbourg, 2009, p. 24; 'Oil Dependence and U.S. Foreign Policy 1850–2017', www.cfr.org/timeline/oil-dependence-and-us-foreign-policy (last accessed 16 August 2021).

[22] On the history of OPEC, see Giuliano Garavini, *The Rise and Fall of OPEC in the Twentieth Century*, Oxford: Oxford University Press, 2019.

[23] *Fortune Global 500*, https://fortune.com/global500/ (last accessed 23 June 2021). The ranking of the ten largest oil and gas companies in the world in the year according to market value in 2022 was as follows: Saudi Aramco (Saudi Arabia, 2.292.1 billion US-D), Exxon Mobil (US, 359.7 billion US-D), Chevron (US, 316.2 billion US-D), Reliance Industries (India, 228.6 billion US-D), Royal Dutch Shell (UK/Netherlands, 211.1 billion US-D), PetroChina (China, 142.3 billion US-D), Total (France, 127.3 billion US-D), ConocoPhilipps (US, 124.4 billion US-D), Equinor (formerly Statoil, Norway, 117.9 billion US-D), BP (UK, 73.5 billion US-D). Cf. Saskia Patermann, 'Das sind die grössten Öl- und Gaskonzerne der Welt', *Handelsblatt*, 23 February 2023, www.handelsblatt.com/unternehmen/energie/shell-total-bp-das-sind-die-groessten-oel-und-gaskonzerne-der-welt/25342258.html?utm_source=pocket-newtab-global-de-DE (last accessed 3 March 2023).

Arabia, China, Venezuela, and Russia – that control most of the world's production (and, increasingly, global trade), even if private Western companies retain importance.

The second story that can be linked to the rise of oil in the twentieth century is geopolitical and strategic. Wars have been fought over resources since time immemorial, whether to control territory, populations, or natural assets. Contrary to the widely held view, however, Western states in the twentieth century rarely relied on direct military force to gain access to oil resources for their corporations. Instead of costly wars, Western companies sought to use concessions to obtain the most advantageous terms possible for extracting resources in producing countries. To secure access to oil for the British navy and reduce the country's then-heavy dependence on American oil imports, the British state, as early as 1912, acquired a majority share in the Anglo-Persian Oil Company (later British Petroleum), which produced oil in the southern part of Iran with a concession, and immediately concluded a long-term supply contract with this company to supply the British navy.[24] The French Compagnie Française des Pétroles (later Total SA), founded in 1924, was another oil company in which the state held a substantial share and which was formed for strategic reasons to secure the supply to the domestic French market.[25]

This model was to be maintained in subsequent decades. Large Western companies, often actively supported by their governments, secured the right to extract natural resources worldwide to supply both domestic and global markets. The best-known example is the American–Saudi de facto alliance, which was formed immediately after the Second World War: in return for American security guarantees, the Saudi Arabian state granted American companies far-reaching concession rights to its oil fields. Negotiations began towards the end of the Second World War. US President Franklin D. Roosevelt lobbied in personal talks with the Saudi king for American economic concerns and convinced him of the merits of an alliance with the United States. In this way, the United States prevailed over the British, who had also shown great interest in Saudi oil concessions.[26] The fact that Western companies, under the protection of their governments, did not shy away even from supporting corrupt regimes in the producing countries or from

[24] R. W.Ferrier, *The History of The British Petroleum Company*, vol. 1, The Developing Years 1901–1932, Cambridge: Cambridge University Press, 1982, especially chapter 4 ('Progress in Persia 1908–14') and chapter 5 ('Fuel Oil and the Admiralty').

[25] Bukold, *Öl im 21. Jahrhundert*, p. 13.

[26] Victor McFarland, *Oil Powers: A History of the U.S.–Saudi Alliance*, New York: Columbia University Press, 2020.

even actively interfering in their politics out of a desire for money or power is also part of the oil story. One of the best-known examples is the case of Iran, where the US and British intelligence services helped to oust Mohammad Mossadegh's government at least in part because it had sought the nationalisation of the oil industry and had thus opposed Western oil interests at the time.[27]

Although oil has rarely been a direct cause of military conflicts, it has played a significant role in wars throughout modern history. Well-known episodes date back to the First World War, when German troops sought to secure oil production sites during their advance into Romania in 1916–17.[28] Shortly afterwards, a German contingent established itself in Georgia and attempted to take possession of the oil near Baku but was unsuccessful. During the Russian Civil War, and with an eye on the oil riches of the Caucasus, the British occupied Baku for only two short periods, but that was enough to deny the Germans access to the South Caucasian oil fields and petroleum infrastructure of the former Russian Empire.[29] In the wake of the collapse of the Ottoman Empire, the British and French played the dominant roles in the reorganisation of the Middle East, establishing borders and spheres of influence largely on their own. Oil played an important part in these considerations. Having already extended their influence into Iran, the British also managed to secure the oil reserves near Mosul in what later became Iraq, in return for ceding control of Syria to France.[30] Contemporary commentators were acutely aware of the oil's importance during this time. The journalist Louis Fischer, a Communist sympathiser who was stationed in Moscow at the time, fiercely denounced the oil greed of Western companies and governments in his widely read book *Oil Imperialism,* published in 1926.[31]

[27] Yergin, *The Prize*, pp. 432–60.

[28] Christian Th. Müller, *Jenseits der Materialschlacht: Der Erste Weltkrieg als Bewegungskrieg*, Paderborn: Schöningh, 2018, p. 176; further, see Ferdinand Friedensburg, *Das Erdöl im Weltkrieg*, Stuttgart: Enke, 1939, especially pp. 25–39.

[29] Yergin, *The Prize*, pp. 166–67; further, see Winfried Baumgart, 'Das "KaspiUnternehmen" – Grössenwahn Ludendorffs oder Routineplanung des Deutschen Generalstabs? Erster Teil: Ein kritischer Rückblick auf die deutsche militärische Intervention im Kaukasus am Ende des Ersten Weltkriegs', *Jahrbücher für Geschichte Osteuropas*, 18, 1 (1970), pp. 47–126; Bülent Gökay, 'The Battle for Baku (May–September 1918): A Peculiar Episode in the History of the Caucasus', *Middle Eastern Studies*, 34, 1 (1998), pp. 30–50.

[30] Charles More, *Black Gold: Britain and Oil in the Twentieth Century*, London: Bloomsbury, 2009, especially chapter 2 ('The World of Oil 1918–39', pp. 23–46); for further reading, see David E. McNabb, *Oil and the Creation of Iraq: Policy Failures and the 1914–1918 War in Mesopotamia*, New York, London: Routledge, 2016.

[31] Louis Fischer, *Oil Imperialism: The International Struggle for Petroleum*, London: International, 1926.

Access to fuel became a crucial concern again during the Second World War. In the summer of 1942, German troops embarked on an unsuccessful advance into the Caucasus, aiming to seize control of the region's valuable oil fields.[32] The first 'oil war' in modern history may well have been the Suez Canal War of 1956. It revolved around control of the vital oil transport route from the Persian Gulf to the Mediterranean, which at the time was the world's most important oil corridor. The conflict pitted Egypt, striving to nationalise the canal, against a coalition of British, French, and Israeli forces. In the end, Egypt emerged victorious, partly due to the lack of US support for its European allies.[33] Oil also played a role in the US-led military offensive to liberate oil-rich Kuwait from Iraqi occupation in 1991 but was even more prominent in the 2003 US-led 'coalition of the willing' campaign to remove Saddam Hussein from power. While the extent of the importance placed on controlling Iraqi oil in American decision-making is debated, economic motives are likely to have been substantial.[34]

For their part, the oil-producing countries have used oil as a 'weapon' against Western consumer states, as in the 1973–74 global oil crisis. During this crisis, the Arab members of OPEC imposed a supply freeze on countries supporting Israel in the Yom Kippur War. They also reduced production, leading to a significant increase in prices worldwide. Unlike an earlier boycott attempt during the 1967 Arab-Israeli war, Western oil companies could not compensate for the tight global supply, leading to unprecedented shortages in industrialised countries. In the short term, this crisis revealed a shift in power from Western energy companies to the producing countries and their national companies. In the longer term, however, the Arab 'oil weapon' became less effective as Western demand weakened during recessions and new suppliers emerged. This led to a global oversupply and a significant fall in prices since the mid-1980s, highlighting the unpredictable nature of oil prices and volatile markets.[35]

[32] Joel Hayward, 'Too Little, Too Late: An Analysis of Hitler's Failure in August 1942 to Damage Soviet Oil Production', *The Journal of Military History*, 64, 3 (2000), pp. 769–94.

[33] For example, see Barry Turner, *Suez 1956: The Inside Story of the First Oil War*, London: Hodder & Stoughton, 2006.

[34] For a critical discussion, see Raymond Hinnebusch, 'The US Invasion of Iraq: Explanations and Implications, Critique', *Critical Middle Eastern Studies*, 16, 3 (2007), pp. 209–28.

[35] Cf. Fiona Venn, *The Oil Crisis*, London: Routledge, 2002; Elisabetta Bini, Giuliano Garavini, and Federico Romero (eds.), *Oil Shock: The 1973 Crisis and Its Economic Legacy*, London: I. B. Tauris, 2016.

A third theme in the history of oil concerns society. The age of oil saw the birth of what Daniel Yergin called the 'hydrocarbon man', who first emerged in the United States in the years after the Second World War and during the 1960s also in Europe and other parts of the world.[36] The 'hydrocarbon man' consumes, indulges in abundance, produces vast amounts of waste, and enjoys his freedoms in the car and on the highways. The exploitation of petroleum for mobility went hand in hand with a new sense of liberty and lifestyle; the car and the highways opened previously undreamed-of possibilities for overcoming distance and borders. This transformation in society brought about by oil has had other far-reaching consequences, shaping patterns of consumption, influencing urban development, and affecting cultural norms and values.

Oil resources may well remain abundant for the foreseeable future, as deposits are still being discovered and new technologies are being developed to profitably exploit reserves that are difficult to tap, such as shale oil. The 'hydrocarbon man' will probably become extinct in the form in which he developed in the twentieth century. Climate policy considerations, decarbonisation of industries, pressure to reduce dependence on imports, and ecological concerns about oil and gas extraction in sensitive ecosystems like the Arctic will be just as influential in determining the future of oil in Western societies as the ability of alternative energy sources and energy technologies to replace fossil fuels. Yet as long as the West continues to rely on a certain amount of oil, gas, and coal, the countries that own and produce these resources will remain important to Europe and the world for some time to come.

The Case of Russia

Russia occupies a special place in the global history of oil. Concerning the first theme of the general history of oil, which describes the emergence of multinational, predominantly private, large companies, Russia has had this experience twice in its history. The first period was in the late Tsarist era when Russia opened up to foreign capital and built up an oil industry in the Caucasus that was highly modern and internationally competitive by the standards of the time. Thanks to the involvement of Western companies, the Russian Empire rose to become one of the world's leading oil powers. Indeed, for a short period around 1900, Russia even produced more oil than the United States. The rapidly modernising empire consumed a significant portion of its oil itself, but

[36] Yergin, *The Prize*, pp. 523–42.

large quantities were also shipped to Europe and other destinations, where cheap Russian oil quickly gained access to the market. While Western capital was crucial for the development of the Russian petroleum industry, however, the Russian share was already about 45 per cent by 1914.[37] This was because foreign involvement in the late Tsarist period had helped to foster genuine Russian entrepreneurship. Considering this, the thesis of the 'colonisation' of Russia by Western capitalists, which was later also raised by Soviet propaganda, hardly seems tenable.[38]

This first 'capitalist' phase of Russian history ended abruptly after the Bolsheviks seized power in October 1917 and nationalised all large industrial enterprises and banks. Only after the collapse of the Soviet Union, when the new Russia abandoned the model of planned economy and the ideology of communism, were parts of the energy sector – and in particular the oil industry – privatised again. The gas sector and the oil and gas export pipelines, meanwhile, remained essentially in the possession of the state. Thanks also to access to foreign technology and investment, modern Russian companies with global operations, such as Yukos and Lukoil, emerged in the 1990s; through joint ventures and production sharing agreements, Western energy companies, including Exxon, Shell, and BP, gained a foothold in Russia's strategically important raw materials sector. The privatisation wave only came to a halt in the mid-2000s when state-owned companies regained market share in the energy industry and some foreign companies were forced out of the country.

Between these two historical phases lies the Soviet period, which lasted about seventy years and in which private property was not permitted, foreign ownership was not allowed, and the state held a monopoly on foreign trade. But even if Russia turned away from the Western-dominated, liberal global economy during the Soviet phase of its history, this does not mean that the Soviet Union did not remain dependent, in one way or another, on its international economic environment. The Soviet Union, like the Russian Empire, also had to establish itself on the international market if it wanted to sell its goods successfully. In the case of oil, this was not done, as in the West, through private corporations with global reach but through the Soviet Ministry of Foreign Trade and the trade organisations and state companies subordinate to it. In the course of the nationalisation of large companies and banks after the revolution of 1917, the Soviet state also seized the property of foreign companies and either imprisoned their owners or drove them out of the country. But this did not mean the end of international cooperation and

[37] Semjonow, *Erdöl aus dem Osten*, p. 105.
[38] Manfred Hildermeier, *Geschichte Russlands*, 2nd ed., Munich: Beck, 2013, p. 1146.

exchanges. From the early 1920s, the Bolsheviks allowed international technical collaboration within the framework of their New Economic Policy and granted foreign companies the right to work in the Soviet Union as part of their concession policy. By the end of the decade, the concession system had been severely restricted, but technology imports, knowledge transfer, and cross-border trade continued to persist.

From about the mid-1930s, during the time of Stalin (who was the party's general secretary from 1922–53), the Soviet Union temporarily withdrew from the global market. After the dictator's death, however, the party's new general secretary, Nikita Khrushchev (1953–64), sought to expand international trade beyond the Eastern European 'socialist camp' and to intensify economic and technical relations with the capitalist West. During the long rule of Leonid Brezhnev (1964–82), the principle of Soviet natural resources in exchange for foreign loans and technology – applied namely through the conclusion of large 'gas-for-pipes' deals – became the most important structural feature of an ever closer relationship with Western Europe. In parallel, from the 1960s and then especially in the 1970s, the Soviet Union became increasingly involved in the global South, providing military aid and engaging in economic and technical cooperation. Economic globalisation thus took place in Soviet times, but it had its own peculiarities and characteristics.

Russia also occupies a special position with regard to the second theme of the history of oil: the strategic and geopolitical dimension. Since Russia has huge natural resource reserves on its territory and has therefore been largely self-sufficient throughout its history, state policy has never sought primarily to control energy deposits outside the country's borders but has rather been aimed at developing its own resources. This does not mean that Russia has never imported modest quantities of energy; after the Second World War, for example, the Soviet Union imported oil from Romania, natural gas from Iran and Afghanistan, and coal from Poland and Czechoslovakia. But even in the late Tsarist period, and especially in the Soviet phase of its history, Russia conducted the struggle for the extraction of raw materials primarily internally; it was a struggle to overcome the distances, adverse climates, and unfavourable natural conditions. For the exploitation of raw materials, the Soviet leadership repeatedly ordered large-scale campaigns to mobilise society to work on big energy development projects.

This internal economic 'colonisation' posed enormous challenges in that the largest deposits were located in far-flung and difficult-to-develop parts of the country. In the 1940s and 1950s, oil deposits were developed in the Volga-Urals region, while the discovery of gigantic oil and gas fields in the northern part of Western Siberia in the second half of the

1960s brought the far north of the country into the Soviet leadership's spotlight. Because their development was technically complex and also extremely costly, the US Central Intelligence Agency (CIA) in its reports repeatedly expressed the suspicion that an energy crisis in the Soviet Union was imminent, the country's abundant resources notwithstanding.[39] When Moscow sent tens of thousands of troops into Afghanistan at the end of 1979 to help the beleaguered communist Afghan regime, which was facing pressure from the Mujahideen, many Western observers, including then-American President Jimmy Carter, perceived it as a threat to Western strategic interests. They saw in the Soviet intervention an intention on the part of Moscow to gain access to Iranian oil and the warm waters of the Persian Gulf.[40] This, however, was inaccurate. The motives behind Moscow's invasion of Afghanistan had little to do with natural resources and the Persian Gulf, not least because by this time the Soviet Union had already set about developing the gigantic raw material deposits of Western Siberia, which would provide the country with an abundance of oil and gas for decades to come.[41]

Geopolitical and strategic considerations did play a role in Soviet energy policy, but they must be considered separately for each historical period. Economic motives were an important impetus for the Bolsheviks to recapture the oil-producing Caucasus and other resource-rich regions during the Russian Civil War. This was also recognised by the then Commissar for Nationalities, Iosif Stalin, who warned in an article in the party newspaper *Pravda* on 10 October 1920 that the 'more developed central Russia ... could not complete the revolution without the help of the less developed peripheral regions of Russia, which are richly endowed with vital resources'.[42]

Towards the end of the Second World War, Iran became the focus of Moscow's foreign policy concern, not least because of its oil wealth, with the result that Soviet troops would occupy the country until 1946.

[39] For example, Central Intelligence Agency, *The Impeding Soviet Oil Crisis*, Intelligence Memorandum, Washington, DC, 1977, www.cia.gov/readingroom/docs/DOC_0000498607.pdf (last accessed 10 July 2021).

[40] See, for example, US President Jimmy Carter's speech to the nation on 21 January 1980, and his State of the Union Address to the US Congress on 23 January 1980, in which he refers to the possibility of a threat to the Persian Gulf from the Soviet invasion of Afghanistan and emphasises US determination to defend the region's oil: Public Papers of the Presidents of the United States, *Jimmy Carter 1980–1981 (In Three Books): Book I – January 1 to May 23, 1980*, Washington, DC: United States Government Printing Office, 1981, pp. 114–80 and pp. 194–200.

[41] David N. Gibbs, 'Reassessing Soviet Motives for Invading Afghanistan: A Declassified History', *Critical Asian Studies*, 38, 2 (2006), pp. 239–63.

[42] I. Stalin, Politika Sovetskoi vlasti po natsional'nomu voprosu v Rossii, *Pravda*, 226, 10 October 1920, p. 2.

Moreover, after the war, Stalin not only had entire factories in those states of Eastern Europe that sided with Nazi Germany, and now controlled by the Red Army, dismantled and transferred to the Soviet Union, but the Soviet Union also took possession of the region's raw materials, including parts of the oil resources of Romania, Hungary, and Austria. Petroleum also repeatedly played a role in foreign policy and diplomacy. Already Lenin understood how coveted this commodity was. At post-war conferences in the early 1920s, he sought to use Russian petroleum to incentivise trade and Western investment to lead the country out of its international isolation. During the Cold War, the geography of oil and gas exports also followed political considerations, and after the break-up of the Soviet Union, the Russian state repeatedly used energy dependencies against its post-Soviet neighbours – namely in the case of Ukraine – even resorting to complete supply interruptions in the hope to achieve certain political and economic goals.

During the Cold War in particular, energy was often subject to different discursive framings. While Moscow never tired of emphasising the peace-promoting and economic character of international energy projects, the Americans interpreted Soviet oil and gas supplies to Europe as an attempt at geopolitical expansion and covert influence. Washington, therefore, tried repeatedly (and in vain) to prevent the construction of Soviet international pipelines by imposing sanctions. In 1962, under pressure from Washington, NATO imposed an embargo on supplying steel pipes to the Soviet Union, mostly to torpedo the construction of the Druzhba pipeline, at that time the longest oil pipeline in the world. This pipeline was designed to transport oil from the fields of the Volga-Urals region to socialist Eastern Europe. In December 1981, Washington again imposed sanctions on the export of steel pipes and pipeline-related technology to stop the construction of the first gas export pipeline between the Urengoi gas fields of Western Siberia and Western Europe. In both cases, the US embargo attempts failed, and the pipelines were completed. This pattern has continued since the end of the Cold War, the most obvious parallel being the controversial debate over the Nord Stream 2 pipeline project, launched in 2015, which runs along the existing Nord Stream 1 gas link from Russia through the Baltic Sea to Germany. Despite US attempts to prevent it, the laying of the pipeline on the seabed was completed in September 2021 – yet due to the outbreak of the Russian-Ukrainian war in February 2022, the German government was halting the certification process thereby effectively stopping the pipeline from becoming operational.

Finally, it is also important to consider the 'hydrocarbon man' in his specific Russian context. Tsarist Russia, with its modern oil industry in the Caucasus, was one of the leading petroleum nations. It both exported this commodity on a large scale and used it for its own consumption. With a population that was still predominantly rural, the domestic oil market was initially relatively small. During industrialisation, however, demand increased rapidly, as imperial Russia used oil not only as a means of illumination but also as a fuel for diesel-powered locomotives and ships' engines. Nevertheless, coal retained its dominance over oil and gas longer in the Soviet Union than in the United States or Europe.[43] The Soviet industrialisation of the 1920s and 1930s was mainly fuelled by coal and peat. As the new symbols of socialist modernity, Soviet propaganda posters featured not oil derricks but the coal miner, gigantic hydroelectric plants, and electricity pylons. This prioritisation was reflected in the energy mix. As late as 1955, oil and natural gas represented only 24 per cent of Soviet primary energy consumption, compared to 68 per cent in the United States and a global average of around 40 per cent.[44]

Under Stalin, the Soviet Union pushed ahead with the motorisation of the army at a rapid pace, especially in the second half of the 1930s.[45] Like other industrialised nations, the Soviet Union became increasingly dependent on oil, but apart from serving as an export commodity, it was mainly used for wasteful state-controlled enterprises, especially the industrial-military complex. This was very different from the American model, where oil fuelled people's individual mobility, as reflected in the rapid rise of the car industry.[46] In the Soviet Union, public transportation was dominant, and the car as a mass phenomenon appeared relatively late: whereas 9.2 million passenger cars were already registered in the United States by 1920, mass motorisation did not take off until the 1950s in parts of Western Europe, while in the Soviet Union, it did not begin until the late 1960s in parallel with the emergence of a consumer society. Once motorisation began, though, it accelerated rapidly: the Soviet Union's automobile production increased from around 200,000 passenger cars per year in 1965 to 1.2 million ten years later.[47]

43 Redwood, 'The Future of Oil Fuel', p. 106.

44 E. V. Bordova et al., *Gosudarstvennaia politika v neftegazovoi sfere v kontekste rossiiskoi modernizatsii*, Moscow: MAORI, 2014, p. 91.

45 An overview can be found in Slavkina, *Neftegazovyi faktor*, p. 77. Continuing on motorisation in the early Soviet period, see Walter Blasi and Martin Malek, 'Eine "Klasse auf Rädern": Die Anfänge der Motorisierung in der Sowjetunion – vom Auto und Traktor zum Panzer', *Zeitschrift für Weltgeschichte*, 20, 1 (2020), pp. 191–224.

46 Alexander Etkind, *Nature's Evil: A Cultural History of Natural Resources*, Cambridge: Polity Press, 2021, p. 261.

47 Lewis H. Siegelbaum, *Cars for Comrades: The Life of the Soviet Automobile*, Ithaca, NY: Cornell University Press, 2008, p. 238.

The 'hydrocarbon man' thus appeared late in the Soviet Union and the other socialist states of Eastern Europe with regard to individual mobility and never attained the same significance as in the West. Moreover, in the authoritarian states of the 'Eastern Bloc' there was a tension between socialist ideals, which emphasised collective values, and the individual aspiration for mobility symbolised by car ownership. This desire for personal transport, even in the later Soviet era, was highly coveted but limited by its scarcity. This was also reflected in the fact that in the Soviet Union – in stark contrast to Western countries – more trucks than cars were still being produced until 1972.[48]

However, awareness of the existence of immense natural resource wealth also became part of political and social identity in the Soviet Union. This could be seen, for example, in the fact that towns built near natural source riches sometimes took on the names of the relevant raw material. In the 1930s, Magnitogorsk, the city on 'Magnet Mountain', was built for the mining of magnetite iron ore. Norilsk, located in the far north of Russia and established in the same period, was named for its huge nickel deposits. The city of Nefteyugansk, founded in 1967, got its name from the oil (*neft'*) discovered a few years earlier on a branch of the Ob River in the central part of Siberia.

Just as the coal and steel worker became the symbol of a new era during the 1920s and 1930s, so too, during the Second World War, mobilisation campaigns started to celebrate the oil worker (*neftianik*) and, in subsequent years, also the gas worker (*gazovik*), although they were never to attain the same status as the industrial workers of the Stalinist era. Oil and gas were part of a local social self-image and a specific 'oil culture' in the producing regions, especially when workers' settlements or cities were established in connection with the discovery of new deposits. This trend persisted in the post-socialist period, as Douglas Rogers notes in his book *The Depths of Russia*, which looks at the case of the Perm region.[49]

From the 1970s onwards, natural gas became ubiquitous in the public sphere as a result of its status as the most important heating fuel for homes and industrial plants, which it reached via a vast network of gas pipes. During the Cold War, the Soviet Union also increasingly presented itself to the outside world as an energy power. The completion

[48] Ibid., p. 6f. For further reading, see Lewis H. Siegelbaum (ed.), *The Socialist Car: Automobility in the Eastern Bloc*, Ithaca, NY: Cornell University Press, 2011.

[49] Douglas Rogers, *The Depths of Russia: Oil, Power, and Culture after Socialism*, Ithaca, NY: Cornell University Press, 2015.

of international oil and gas pipelines was celebrated in the Soviet state media or on pictorial representations such as postage stamps, which painted them as symbols of 'friendship among nations' or as transnational 'bridges of peace'. The power to unite peoples was also emphasised when the Soviet leadership gave the westbound pipelines such symbolic names as Druzhba ('friendship'), Bratstvo ('brotherhood'), and Soiuz ('union').[50]

Russian energy history, with all its peculiarities, is part of a global history. The value attributed to natural resources was contingent on the historical context. The two great historical upheavals of the twentieth century – the socialist revolution of 1917 and the dissolution of the Soviet Union in the wake of the democratic changes of 1991 – brought about sweeping economic, political, and social transformations. Radical as these transformations were, however, they did little to change the deeper structural conditions that resulted not least from Russia's spatial, climatic, and geological situation. Moreover, since Russia was 'poor' in financial capital, it was always dependent on foreign investment and credit, because, as Count Witte wrote in his memoirs, 'no country had ever developed without foreign capital'.[51] Then, as now, however, resistance to foreign involvement in the exploitation of mineral resources was strong: Witte complained that many would oppose the opening of the country out of 'purely nationalistic considerations' because they believed that 'Russian natural resources should only be exploited by "true" Russians and with the aid of Russian money'.[52]

This proved to be an illusion not only then but also later. The Soviet Union, and later the new Russia, were dependent on capital, technology, and knowledge from abroad for their economic development, and the export of raw materials represented a possibility to gain this access. The commodity in question, however, changed with each historical period. Whereas grain was by far the most important export commodity in late Tsarist Russia, the Soviet Union initially exported mainly wood, flax, crude oil, petroleum products, and other valuable goods such as gold to Western countries. It was not until the late Soviet period that hydrocarbon-based fossil fuels and raw materials – namely oil, oil products, and natural gas – rose to become the most important commodities. These commodities have been dominating Russia's export since the end of the Soviet Union.

[50] Klaus Gestwa, '"Energetische Brücken" und "Klimafabriken": Das energetische Weltbild der Sowjetunion', *Osteuropa*, 54, 9/10 (2004), pp. 15–38, here p. 28.
[51] *The Memoirs of Count Witte*, p. 74. [52] Ibid.

Twentieth-century Russian history was marked by major social and political disruptions. Regarding modernisation, the country's leaders faced similar challenges in all periods. How the Bolsheviks approached the energy question in the early Soviet period and the importance they attached to oil will be discussed in Chapter 2.

2 The Bolsheviks and Oil

Upon taking power in 1917, the Bolsheviks vowed to free the peoples of Russia from the 'yoke' of tsarism. When numerous non-Russian nationalities, including in the multi-ethnic Caucasus region, declared their independence following the revolution, however, the new rulers fought tooth and nail against the dissolution of the former Russian Empire. In the Caucasus, where almost the entire oil industry of the time was concentrated, the Bolshevik-led Red Army also battled for access to the oil fields near Grozny and Baku – for the leaders of the revolution knew that their new state would be no more viable without Caucasian oil than it would without the coal and grain of Ukraine or the cotton of Central Asia.

After the Red Army conquered the Caucasus, the Bolsheviks nationalised the oil companies, expropriated their assets, and drove the foreign owners out of the country. Although Vladimir Lenin never tired of demonising the capitalists of the West, already in the early 1920s, and against not insignificant opposition within his own party, he vehemently advocated bringing Western companies back into the country by granting them concessions. This policy also aimed to rebuild the oil industry, which had been badly damaged by the Civil War, as quickly as possible in order to resume exports abroad. The Bolsheviks also realised that oil could be used as a diplomatic tool. At the great post-war conference in Genoa in 1922, the representatives of Soviet Russia sought to attract foreign investment and boost trade by granting oil concessions, thus paving the way out of their country's international isolation and breaking out of the blockade policy imposed on Soviet Russia by the victorious Entente powers, namely the United Kingdom and France.

With the help of technology, knowledge, and investment from Western countries, the Soviet Union was able to rebuild its oil industry and ramp up production in just a few years. By the end of the 1920s, the country had once again become one of the world's major oil suppliers, and its cheap oil quickly gave it a significant market position in Britain, Germany, Italy, and several other countries. Ideology was not an insurmountable barrier to trade relations: the first socialist state supplied oil to fascist Italy in large quantities and did not stop providing oil to Germany when the Nazis took power in 1933.

By the mid-1930s, however, the Soviet Union's importance as a supplier of crude oil and petroleum products had declined significantly. The country expended most of its oil on domestic consumption, leaving little capacity for exports. Although the Soviet leadership considered the oil industry to be strategically important, especially for the military, oil was for a long time underfunded compared to coal, which, along with peat, was still by far the most important primary energy source at the time. As a result, the Soviet leadership failed to develop new deposits in places like the Volga-Urals region, where oil had already been discovered in the late 1920s. It was only when Hitler's armies advanced into the oil-rich Caucasus during their war against the Soviet Union that Stalin was prompted to order a mobilisation campaign for the rapid development of the fields in the Volga-Urals region.

This chapter focuses on the role of oil in the early Soviet period. It explains the importance that Soviet leaders attached to this commodity for domestic development and international trade and examines the problems and challenges that accompanied oil trade between the Bolshevik Soviet Union and the outside world in the interwar period.

Energy Policy in the Early Soviet Period

The Bolsheviks were anything but modest. They swept into power with nothing less than the claim to create a new world. To lead the first socialist state into the communist future, the Communist Party was declared the guiding force in the project of socialist transformation. For Lenin and his comrades-in-arms, communism was not an abstract concept but a goal to be realised in the present. According to Marxist doctrine, the future followed neither chance nor a divine plan incomprehensible to man. Rather, the future was predictable because it obeyed certain rational principles. Inspired by the prevailing belief in progress at the time, Lenin and his fellow revolutionaries firmly believed in the potential of modern technology to expedite the country's journey towards the utopian future of communism. They were convinced that harnessing the power of technological progress would act as a catalyst to accelerate the transformation of society. The view that man would become more powerful the more energy he acquired was not only prominent among Soviet scientists but also formed part of the state's self-image. In the opinion of the Bolsheviks, the new energy possibilities enabled states to transform landscapes and nature for people's use, which in turn served people and societies. When people participated in the transformation project, they were torn out of their conventional traditions and habitual ways of thinking and became part of a new socialist order in which they themselves participated. As the famous Soviet writer Maksim Gorkii was convinced, 'Man, in changing nature, changes himself.'[1]

Technical innovations, whether the steam engine, the internal combustion motor, or the light bulb, have never only opened new economic and labour possibilities but have also always produced new desires and life designs. In view of important discoveries in the field of energy use, there was a widespread tendency among Western scientists and scholars from the mid-nineteenth century onwards to see energy as the driving force of history in general.[2] Electricity was given a central place because, unlike coal, electricity was seen as a clean form of energy, a 'white coal' with no harmful emissions. The use of electricity was sometimes even seen as a measure of social progress. In their political programmes, conservative as well as socialist parties linked their social visions of the future to the availability of electricity. Electricity was understood not merely as usable energy in the form of electric current but as a means of empowering and emancipating the population. For example, the well-known German socialist August Bebel sketched a picture of an electrified paradise as a prerequisite for the emancipation of women in his publication *Die Frau und der Sozialismus* ('Woman and Socialism'), first published in 1879 and subsequently in fifty further editions. The electrification of kitchens and the elimination of the private kitchen were supposed to relieve women of household work, thus freeing them for other social tasks.[3]

Like many of his contemporaries, Lenin was enthusiastic about electricity. He saw it as a kind of 'fifth element', an energy revolution that would fundamentally change people's lives. In his view, energy use would be a powerful catalyst not only for economic development but also for social transformation. He was therefore convinced that the future of the socialist project depended on the successful use of energy – and electrification seemed like a particularly good way of approaching the

[1] Gorkii made this statement in reference to a famous dictum by Karl Marx in M. Gork'ii, L. Averbakh, and S. Firin (eds.), *Belomorsko-Baltiiskii Kanal imeni Stalina: Istoriia stroitel'stva, 1931–1934 gg.*, Moscow: OGIZ, 1934 [new edition 1998], pp. 280, 318.

[2] Karin Zachmann, 'Past and Present Energy Societies', in Nina Möller and Karin Zachmann (eds.), *Past and Present Energy Societies: How Energy Connects Politics, Technologies and Cultures*, Bielefeld: transcript, 2012, pp. 7–41.

[3] August Bebel, *Die Frau und der Sozialismus*, Zurich-Hottingen: Verlag der Volksbuchhandlung, 1879.

social utopian vision of communism, the classless society, in large steps.[4] As early as 1920, Lenin ordered a comprehensive plan for electrification of the whole country to be drawn up, known as the GOELRO plan. This ambitious scheme involved the participation of hundreds of scientists from across the country, who worked together under the leadership of Gleb Krzhizhanovskii, who was appointed as the head of the planning commission.

The ten-year plan, which Lenin first presented to the Soviet Congress on 22 December 1920, outlined in detail how the industrialisation and electrification of the country were to be carried out. The roughly 600-page document, which according to Lenin was to be treated like a 'second party programme', prescribed not only how many tonnes of cement and bricks would be needed to build hydroelectric power stations and canals but also how much coal, peat, and oil had to be produced to fuel the socialist transformation.[5] The GOELRO plan was thus a precursor to the five-year plans that would be promulgated at regular intervals beginning in 1928. These plans were each prepared by the Gosplan, the State Committee for Economic Planning, according to instructions from the top party leadership. From the early 1920s, Gosplan was the most important planning body in the nascent Soviet central administrative system. Not coincidentally, it was Krzhizhanovskii, the man responsible for elaborating the GOELRO plan, who was to become the first chairman of Gosplan.[6]

Lenin's determination to transform the country was fuelled by Russia's challenging post–Civil War circumstances, marked by millions of casualties, widespread destruction, and massive shortages. Industrial production had collapsed and trade with foreign countries had come to a standstill. Soviet Russia was largely isolated internationally and was not initially recognised diplomatically by any Western state. In the early 1920s, the Bolsheviks were still seeing their hold on power being threatened by uprisings in Ukraine, the Caucasus, and Central Asia; a war with Poland was raging over the delineation of the western border of Soviet Russia. Moreover, the experience of wartime communism had

[4] Klaus Gestwa, *Die Stalinschen Grossbauten des Kommunismus: Sowjetische Technik- und Umweltgeschichte, 1948–1967*, Munich: Oldenbourg, 2010, p. 12.

[5] V. I. Lenin, *Collected Works*, vol. 31, Moscow: Progress, 1966, pp. 483–515, here pp. 510–15.

[6] Jonathan Coopersmith, *The Electrification of Russia, 1880–1926*, Ithaca, NY: Cornell University Press, 1992. On the GOELRO plan, see 'GOELRO: The Creation of a Dream, 1920–1921', in ibid, pp. 151–91; Heiko Haumann, *Beginn der Planwirtschaft: Elektrifizierung, Wirtschaftsplanung und gesellschaftliche Entwicklung Sowjetrusslands 1917–21*, Dusseldorf: Bertelsmann, 1974.

proved disastrous: the forced collectivisation and confiscations that the Bolsheviks carried out during the Civil War provoked large-scale peasant uprisings and resulted in crop failures and catastrophic famines. The permanent state of war and crisis in which Russia had persisted since the outbreak of the First World War in 1914 had emaciated the country and demanded a high blood toll from the population.[7]

From the Bolsheviks' perspective, even after the end of the Civil War, socialism remained threatened by enemies within and by 'imperialist' forces from outside and therefore had to be put on a firm footing as quickly as possible. For Lenin, socialist reconstruction was a struggle for survival, and he saw his socialist project as being in fierce competition with the capitalist world. This contest was not only about the persistence of the Soviet state but also the future of socialism as a global venture. If Russia's Bolsheviks failed, then world revolution was also threatened. Lenin thus saw the creation of a modern large-scale industry, with the energy sector at its core, as essential for validating his ideological vision.

Yet Lenin's electrification plan was too ambitious and too expensive to be fully realised in the time allotted. True, some of its goals were achieved earlier than envisaged. The first large dam on the Dnieper River, for instance, was inaugurated already in 1932. It was built in only five years and was to become the showcase project of the modern Soviet state. Other projects, however, were delayed by several decades, among them the massive dam project on the Volga, construction of which did not begin until 1949 and would reach its full capacity only in 1957.[8] For gigantism and megalomania, the Soviet leadership mobilised millions of workers and, during Stalin's rule, also employed a large number of camp prisoners who laboured under inhumane conditions on the 'construction sites of communism' and gave their lives in their thousands for the accomplishment of large-scale energy projects.[9]

Although Soviet propaganda tried to conceal this fact, the construction of even the great dams would not have been possible without the Soviet Union's success in attracting foreign capital and technology. In the case of the colossal construction on the Dnieper, it was an American company, Hugh L. Cooper Co., that planned and supervised the construction of the dam, and it was with the help of turbines and generators designed and built in the United States that the project was successfully

[7] On the situation in Russia during the years of the First World War, the Revolution, and the Russian Civil War, see Laura Engelstein, *Russia in Flames: War, Revolution, Civil War 1914–1921*, New York: Oxford University Press, 2018.

[8] Gestwa, *Die Stalinschen Grossbauten des Kommunismus*, p. 29.

[9] O. V. Khlevniuk et al., *Zakliuchennye na stroikakh kommunizma: Gulag i ob''ekty energetiki v SSSR; Sobranie dokumentov i fotografii*, Moscow: ROSSPEN, 2008.

completed.[10] Lenin was certainly aware of the need for this support, making it clear to party comrades already at the presentation of the GOELRO plan on 22 December 1920 that neither the gold reserves nor the food fund would amount to the 1–1.2 billion gold roubles that would be needed to implement the plan.[11] He, therefore, advocated landing the necessary investment by opening up the country to the capitalist world and granting concessions to foreign companies. Subsequently, the oil industry in the Caucasus was to benefit from this policy.

Oil, Concessions, and Diplomacy

Oil was not initially the focus of the Bolsheviks' energy policy, driven as it was by social utopian ideas. Yet the leaders of the Russian Revolution were aware of the importance of oil and other natural resources. They were sensitised to the relevance of having access to natural resources during the Russian Civil War, when the anti-Bolshevik forces of the so-called White Army briefly succeeded in cutting off the Bolshevik-controlled areas in central Russia from Ukrainian wheat, coal from the Donbas, and oil supplies from the Caucasus. This blockade led to supply shortages that had devastating effects on industrial production. The reconquest of the resource-rich periphery was therefore a declared goal of the Bolsheviks and their Red Army. Almost the entire oil production of the former Tsarist empire was concentrated in the Caucasus, with the plants near Grozny and Baku contributing by far the largest share of output.[12] Whoever controlled the Caucasus, Stalin told the newspaper *Pravda* in an interview published on 30 November 1920, controlled not only the most important source of fossil fuels but also the trade and transport routes between Europe and Asia.[13]

Although the Bolsheviks and their Red Army eventually managed to recapture all of the Caucasus and its oil by early 1921, they inherited a decimated industry. The destruction wrought by the war, combined with the policies of the Bolsheviks – nationalisation of industrial enterprises and banks, expropriation of foreign property, and arbitrary cancellation of all foreign debt accumulated during the Tsarist period – had led to the

[10] Gestwa, *Die Stalinschen Grossbauten des Kommunismus*, p. 61; Harold Dorn, 'Hugh Lincoln Cooper and the First Détente', *Technology and Culture*, 20, 2 (1979), pp. 322–47.

[11] Lenin, *Collected Works*, vol. 31, p. 513.

[12] Ferdinand Friedensburg, *Das Erdöl im Weltkrieg*, Stuttgart: Enke, 1939, pp. 39–43.

[13] 'Polozhenie na Kavkaze: (Beseda s tov. Stalinym)', *Pravda*, 269, 30 November 1920, p. 1.

effective isolation of Soviet Russia from foreign capital. This, in turn, cut off the supply chains for spare parts for necessary equipment and access to new technology from abroad. There was also a shortage of skilled workers who could repair and operate the plants: many had been mobilised for the war effort and were killed, wounded, or became prisoners of war – with the result that they were absent from construction sites and operating plants. The former owners, meanwhile, had fled abroad after the expropriations.

All this had a dramatic effect on production figures. In 1921, Soviet Russia produced only about 3.8 million tonnes of oil, which was around one-third of the volume that Tsarist Russia had produced in 1916.[14] Of the approximately 3,500 wells that had been in operation near Baku before the war, only 960 were still working after the war.[15] The slump in industrial production also led to an almost complete collapse in exports, including oil.[16]

Only a few months after the revolution, Lenin declared in his well-known essay 'The Immediate Tasks of the Soviet Government', first published in the newspapers *Pravda* and *Izvestiia* on 28 April 1918, that in view of its 'momentary weakness', Soviet Russia would have to pay a 'certain tribute to foreign capital during a transitional period' in order to 'safeguard [the country's] internal economic independence'.[17] Against the backdrop of the enormous devastation of the Civil War, his view that reconstruction could not succeed without the help of capitalist foreign countries eventually prevailed. Lenin identified the granting of concessions as the solution; and as early as 23 November 1920, he signed the decree 'On the General Economic and Legal Conditions of Concession'.[18] Repeatedly, the revolutionary leader advocated finding concessionaires as quickly as possible in the face of the looming 'disaster' and condemned as 'fools' those within the party who opposed his approach.[19]

[14] Marshall I. Goldman, *Petrostate: Putin, Power and the New Russia*, New York: Oxford University Press, 2010, pp. 5–6.

[15] V. Iu. Alekperov, *Neft' Rossii: Proshloe, nastoiashee i budushchee*, Moscow: Kreativnaia ekonomika, 2011, p. 214.

[16] Ministerstvo vneshnei torgovli SSSR, *Vneshniaia torgovlia SSSR za 1918–1940 gg.: Statisticheskii obzor*, Moscow: Vneshtorgizdat, 1960, pp. 13–15.

[17] V. I. Lenin, *The Immediate Tasks of the Soviet Government*, Moscow: Foreign Languages Publishing House, 1951, pp. 8, 29.

[18] Reprinted in *Dekrety Sovetskoi vlasti*, vol. 11, October–November 1920, Moscow: Politizdat, 1983, pp. 251–54.

[19] Thus, for example, in his 'Letter on Oil Concessions' to the members of the Politburo of 12 February 1921, in V. I. Lenin, *Collected Works*, vol. 32, Moscow: Progress, 1973, pp. 134–36, here p. 129.

For Lenin, a concession meant that the Soviet state granted a foreign company the right to take over an existing factory or to build its own production facility in Soviet Russia. The capitalist enterprise was, in this understanding, a 'contractor leasing socialist means of production', among which Lenin counted raw materials, mines, oilfields, minerals, and even factories. In exchange for 'making a profit on his capital', the capitalist contractor was to deliver 'a part of his output to the socialist state'.[20] A quarter of Baku, a quarter of Grozny, and a quarter of the 'best forest reserves', Lenin argued, should be given to the 'biggest imperialist trusts' to enable the reconstruction of the economy and allow Soviet Russia to catch up with the 'advanced trusts of other countries'.[21]

On Lenin's initiative, the Council of People's Commissars approved in principle the possibility of granting oil concessions in Grozny, Baku, and other oil fields as early as 1 February 1921.[22] There was, however, great resistance in the ranks of the party, as not a few saw the concession policy as a betrayal of the aims of the revolution.[23] Many comrades feared that the participation of capitalist enterprises would cause large-scale industry to 'cease to be socialist'.[24] But Lenin was convinced that there was no other viable approach. At the 10th Party Congress in March 1921, he prevailed over internal opponents to officially announce the abandonment of War Communism and the introduction of the New Economic Policy. The latter aimed to restore private property and private trade on a modest scale. On the same occasion, he reminded the comrades present of the importance he attached to concessions for the future of the oil industry in particular:

> Unless we grant concessions, we cannot hope to obtain the assistance of well-equipped modern capitalist industry. And unless we utilise the latter, we shall be unable to lay a proper foundation for our own large-scale production in such industries as oil, which is of exceptional importance for the whole of the world economy.[25]

Lenin's new political course also made itself felt internationally, as his negotiators worked hard to re-establish economic and trade relations and gain diplomatic recognition for their country. On 16 March 1921, Moscow achieved a first major diplomatic success with the signing of

[20] See his 'Report on the Tax in Kind' of 9 April 1921, in ibid., pp. 286–98, here p. 297.
[21] From Lenin's 'Report on the Political Work of the Central Committee of the R.C.P (B)', in ibid., pp. 170–91, here pp. 182–83.
[22] Ibid., p. 183.
[23] On this, see E. S. Kosykh, 'Diskussii v RKP (b): Argumenty "za" i "protiv" inostrannykh kontsessii', *Universum: Obshchestvennye nauki; Elektron. nauchn. zhurn.*, 16, 6 (2015), http://7universum.com/ru/social/archive/item/2270 (last accessed 8 July 2021).
[24] Lenin, *Collected Works*, vol. 32, p. 235. [25] Ibid., p. 266.

the Anglo–Soviet Trade Agreement. Admittedly, Soviet Russia remained far from establishing full diplomatic relations or even integration into the European balance of power. But it was a milestone, as it provided the Soviet state with at least de facto recognition by one of the victorious powers of the First World War.[26] The agreement allowed for the resumption of economic and political relations and paved the way for de jure recognition by the United Kingdom, which finally took place in August 1924. Following the British example, Italy and other countries also concluded trade agreements with Soviet Russia in the early 1920s, with a view to later recognising its government diplomatically. By the mid-1920s, most European countries and many states around the world had recognised the Soviet government. Only the United States waited until 1933 to do so.[27]

The driving force behind the negotiation of the Anglo–Soviet agreement on the Soviet side was Leonid Krasin. Krasin, who was responsible for foreign trade issues within the Bolshevik government from 1920 to 1924, proved to be both a skilled diplomat and knowledgeable about economic affairs. As a trained engineer, he benefitted from the vast experience of industrial and commercial matters that he had gained before the revolution as an employee of the Siemens-Schuckertwerke in Berlin and Moscow. He had also previously worked in Baku for four years, during which time he had become familiar with the needs and functioning of the Russian oil industry.[28]

That the United Kingdom was the first European country to conclude a trade agreement with Soviet Russia was due in part to the efforts of Liberal British Prime Minister David Lloyd George, who believed that trade with capitalist states would have a civilising influence on the Russian revolutionaries. However, the normalisation of trade relations was also in Westminster's interest because Britain had had close economic relations with the Russian Empire before the First World War when Russia had supplied the British economy with much needed raw materials such as grain, timber, flax, and petroleum.[29] Although other

[26] Friedrich Asschenfeldt and Max Trecker, '"Den Bolschewismus in der Wiege erdrosseln": Die Blockade der Entente gegen Sowjetrussland', *Osteuropa*, 71, 10/11 (2021), pp. 47–58, here p. 55.

[27] A. N. Makarov, 'Die Anerkennung der Sowjetregierung durch die Vereinigten Staaten', *Zeitschrift für ausländisches Recht und Völkerrecht*, 4 (1934), pp. 1–24.

[28] Juri Semjonow, *Erdöl aus dem Osten: Die Geschichte der Erdöl- und Erdgasindustrie in der Sowjetunion*, Düsseldorf: Econ, 1973, p. 139; for further information on Krasin, see Semen S. Khromov, *Leonid Krasin: Neizvestnye stranitsy biografii, 1920–1926 gg.*, Moscow: Institut rossiiskoi istorii RAN, 2001.

[29] Christine A. White, *British & American Commercial Relations with Soviet Russia, 1918–1924*, Chapel Hill: University of North Carolina Press,1992, pp. 10–13.

states, including the United States, stepped into the breach after Russian imports were lost due to revolution and war, their products were often much more expensive than the goods previously imported from the Tsarist empire.[30] Not only had it become increasingly clear towards the end of 1920 that the blockade policy of the Entente powers failed to prevent the Bolsheviks from winning the Civil War, but the lack of Russian raw materials on the European market also led to shortages and price increases. Grain prices in particular soared massively. Therefore, it seemed time to reintegrate the Russian economy into world trade.[31]

Lloyd George's efforts to normalise relations with Soviet Russia were not met with universal sympathy, however. In addition to opposition from within the ranks of his own cabinet and in the British parliament, he also came under fire from representatives of the expropriated British oil companies, who fiercely opposed a rapprochement with Soviet Russia. They had expected their government to settle the compensation question before signing any agreement. After all, some sixty British oil companies had operated in Russia before the outbreak of the revolution, and nearly 70 per cent of the foreign capital invested in the Russian oil industry was of British-Dutch origin. In addition, French, German, and Belgian companies had made substantial investments in the Russian petroleum sector.[32] The majority of British companies had invested in the Maikop production area, which was considered a particularly promising oil region at the time. British companies were also represented at other production sites in the Caucasus, namely in Grozny and in the Kuban region.[33] British capital had further accounted for a large share of the Russian General Oil Corporation, founded in London in 1912. This association was not itself involved in the extraction and processing of oil but acquired shares in numerous oil companies operating in the Caucasus, including Russian ones, and thus gained control over their production.[34] Through this merger, the Russian General Oil Corporation rose to become the most important oil producer in the

[30] Norbert H. Gaworek, 'From Blockade to Trade: Allied Economic Warfare Against Soviet Russia, June 1919 to January 1920', *Jahrbücher für Geschichte Osteuropas*, 23, 1 (1975), pp. 39–69, here p. 62.

[31] Asschenfeldt and Trecker, 'Den Bolschewismus in der Wiege erdrosseln', p. 54.

[32] Hans Heyman, 'Oil in Soviet-Western Relations in the Interwar Years', *The American Slavic and East European Review*, 7, 4 (1948), pp. 303–16, here p. 304.

[33] Nat Moser, *Oil and the Economy of Russia: From the Late Tsarist to the Post-Soviet Period*, London, New York: Routledge, 2018, p. 32.

[34] Semjonow, *Erdöl aus dem Osten*, p. 79.

Tsarist empire.[35] Along with other companies, the British were also instrumental in the modernisation of the Russian oil industry. The British-Dutch company Royal Dutch Shell, for example, introduced modern rotary drilling technology in Baku shortly before the outbreak of the revolution.[36]

Indeed, considering the significant presence of British companies in Tsarist Russia, it was to be expected that protests against the Anglo–Soviet agreement would emerge. On 20 June 1921, British companies formed the Association of British Creditors of Russia, which included some 350,000 investors, traders, and entrepreneurs from a variety of industries, whose initial claim for compensation amounted to some 300 million pounds sterling.[37] The aim was to use this association to lend as much weight as possible to demands for compensation from Soviet Russia and at the same time to exert pressure on their own government. British petroleum interests were particularly prominent in this association, but not all firms went along. The Anglo-Maikop Corporation, for example, negotiated directly with the Soviet side and did not apply for membership until 1925, when hopes of a settlement had been dashed.[38] For it was soon to become apparent that the Bolsheviks were intransigent. Instead of engaging in talks regarding compensation, they sought to lure foreign companies into the country by offering attractive concession deals. An opportunity to do so presented itself in the context of the great international post-war conference of Genoa, which took place in the spring of 1922 and aimed to bring order to the financial and economic system of Europe, which had been shattered by the First World War. All the former participants in the war took part; only the United States refused to participate officially and just sent observers.[39]

Oil may not have been on the official conference agenda, but this international meeting in fact revolved very much around the issue of oil, not least because after the First World War there were fears of a worldwide oil shortage. Although demand was steadily increasing, no substantial new reserves had yet been discovered. Russian oil was therefore in great demand.[40] Over 150 companies had filed suits against the

[35] Geoffrey Jones and Clive Trebilcock, 'Russian Industry and British Business, 1910–1930: Oil and Armaments', *Journal of European Economic History*, 11 (1982), pp. 61–103, here p. 87; on the shares in 1913, see Moser, *Oil and the Economy of Russia*, p. 37.

[36] Jones and Trebilcock, 'Russian Industry and British Business', p. 86.

[37] Andrew J. Williams, *Trading with the Bolsheviks: The Politics of East-West Trade, 1920–39*, Manchester, New York: Manchester University Press,1992, p. 66.

[38] Clara Müller, *Zwischen Verhandlungsbereitschaft und Boykott: Grossbritannien und sowjetisches Erdöl 1920–1927*, master's thesis, University of Zurich, 2019, p. 28.

[39] Semjonow, *Erdöl aus dem Osten*, p. 141.

[40] Bukold, *Öl im 21. Jahrhundert*, p. 14.

new government of Soviet Russia over confiscated oil properties, and many company representatives sought to use the Genoa conference to press their claims.[41] But Lenin did not send his representatives to reverse the expropriations. Rather, he was concerned with softening the international economic blockade against Bolshevik Russia and attracting investment. To this end, he had a high-profile delegation dispatched to Genoa, led by Foreign Minister Georgii Chicherin and including such prominent figures as Krasin and Maksim Litvinov. Lenin specifically instructed his delegates to deal with the capitalists 'as merchants' in order to secure 'the most favourable terms for promoting trade', which he considered vital to the economic recovery of Soviet Russia.[42] In his opening speech, given in French on the first day of the conference, Foreign Minister Chicherin spoke not of a struggle between systems but of the possibility of 'parallel coexistence' between the 'old order and the emerging order', which he considered necessary for the reconstruction and recovery of war-torn Europe.[43]

The Soviet delegation also had in their bag a list of possible oil concessions. However, this contained only a fraction of the oil fields seized from Western companies. Moreover, Moscow refused to offer the expropriated companies the prospect of concessions that included their former oil-producing areas. Soviet officials justified this on the grounds that the entire Soviet oil industry had been reorganised and the scattered former holdings of foreign companies consolidated into larger units that were now administered by state 'trusts'. Thus, Azneft was responsible for production near Baku, while Grozneft managed production near Grozny. These companies had union status, which meant that they answered directly to Moscow rather than to the authorities in their respective territorial administrative units.[44]

Despite their reservations, the British government and individual British oil companies showed interest in the possibility of concessions instead of restitution of former property. However, other major former

[41] Robert W. Tolf, *The Russian Rockefellers: The Saga of the Nobel Family and the Russian Oil Industry*, Stanford, CA: Hoover Institution Press, 1976, p. 221.

[42] From the 'Political Report of the Central Committee of the R.C.P. (b)', 27 March 1922, in V. I. Lenin, *Collected Works*, vol. 33, Moscow: Progress, 1973, pp. 263–309, here p. 266.

[43] Chicherin's speech of 10 April 1922 is contained in Russian in Narodnyi komissariat po inostrannym delam [RSFSR], *Materialy Genueskoi Konferentsii (podgotovka, otchety zasedanii, raboty komissii, diplomaticheskaia perepiska i pr.)*, Moscow: n.p., 1922, pp. 78–82, here p. 78.

[44] Sara Brinegar, 'The Oil Deal: Nariman Narimanov and the Sovietization of Azerbaijan', *Slavic Review*, 76, 2 (2017), pp. 372–94, here p. 382.

investors – namely the Belgians and the French – did not want to back down from their hard-line stance. In order not to strain its already tense relations with France, the British temporarily moved closer to the French and Belgian position, signalling to the Soviet delegation that it was only willing to negotiate financial aid once the debt issue had been settled. However, the already fragile European unity was shattered when, unexpectedly for all concerned, the representatives of Germany and Soviet Russia present at the conference signed an agreement to resume economic and diplomatic relations in the Ligurian coastal town of Rapallo, not far from Genoa, on 16 April 1922. This agreement meant that the two states normalised their relations and renounced all indemnities and claims for restitution. As a result, the German delegation was immediately excluded from the negotiations in Genoa, while the Soviet representatives were allowed to stay.[45]

Even though the Soviet delegation remained, the Allies did not back down, as they believed they could act from a position of strength vis-à-vis Moscow. Some assumed that the communists would not be able to hold on to power in the long term, while others believed that the precarious economic and social situation in Russia would sooner or later drive the Bolsheviks to compromise. Lloyd George, for example, interpreted Lenin's rejection of War Communism and the introduction of the New Economic Policy as signs of a fundamental turn away from communist ideology. Among the representatives of Western oil companies, too, there were those who still believed that time was on their side and that the Bolsheviks would eventually agree to return the confiscated properties.

This is the only explanation for the fact that individual Western companies were still taking over shares in expropriated oil firms in the Caucasus in the summer of 1920 when the victory of the Red Army in the Civil War was largely certain. The illustrious industrialist Henri Deterding, majority shareholder and general manager of Royal Dutch Shell, had already acquired all the Rothschilds' business in Russia by 1912.[46] After the Russian Revolution, the Anglo-Dutch company showed interest in taking over Branobel, whose leadership had fled the Caucasus in 1918 and henceforth run the business from Paris and Stockholm.[47] Negotiations failed, however, and instead, Branobel in

[45] Cf. Stephanie Salzmann, *Great Britain, Germany and the Soviet Union: Rapallo and After, 1922–1934*, Woodbridge: The Boydell Press, 2003.

[46] Pierre Jaloustre, *The Oil Interests of the Rothschild of Paris: Between World Competition and the Russian Government (1883–1912)*, unpublished paper, EBHA – 11th Annual Conference, Geneva, 13–15 September 2007, p. 2.

[47] Jones and Trebilcock, 'Russian Industry and British Business', pp. 88f.

July 1920 ceded about half of its Russian holdings, located mainly in Baku and Grozny, to Standard Oil of New Jersey, Shell's major competitor.[48] This happened at a time when the Bolsheviks had already confiscated all of Branobel's Russian property, the Red Army having invaded Azerbaijan in April 1920. Strictly speaking, Branobel was thus selling off assets it no longer owned – but this did not deter Shell.[49] Nor did the new power constellation stop Deterding from taking over shares in other companies that had operated in Russia in July 1920, namely A. I. Mantashev & Co. and G. M. Lianozov Sons, whose owners had also fled the Caucasus after the October Revolution and had henceforth managed their business from Paris.[50]

The fact that many in the West did not believe in the victory of the Bolsheviks and the permanence of Soviet power stemmed from a gross misjudgement of the political situation within Soviet Russia. Moreover, it soon became clear that the Europeans and Americans could only hope to act from a position of strength if they presented a unified front to Moscow on the questions of debt repayment and the return of expropriated property. But even before Germany pulled out, unity between the Western states was badly damaged. The expropriated companies were likewise unable to close ranks in the long term. Especially in the lucrative oil sector, the Bolsheviks' concession offers were simply too tempting. Shortly after the end of the Genoa Conference, rumours of an 'oil scandal' began to circulate: various Western newspapers reported that Shell had secretly negotiated an oil agreement with Soviet government representatives during the conference.[51] This news met with great displeasure, especially on the American side. Standard Oil of New Jersey, which had been hit particularly hard by the expropriations in the Caucasus and felt ignored by the British and French in the awarding of concessions in the Middle East, protested vehemently and demanded that the British government clarify that they had not approved such a concession. Although it could not be ascertained that Shell had indeed negotiated a concession with Soviet Russia, the British government

[48] Philip S. Gillette, 'American Capital in the Contest for Soviet Oil, 1920–23', *Soviet Studies*, 24, 4 (1973), pp. 477–90, here p. 480; Tolf, *The Russian Rockefellers*, pp. 216–17.

[49] George Sweet Gibb and Evelyn H. Knowlton, *History of Standard Oil Company New Jersey*, vol. 2, The Resurgent Years 1911–1927, New York: Harper, 1956, pp. 328–35; Brita Åsbrink, 'Emanuel Nobel Is Forced to Leave Everything and Flee', *The Nobel Brothers*, www.branobelhistory.com/themes/the-nobel-brothers/-emanuel-nobel-is-forced-to-leave-everything-and-flee/ (last accessed 16 August 2021).

[50] Glyn Roberts, *The Most Powerful Man in the World: The Life of Sir Henri Deterding*, New York: Covici Friede, 1938, p. 228.

[51] Karl Hoffmann, 'Die russische Erdölfrage in der Politik', *Zeitschrift für Politik*, 19 (1930), pp. 657–75, here pp. 661–62.

refused to issue an appropriately worded denial, presumably to leave open the possibility of British companies conducting business in the former Tsarist empire in the future.[52]

When the follow-up conference in The Hague in the summer of 1922 also failed to produce any resolution to the restitution issue, those Western oil companies affected by expropriation attempted a formal merger to prevent Soviet oil from reaching the international market. In September 1922, they formed the Groupement International des Société Naphtifères en Russie, commonly known as the 'Front Uni' (United Front), in Paris.[53] This front, led by Deterding, would eventually comprise more than a dozen companies, including such market giants as Royal Dutch Shell, Standard Oil of New Jersey, and Branobel, as well as smaller companies like the Spies Petroleum Company. However, several major players with claims in the Caucasus – notably the Anglo-Maikop Corporation and Baku Consolidated Oilfields – were not among them.[54]

The 'front' did not last long. When Shell heard a rumour that another member of the group had been brokering Soviet petroleum products to a newly formed British distribution company, the Asiatic Petroleum Company (which was part of the Shell Group) bolted and bought substantial quantities of Soviet petroleum to sell on the international market. This led to further unrest and disputes within the group.[55] However, it was not only internal squabbles and boycott evasions that led to the dissolution of the Front Uni by the end of 1923 but also the fact that by that time a number of Western companies had already responded to concession offers from the Soviet government. The best-known case in the Caucasus was the concession negotiated with the American company International Barnsdall Corporation.

The Americans in Baku

The Bolsheviks' primary goal in the early 1920s was to break Soviet Russia's economic and political isolation. They saw cooperation with the leading Western industrial nations as a prerequisite for the restoration of their country's economy and rapid industrialisation. However, the Bolsheviks made the granting of concessions subject to strict conditions, and the conclusion of agreements with foreign

[52] Müller, *Zwischen Verhandlungsbereitschaft und Boykott*, pp. 39–40.
[53] Wilhelm Mautner, 'Das russische Erdöl und die Petroleumpolitik', *Osteuropa*, 2, 5 (1927), pp. 241–60, here pp. 253–54.
[54] Müller, *Zwischen Verhandlungsbereitschaft und Boykott*, p. 43.
[55] Semjonow, *Erdöl aus dem Osten*, p. 153.

concessionaires was often preceded by long and tough negotiations. To obtain a concession, foreign companies had to pay a license fee. They had to commit themselves to a contractually fixed financial investment and the import of the latest technologies. These were not always 'pure' concessions but often 'mixed' concessions with Soviet and foreign participation. In addition to these, some concessions existed in the form of technical-economic cooperation. In such cases, the foreign company did not participate directly in production but merely undertook to provide support to the Soviet company in the form of technical equipment and on-site training. In return, the concessionaire received money or a certain share of the goods produced by the Soviet company. Although this form of cooperation was often referred to as a concession, strictly speaking, it was not.

Over the course of the decade, the Soviet state would conclude concession agreements with numerous foreign companies. According to British economic historian Antony Sutton, by 1926 the Soviet Union had granted foreign firms a total of 330 concessions of the first and second types ('pure' concessions and 'mixed' concessions), and by the end of the 1920s a further 134 concessions of the third type ('technical cooperation').[56] Based on analysis of Soviet archival documents, more recent Russian-language research gives lower figures. Soviet Russia (that is, the Soviet Union from December 1922) is said to have received a total of 2,211 concession offers from foreign companies by 1927, most of them from Germany (35.3 per cent), Great Britain (10.2 per cent), the United States (9.4 per cent), and France (7.9 per cent); however, the Soviet government is claimed to have ultimately approved less than 10 per cent of these.[57]

The literature contains differing accounts of the precise significance of the concession system for the reconstruction of the Soviet economy. While Sutton, in his pioneering study, ascribes great importance to concessions overall for the upswing in individual industrial sectors, including the oil industry,[58] the topic initially received little attention in the Soviet literature and is treated controversially in more recent studies carried out by Russian historians.[59] The reason for this is obvious: the

[56] Antony C. Sutton, *Western Technology and Soviet Economic Development 1917 to 1930*, 2nd ed., Stanford, CA: Hoover Institution on War, Revolution and Peace, 1970, p. 9.

[57] See the data in Semen S. Khromov, *Inostrannye kontsessii v SSSR: Istoricheskii ocherk; Dokumenty*, part I, Moscow: Institut rossiiskoi istorii RAN, 2006, p. 26.

[58] Sutton, *Western Technology*, especially the chapter 'The Western Contribution to Production and Productivity, 1917–30', pp. 327–40.

[59] See the discussion in I. P. Zolotova, 'Opyt ispol'zovaniia kontsessii v narodnom khoziaistve Rossii', *Vestnik BNTU*, 4 (2010), pp. 75–80.

Soviet leadership from the end of the 1920s, when the concession system was significantly scaled back, was not very keen on publicising the role of foreign support. Information on the number of concessions and their economic significance was subject to censorship throughout the Soviet period.[60] The fact of cooperation with the capitalist West was never entirely concealed, but its importance to the country's industrialisation was downplayed so as not to diminish the Soviet Union's own achievements and the alleged superiority of socialism. This attitude was reflected already in early Soviet writings on the subject of concessions. According to a 1931 essay penned by a Soviet author, concession enterprises were 'nothing but small bourgeois islands in the great communist sea' and played a 'very small role' in the Soviet economy; even at the height of the concession system in the late 1920s, they allegedly contributed no more than 1 per cent to the overall output of the Soviet economy.[61]

The role of the concession system in the upswing of the Soviet economy is also difficult to measure because Western companies engaged in business with Soviet Russia often had little interest in providing precise information about their activities, at least as long as the question of repayment of foreign debts and the problem of expropriation of foreign property remained unresolved. After all, companies that received concessions had to expect that they would also receive the land of expropriated foreign companies for lease, even if the Soviet side tried to deny this. Accordingly, foreign investors were usually very reluctant to provide detailed information on the nature and scope of their activities in Soviet Russia; some even sought to suppress it altogether. The International Barnsdall Corporation – which was one of the first foreign companies to be granted a concession for oil production near Baku, receiving it as early as September 1922 – was no exception.

The central mediator in the granting of this concession was Henry Mason Day, who, as president of the American Foreign Trade Corporation after the First World War, had represented the interests of several American businessmen at the 1920 Constantinople Conference. Day toured the south of the former Tsarist empire in 1921, explored the oil fields of the South Caucasus, and as early as October 1921 concluded

[60] M. Levin, and I. Sheveleva, 'Inostrannye kontsessii v 1920-kh godakh v SSSR: "Pochemu rasstalis'"?', *Voprosi ekonomiki*, 1 (2016), pp. 1–20, here p. 3. On the Russian-language state of research, see Irina V. Shilnikova, 'Foreign Concessions in the USSR Textile Industry in the 1920s and early 1930s: The Public-Private Partnership Experience', *Russian Journal of Economics*, 7 (2021), pp. 160–84, here p. 161.

[61] A. A. Bogolepov, 'Die Konzessionen in Sowjetrussland', *Zeitschrift für die gesamte Staatswissenschaft / Journal of Institutional and Theoretical Economics*, 91, 1 (1931), pp. 86–114, here p. 88.

temporary concession contracts that he sought to make palatable to American investors upon his return to the United States. The Barnsdall Corporation showed interest and subsequently established a Baku-based subsidiary, the International Barnsdall Corporation. Day became its president and acquired a quarter of the stock.[62] The public did not learn of the Barnsdall Corporation's activities until March 1922, when they were publicised in a *New York Times* article. The newspaper report stated that the American company was about to sign an agreement for oil production near Baku but that this would be limited mainly to drilling new wells 'in return for which the exclusive oil development rights in the Baku fields are to be given'.[63]

It was to take a good six months of intensive talks before the American and Soviet representatives reached a definitive agreement in September 1922. The focal point of the agreement was determining the designated area and the duration of the concession. According to the contract, the International Barnsdall Corporation received 400 dessiatines (about 4.4 km^2) of land for fifteen years. In return, the American company committed to importing electric pumping systems, rotary drills, and other technical equipment, while US engineers would provide training to the local workforce in the application of these advanced technologies. In addition, the agreement specified exactly how many metres were to be drilled per year and how wide and deep the boreholes were to be. In exchange, the International Barnsdall Corporation was to receive 20 per cent of the output of the newly drilled wells and 15 per cent of the output of those old fields that were to be equipped with new pumps. The contract was signed between the International Barnsdall Corporation, represented by Henry Mason Day, and the Soviet oil trust Azneft, represented by its chairman, Aleksandr Serebrovskii.[64]

The fact that the contract was signed on the Soviet side by the oil company Azneft is significant because the Soviet trusts still enjoyed a relatively large degree of autonomy at that time. These companies were state-owned, and their production targets were prescribed by the central state authorities in Moscow. The concession agreement with the International Barnsdall Corporation, too, was ultimately examined and approved by the centre. However, the Soviet trusts initially had a

[62] Gillette, 'American Capital in the Contest for Soviet Oil', p. 486.
[63] 'Barnsdall Confirms Baku Oil Negotiations', *The New York Times*, 29 March 1922, p. 30.
[64] Iu. V. Evdoshenko, '"Barnsdal'skaia istoriia", ili neftianaia kontsessiia, kotoraia okazalas' nikomu ne nuzhno', *Ekonomicheskaia istoriia: Ezhegodnik 2014/15*, Moscow: Institut rossiiskoi istorii RAN, 2016, pp. 393–436, here p. 400.

relatively large amount of leeway with regard to the implementation of these goals and the conduct of the work on the ground.[65] It was not until 1929, when the oil trusts were subordinated to the newly founded All-Union Petroleum and Natural Gas Industry Association Soiuzneft, that the economic autonomy of these units was formally curtailed.[66] The director of Soiuzneft was Georgii Oppokov (also known as Afanasii Lomov), who had previously headed the Neftesindikat, the state trading organisation for petroleum.[67]

On 21 September 1922, immediately after the contract was signed, Serebrovskii published details of the agreement with the International Barnsdall Corporation in a lengthy article on the front page of *Pravda*, which was immediately picked up by Western newspapers.[68] While Day was not pleased with Serebrovskii's actions because of the sensitive restitution issue and immediately voiced his displeasure to Krasin,[69] the Soviet side clearly wanted to use the deal to lobby for further concession agreements – in which effort it was at least somewhat successful. The *New York Times*, for example, in an article of 24 September 1922, largely adopted the Soviet reading when it stressed that the land that the Soviet government had ceded to the American company would be 'State lands' and that 'there is no question of former owners in the region of Baku'.[70] The newspaper quoted lengthy excerpts from a statement by Krasin, who praised this agreement as a model for a profitable partnership between America and Russia. Krasin stressed that 'because this was the first deal of the kind', the International Barnsdall Corporation had also been granted 'most favorable' terms.[71] The propagation of the award of this oil concession was so important to the Soviet side because it effectively broke the embargo that Western oil companies had previously attempted to impose. This was to pave the way for business activities by other Western companies in the Soviet Union.

[65] R. N. Bakhtizin, A. S. Vereshagin, and M. Iu. Kiiko, *'Neftianoi faktor' v Rossiiskoi gosudarstvennoi politike: Dorevoliutsionnyi i sovetskii periody*, Ufa: Neftegazovoe delo, 2007, p. 75.

[66] Alekperov, *Neft' Rossii*, pp. 264–65.

[67] Aleksandr Matveichuk, 'V tiskakh pervoi piatiletki', *Neft' Rossii*, 2 (2011), www.oilru.com/nr/214/5271/ (last accessed 7 July 2021); on the organisation of the Soviet oil industry in the early Soviet period, see Ts. Kh. Sergeeva, 'Bor'ba za neft', teoreticheskie diskussii i stanovlenie sovetskoi modeli upravleniia neftianoi otrasl'iu 1910–1940-e gg.', *Vestnik Kazanskogo tekhnicheskogo universiteta*, 15, 5 (2012), pp. 154–62.

[68] [A.] Serebrovskii, 'Amerikantsi i burenie na bakinskikh promyslakh', *Pravda*, 212, 21 September 1922, p. 1.

[69] Evdoshenko, 'Barnsdal'skaia istoriia', p. 402.

[70] 'Americans to Work Russian Oil Tract', *New York Times*, 24 September 1922, p. 9.

[71] Ibid.

However, the cooperation between Azneft and the International Barnsdall Corporation did not run smoothly. The venture was not very promising from the outset. Since the United States had not recognised the Soviet government officially, the US State Department stressed that it would not be able to support the company diplomatically 'in case of a controversy'.[72] Moreover, the State Department had doubts about the Soviet official representation that the land made available to the International Barnsdall Corporation for production was indeed former crown land. US Secretary of State Charles E. Hughes made clear in a letter to the company dated 30 January 1923 that even though he demanded a 'written confirmation' that the agreement did not 'encroach upon the property rights of others', no such statement 'has been received up to the present'.[73]

There were also problems in the Soviet Union: although the arrival of the Americans at the beginning of 1923 was celebrated in the local Soviet press, this did not mean that the awarding of the concession met with goodwill everywhere. Even Krzhizhanovskii, then head of Gosplan, explicitly opposed foreign concessions in the oil industry because he believed that oil, as one of the basic sources of energy in both its raw and refined forms, should remain 'completely and indivisibly' under government control, a point he had made in a January 1922 internal report to the Politburo titled 'Why We Should not Offer the Industrial Regions of Baku or Grozny for Concessions'.[74] Krzhizhanovskii also expressed his belief that the oil industry, if granted access to its profits, could fund its own reconstruction. Obsolete equipment, he argued, should be replaced with loans floated on gold or refined petroleum products. Furthermore, he maintained that the granting of concessions would make it impossible for the Soviet government to extract short-term profits from the petroleum industry, as these would be siphoned off by foreigners.[75]

Azneft director Serebrovskii supported concessions in line with government requirements. Personally, however, he did not seem to be very fond of such agreements either. In a letter to his party colleague Georgii

[72] The refusal on the part of the American government to support the company was made public in an article published in the *New York Times*: 'Sending Engineers to Baku: Barnsdall Corporation Will Have No Backing from Washington', *New York Times*, 21 January 1923, p. 5.

[73] The letter can be found in *Papers Relating to the Foreign Relations of the United States 1923*, vol. II, Washington, DC: United States Government Printing Office, 1938, pp. 812–13.

[74] Gosudarstvennyi Arkhiv Rossiiskoi Federatsii (GARF), fond (f). 8350, opis' (op.). 1, delo (d.). 51, listy (ll.) 17–20, here l. 17; citation included in Sara G. Brinegar, *Baku at All Costs: The Politics of Oil in the Soviet State*, PhD dissertation, University of Wisconsin–Madison, 2014, p. 90.

[75] Ibid., pp. 90–91.

Piatakov, then deputy chairman of Gosplan, Serebrovskii even claimed to be a convinced 'counter-concessionaire' who longed to 'rid Baku in the near future of these concessionaires, who are now unnecessary'.[76] This did not mean that Serebrovskii was not interested in importing modern Western technology and profiting from foreign knowledge. But this is precisely where problems arose in the cooperation with the International Barnsdall Corporation. The Soviet side repeatedly complained that the Americans did not deliver the promised technology to the extent stipulated in the contract, and therefore the deadlines for the work on the wells were not met. After the contract had been renegotiated in the spring of 1923, the equipment finally arrived on site that summer. However, the disputes and mutual accusations of contract violations did not abate in the months that followed. The conflict escalated over the course of 1924 and the concession agreement was formally dissolved in the spring of 1925.[77]

Nevertheless, cooperation with the International Barnsdall Corporation proved extremely profitable for the Soviets. The American company organised the import of the latest technology, such as ultra-modern rotary drills from the American Lucey Manufacturing Company, which became the full property of Azneft due to the premature termination of the contract. Drilling with a rotary drill string proved crucial to increasing production, as this method allowed deeper and therefore more productive wells to be developed. While the rotary drilling technique was known before the revolution, it was not until after 1923 that this method, pioneered by American companies, was extensively employed in the Caucasian oil fields. The introduction of electric pumps from the United States had a similarly transformative impact, replacing the outdated practice of manually extracting oil from wells using buckets and barrels.[78]

The experience of working with the International Barnsdall Corporation also showed that the granting of concessions in the strict sense was not a prerequisite for the establishment of a modern industry but that the main thing was to introduce technology and knowledge from abroad. It was vital that the local workforce was trained in the new technology and procedures, as the International Barnsdall Corporation

[76] The letter is dated 22 April 1923 and excerpts are printed in Evdoshenko, 'Barnsdal'skaia istoriia', p. 410.

[77] Ibid., p. 417.

[78] Sutton, *Western Technology*, pp. 24–25; *Russia: The Official Report of the British Trades Union Delegation to Russia and Caucasia Nov. and Dec., 1924*, London: Co-Operative Printing Society, 1925, p. 222.

had done by sending its own engineers to Baku.[79] The allocation of Russian land to foreigners, however, seemed unnecessary. The planned granting of large oil concessions to other American firms, notably the Sinclair Oil Corporation, was thus not to materialise.[80] More broadly, Lenin's original idea to lease a substantial part of the oil fields of Baku and Grozny to foreigners was never realised. A 'pure' concession for oil production near Baku was awarded in 1923 to the French Duverger Group, which also received a concession near Emba.[81] Individual oil concessions were granted by the Soviet government in less productive or still largely undeveloped areas, including Sakhalin Island in the Far East. In fact, the only concession in the petroleum sector that was to last into the Second World War was the one awarded to a Japanese company on Sakhalin on 14 December 1925 for a term of forty-five years.[82]

In the oil sector, it was not concessions in the strict sense that were to play a role in restoring the industry but rather the expansion of technology imports and cooperation with Western companies that trained personnel and assisted Soviet engineers in the construction of industrial projects. This model of cooperation, in various forms, would become prevalent and persist throughout the subsequent years and decades. Since the Soviet state lacked the financial resources to purchase all its equipment abroad, Soviet engineers soon started copying Western technology as best they could in their own industrial plants. As early as 1924, for example, the Soviet Union built production facilities based on American plans that were capable of manufacturing some of the technology needed for oil production, including derricks, deep drilling pumps, and rotary drilling rigs.[83] Nevertheless, the proportion of material imported from abroad remained significant: according to Russian oil historian Aleksandr Igolkin, in 1925–26 around one-fifth of the equipment supplied to the Soviet oil companies Azneft and Grozneft was of

[79] Sutton, *Western Technology*, p. 21.

[80] Katherine Siegel, *Loans and Legitimacy: The Evolution of Soviet-American Relations 1919–1933*, Lexington: The University Press of Kentucky, 1996, especially the section 'American Concessionaires in the Soviet Union', pp. 118–26.

[81] Sutton, *Western Technology*, p. 29.

[82] V. N. Elizar'ev, 'Inostrannyi kapital v sakhalinkikh neftegazovykh proiektakh: Kak eto nachalos'', *Aktual'nye problemy gumanitarnykh i estestvennykh nauk*, 2/1 (2016), pp. 74–77; G. A. Shalkus, 'Sozdanie i deiatel'nost' iaponskikh kontsessii na Severnom Sakhaline v 1925–1944 gg.', *Sibirskii torgovo-ekonomicheskii zhurnal*, 7 (2008), pp. 87–91.

[83] A. A. Igolkin, 'Import oborudovaniia kak faktor razvitiia neftianoi promyshlennosti v gody dovoennykh piatiletok', *Ekonomicheskii zhurnal*, 9 (2005), pp. 208–20 [online pp. 1–16, here p. 1], https://cyberleninka.ru/article/n/import-oborudovaniya-kak-faktor-razvitiya-neftyanoy-promyshlennosti-v-gody-dovoennyh-pyatiletok (last accessed 13 July 2021).

foreign origin with the Americans, the British, and the Germans being the main suppliers to the Soviet oil industry at that time.[84]

Not only in the production but also in the processing and transportation of oil, there was close cooperation with Western companies in the early Soviet period. American, British, and German companies were heavily involved in the construction of refinery complexes.[85] Between 1925 and 1928, steel pipes and pipeline technology from the United States, Germany, and Great Britain were used to build two important export pipelines to the Black Sea, where Soviet crude oil was processed and shipped. One oil line ran from Baku to Batumi in Georgia, the other from Grozny to Tuapse in southern Russia.[86] However, not all the technology for the construction of the pipelines was imported from abroad: in addition to the equipment supplied by German and British companies for the pumping stations of the Baku-Batumi pipeline, parts were made in Soviet factories according to German plans.[87] The American company J. I. Allen Co. was responsible for the demanding welding work. The company not only supervised the work on site but also invited around 150 Soviet welders to the United States to train in its factories near Los Angeles.[88]

'Red Oil' on the World Market

The Bolsheviks' success in purchasing foreign technology in the early 1920s was made possible by the fact that the Soviet state initially still had relatively large gold reserves. But these were gradually depleted. In their quest to obtain convertible currency, the Bolsheviks went so far as to sell abroad art and cultural assets that they had previously taken from monasteries, museums, and former aristocratic houses as part of their policy of expropriation. Measured against their actual value, however, the proceeds from the export of cultural objects were rather small.[89] In the longer term, the Bolsheviks would need stable access to international markets for their goods – and they saw the concession policy as a means of achieving this. At its core, this policy functioned largely according to the principle of barter: raw materials in return for technology. The agreement with the International Barnsdall Corporation, which provided for the supply of American drilling and oil production technology in

[84] Ibid., p. [2]. [85] Sutton, *Western Technology*, p. 37. [86] Ibid., p. 33.
[87] Igolkin, 'Import oborudovaniia', pp. [2–3]; Sutton, *Western Technology*, p. 35 (n. 53).
[88] Sutton, *Western Technology*, p. 34.
[89] Waltraud Bayer, 'Der legitimierte Raub: Der Umgang mit Kunstschätzen in der Sowjetunion, 1917–1938', *Osteuropa*, 56, 1/2 (2006), pp. 55–70.

exchange for a certain share of the crude oil produced, precisely followed this pattern. Later deals often operated on the same model: when Standard Oil of New York was commissioned by Azneft to build a refinery in Batumi for processing crude oil in 1927, the Soviet side paid for it with a share of the petroleum products produced at that refinery and made available to the Americans for sale on international markets.[90]

This business model had its limits. After all, to make purchases abroad, the Soviet Union was ultimately dependent on foreign currency. It could only earn this by selling its products directly on international markets. However, the Western blockade policy initially made it difficult to gain this access. It was not until 1923, in parallel with the granting of the first concessions, that the Soviet Union was once again to appear on the global stage as an exporter of crude oil and petroleum products; at the same time, the Soviet Union was also to gain increased access to international credit markets.

Foreign oil trade was handled by the state-owned Neftesindikat. This organisation was founded in July 1922, but it was not until September 1923 that the monopoly on oil trade was transferred to it (the monopoly on foreign trade had been formally in the hands of the state since March 1922). Neftesindikat represented a kind of umbrella organisation of the most important Soviet oil companies (among them Grozneft, Azneft, and Embaneft), some of which were still marketing their oil themselves in the early 1920s.[91] Although Neftesindikat was formally subordinated to the Supreme Council of the National Economy and, within that institution, to the Leading Oil Committee, the syndicate enjoyed relatively wide latitude in its activities abroad. The organisation's strategy was initially aimed at paving its way into international business through low prices and agreements with Western oil companies. In the spring of 1923, Neftesindikat agreed with the London-based firm Sale and Company for the sale of 30,000 tonnes of crude oil and follow-on sales of 100,000 tonnes of kerosene per year for the British market. In the deal, Neftesindikat received a 50 per cent stake in the company's share capital and reserved the right to buy all the shares at a later date.[92] Following this first major breakthrough for Soviet oil on the international market, other companies did not want to be left behind; Neftesindikat subsequently succeeded in concluding further agreements

90 Igolkin, 'Import oborudovaniia', p. [3].

91 Alekperov, *Neft' Rossii*, p. 217; A. A. Igolkin, 'Sovetskii neftianoi eksport v gody predvoennykh piatiletok', *Neftianoe khoziastvo*, 9 (2006), pp. 139–41, here p. 139; A. A. Igolkin, *Sovetskaia neftianaia politika v 1940-m–1950-m godakh*, Moscow: Institut rossiiskoi istorii RAN, 2009, pp. 26, 29.

92 Sutton, *Western Technology*, p. 41; Marshall, *Petrostate*, p. 28.

for the marketing of its oil, including with the major Western companies Royal Dutch Shell and Standard Oil of New Jersey.[93] Together, these two companies were responsible for 44 per cent of Soviet petroleum sold on the international market in 1924–25 and for about a third of sales in 1925–26.[94]

Not insignificant for the success of Soviet oil were Serebrovskii's own international activities. In the spring of 1924, he received an order from the Politburo to travel to Europe 'in matters of the Neftesindikat' to explore the market and the possibilities for international business.[95] In England, Serebrovskii visited, among others, the British engineering firm Vickers, concluding substantial contracts for the purchase of equipment for the Soviet oil industry.[96] Vickers – which had done extensive business in Russia prior to the revolution and was anxious to re-establish its trade relations – was to become a major supplier of equipment for drilling, cracking, and refining oil in the Soviet Union.[97]

After various stops in Europe, a Soviet delegation led by Serebrovskii visited the United States in the summer and autumn of 1924. This choice of visit was no accident: the Soviet Union's industrialisation at this time was strongly oriented towards American models, not only in terms of technology and equipment but also with regard to the functioning and organisation of large industrial enterprises.[98] During his months-long stay, Serebrovskii visited oil production plants in various parts of the country in order to gain insight into the internal structure of the American petroleum industry, and in early October he took part in an international congress of petroleum specialists in Tulsa (Oklahoma) that lasted several days and at which he himself gave a lecture.[99]

During his US tour he also met with John D. Rockefeller. The two men agreed at that meeting to grant Standard Oil of New Jersey distribution rights for Soviet oil in the Middle and Far East.[100] At least as important, in Serebrovskii's view, was that Soviet companies would

[93] Sutton, *Western Technology*, p. 41. [94] Alekperov, *Neft' Rossii*, p. 230.

[95] Evdoshenko, 'Barnsdal'skaia istoriia', p. 414.

[96] M. M. Zagorul'ko, V. V. Bulatov, and V. N. Kostornichenko, *'Vikkers' v Rossii*, Volgograd: Izd-vo VolGU, 2012, pp. 195–96.

[97] Roger Munting, 'British Business and the Politics of Trade with the USSR during the New Economic Policy (NEP)', *Business History*, 48, 2 (2006), pp. 254–71, here p. 261.

[98] B. M. Shpotov, 'Ispol'zovanie opyta SShA v rekonstruktsii sovetskoi neftianoi promyshlennosti v 1920–30-e gg.', *Rossiiskii zhurnal' menedzhmenta*, 4, 1 (2006), pp. 163–78.

[99] V. N. Kostornichenko, 'Deiatel'nost' A. P. Serebrovskogo po modernizatsii otechestvennoi neftianoi promyshlennosti perioda NEPA: Privlechenie amerikanskogo kapitala', *Vestnik RUDN: Seriia 'Istoriia Rossii'*, 4 (2007), pp. 64–71, here p. 66.

[100] Jonathan Sicotte, 'Alexandr Serebrovskii and the Modernization of the Soviet Oil Industry – 1924 to 1929', *The Soviet and Post-Soviet Review* (2021), pp. 1–30, here

henceforth be granted access to American credit markets, which was necessary to provide financial security for commercial transactions. Rockefeller was to receive 10 per cent of the proceeds from the business of selling Soviet oil; in return, the Soviets would receive greater access to both the international oil market and American credit institutions.[101] In the years that followed, the Soviet Union would make extensive use of its ability to take out loans: between 1926 and 1929, the Soviet oil industry ordered over 20 million US dollars' worth of equipment from the United States alone, the purchase of which it financed to a large extent with long-term credits.[102]

After Soviet oil gained access to the international market through low prices and collaboration with Western oil companies, Neftesindikat set about building up distribution networks abroad by founding its own companies. The most obvious locations were those countries where Soviet crude oil and petroleum products were already on the market. It was therefore only natural that Neftesindikat should set up one of its first subsidiaries in Great Britain. Together with ARCOS (All-Russian Co-operative Society Ltd.), a foreign trade organisation under the Soviet Ministry of Foreign Trade, Neftesindikat arranged in August 1924 for the registration of Russian Oil Products Ltd. (R.O.P.) as a private company with a share capital of 100,000 British pounds.[103] The London-based company succeeded in establishing its own large trading system on the British market the very next year. The company constructed oil storage facilities, maintained a network of filling stations, and even had sea terminals built on the British coast for its fleet of tankers.[104] Thanks to an aggressive low-price strategy, R.O.P. succeeded in conquering a large share of the market in a relatively short time. Indeed, of the 250,000 tonnes of oil imported into Great Britain in the first nine months of 1925, Soviet petroleum products accounted for about one-fifth.[105]

Soviet petroleum expanded into other parts of Europe at the same time. In 1926, Neftesindikat founded the German-Russian Naphta-Gesellschaft (Derunapht), based in Berlin, for the import and

p. 14, https://doi.org/10.30965/18763324-BJA10032 (last accessed 16 August 2021); Sutton, *Western Technology*, p. 42.

101 Sicotte, 'Alexandr Serebrovskii', p. 14.

102 Igolkin, 'Import oborudovaniia', p. [2].

103 Sutton, *Western Technology*, p. 42; Alekperov, *Neft' Rossii*, p. 231; for further reading, see Julian Bowden, 'That's the Spirit! The Russian Oil Products Ltd. (ROP) and the British Oil Market, 1924–39', *Journal of European Economic History*, 17, 3 (1988), pp. 641–63.

104 Alekperov, *Neft' Rossii*, p. 231.

105 'Russian Oil Products Ltd', www.blisworth.org.uk/images/Canal/Arm/ROP.htm (last accessed 28 April 2021); Bakhtizin, Vereshchagin, and Kiiko, *'Neftianoi faktor'*, pp. 81–82.

distribution of petroleum and petroleum products in Germany. Through the Soviet company Derop, which was established shortly thereafter, Derunapht also maintained a network of tank farms, supply depots, and service stations throughout Germany.[106] Neftesindikat also established branches and joint ventures to distribute its products in several other countries, including Italy, Austria, Czechoslovakia, France, Turkey, Sweden, and Finland. In Spain, Neftesindikat joined forces with Argus Bank of Barcelona to form a company that was awarded the exclusive right to distribute Soviet crude oil in Spain, Portugal, and their colonies. Trade with states outside Europe also increased, one example being Persia, where Soviet petroleum was sold through the Persian-Soviet company Persaneft. Soviet oil products first appeared in South China and Korea in the early 1930s and in Canada and New Zealand in 1932.[107]

By the end of the 1920s, Soviet oil production had surpassed its 1901 peak and the Soviet Union rejoined the ranks of the world's leading oil exporters.[108] By selling crude oil and petroleum products – namely gasoline, kerosene, and fuel oil – the Soviet Union had gained a fairly important position in the energy mix of many countries in Europe and beyond. By the late 1920s, Neftesindikat was responsible for 4 per cent of gasoline sold to the Western European market, 16 per cent of kerosene, 12 per cent of lubricating oil, 13 per cent of fuel oil, and 6 per cent of crude oil.[109] It is true that the Soviet Union's share of the global trade volume as of 1928 was just 1.7 per cent, still far below the Tsarist empire's 3.7 per cent share in 1913.[110] Within a few years, however, oil – along with timber and gold – would become the Soviet Union's most important export commodities. By the end of the 1920s, petroleum and petroleum products generated between 15 and 20 per cent of the total value of Soviet exports and thus contributed considerably to Soviet foreign exchange earnings.[111] Thus, petroleum also replaced grain to

[106] Alekperov, *Neft' Rossii*, p. 231; Titus Kockel, *German Oil Policy 1928–1938*, Berlin: Akademie Verlag, 2015, p. 353.

[107] Alekperov, *Neft' Rossii*, pp. 231–333; Igolkin, 'Sovetskii neftianoi eksport', p. 139; A. K. Sokolov, 'Sovetskii "Neftesindikat" na vnutrennem i mezhdunarodnom rynkakh v 1920-e gg.', in L. I. Borodkina (ed.), *Ekonomicheskaia istoriia: Obozrenie*, vol. 10, Moscow: n.p., 2005, pp. 101–31, here pp. 120–27.

[108] Goldman, *Petrostate*, pp. 4–6.

[109] Bakhtizin, Vereshagin, and Kiiko, *'Neftianoi faktor'*, p. 74.

[110] Anna Kashurina, '1917–2017: Sto let vneshnei torgovli po-russki – II vypusk', *Proved*, 4 April 2017, http://провэд.рф/economics/fea/41508-1917-2017-sto-let-vneshney-topgovli-po-pusski-ii-vypusk.html (last accessed 13 July 2021).

[111] Sutton, *Western Technology*, p. 44; Aleksandr Igolkin puts the figure at 18.7 per cent for 1932: Igolkin, 'Sovetskii neftianoi eksport', p. 140; according to Marshall Goldman, oil revenues accounted for 14 per cent of the Soviet Union's total foreign exchange earnings in 1928, see Goldman, *Petrostate*, p. 29.

some extent. The most important commodity in late Tsarist Russia could no longer be exported in the same quantities after the devastation of the Civil War and the famines that followed.[112]

The triumphant advance of Soviet oil did not go entirely smoothly. In Great Britain in particular, there was great resistance to importing Soviet oil considering the still unresolved restitution issue. The general deterioration in British–Soviet relations was due not only to the anti-Soviet policy of the Conservative Party, which had been in power since 1924, but also to the fact that business organisations and political circles were increasingly calling for public boycotts of Soviet oil imports, warning of the growing political influence of the Soviet Union and the spread of world communism. In May 1927, the situation came to a dramatic head when Metropolitan Police officers raided the headquarters of ARCOS, whose offices were in the same building as the Soviet trade delegation. The material seized during the raid largely confirmed suspicions that the Soviet Union was engaged in propaganda activities under the guise of trade.[113] In light of this, the British Cabinet decided to break off diplomatic relations with the Soviet Union, a decision that was confirmed by a large majority in the British Parliament. The action caused a great stir in the British and international press at the time. Soviet diplomats and business representatives in Britain strongly contested the official account, claiming that it was a plot to sabotage a forthcoming loan and damage the economic interests of the Soviet Union.[114]

The severance of diplomatic relations did not extend to trade relations, as the British government refrained from implementing a formal boycott of Soviet oil. Nevertheless, the volume of British–Soviet trade, which had already been declining, fell once again as a result of the political upheavals; oil exports to Great Britain also declined. However, this was only temporary: the following year Great Britain imported more Soviet crude oil and in 1929 the Soviet Union figured as the country's third most important oil supplier behind the United States and Iran.[115] Great Britain thus represented the most important market for Soviet petroleum and petroleum products, followed by Italy, Germany, France, and Spain. Together, these five states absorbed about two-thirds of all Soviet petroleum

[112] See the compilation in Sanchez-Sibony, *Red Globlization*, p. 36.

[113] Harriette Flory, 'The Arcos Raid and the Rupture of Anglo-Soviet Relations, 1927', *Journal of Contemporary History*, 12, 4 (1977), pp. 707–23.

[114] Alekperov, *Neft' Rossii*, p. 234; Hoffmann, 'Die russische Erdölfrage in der Politik', pp. 657–58, 666.

[115] Alekperov, *Neft' Rossii*, p. 237.

exports.[116] Other important customers of Moscow during this period were Egypt, Turkey, British India, South Africa, and Belgium.[117]

Although there were already voices in Europe warning that the Soviet Union was preparing a large-scale 'oil offensive' to flood the market with cheap raw materials and displace Western international companies, European governments did not generally see 'red oil' as a major security risk, also because oil still accounted for a relatively small share in the coal-based economies of Europe at that time.[118] But it was in the military sphere that oil played an increasingly important role. In fact, the Soviets supplied a not insignificant portion of their oil by order of Western governments interested in purchasing relatively cheap Soviet fuel primarily for their war fleets. Thus, the Soviet Union supplied fuel to the British and French navies; Greece and the United States also ordered Soviet fuel for their warships. Soviet companies supplied oil to Mussolini's fascist Italy, even though the Italian government was persecuting socialists and communists at home. Similarly, Hitler's rise to power did not stop the Soviets from selling their oil to Germany. Soviet oil was simply too cheap for Western governments to refuse on political or ideological grounds.[119] Responsible for all international trade in crude oil and petroleum products on the Soviet side at this time was the company Soiuznefteeksport, which was subordinate to the Soviet state petroleum organisation Soiuzneft and from 1931 had a monopoly on all trade in petroleum and petroleum products; all shareholdings of Soviet petroleum companies operating abroad had also been transferred to Soiuznefteeksport.[120]

Oil Shortage and World War

The triumph of Soviet oil was possible because the representatives of Soviet companies and trade organisations quickly familiarised themselves with the rules of the international oil business and became important

[116] A. A. Igolkin, Neftianaia promyshlennost' SSSR (1928–1950-e gody), Moscow: Institut ekonomiki RAN, 2011, p. 245.

[117] Igolkin, 'Sovetskii neftianoi eksport', p. 141.

[118] J. Trachtenberg, 'The Soviet Oil Offensive', *The Living Age* (September 1933), pp. 35–37; this is an article translated into English that originally appeared in the conservative Viennese daily *Neues Wiener Tagblatt.*

[119] Claudia Wörmann, *Osthandel als Problem der atlantischen Allianz: Erfahrungen aus dem Erdgas-Röhren-Geschäft mit der UdSSR*, Bonn: Europa Union Verlag, 1986, p. 27; Semjonow, *Erdöl aus dem Osten*, p. 185; Bakhtizin, Vereshchagin, and Kiiko, *'Neftianoi faktor'*, p. 80; Goldman, *The Enigma of Soviet Petroleum*, p. 26.

[120] 'Ob organizatsii v vedenii Narodnogo komissariata vneshnei torgovli Vsesoiuznogo ob"edineniia po eksportu nefti i nefteproduktov ("Soiuznefteeksport")', Moscow, Kremlin, 26 February 1931', *Istoricheskie materialy* (Istmat), http://istmat.info/node/54632 (last accessed 30 April 2021).

players in this market themselves. In doing so, they did not behave much differently from their capitalist counterparts. With its aggressive low-price policy, the Soviet Union initially flooded selected countries with cheap oil to secure market shares. The Soviet Union could afford these low prices primarily because the labour force in the country was relatively inexpensive. Only after market share had been secured were prices cautiously increased. In this, the Soviet Union used a strategy that had been common practice among international oil companies since the late nineteenth century. Even political upheavals, as in the case of Great Britain, were ultimately unable to drive Soviet oil away. Rather, the real danger lurked in the invisible forces of the market itself. These made themselves felt in the global economic depression of the 1930s, because of which global demand for oil fell sharply and, consequently, world market prices also collapsed. The oil market was faced with an even more striking situation as the discovery of new fields, such as the Black Giant field in east Texas in 1930, which happened to be the largest field in the world at the time, led to a further decline in already relatively low prices. Concerns about scarcity, which had existed since the early 1920s, turned into a tangible oil glut, exacerbating the market's challenges.[121]

This unfavourable constellation was felt directly by the Soviet Union. While in 1930 the country earned 157 million roubles from the export of 4.7 million tonnes of crude oil, by 1932 revenue had fallen by more than 30 per cent, even though the country had increased its export volume by 30 per cent.[122] Given the low prices at which Soviet companies sold their petroleum on the international market, already tight profit margins were also shrinking. The Soviet Union attempted to compensate temporarily for the collapse in oil prices by increasing grain exports and continued to export its grain even as famine caused millions of deaths in 1932–33, especially in Ukraine but also in other parts of the country, due to mismanagement, crop failures, and confiscations ordered by the Soviet leadership in the aftermath of forced collectivisation of farms.[123]

The withdrawal of Soviet oil in the 1930s was paralleled by a general collapse in global economic trade. In the case of the Soviet Union, however, the reduction in international trade volume was not, as sometimes assumed in the Western literature, due to a deliberate policy on the part of the Soviet government to disconnect the country's economy from

121 Bukold, *Öl im 21. Jahrhundert*, p. 16.
122 Igolkin, 'Sovetskii neftianoi eksport', p. 140.
123 R. W. Davies, M. B. Tauger, and S. G. Wheatcroft, 'Stalin, Grain Stocks and the Famine of 1932–1933', *Slavic Review*, 54, 3 (1995), pp. 642–57, especially the table from p. 645.

global trade flows. Rather, it should be understood as a concomitant of the sharp fall in commodity and energy prices in the wake of the global economic crisis and surging nationalism in Europe.[124]

The fact that the Soviet Union almost completely stopped exporting oil abroad by the end of the 1930s also had to do with the fact that Soviet oil production had reached its capacity limits and that the specifications of the five-year plans created misguided incentives. For to be able to implement the state's demands for the maximum possible fulfilment of the plan targets, which were in any case often completely unrealistic, the heads of the individual companies felt increasingly compelled to pump the existing wells relentlessly instead of investing in the exploration of new fields. However, if the old fields were exhausted and no alternative sources of production were available, then a decline in production could hardly be avoided.

The production targets set for the oil industry in the first five-year plan were already excessive and could not be met.[125] The same would be true of later plans: of the 44.3 million tonnes of petroleum envisaged in the second five-year plan for 1937, for instance, only 28.4 million tonnes were actually produced.[126] Thousands of skilled workers and engineers fell victim to the repressions of the 1930s initiated under Stalin, which were carried out under the pretext of liquidating internal 'saboteurs' and 'enemies'. These purges also had a disastrous impact on the Soviet economy, including the petroleum industry, which showed almost no growth by the late 1930s.[127] Given that the demand for fuel within the modernising Soviet state had also soared, there was thus little left for export.

Despite the strategic importance of oil, it now became apparent that too little had been invested in the oil industry following the boom of the 1920s. As a result, coal and even peat remained the prevailing energy sources. But coal and peat could not fuel tractors, which were used in ever greater numbers from the 1930s onwards because of the mechanisation of agriculture, nor could they power diesel-driven ships, lorries, and locomotives. Although oil and fuel production increased in absolute terms, coal production also increased sharply. This becomes clear when

124 On the autarky discussion, see Michael R. Dohan, 'The Economic Origins of Soviet Autarky 1927/28–1934', *Slavic Review*, 35, 4 (1976), pp. 603–35; Sanchez-Sibony, *Red Globlization*, pp. 4–7.

125 Matveichuk, 'V tiskakh pervoi piatiletki'.

126 A. A. Igolkin, *Neftianaia politika SSSR v 1928–1940-m godakh*, Moscow: Institut rossiiskoi istorii RAN, 2005, p. 63.

127 Rehschuh, *Aufstieg zur Energiemacht*, especially pp. 76–79; on production figures, see Slavkina, *Neftegazovyi faktor*, p. 93.

looking at developments in overall energy consumption. While the share of oil in total Soviet energy consumption rose from about 11 per cent after 1927–28 to just under 19 per cent by 1937, the coal sector also grew during this period: its share of the energy mix increased from 30 per cent to 47.5 per cent over the same period.[128] While this was in line with developments in most European countries, whose economies were still largely based on coal, it represented a reversal of the trend in the United States, where a marked decline in the share of coal and an increase of oil in the energy mix was already evident in the 1930s.

The reasons behind this trajectory were complex and probably had to do with the fact that it was considered costly to transport the oil, which at that time was only produced in the Caucasus, throughout the entire country. In contrast, the local extraction of coal, which was available in many parts, was thought to make more sense strategically and in terms of transportation.[129] Moreover, a number of well-known personalities from the Caucasus region who had belonged to the closest circle of leaders around Stalin died, were deposed, or were murdered in the course of the purges. As a result, there were fewer and fewer Caucasian representatives in the country's top party leadership to champion petroleum affairs. In contrast, supporters of the much broader coal industry, which had large production centres in the Donbas and elsewhere, were able to gain a stronger hearing from the country's top leadership. This corresponded to the Soviet Union's industrial development model, which was still heavily centred on coal and steel.

In the early Soviet time, and compared to coal, petroleum was a low-labour intensity industry. Whereas, according to Soviet statistics, some 344,000 people were employed in the country's coal mines as of 1933, the petroleum extraction and petroleum processing industry employed only some 54,000. Of these, 40,000 worked for the country's two largest oil companies, Azneft and Grozneft.[130] Overall, oil workers accounted for only about 2.5 per cent of all Soviet heavy industry employees during this period.[131] The oil industry thus had the potential to mobilise just tens of thousands of workers compared to the hundreds of thousands in the coal industry. Consequently, oil did not figure prominently in official propaganda of socialist utopia that promoted light bulbs, utility poles, hydroelectric power plants, and the coal miner. Depictions of Soviet posters of the 1920s and 1930s, which were printed in large numbers

[128] Igolkin, *Neftianaia politika SSSR v 1928–1940-m godakh*, p. 19.
[129] Rehschuh, *Aufstieg zur Energiemacht*, p. 85.
[130] Igolkin, *Neftianaia politika SSSR v 1928–1940-m godakh*, p. 156. [131] Ibid., p. 157.

to convey the goals of the Soviet project, are thus lacking oil derricks and the oil worker, the *neftianik*.[132]

The fact that not enough funds flowed into the further development of the oil industry was also due to the special status of oil in the overall view on energy at the time. As early as the 1920s, geologists began to express the opinion that global oil reserves were limited and that the world could soon run out of oil. David White of the US Geological Survey wrote in a well-received 1920 journal article that if the pace of production remained steady, known exploitable oil reserves in the United States would be exhausted in about seventeen years.[133] Fear of an impending oil shortage was a worldwide phenomenon but caused particular concern in the United States. The search for new reserves at home and the global expansion of American oil companies to secure and develop new oil deposits were an expression of this (ultimately unfounded) concern.[134]

The Soviet side was likewise aware of the immense strategic importance of oil and the looming threat of a global shortage.[135] In the battle for oil, however, the Soviet Union believed it had an advantage because it assumed that it had huge reserves of its own that would secure the country a dominant position in the future: 'The country that controlled the oil', the author of a 1924 essay in the newspaper *Moskovskii Komsomolets* declared, would also dominate 'world trade':

> The army, the fleet, the money, and even the population – all this is nothing if the oil is missing. And if in the world the oil is present on average for another 22 years, our reserves will last for another 64 years. At the same time, America, which is now in first place in oil production (the USSR is in third place), will run out of oil in seven years .... [This situation] will [ensure] us total domination of world trade.[136]

Looking to the future, many in the Soviet Union were therefore of the opinion that oil should be hoarded rather than immediately exploited and consumed on a large scale. In view of the decline in oil exports at the beginning of the 1930s, the most famous Soviet geologist of the time, Ivan Gubkin, defended himself in a 1932 essay addressed to a European audience against 'rumours of the alleged catastrophic drying-up of the

132 Jeronim Perović, 'Russlands Aufstieg zur Energiegrossmacht: Geschichte einer gesamteuropäischen Verflechtung', *Osteuropa*, 63, 7 (2013), pp. 5–28, here p. 8.

133 David White, 'The Petroleum Resources of the World', *The Annals of the American Academy of Political and Social Science*, 89 (1920), pp. 111–34.

134 Bukold, *Öl im 21. Jahrhundert*, pp. 14–16.

135 A. M. Morgoliusov-Turkovskii, *Spravochnik po toplivu, osveditel'nym produktam i smazochnym materialam*, Moscow: Gosudarstvennoe tekhnicheskoe izdanie, 1926, p. 154.

136 Quoted in Bakhtizin, Vereshchagin, and Kiiko, *'Neftianoi faktor'*, p. 82.

naphtha wells' spread by the 'foreign press' in order to 'discredit' the Soviet Union.[137] Gubkin asserted that the Soviet Union, with '37.5% of the world's total supply', possessed the largest deposits worldwide.[138] Due to its 'relatively weakly developed naphtha industry', the 'profit opportunities [were] far from exhausted, whereas the United States had apparently already developed and explored everything that could be exploited'.[139] In a book published contemporaneously, the Soviet geologist expressed his conviction that the 'Soviet Union was a rising star' in the realm of natural resources, while the United States was 'facing inevitable defeat'.[140] In 1937, Gubkin even claimed that the Soviet Union was in possession of 54.8 per cent of all known oil reserves.[141]

Irrespective of such (mis)conceptions, the Soviet Union was confronted with ever-greater problems in oil production, which led to a serious fuel shortage at the end of the 1930s. Given the growing threat of war in Europe, this must have seemed extremely menacing to the Soviet leadership, as the Bolsheviks had already been acutely aware of the importance of oil to mechanised warfare due to their experiences in the Civil War. Stalin himself expounded on the subject of oil on several occasions. Already in a December 1925 political report to the Central Committee (CC) of the Communist Party of the Soviet Union (CPSU), he described the 'problem of oil' as a 'vital' one 'because who will command in the next war depends on who will have the most oil' and 'who will command world industry and trade depends on who will have most oil'. Stalin was convinced that the imperialist states would ultimately wear themselves out over the question of oil.[142] Two years later, in another political report to the CC of the CPSU, he once again underlined that 'without oil, it is impossible to wage war' and 'whoever has the advantage as regards oil has a chance of victory in the coming war'.[143]

However, the country's leadership did not subsequently derive from this a strategy that would have placed oil at the centre of energy policy in

[137] I. M. Gubkin, 'Die Naphtavorkommen in der Sowjetunion', *Die Volkswirtschaft der Union der Sozialistischen Sowjet-Republiken*, 11, 10 (1932), pp. 8–16, here p. 8.
[138] Ibid., p. 11. [139] Ibid., p. 13.
[140] I. M. Gubkin, *Die Naturschätze der UdSSR und ihre Auswertung*, Moscow: Verlagsgenossenschaft ausländischer Arbeiter in der UdSSR, 1932, p. 38.
[141] Gubkin quoted in 'Der Reichtum natürlicher Energie in der UdSSR', *Sowjetwirtschaft und Aussenhandel: Halbmonatszeitschrift der Handelsvertretung der UdSSR in Deutschland*, 16, 21/22 (1937), pp. 7–10, here p. 8.
[142] 'Political Report of the Central Committee', 18 December 1925, in J. V. Stalin, *Works*, vol. 7, Moscow: Foreign Languages Publishing House, 1954, pp. 267–361, here p. 284.
[143] 'Political Report of the Central Committee', 3 December 1927, in J. V. Stalin, *Works*, vol. 10, Moscow: Foreign Languages Publishing House, 1954, pp. 277–363, here p. 283.

the longer term. This only began to change at the end of the 1930s, when the signs in Europe pointed to war due to Nazi Germany's expansionist policy. Although Stalin did not expect Germany to launch an immediate military attack on his country (which proved to be a grave misjudgement), the Soviet Union mobilised and modernised its armed forces on an unprecedented scale: between 1939 and 1941 the Red Army grew from two to five million men.[144] Simultaneously, the Caucasus and its petroleum industry became the focus of the Soviet party leadership, for this region still accounted for well over 90 per cent of total oil production and almost as much refining capacity. Thus, it was in the Caucasus that the fuel for Soviet tanks, aircraft, and motor vehicles was produced. Hence it was certainly no coincidence that the Politburo in April 1940 chose Viktor Ivanov, an experienced petroleum manager, as the new First Secretary of the Chechen-Ingush ASSR. Ivanov was not only to get a grip on the growing problem of 'banditry' in this troubled part of the Soviet empire but also to revive oil output after production rates at the facilities around Grozny were declining for some time. And indeed, as early as mid-November 1940, Ivanov announced to the 4th Plenum of the Chechen-Ingush Party Bureau that the 'enemy theory', according to which there was not enough oil at Grozny, had already been refuted by an increase in production. The oil-processing industry near Grozny, which at that time processed about a third of all Soviet oil, had also been able to stabilise its production, according to Ivanov. However, the successes were minimal and short-term and came partly at the cost of damaging existing oil fields.[145]

Only a week before Germany's invasion of Poland on 1 September 1939, which triggered the Second World War, Moscow still believed that it could reach an agreement with Berlin within the framework of a non-aggression pact to protect the country's western flank from a German attack. The Nazi-Soviet Nonaggression Pact, signed on 23 August 1939 between German Foreign Minister Joachim von Ribbentrop and his Soviet counterpart, Viacheslav Molotov, included a secret additional protocol that established the division of Poland and the two parties' respective spheres of interest in the Baltic states, Bessarabia and Finland, in the war that had now been decided upon. The agreement stipulated that the Soviet Union would supply the German Reich with

[144] A. Iu. Bezugol'nyi, *Narody Kavkaza i Krasnaia Armiia, 1918–1945 gody*, Moscow: Veche, 2007, p. 140.

[145] Rossiiskii Gosudarstvennyi Arkhiv Social'no-Politicheskoi Istorii (RGASPI), f. 17, op. 22, d. 3725, l. 2; cf. also Jeronim Perović, *From Conquest to Deportation: The North Caucasus under Russian Rule*, New York: Oxford University Press, 2018, p. 266.

industrial products, raw materials, and food. Although the Soviet Union had largely halted oil exports due to its own shortage, the country nevertheless supplied its valuable fuel to the German Reich. The Soviet Union thus filled the fuel stocks of the Wehrmacht, which had secretly been preparing for a war against the Soviet Union for some time.[146] Although the main supplier of foreign oil to the German Reich during this period was Romania, Soviet deliveries accounted for around 30 per cent of total German oil imports, as indicated by Russian historian Mariia Slavkina in her study on the history of Soviet oil and gas.[147]

The Soviet leadership now finally ordered an increase in investment in the oil industry and in the spring of 1941 for the first time launched a large-scale public mobilisation campaign, which called on the *neftianiki* to increase production to '38 million tonnes of oil with gas in 1941'.[148] Although these measures led to a short-term increase in production, they came far too late. When Nazi Germany launched its surprise attack on the Soviet Union on 22 June 1941, the country was inadequately prepared – and not only in military terms. The Soviet leadership's omission to build new oil production facilities and refineries outside the Caucasus was about to have severe repercussions. The Caucasus and its industry were exposed and therefore vulnerable, a fact known to Hitler, who ordered a southward attack in the summer of 1942. This was to involve the German Luftwaffe destroying pipelines and rail links near Baku to cut off the Soviet Union from most of its oil. Simultaneously, the occupation of the Caucasus aimed to secure a sustainable additional source of oil for the German military forces in the long run.[149] While the Wehrmacht was marching south, Stalin ordered the resettlement of more than 10,000 oil workers from the Caucasus and the dismantling of entire plants, which were moved at a rapid pace to the east in order to build up an oil industry in the Volga-Urals region in the shortest time possible.[150]

The Wehrmacht operation failed. The German advance came to a halt before reaching Grozny. The Germans only succeeded in capturing the previously destroyed oil installations near Maikop in the present-day North Caucasian Republic of Adygeia. However, because some of the

[146] Rehschuh, *Aufstieg zur Energiemacht*, pp. 89–106. For further reading, see Claudia Weber, *Der Pakt: Stalin, Hitler und die Geschichte einer mörderischen Allianz 1939–1945*, Munich: Beck, 2019.

[147] Slavkina, *Neftegazovyi faktor*, p. 89.

[148] The poster from 1941 with the inscription 'For 38 million tonnes of oil with gas in 1941!' (*Za 38 mln. tonn nefti s gazom v 1941 godu!*) by Pavel P. Golrelyj is reprinted in Aleksandr Snopkov, Pavel Snopkov, and Aleksandr Shkliaruk, *Shest'sot plakatov*, Moscow: Kontakt-Kul'tura, 2004, p. 414.

[149] Hayward, 'Too Little, Too Late', p. 771.

[150] Rehschuh, *Aufstieg zur Energiemacht*, pp. 110–22.

installations in the unconquered production areas of Grozny and Baku had been dismantled and many wells had been partially cemented over – in some cases causing irreparable damage – and production in the Volga-Urals had not yet reached the necessary levels, Soviet oil production collapsed by about a third between 1940 and 1946.[151] Despite its huge wealth of raw materials, the Soviet Union subsequently ran into such a major supply bottleneck that it had to rely on aid supplies from the Western Allies. Without fuel imports from the United States under the Lend-Lease Act, the Red Army would probably have been able to deploy its mechanised troops, especially its air force, only to a limited extent.[152]

Developments during the war did not merely change the geography of Soviet oil production, with the Volga-Urals region becoming responsible for an increasingly large share of production during the 1950s.[153] The war also sharpened the Soviet leadership's awareness of the economic and military strategic importance of oil. This was to shape Soviet foreign policy in the immediate post-war period: in 1946, for example, the Soviet leadership attempted to force concessions on the exploitation of Iran's oil fields through a military presence on the ground and political pressure, seized the oil sector in Red Army-occupied Romania, and secured control over the not-inconsiderable oil production of Austria and Hungary.

This reassessment of oil further manifested itself in Soviet domestic policy. Oil was now treated with the necessary priority in the context of Soviet energy policy, and the oil worker took up a permanent place in the pantheon of celebrated 'heroes of labour' alongside the coal and metal workers. For the first time, the *neftianik* appeared prominently on Soviet propaganda posters.[154] The image of oil in the Soviet Union's trade policy also changed: a Soviet poster from 1950 celebrated oil exports, which the country resumed on a very modest scale at this time, as a contribution to 'the beloved fatherland'.[155] In this way, the Soviet Union

[151] Goldman, *Petrostate*, p. 6; Slavkina, *Neftegazovyi faktor*, p. 118.

[152] Natalya V. Butenina, 'Lend-Lease: The Oil Factor', *Oil of Russia*, 12, 1 (2005), www.oilru.com/or/22/360/ (last accessed 1 January 2013).

[153] Nataliia Egorova, 'Stalin's Oil Policy and the Iranian Crisis of 1945–1946', in Perović (ed.), *Cold War Energy*, pp. 79–104.

[154] The new importance of the oil worker was expressed by P. Krivonogov's 1948 poster, which bore the headline 'Oilmen, more oil for the homeland! Let's fulfill the five-year plan in four years! (*Neftianiki, bol'she nefti Rodine! Vypolnim piatiletku v 4 goda!*), www.sovietposters.com/posters/oilmen-more-oil-to-the-motherland (last accessed 13 July 2021).

[155] The poster was designed by V. N. Elkin in 1950 and is entitled 'Let us transport more oil for the needs of the beloved fatherland' (*Bol'she perevezem nefti dlia nuzhd liubimoi rodiny*), in Snopkov, Snopkov, and Shkliaruk, *Shest'sot plakatov*, p. 418.

not only expressed a new patriotic feeling but also acknowledged oil as an integral part of its international great power identity.[156]

Between Isolation and Trade

Western scholarship from the Cold War period has been dominated by the idea that Soviet economic policy under Stalin was fundamentally geared towards becoming as self-sufficient as possible in order to protect the country from capitalist influence and outside interference. Indeed, the decline of the concession system and the reduction in the total volume of trade in the course of the 1930s can be interpreted as an expression of autarkic aspirations. However, these developments were not the product of a deliberate decoupling of the Soviet Union from the world economy. This was evident from the fact that Soviet representatives, in their rhetoric directed at an international audience, explicitly rejected the use of the term 'autarky' to characterise their country's economic policy. The Bolsheviks were realistic enough to understand that their economy could not develop in complete isolation from the capitalist West. The declared goal was therefore not to decouple from the world economy but to build up as independent an economy as possible in the long term through continuous exchange with the capitalist world.[157]

In conversations with foreign representatives, Stalin saw no inherent contradiction in establishing trade links between capitalist and socialist systems. Indeed, he recognised that trade provided the ideal platform for agreements and cooperation between the two. Speaking to an American workers' delegation in September 1927, Stalin emphasised that trade was 'the most suitable ground' for promoting understanding and cooperation between capitalist and socialist nations:

> Exports and imports are the most suitable ground for such agreements. We need: equipment, raw materials (raw cotton for example), semi-manufactures (from metals, etc.), while the capitalists need a market for those goods. There you have a basis for agreements. The capitalists need: oil, timber, grain products; we need a market for those goods. There you have a basis for agreements. We need credits; the capitalists need good interest for their credits. There you have still further basis for agreements, namely, in the field of credit.[158]

This basic pattern remained essentially the same into the 1930s. Soviet diplomats and foreign trade representatives continued to actively seek

[156] Perović, 'Russlands Aufstieg zur Energiegrossmacht', p. 11.
[157] Rehschuh, *Aufstieg zur Energiemacht*, p. 51.
[158] 'Interview with the First American Labour Delegation', 9 September 1927, in Stalin, *Works*, vol. 10, pp. 97–153, here p. 129.

cooperation with foreign companies. The prerequisite for this cooperation was that they saw a concrete benefit for the development of the Soviet Union into an 'independent economic entity', as an anonymous Soviet author explained to his readership in an article published in 1933 in the German-language bimonthly journal *Sowjetwirtschaft und Aussenhandel.*[159] In this essay, entitled 'Economic Independence and Autarky', the author decisively rejected the concept of autarky, understood as the 'dwindling of world economic connections' and the 'reduction of these connections to a minimum', as the guiding principle of Soviet economic policy.[160] In this spirit, Soviet Foreign Minister Litvinov emphasised in his speech at the World Economic Conference in London on 14 June 1933 that the Soviet Union, 'unlike other countries and despite the tremendous increase in its own production', would not strive for autarky and would not oppose the 'advantageous import of foreign goods'.[161]

The problem was that the Soviet Union's ability to offer the West raw materials and other commodities in return for imports of foreign goods was increasingly limited during this period because of rising domestic demand and stagnating growth rates, the effects of which extended beyond the oil sector. From the point of view of the Soviet leadership, the uncertainties created by the Great Depression in the first half of the 1930s, and then the growing fear of war from the mid-1930s, made it more necessary than ever to take precautions to protect the country's national economy. In other words: 'autarky' was not a choice but an outcome of international developments.

This was not a Soviet peculiarity but corresponded to a trend that was also noticeable in other states at this time, especially Germany. Thus, we learn from Hitler's *Denkschrift* ('memorandum') on the Four-Year Plan, written in August 1936 (but not made public in full until 1955), that the aim was to strengthen the self-sufficiency and war-worthiness of the German economy.[162] Within this framework, the German Reich also

[159] [B. R.], 'Wirtschaftliche Unabhängigkeit und Autarkie', *Sowjetwirtschaft und Aussenhandel: Halbmonatszeitschrift der Handelsvertretung der UdSSR in Deutschland*, 12, 6 (1933), pp. 2–7, here p. 5.

[160] Ibid.

[161] Litvinov's speech is included in German in 'Die Sowjetunion auf der Weltwirtschaftskonferenz: Rede des Aussenkommissars der Sowjetunion, M. M. Litwinow, gehalten am 14. Juni 1933 auf der Londoner Weltwirtschaftskonferenz', *Sowjetwirtschaft und Aussenhandel: Halbmonatszeitschrift der Handelsvertretung der UdSSR in Deutschland*, 12, 11 (1933), pp. 2–8, here p. 2.

[162] Hitler's memorandum is reprinted in [Adolf Hitler], 'Denkschrift Hitlers über die Aufgaben eines Vierjahresplans', *Vierteljahrshefte für Zeitgeschichte*, 3, 2 (1955), pp. 204–10.

intensified its efforts to reduce its dependence on petroleum imports by extracting synthetic fuel from coal – for while Germany had hardly any petroleum of its own, it had coal in abundance. Even though the synthetic production of fuel was expensive and complex, by the beginning of the war in 1939 German chemical companies were managing to meet an astonishing 46 per cent of Germany's oil needs through the production of synthetic oil and increased this share to 57 per cent for a short time during the war in 1943, most of it for military use.[163]

The German war of aggression, which threatened the Soviet Union in its very existence, highlighted the vulnerability of the Soviet economy despite its efforts to achieve economic independence. It was against this background that the Soviet leadership decided immediately after the end of the war to once again significantly increase its own industrial production. Ultimately, however, this did not change the fact that the Soviet Union remained interested in importing technology and goods from the West and sought to gain access to these imports by selling its raw materials. This remained the basis of exchange relations with the West throughout the Soviet period, although – as will become clear in Chapter 3 – there were efforts, particularly during Khrushchev's tenure, to reverse this pattern by developing a modern petrochemical industry and transforming the country into a producer and exporter of manufactured goods. These, however, did not meet with success. It was the fossil commodities – oil and later natural gas – that came to structure the Cold War economic ties between the Soviet Union and the capitalist West.

[163] Cf. Bukold, *Öl im 21. Jahrhundert*, p. 18.

3 Energy in the Cold War

In the immediate post-war period, the Soviet Union experienced an industrial revival. Faced with a significant decline in oil production from the Caucasian fields during the war with Nazi Germany, the Soviet Union stepped up its efforts to develop new oil reserves in the Volga-Urals and other parts of the country. In addition, as the Red Army advanced into east-central Europe in the final months of the war, the Soviet Union acquired vital fuel resources by effectively seizing oil production facilities in Romania, Austria, and Hungary in order to alleviate its own fuel shortage. Moscow's attempt to force concessions on the northern Iranian oil fields likewise testified to the Soviet leadership's heightened awareness of the strategic value of 'black gold'. During the incipient Cold War, Moscow focused primarily on supplying its own war-ravaged country and on deepening economic and trade relations in the consolidating Eastern European 'socialist camp'. Trade with the capitalist industrialised countries barely developed during this period, partly because the West, for reasons of military strategy, severely curtailed its economic relations with the Soviet Union and the socialist states of Eastern Europe and stopped granting loans to these countries.

This did not mean the Soviet Union's permanent retreat into economic isolation. Shortly after Stalin's death in 1953, the volume of trade with the countries of Western Europe began to increase again. In the time of Khrushchev, who led the Soviet Union as First Secretary of the Communist Party from 1953 to 1964, Moscow increasingly supplied the socialist 'fraternal states' in Eastern Europe with cheap energy. This marked a change from the late Stalin era when these countries had been exploited primarily as suppliers of raw materials and equipment for Soviet industry. But it was not until the late 1950s, after an absence of some twenty years, that the Soviet Union re-emerged as a serious supplier of oil on the international market.

Although Soviet oil represented a relatively modest share of total Western European imports in the early Cold War – these countries imported most of their oil from North Africa and the Persian Gulf – the trade in 'red oil' soon became part of the Western security discourse on the perceived Soviet threat. Washington saw the alleged 'oil offensive' from the East as a politically motivated expansionist strategy that needed to be contained to the maximum extent possible. In the aftermath of the crises over Berlin and Cuba, the NATO Council decided in a resolution in November 1962 to tighten the Western sanctions regime against the Soviet Union and to block even contractually agreed deliveries of steel pipes. In particular, this was intended to prevent the completion of the Druzhba oil pipeline, which was to carry oil from the Volga-Urals region via the Soviet republics of Ukraine and Belarus to Poland, Hungary, Czechoslovakia, and the German Democratic Republic (GDR) – and thus to the immediate borders of Western Europe.

However, the NATO sanctions did not have the desired effect. The pipeline was completed in 1964, and in the following years the Soviet Union was able to steadily increase its exports to both the socialist states of Eastern European and the capitalist countries of Western Europe. The Soviet Union also began to export natural gas, which it was producing in growing quantities in the fields of the Volga-Urals region and in new deposits in Western Siberia, to supply the states of the socialist camp. As early as 1968, Soviet natural gas reached Austria via an extension of the existing Eastern European pipeline system – and thus for the first time the USSR supplied a country on the western side of the Iron Curtain. This was the beginning of the natural gas 'bridge' that was to develop between Western Europe and the Soviet Union in the years and decades to come.[1]

This chapter shows how Soviet decision-makers thought about trade, economic exchange, and the role of natural resources in the early Cold War. Beginning with an overview of developments in the late Stalin years, it focuses on the Khrushchev period and the conflicting views on the use of the country's energy resources. In the final section, this chapter delves into Soviet deliberations on external economic relations during the latter half of the 1960s, culminating in the establishment of the first substantial agreements on gas supplies with Austria and other Western European countries.

The World in Two Camps

On 9 February 1946, in a much-publicised speech to supporters in a Moscow constituency, Stalin called for a new 'powerful upswing' of the national economy. To be certain that the 'Motherland [would] be

[1] Thane Gustafson, *The Bridge: Natural Gas in a Redivided Europe*, Cambridge, MA: Harvard University Press, 2020, p. 40.

insured against all contingencies', Stalin wanted Soviet industry to produce annually about 50 million tonnes of pig iron, 60 million tonnes of steel, 500 million tonnes of coal, and 60 million tonnes of oil. This target, the Soviet leader estimated, would probably take three five-year plans to achieve.[2] The German war of aggression had made clear the vulnerability of the Soviet Union and its dependence on the oil industry of the Caucasus; that energetic measures should now be taken to arm the country 'against all contingencies', but especially against a new war of aggression, was understandable. In the years that followed, the Soviet Union managed to significantly increase its production of raw materials and metals, even exceeding the growth rates for oil production that Stalin had stipulated.[3]

Stalin's statement, however, was not to be interpreted as an economic policy characterised by 'the pursuit of autarky for the Soviet Union and the Soviet-dominated adjacent areas', as George F. Kennan, a staff member at the US Embassy, reported to the US State Department in his famous 'Long Telegram' of 22 February 1946.[4] Although the Soviet Union was concerned with consolidating its influence in the areas it controlled in Eastern Europe, this was not yet a rejection of continued cooperation with the Western Allies. The billions of dollars of US assistance provided to the Soviet Union and other Allied states under the Lend-Lease Act during the war had demonstrated to Moscow the benefits of cooperation with Western states, and especially with the United States as the world's most potent economic power. The United States had not only supported the Soviet Union with state-of-the-art weapons systems, including thousands of tanks, aircraft, and guns, but also supplied it with food, raw materials, machinery, and industrial equipment. The supplies were substantial, accounting for about 10 per cent of Soviet economic output during the war years, according to calculations by

[2] See the English translation of Stalin's speech at [J. V. Stalin], 'Speech Delivered by Stalin at a Meeting of Voters of the Stalin Electoral District, Moscow, 9 February 1946', *History and Public Policy Program Digital Archive*, Gospolitizdat, Moscow, 1946, p. 41, http://digitalarchive.wilsoncenter.org/document/116179 (last accessed 3 November 2021).

[3] According to internal Soviet data, the Soviet Union produced only 21.6 million tonnes of oil in 1946 (Rehschuh, *Aufstieg zur Energiemacht*, p. 227), but by 1955 it had increased production to 71 million tonnes: Petroleum Industry Research Foundation, 'Special Report: The Role of Oil in the Soviet Economy', *Pirinc Reports on World Business*, 15 October 1956, p. 4.

[4] 'The Chargé in the Soviet Union (Kennan) to the Secretary of State', Moscow, 22 February 1946, in US Department of State (ed.), *Foreign Relations of the United States 1946*, vol. VI, Eastern Europe, The Soviet Union, Washington, DC: United States Government Printing Office, 1969, pp. 696–709, here p. 703.

British economic historian Mark Harrison.[5] The oil industry benefitted directly from the extensive transfer of technology and equipment. In the summer of 1943, for example, the Soviet leadership sent a group of senior oil specialists to the United States to familiarise themselves with American technology and equipment in the oil industry. The material ordered by the Soviet Union, including modern pumps, pipes, and drills, was only able to cover a small part of the country's actual demand at the time but made an important contribution to the recovery and further development of the Soviet oil industry after the war.[6]

The Marshall Plan, the large-scale American financial aid programme for the reconstruction of Europe announced in June 1947, was essentially a continuation of the Lend-Lease programme under new auspices. Given the already strained relations between the Western Allies and the Soviet Union, mainly due to disagreements over the resolution of the German question and other post-war issues, hardly anyone in the West expected Soviet participation in the American programme. Officially, however, the country was not excluded, and there was nothing to stop Moscow from sending a delegation of about 100 people, led by Soviet Foreign Minister Molotov, to Paris in July 1947 to take part in the negotiations. With this large mission, the Soviet side underlined the seriousness of its intention to participate. Indeed, Molotov decided to withdraw from the negotiations only when it became clear to him that Washington and Westminster did not want the Soviet Union to participate in the Marshall Plan. This was primarily because the provision of loans was contingent upon terms that Moscow could not agree to. American aid to the Europeans was conditional on cooperation among them and covered Germany as a whole, including the Soviet-administered zone. The Soviet Union rightly feared that this would undermine its influence not only in the part of Germany it occupied but also in the Moscow-controlled Eastern European states, some of which at that time were also showing interest in participating in the Marshall Plan.[7]

To be sure, there were tensions between Moscow and the Western Allies even before this point in time. However, it was the Soviet Union's withdrawal from the Marshall Plan that marked Moscow's final break with the West and the beginning of the Cold War. As a result, in September 1947, the Soviet party leadership summoned the leaders of

[5] Mark Harrison, *Accounting for War: Soviet Production, Employment, and the Defence Burden, 1940–1945*, Cambridge: Cambridge University Press, 1996, pp. 132–42.

[6] Rehschuh, *Aufstieg zur Energiemacht*, pp. 135–40.

[7] Scott D. Parish and Mikhail M. Narinsky, *New Evidence on the Soviet Rejection of the Marshall Plan 1947: Two Reports*, Cold War International History Project, Working Paper 9, Washington, DC: Woodrow Wilson International Center for Scholars, 1994.

the Communist parties of Eastern Europe, including those of Italy and France, to a secret meeting in the Polish town of Szklarska Poręba to create the Communist Information Bureau (Cominform). This was to succeed the Comintern, which had been dissolved in 1943, as the new coordinating organ among the Communist parties. However, the Cominform was nothing more than a means of consolidating Moscow's influence in Eastern Europe. At the inaugural meeting, the then Soviet chief ideologist, Andrei Zhdanov, announced his famous two-camp theory. In this speech, he branded the Marshall Plan as an American 'plan to enslave Europe' and outlined a world divided into a US-dominated 'anti-democratic' and 'imperialist' camp, on the one hand, and a Soviet-led 'anti-imperialist' and 'democratic' camp, on the other.[8] At this meeting, the Eastern European comrades were made to adhere to Soviet ideas for building socialism, while the Italian and French Communists were called upon to obstruct the Marshall Plan in their countries.[9]

The meeting marked the formal birth of the socialist camp under strict Soviet leadership. Moscow signalled that henceforth it wanted to be consulted on all important policy issues. The fact that deviations from the line laid down by Moscow were not tolerated became apparent no later than June 1948, when the Communist Party of Yugoslavia was excluded from the Cominform on the pretext of ideological differences and isolated politically and economically within the socialist camp. In fact, however, this dispute was less about ideology than about tangible power-related interests. Moscow was annoyed by the increasingly idiosyncratic foreign policy course of the Yugoslav Communists under their leader Josip Broz Tito, who, despite Soviet reservations, stuck to the project of uniting Yugoslavia with Albania and in the spring of 1948 was at the point of moving Yugoslav military forces into the small Balkan state. The Belgrade leadership also angered the Kremlin because Tito continued to support the Communist rebels in Greece, even though Stalin and Molotov had repeatedly and unequivocally urged the Yugoslavs to exercise restraint in the Greek Civil War.[10]

Moscow used the ostracism of the Communist Party of Yugoslavia as an opportunity to consolidate its influence in the rest of the camp and to

[8] The final version of Zhdanov's lecture can be found in RGASPI, f. 77, op. 3, d. 94, ll. 1–49.

[9] The proceedings of the Cominform conferences are contained in Giuliano Procacci et al. (eds.), *The Cominform: Minutes of the Three Conferences 1947/1948/1949*, Milano: Feltrinelli Editore Milano, 1994, pp. 35–451 (minutes of the first conference in Szklarska Poręba).

[10] Jeronim Perović, 'The Tito-Stalin Split: A Reassessment in Light of New Evidence', *Journal of Cold War Studies*, 9, 2 (2007), pp. 32–63.

carry out purge campaigns against supposed dissenters and 'Titoists'.[11] The Soviet leadership now accorded the highest priority to socialist cohesion; accordingly, economic exchanges within the camp were also promoted, which for many of these states meant a radical reorientation of their trade and economic relations away from Western Europe. The Council for Mutual Economic Assistance (CMEA), which was founded in 1949 and initially included Poland, Romania, Bulgaria, Hungary, and Czechoslovakia as well as the Soviet Union, was the Soviet response to the economic integration process in Western Europe, giving the Moscow-dominated camp an institutional appearance for the first time.[12]

The impact of these dynamics can be illustrated by the changes in the trade figures. While the Soviet Union's total volume of trade with Western capitalist states remained low between 1946 and 1950 and even declined slightly, the volume of trade with the CMEA states tripled, according to official Soviet statistics. These states' share of total Soviet trade rose from around 45 per cent in 1946 to almost 60 per cent by 1950; the share of all socialist states with which the Soviet Union traded, including China and North Korea in particular, was over 80 per cent in 1950.[13] Trade with the United States experienced a particularly dramatic collapse during this period: even before the Marshall Plan came into effect, the United States had restricted East–West trade by means of a selective embargo and had imposed a ban on the export of goods that could directly or indirectly benefit the Soviet arms industry. Following the hardening of relations in the incipient Cold War, this sanctions regime was again tightened with the passage of the Export Control Act of 1949, by which the US Congress prohibited the export of strategically important goods to communist states altogether. Thereafter, the total value of American shipments of goods to the socialist states of Eastern Europe shrank from 400 million US dollars in 1948 to a mere two million US dollars in 1953.[14] An exception to the American boycott

[11] Ibid., pp. 61–62.

[12] Leonid Gibianskij, 'Die Gründung des Rates für Gegenseitige Wirtschaftshilfe', in Walter M. Iber and Peter Ruggenthaler (eds.), *Stalins Wirtschaftspolitik an der sowjetischen Peripherie: Ein Überblick auf der Basis sowjetischer und osteuropäischer Quellen*, Innsbruck, Vienna, Bolzano: Studien Verlag, 2011, pp. 21–41; Martin Dangerfield, 'Sozialistische Ökonomische Integration: Der Rat für Gegenseitige Wirtschaftshilfe (RGW)', in Greiner, Müller, and Weber (eds.), *Ökonomie im Kalten Krieg*, pp. 348–69; Erik Radisch, *Der Rat für Gegenseitige Wirtschaftshilfe als Konsensimperium (1949–1971)*, Stuttgart: Franz Steiner Verlag, 2022.

[13] Calculated based on official Soviet statistics; the notes are contained in 'Foreign Trade Statistics', *Soviet and Eastern European Foreign Trade*, 3, 1 (1967), pp. 39–64, here p. 40.

[14] Roland Schönfeld, 'The USA in the Economic Relations between East and West', *Soviet and Eastern European Foreign Trade*, 10, 1 (1974), pp. 3–18, here pp. 3–4.

was Yugoslavia, which in the years following the break between Stalin and Tito enjoyed initially covert American military aid and economic support.[15]

What the official Soviet statistics do not reveal, however, is the fact that the Soviet Union remained a net importer of energy from east-central Europe until the mid-1950s, importing namely coal from Poland and Czechoslovakia in large amounts. Except for Romania, crude oil still played little role in the energy mix of most Eastern European states; coal was the dominant energy source. According to its own statistics, the Soviet Union exported small quantities of crude oil and petroleum products to its CMEA allies after the war. In reality, until Stalin's death, the Soviet Union, in its Eastern European sphere of influence, pursued a policy bordering on exploitation. Immediately after the end of the war, for example, the Soviet Union set about dismantling hundreds of industrial and infrastructural plants – including thousands of kilometres of railway lines – in the zone it occupied in Eastern Germany and transferring them to the Soviet Union to help cover reparations claims.[16] Based on an analysis of Soviet archival material, German researchers have concluded that the total value of the goods removed from the Soviet zone may have been equivalent to 14 billion US dollars at 1938 prices. No country in the world made such high reparations payments after the Second World War as the GDR.[17]

Among the Eastern European states, Hungary and Romania also had to pay substantial reparations to the Soviet Union because of their collaboration with Nazi Germany. These were also mainly in material form. In the case of Romania, the most important oil producer in Europe behind the Soviet Union and the most important fuel supplier to the German war machine during the Second World War, Moscow secured access to this country's industrial production shortly after the war through the establishment of a number of joint Soviet–Romanian enterprises, including the oil company Sovrompetrol founded in

[15] Lorraine M. Lees, *Keeping Tito Afloat: The United States, Yugoslavia, and the Cold War*, University Park: Pennsylvania State University Press, 1997.

[16] According to Siegrid Wenzel, around 2,400 industrial enterprises were dismantled; André Steiner even gives a figure of 3,400: Siegfried Wenzel, 'Die DDR-Wirtschaft im Spannungsfeld zwischen objektiven Bedingungen und Politik der SED', in Ludwig Elm, Dietmar Keller, and Reinhard Mocek (eds.), *Ansichten zur Geschichte der DDR*, vol. 6, Wirtschaft, Eggersdorf: Verlag Matthias Kirchner, 1996, pp. 89–164, here p. 91; André Steiner, *Von Plan zu Plan: Eine Wirtschaftsgeschichte der DDR*, Munich: Deutsche Verlags-Anstalt, 2004, p. 29.

[17] Lothar Baar, Rainer Karlsch, and Werner Matschke, *Kriegsfolgen und Kriegslasten Deutschlands: Zerstörungen, Demontagen und Reparationen*, Studien zur Wirtschaftsgeschichte 1, Berlin: Humboldt-Universität, Institut für Wirtschaftsgeschichte, 1993, p. 100.

July 1945.[18] Similar developments can be seen in Hungary, where in April 1946 two oil companies were established with Soviet participation.[19] The Soviet Union also imported human resources after the war. In addition to the GDR, this affected other states occupied by the Red Army, especially Hungary, from whence up to 600,000 people were presumably deported to Soviet labour camps after the war.[20] In Austria, the Soviet Union was involved in oil production through the Sowjetische Mineralölverwaltung (Soviet Mineral Oil Administration – SMV), established in September 1945.[21] A large part of the oil produced in these three countries was shipped abroad to meet the demands of other CMEA countries, as well as the Soviet Union itself. Some was also used for re-export to third countries, with Finland being a notable example. In the case of Austria, most of the oil produced at the beginning of the 1950s, around ten million tonnes, was exported to Eastern Europe, namely Poland, the GDR, and the Soviet Union (to Mukachevo in Western Ukraine and as far as Batumi in Georgia).[22]

Stalin's foremost objective was to expedite the recovery of his country's war-ravaged economy. If international circumstances made cooperation with the United States and other Western industrial nations difficult, then the goal was to extract maximum economic benefit from Soviet supremacy in Eastern Europe. Without considering the difficult economic situation of these states, the Kremlin leadership prioritised meeting the needs of its own country. With imports from Romania, Austria, and Hungary, the Soviet Union cushioned the blow of fuel shortages at home,[23] using oil imports from east-central Europe as a 'gap filler' for its own deficits.[24] However, it was understood in Moscow that this could not be a sustainable economic policy in the long run. Apart from the fact that Soviet behaviour met with little approval in the states of Eastern Europe, Soviet planners realised as early as the late 1940s that the steady growth in energy demand would make Stalin's planned production target of 60 million tonnes of crude oil insufficient to meet projected fuel needs

[18] László von Taubinger, 'Die sowjetisch-rumänischen Gesellschaften', *Osteuropa*, 5, 2 (1956) 2, pp. 145–49; Mihaela Sitariu, 'British–Romanian Relations during the Cold War', PhD thesis, Western University, London [Canada] 2013, pp. 28, 121.

[19] László Borhi, *The Merchants of the Kremlin: The Economic Roots of Soviet Expansion in Hungary*, Cold War International History Project, Working Paper 28, Washington, DC: Woodrow Wilson International Center for Scholars, 2000, p. 35.

[20] Tamás Stark, '"Malenki Robot" – Hungarian Forced Labourers in the Soviet Union (1944–1955)', *Minorities Research*, 7 (2005), pp. 155–67, here p. 158.

[21] Walter M. Iber, 'Erdöl statt Reparationen: Die sowjetische Mineralölverwaltung in Österreich 1945–1955', *Vierteljahrshefte für Zeitgeschichte*, 57, 4 (2009), pp. 571–605.

[22] Ibid., p. 594. [23] Rehschuh, *Aufstieg zur Energiemacht*, p. 183. [24] Ibid., p. 189.

by the mid-1950s.[25] Moreover, against the background of the uncertain international situation, Moscow wanted to avoid at all costs a longer-term dependence on imports of strategically important goods.

The problems that such dependence could entail became apparent in the so-called Iran crisis of 1946, which is sometimes seen in Western historiography as the prelude to the Cold War.[26] As early as 1941, Soviet troops had invaded the north, and British troops the south, to strengthen their defensive position against the Third Reich and to secure supply and transport routes via Iran. Britain and the Soviet Union, who had been allies during the war against Nazi Germany, divided the country into a British zone of influence in the south and a Soviet zone of influence in the north and – with the participation of American forces sent to Iran – took control of roads, railways, airports, pipelines, and shipping lanes. Securing the Persian route was primarily intended to facilitate Allied aid deliveries to the Soviet Union. Washington, Westminster, and Moscow assured the Iranian government that Iran's territorial integrity and independence would be guaranteed.[27]

Contrary to Western assumptions at the time, Soviet archival documents show that even after the end of the Second World War, Moscow was not interested in permanently annexing the parts of northern Iran occupied by Soviet troops and populated predominantly by ethnic Azerbaijanis, nor in escalating tensions with the United States and Great Britain. Rather, the Soviet leadership's main interest was in the country's oil resources, and Moscow withdrew its troops only after an agreement had been reached with the Iranian government on the oil issue. The Soviet–Iranian agreement provided that the Soviet Union would obtain rights to produce oil in the northern part of Iran as part of a joint Soviet–Iranian enterprise. Shortly after Stalin received assurances of oil extraction in Iran and the Soviet Union withdrew its troops in 1946, the Iranian parliament decided to rescind the agreement with the Soviet Union. In doing so, Iran relied on a December 1944 law that prohibited the granting of oil concessions to foreigners.[28]

During the early Cold War, the Soviet leadership's focus on expanding its industrial capacity was not solely driven by economic motives. Increasing oil production was also seen as a crucial factor in

[25] Ibid., p. 232.

[26] Fraser Harbutt, 'American Challenge, Soviet Response: The Beginning of the Cold War, February–May, 1946', *Political Science Quarterly*, 96, 4 (1981/82), pp. 623–39.

[27] On this subject in detail, see Jana Forsmann, *Testfall für die 'Grossen Drei': Die Besetzung Irans durch Briten, Sowjets und Amerikaner 1941–1946*, Cologne, Weimar, Vienna: Böhlau, 2009.

[28] Egorova, 'Stalin's Oil Policy and the Iranian Crisis of 1945–1946'.

strengthening national defence capabilities. As Felix Rehschuh demonstrates in his study of Soviet oil policy during the Stalin era, it was primarily national security concerns that prompted Stalin to sign a decree on 20 July 1949 stipulating an increase in oil production to 90 or even 100 million tonnes over a ten-year period. The investments earmarked for this purpose were not only to flow into the existing oil-producing areas and industries but were also to be used for the exploration and development of new deposits. The person responsible for the implementation of these ambitious measures was none other than Lavrentii Beriia, the notorious head of the Soviet Ministry of the Interior and at that time one of Stalin's closest confidants.[29] It was in the context of Western sanctions policy and a heightened sense of threat that the Soviet Union from this point on began to show more clearly those autarkic tendencies that, according to Kennan, had characterised Soviet economic policy already in 1946.

Oil and Politics under Khrushchev

The turbulent period after Stalin's death was marked by political struggles among the members of the 'collective leadership', which until the mid-1950s consisted of Khrushchev, Molotov, and Georgii Malenkov. These disputes also revolved around setting priorities for economic development and deciding on the allocation of funds to different sectors of the economy. Accordingly, the various lobby groups sought to exert as much influence as possible through their contacts with the relevant decision-makers in the state and party apparatus.[30] With the final consolidation of Khrushchev's power in 1956–57, those groups that gave priority to the oil and gas industry prevailed. The preconditions for this had been laid in the late Stalin years. What was new was that the decades-long primacy of coal as the basis of Soviet energy policy was now officially declared to be over.[31] The result of this change of direction was expressed in remarkable growth for the oil and gas sectors: if the Soviet Union had produced 71 million tonnes of petroleum in 1955,[32] this volume rose to over 166 million tonnes by 1961. During this period,

[29] Rehschuh, *Aufstieg zur Energiemacht*, pp. 233–34.

[30] Viacheslav Nekrasov, 'Decision-Making in the Soviet Energy Sector in Post-Stalinist Times: The Failure of Khrushchev's Economic Modernization Strategy, in Perović (ed.), *Cold War Energy*, pp. 165–99.

[31] This was announced by Khrushchev at the 21st Party Congress in 1959: Rehschuh, *Aufstieg zur Energiemacht*, p. 330.

[32] Petroleum Industry Research Foundation, 'Special Report: The Role of Oil in the Soviet Economy', p. 4.

the country increased the volume of natural gas produced annually almost six-fold, from 10.4 billion cubic metres to 59 billion cubic metres.[33] The oil rush of the 1950s was mainly due to the rapid upswing in production in the Volga-Urals region, while oil production near Baku largely recovered.[34]

The Soviet Union consumed most of the oil it produced, but there was now also more oil available for export. By the early 1950s, the Soviet Union was again supplying modest quantities of oil to those countries that had been traditional customers for Soviet raw materials before the war, including Italy, France, Great Britain, and (after Stalin's death) West Germany. In the beginning, however, smaller European countries became the most important buyers: In 1954, Finland, Sweden, and Ireland absorbed about three-quarters of the total volume of Soviet petroleum exports to non-communist countries.[35] On the whole, however, the Soviet Union's oil shipments to Western Europe were insufficient to have significant economic relevance. Accordingly, Soviet oil supplies presented little cause for concern about excessive dependence on the Soviet Union, especially since Moscow was anxious to prove itself a reliable trading partner to its Western European customers.

Much as it had before the war, the Soviet Union regarded the large Western European states as important potential customers and sources of hard currency revenue. It did not necessarily see the smaller European economies or the countries of the so-called Third World in the same way. Under certain conditions, the Moscow leadership considered oil deliveries to these countries a political instrument. This was particularly true in the case of Finland, which in the 1950s purchased between 80 and 90 per cent of its oil from the Soviet Union. Some of this was oil from Romania that the Soviet Union re-exported.[36] Neutral Finland, which shared a long border and a bloody history with the Soviet Union, was interested in good trade relations with its large eastern neighbour, and the Finnish government was even willing to forego economic support from the West as part of its policy of appeasement toward Moscow. When the Soviet Union curtailed its oil exports to Finland in 1958 because it was unhappy

33 Rossiiskii Gosudarstvennyi Arkhiv Noveishei Istorii (RGANI), f. 80, op. 1, d. 322, l. 39.

34 Rehschuh, *Aufstieg zur Energiemacht*, pp. 246f., 283–86.

35 Jennifer I. Considine and William A. Kerr, *The Russian Oil Economy*, Cheltenham: Edward Elgar, 2002, p. 64.

36 Niklas Jensen-Eriksen, 'The First Wave of the Soviet Oil Offensive: The Anglo-American Alliance and the Flow of "Red Oil" to Finland during the 1950s', *Business History*, 49, 3 (2007), pp. 348–66, here p. 354; Rehschuh, *Aufstieg zur Energiemacht*, p. 305.

with the composition of the new Finnish government, the government in Helsinki decided to resign and form a new cabinet, an episode that came to be known as the 'Night Frost Crisis'.[37] Instead of accepting economic support from the United States and sourcing oil from Western energy companies such as Shell, the Finnish leadership turned down these offers out of concern for Soviet sensitivities.[38]

Oil and politics also went hand in hand in other parts of the world. After the exclusion of the Yugoslav Communist Party from the Cominform, the Soviet Union imposed an economic blockade on the Balkan country, resuming oil supplies only with the rapprochement between Khrushchev and Tito from 1954 onwards. As a result of the Suez crisis, Moscow stopped oil supplies to Israel in 1956. When Soviet–Chinese relations deteriorated in the late 1950s, the Soviet Union cut its oil exports to Communist China. Moscow also halted oil exports to Albania when this small Balkan state drifted away from Soviet control in the early 1960s. Although the Soviet embargoes against Yugoslavia, China, and Albania were not effective, they demonstrated that, especially in the case of socialist states, Moscow was ready to apply economic pressure to punish these countries for deviating from Moscow policies.[39]

Especially in former colonial states and 'Third World' countries, Moscow saw trade and economic relations as a way to engage in systemic competition with the capitalist West. In the 1950s, for example, the Soviet Union supplied Egypt and Syria but also select 'Third World' states – such as Guinea, Ethiopia, India, and Cuba – with oil and other products, seeking to exploit this propagandistically as a contribution to these countries' emancipation from the former Western colonial powers. The Soviet Union held a certain appeal as a trading partner for many of these countries because, in contrast to the international oil companies, it was prepared to conduct trade on the basis of compensation deals. In the 1950s, the Soviet Union traded oil for Egyptian cotton, Cuban sugar, Uruguayan wool, and Israeli citrus fruits.[40] Trade with Finland, its most important European economic partner at the time, also took place to a large extent through the exchange of goods. Indeed, Helsinki's exports were strongly oriented towards Soviet demand: the Finns supplied

[37] Johanna Rainio-Niemi, 'Neutrality as Compromises: Finland's Cold War Neutrality', in Mark Kramer, Aryo Makko, and Peter Ruggenthaler (eds.), *The Soviet Union and Cold War Neutrality and Nonalignment in Europe*, Lanham: Lexington Books, 2021, pp. 75–100, here pp. 86–88.

[38] Jensen-Eriksen, 'The First Wave', pp. 358–89.

[39] Klinghoffer, *The Soviet Union & International Oil Politics*, pp. 12, 195–201.

[40] Perović, 'Russlands Aufstieg zur Energiegrossmacht', p. 14.

machinery, ships, and other finished products in exchange for oil and other raw materials from the Soviet Union.[41]

Raw Materials and Socialist Integration

After Stalin's death, the Soviet Union also changed its attitude towards the Eastern European socialist camp. The mass uprisings in the GDR in June 1953 were an expression of the disastrous economic and social situation in which this country found itself after the war. As a direct result of these riots, Moscow declared the reparations claims against the GDR to be fulfilled and granted the East German government a loan worth millions of US dollars to provide the country with the funds to purchase urgently needed raw materials and equipment.[42] Discontent also made itself felt in other countries, such as Poland, where thousands of workers organised in a major uprising in June 1956 to demonstrate for a change of political direction and against shortages. It was the Hungarian national uprising in the late autumn of 1956, however, that demonstrated most clearly to the Soviet leadership how unstable the situation in the states of east-central Europe was. Although Soviet troops were to put down the popular uprising in Hungary using brute military force, Moscow understood that it had to realign its policy in order to defuse the social and economic crisis in these countries and to support the communist regimes there.[43] The increased supply of subsidised Soviet commodities was one of the means of stimulating economic growth, which was also intended to bring greater political and social stability to the region.[44] A primary aim of this policy was to shape perceptions of the Soviet Union as a benefactor, rather than an oppressor, of the Eastern European 'people's democracies'. Providing these countries with energy also sought to mitigate the lingering negative

[41] Niklas Jensen-Eriksen, 'The Cold War in Energy Markets: British Efforts to Contain Soviet Oil Exports to Non-Communist Countries, 1950–1965', in Alain Beltran (ed.), *Le pétrole et la guerre: Oil and War*, Brussels: Peter Lang, 2012, pp. 191–207, here p. 201; for further reading, see G. Oblath and P. Pete, 'Trade with the Soviet Union: The Finnish Case', *Acta Oeconomica*, 35, 1/2 (1985), pp. 165–94.

[42] Michel Vale and Jochen Bethkenhagen, 'The Development of GDR Economic Relations with the USSR', *International Journal of Politics*, 12, 1/2 (1982), GDR Foreign Policy (Part II), pp. 232–60, here p. 236.

[43] G. Iu. Koleva, 'Neft' vmesto uglia: Vliianie vengreskikh sobytii 1956 g. na izmeneiia v energeticheskoi politike SSSR', *Vestnik Tomskogo gosudarstvennogo universiteta*, 399 (2015), pp. 74–79.

[44] Margarita M. Balmaceda, 'Der Weg in die Abhängigkeit: Ostmitteleuropa am Energietropf der UdSSR', *Osteuropa*, 54, 9/10 (2004), pp. 162–79, here p. 163.

legacy of Stalin's policies in the region and to portray the Soviet Union as a positive force for Eastern European nations.[45]

As a result of this change of course, the Soviet Union significantly increased its exports of crude oil and petroleum products to Eastern Europe. According to its own statistics, the Soviet Union supplied 2.2 million tonnes of crude oil to the countries of the CMEA in 1955, a figure that rose to almost 18 million tonnes by 1964. In the same period, the Soviet Union increased its exports of petroleum products eightfold.[46] This greatly enhanced the dependence of these countries on Soviet oil: with the exception of Romania, Soviet oil and oil derivative imports comprised between 85 per cent (Poland) and 95 per cent (GDR) of the socialist countries' total oil imports in 1965.[47] The construction of the Druzhba oil pipeline, completed in 1964, accelerated this shift by allowing Soviet crude oil from the fields of the Volga-Urals region to be transported westwards faster and in larger quantities than before. While the first concrete plans for the project had been presented as early as 1957, the actual construction of the pipeline began in 1960; both this and later pipelines were infrastructure projects organised and coordinated within the framework of the CMEA.[48] The Druzhba oil pipeline was intended to advance the integration of CMEA and contribute to the prosperity of the socialist countries: the Soviet Union supplied Poland and the GDR with oil via a northern route and Hungary and Czechoslovakia via a southern route. However, Moscow required the recipient states to provide workers to help build the 'oil artery', as the pipeline was sometimes called.[49]

An important goal of the Soviet leadership was to use oil supplies to help neighbouring socialist states develop energy-intensive petrochemical industries, in line with Khrushchev's new economic policy focus. His petrochemical project, which he tried to push through in the face of sometimes fierce internal resistance, was designed to provide the basis for agricultural industry and the production of consumer goods, which would have enabled the Soviet Union to export not only raw materials but increasingly processed petroleum products and finished goods that could compete internationally. On 10 October 1957, the Presidium of

45 Marshall I. Goldman, 'Soviet Trade and Aid', *Challenge*, 12, 3 (1963), pp. 30–33, here p. 32.
46 'Foreign Trade Statistics', p. 47.
47 Jeremy Russell, *Energy as a Factor in Soviet Foreign Policy*, Saxon House Studies, Lexington, MA: Lexington Books, 1976, p. 95.
48 Falk Flade, 'Creating a Common Energy Space: The Building of the Druzhba Oil Pipeline', in Perović (ed.), *Cold War Energy*, pp. 321–44, here pp. 325–28.
49 Ibid., p. 328f.

the CC of the CPSU adopted the resolution 'On Fundamental Directions in the Formulation and Preparation of the Five-Year Plan for the Economic Development of the USSR', which stated the need to 'pay special attention to the rapid growth and development of the chemical industry … and to concentrate on the decisive increase of oil production and the use of gas in the economy'.[50] Coal, which at that time was still the most important source of energy, took a back seat in this rhetoric. In Khrushchev's view, the new foundations of the economy were oil, gas, and electricity. The plants created for coal mining were to be closed. This was done not only because coal mining was relatively expensive but also because Khrushchev believed that the Soviet Union did not need coal, 'as [it] would convert the economy to a new, more advanced energy'.[51]

The new policy made itself felt in the Soviet Union's primary energy production. According to an internal Gosplan report compiled in February 1962, the share of coal declined from 59.8 per cent in 1958 to 51.3 per cent in 1961, while the share of oil rose from 27 per cent to 33 per cent and that of gas from 5.6 per cent to 9.7 per cent in the same period.[52] Coal's importance would continue to decline, but it would remain dominant in the Soviet energy mix for a long time, still providing 29 per cent of the country's energy needs in the late 1970s.[53] This was partly because a significant proportion of electricity was still generated in coal-fired power stations. Thus, even in the Khrushchev era, coal-fired power continued to have a very high priority.[54] However, as more and more oil and gas reserves were discovered, the enormous potential of these resources seemed to provide the basis for a fundamental energy turnaround.

The exploration of new promising regions intensified already in the second half of the 1950s. By this time, the Soviet Union had built up a staff of some 25,000 geologists, who were now available to systematically

[50] A. A. Fursenko (ed.), *Prezidium TsK KPSS 1954–1964: Chernovye protokol'nye zapisi zasedanii; Stenogrammy; Postanovleniia*, in 3 vols, vol. 1, Chernovye protokol'nye zapisi zasedanii: Stenogrammy, Moscow: Politicheskaia entsiklopedia, 2003, p. 283; A. A. Fursenko (ed.), *Prezidium TsK KPSS 1954–1964: Chernovye protokol'nye zapisi zasedanii; Stenogrammy; Postanovleniia*, in 3 vols, vol. 1, Postanovleniia, Moscow: Politicheskaia entsiklopedia, 2015, pp. 695–96.

[51] Quotations from Khrushchev's speech on 4 September 1958 at a meeting of the Committee for the Elaboration of Theses for the 21st Party Congress of the CPSU: RGANI, f. 52, op. 1, d. 170, l. 5.

[52] The report bears two dates, 24 and 19 February 1962, and is contained in Rossiiskii Gosudarstvennyi Arkhiv Ekonomiki (RGAE), f. 4372, op. 80, d. 266, ll. 6–13, here l. 7.

[53] Cf. 'The Soviet Coal Industry' in *Technology & Soviet Energy Availability*, Washington, DC: United States Government Printing Office, 1981, pp. 81–108, here p. 81.

[54] Felix Frey, *Arktischer Heizraum: Das Energiesystem Kola zwischen regionaler Autarkie und gesamtwirtschaftlicher Verflechtung 1928–1974*, Osteuropa in Geschichte und Gegenwart 4, Vienna, Cologne, Weimar: Böhlau, 2019, pp. 236–38.

scour the vast country for new prospective producing regions.[55] During the late 1950s and early 1960s, new reports of discoveries were regularly received, predominantly in the far north of the country, in Western Siberia, and in Central Asia.[56] At the same time, the Soviet planners were fully aware that although the rapid growth of oil and gas production was made possible by the discovery of new large oil and gas fields in various parts of the country, major additional prospecting and exploration work was required to find and develop new reserves, if the planned increase in production was to be maintained over the next years. This was especially true for the huge Siberian territory, which was still inadequately explored. As noted by a major report compiled by Gosplan's own Department of Geology in March 1960, while 'such geological areas as the Volga-Urals oil-region, the North Caucasus, and Azerbaijan' have been sufficiently studied, 'the degree of geological study' in 'Siberia, Kazakhstan and some areas of the Turkmen SSR' was considered still insufficient. 'Ten years of geophysical, prospecting and exploratory work have found indications of oil-bearing potential in some areas of Siberia, but no commercial oil fields have yet been identified.'[57]

This was to change in the years to come with discoveries of new large oil and gas fields, and it soon became very clear that the Soviet Union did not need to worry about the availability of natural resources. According to a May 1962 report by the All-Union Geological Fund entitled 'Summary of the Status of Reserves and Production of Major Minerals in the Countries of Socialism and Capitalism', the Soviet Union's shares of world reserves and production of petroleum were 11 per cent and 14 per cent, respectively; for natural gas, these were 13 per cent and 10 per cent.[58] The Soviet Union was thus still behind the United States in terms of reserves and production, but Soviet planners were confident that their country would soon be able to close this gap. The challenge, however, was how to develop these resources efficiently and transport them over long distances to the country's consumer centres. Regarding transportation, this required, among other things, millions of tonnes of high-quality steel pipes.

As early as the late 1950s, Gosplan repeatedly pointed out the problem of serious production shortages in this area.[59] As it turned out, the Soviet Union had neither a sufficient amount of steel nor enough capacity to build large-diameter pipelines. It seemed, therefore, only reasonable to

55 Petroleum Industry Research Foundation, 'Special Report: The Role of Oil in the Soviet Economy', p. 4.
56 RGAE, f. 4372, op. 81, d. 1812, ll. 277, 278.
57 RGAE, f. 4372, op. 79, d. 180, ll. 79, 94–178, here l. 102.
58 RGAE, f. 4372, op. 80, d. 418, ll. 79, 81, 82.
59 Cf. Gosplan SSSR, 9 December 1958, in RGAE, f. 4372, op. 77. d. 123, ll. 77–78.

seek closer cooperation with foreign countries, and Gosplan at that time urged to acquire the necessary pipes abroad, compiling a precise list of all the goods to be purchased in order to develop the domestic oil and gas pipeline system.[60] In the late 1950s, Gosplan representatives repeatedly travelled to Western European countries to buy steel tubes in order to fill the gaps in Soviet domestic production. In 1958, a certain Iushin, a member of Gosplan, was sent to West Germany with the task of procuring large diameter welded pipes in the amount of 110–20,000 tonnes, which corresponded to about 10 per cent of the total demand for pipes at that time and was to be paid for in Soviet gold.[61]

'Let's Trade!'

In political terms, the Khrushchev years were marked by efforts to end the personality cult around Stalin and to denounce the mass crimes committed during his rule. Even before his famous 'secret speech' on 25 February 1956 at the end of the 20th Party Congress, hesitant steps towards de-Stalinisation had been taken. Only a few days after Stalin's death, the Soviet leadership issued an amnesty for imprisoned party members. As a result, as many as half of all Gulag prisoners were released.[62] The 1950s also saw a liberalisation of the cultural sphere, which made criticism of Stalin and his policies possible, although fundamental questioning of socialism and the CPSU was not permitted. Khrushchev's economic policy did not only emphasise military rearmament and heavy industry but focused on the development of light industry, agriculture, and the petrochemical industry, stressing the importance of consumption and the production of consumer goods. Soviet citizens were not to have to tighten their belts even further to achieve Soviet goals, as Stalin had demanded, but should be given the right to consume and enjoy the fruits of socialist prosperity.[63]

Accordingly, Khrushchev introduced a series of reforms that, although often not very well thought out, were essentially aimed at raising the population's standard of living. This was also a central argument for building up a petrochemical industry as quickly as possible. Among other things, this industry was to produce consumer goods for the broad mass

[60] RGAE, f. 4372, op. 77. d. 123, ll. 78, 81.

[61] RGAE, f. 4372, op. 77. d. 147, ll. 284–85.

[62] Jochen Krüger, 'Entstalinisierung unter Chruschtschow', *dekoder*, 20 December 2018, www.dekoder.org/de/gnose/entstalinisierung-chruschtschow-geheimrede-tauwetter#fuss4 (last accessed 17 May 2021).

[63] O. Pick and A. Wiesman, 'Sputniks and Sausages: Soviet Drive for Consumer Goods', *The World Today*, 15, 12 (1959), pp. 472–81.

of the population. Other important reform projects were aimed in the same direction. To combat the rampant housing shortage, for instance, smaller apartment blocks made of mass-produced prefabricated components (so-called *Khrushchevki*) were built instead of Stalin's neoclassical showpieces. Millions of Soviet citizens who had previously lived in communal flats (*kommunalki*) thus found themselves in their own living space for the first time, even if the buildings were often of very poor quality.[64] In the context of Khrushchev's 'thaw' (a term coined by Ilya Ehrenburg), travel abroad became possible again and hundreds of thousands of tourists crossed the Iron Curtain in both directions. International festivals were organised in Moscow, allowing young people from the West to meet Soviet students. The resumption of the Moscow Film Festival and the opening of the International Tchaikovsky Competition were also results of the reform policy initiated under Khrushchev.[65]

These developments were in complete accord with the new foreign policy line, which, after Stalin's confrontational policy, sought to open the country to the capitalist West. With a view to returning to Lenin's principle of 'peaceful coexistence' between capitalism and communism, economic relations with the West were also expanded again. 'Let's trade!' (*Davaite torgovat'!*) read the title emblazoned on an essay in the well-known Soviet weekly *Ogonek* on 26 April 1959, describing one of the guiding principles of this time marked by a spirit of optimism.[66] In order to revive the broken trade contacts with the West, Khrushchev also drew on the experience of people who had been active already during the New Economic Policy era. An important role was played by Anastas Mikoian, who had held the post of foreign trade minister from 1926 to 1946. Shortly after Stalin's death, Mikoian took up this post again. After his appointment as deputy prime minister in 1955, he continued to vigorously advocate the expansion of Soviet foreign trade.[67]

Economic and trade issues were high on Mikoian's list of priorities when he visited the United States in January 1959 and repeatedly spoke out in favour of expanding US–Soviet trade relations. To achieve this, however, it was first necessary to lift what Mikoian saw as discriminatory restrictions that hindered US–Soviet trade. Moreover, due to a lack of foreign exchange reserves, the Soviet Union was dependent on loans to

[64] Krüger, 'Entstalinisierung unter Chruschtschow'.

[65] Aleksandr Zadorozhnyi, '"Ne pripomniu lichnosti so stol' tragicheski razdvoennym soznaniem": Posle Stalina; Kak Nikita Khrushchev pytalsia izmenit' SSSR i shto iz etogo vyshlo', 17 April 2019, www.znak.com/2019-04-17/posle_stalina_kak_nikita_hruchev_pytalsya_izmenit_sssr_i_chto_iz_etogo_vyshlo (last accessed 17 May 2021).

[66] Ia. Miletskii, 'Davaite torgovat'!', *Ogonek*, 18, 26 April 1959, pp. 24–25.

[67] Sanchez-Sibony, *Red Globalization*, pp. 108–11.

be able to start trade at all. Mikoian made this clear to US Under Secretary of State for Economic Affairs C. Douglas Dillon, explaining during a meeting:

> We want to trade. But first you must give us credit so that we can start. If you can't make credit available, then we must do without trade. Our plans don't take into account credits, but if you give us credits we can make changes in our plans.[68]

Khrushchev, who from 1958 onwards held the office of Chairman of the Council of Ministers in addition to his role as General Secretary of the Communist Party, also distinguished himself through active travel. In April 1956, he visited the United Kingdom, where he complained repeatedly to his British interlocutors about the 'policy of discrimination' against the Soviet Union in international trade matters, which showed, he claimed, that 'in certain quarters' there was still no desire to end the Cold War.[69] In September 1959, he became the first Soviet leader to travel to the United States. During his two-week stay, he forcefully advocated closer trade relations, which he also framed as a contribution to the promotion of global peace and stability. In a speech to journalists in Washington, DC, on 16 September 1959, he opined:

> Trade is like a barometer. It shows the trend in political development whether clouds are gathering as before a storm or whether it will be fair and fine. We sincerely hope the barometer will always point to 'Fair', and this, we are deeply convinced, requires all-around expansion of international trade.[70]

Eager to acquire technological knowledge, Soviet representatives, including energy experts from the oil and gas sectors, travelled abroad to explore cooperation opportunities; they visited oil production facilities and attended energy conferences to exchange views with their Western counterparts.[71] Western experts and representatives of foreign

[68] 'Memorandum of Conversation', Washington, DC, 19 January 1959, in US Department of State (ed.), *Foreign Relations of the United States 1958–1960*, vol. X, part 1, Eastern Europe Region; Soviet Union; Cyprus, Washington, DC: United States Government Printing Office, 1993, pp. 241–52, here p. 252.

[69] The transcripts of the conversations can be found in 'Visit to the United Kingdom of Bulganin and Khrushchev, 19–27 April 1956', *History and Public Policy Program Digital Archive*, FO 371/122836, Document obtained by James Vaughan, https://digitalarchive.wilsoncenter.org/document/123798 (last accessed 6 November 2021).

[70] 'N. S. Khrushchev Meets Journalists at the National Press Club', in *Khrushchev in America: Full Texts of the Speeches Made by N. S. Khrushchev Chairman of the Council of Ministers of the USSR on His Tour of the United States, September 15–27, 1959; Translated from the Book Published in the USSR Entitled 'Live in Peace and Friendship!'*, New York: Crosscurrents Press, 1960, pp. 15–32, here p. 25.

[71] Högselius, *Red Gas*, pp. 26–27; on this, see also L. D. Churilov, *Moia istoriia sovetskoi nefti (zapiski poslednego ministra)*, Moscow: Izd-vo 'Neftianoe khoziaistvo', 2016, pp. 61, 147–49, 130–31, 298.

companies also came to energy conferences held in the Soviet Union. When Aleksei Kortunov, head of the Central Administration for the Soviet Natural Gas Industry (Glavgaz), hosted a meeting of the International Gas Union for the first time in the summer of 1960, hundreds of foreign gas experts and company representatives travelled to the Soviet Union and were given their first opportunity to become familiar with the workings of the Soviet gas industry on the ground.[72]

However, this more liberal policy encountered various difficulties – and not only because of continued Western trade restrictions against communist states. Despite Khrushchev's official announcement of a willingness to increase participation in international cooperation and to admit foreign expertise, the opening of the Soviet Union turned out to be quite complicated. In July 1959, the CC of the CPSU denied an American delegation access to Soviet oil industry facilities because the production sites were in zones closed to foreigners. Reciprocal visits would have been useful to the Soviet Union, however, because the oil industry depended on modern American drilling technology. The problem of secrecy also arose when Soviet specialists were sent abroad. Following the visit of a Soviet expert to the United Kingdom, information about Soviet metallurgy appeared in a British journal. Soviet foreign intelligence regarded such leaks as damaging and demanded a stricter information policy. Consequently, links with the Western press and opportunities to publish scientific information within the Soviet Union were tightened.[73]

Despite good intentions, the expansion of trade relations with the countries of the capitalist West did not go as desired from the Soviet point of view. In absolute terms, the volume of trade did increase, as did the number of trading partners: by the end of the 1950s, the Soviet Union had concluded trade agreements with seventy countries.[74] This positive development was only partly due to Khrushchev's policy; it also had to do with changes taking place internationally. Western Europe, but also Japan, had now recovered economically to the point that they were once again able to offer themselves as strong and attractive trading partners able to shape their economic policy relatively independently of the United States. Moreover, with the decolonisation of the developing

[72] Högselius, *Red Gas*, p. 27.
[73] Sari Autio-Sarasmo, 'Khrushchev and the Challenge of Technological Progress', in Melanie Ilic and Jeremy Smith (eds.), *Khrushchev in the Kremlin: Policy and Government in the Soviet Union, 1953–1964*, London, New York: Routledge, 2011, pp. 133–49, here p. 138.
[74] D. O. Churakov (ed.), *Istoriia Rossii XX – nachala XXI veka*, vol. 2, 1941–2016: Uchebnik dlia akademicheskogo bakalavariata, 2nd rev. and expanded ed., Moscow: Izdatel'stvo Iurait, 2017, p. 168.

states of Asia, Africa, and the Middle East in the 1950s and 1960s, new actors emerged who also demonstrated a strong interest in cooperation with the Soviet Union and to whom the Soviet Union was willing to offer technical and economic assistance in return for trade.[75]

However, even towards the end of the Khrushchev era, socialist countries – specifically the members of the CMEA – were still responsible for over two-thirds of total Soviet trade turnover.[76] This posed a problem for the Soviet Union in that the socialist countries were only partially able to meet the Soviet Union's enormous demand for high technology goods, and in any case, Moscow did not trust them to supply these products in the necessary quality. When the Soviet Union commissioned the GDR to build a ship, the Soviet foreign trade department demanded that the ship's engine be of West German production. This cost the GDR 20,000 German marks, even though the engine, 'could [have been] produced just as well in the socialist camp', as Walter Ulbricht, the party leader of the GDR, complained to Khrushchev at a meeting in August 1961.[77] However, Ulbricht was also aware that this would have required the will within CMEA to exchange technical knowledge – such as Western plans for the production of certain machines. Since 'there is no cooperation among socialist countries … [and] everyone is working for himself', bemoaned Ulbricht, the socialist states would fall 'into great dependency on the West'.[78]

The Soviet leadership was well aware of this. Although it sought to expand trade relations, Moscow wanted to avoid too great a dependence on the capitalist West. Khrushchev was still firmly convinced of the superiority of his own system and believed that communism would ultimately emerge as the victor from the system struggle, a claim that he declared loudly and often. The motto of being able to 'catch up with and overtake' the United States in per-capita production within a few years was elevated under him to the credo of Soviet industrial development.[79] This included the energy sector, which was regarded as the basis

75 Gu Guan-Fu, 'Soviet Aid to the Third World: An Analysis of Its Strategy', *Soviet Studies*, 35, 1 (1983), pp. 71–89.

76 For a compilation, see Sanchez-Sibony, *Red Globalization*, pp. 206–7.

77 'Notes on the Conversation of Comrade N. S. Khrushchev with Comrade W. Ulbricht on 1 August 1961', *History and Public Policy Program Digital Archive*, RGANI, f. 52, op. 1, d. 557; obtained and translated by Hope M. Harrison and included in CWIHP e-Dossier No. 23, https://digitalarchive.wilsoncenter.org/document/110206 (last accessed 6 November 2021).

78 Ibid.

79 Cf. Jutta Scherrer, '"To Catch Up and Overtake" the West: Soviet Discourse on Socialist Competition, in Katalin Miklóssy and Melanie Ilic (eds.), *Competition in Socialist Society*, London, New York: Routledge, 2014, pp. 10–22.

for economic development. Frol Kozlov, Politburo member and First Deputy of the Council of Ministers, expressed conviction during a debate in the Presidium of the Central Committee on 14 December 1959 that the Soviet Union would catch up with the United States in the production of all kinds of energy resources by 1970: 'We have gigantic energy resources. We are the richest country on earth in energy resources, no one is richer. This serves to consolidate our material base.'[80]

When, in the course of the 1950s and early 1960s, ever-new and ever-larger oil and gas deposits were discovered in the southern and middle part of Western Siberia, including the 'super-giant' oil field Samotlor in 1965 (still today Russia's largest oil field), it fuelled the debate not only within the Party but also in Soviet newspapers and academic circles about how to deal with these riches.[81] While the first commercial-scale oil well at Samotlor was completed already in April 1968,[82] it would take more than a decade before the Soviet leadership finally ordered the systematic development of the Western Siberian natural gas resources, the largest of which were discovered in the second half of the 1960s. But the knowledge of energy wealth fuelled the fantasies of economic planners even earlier. This enthusiasm was expressed, for example, in the party programme adopted at the 22nd Congress of the Communist Party in October 1961, which prophesied that already the 'present generation of Soviet people' would enjoy life under communism.[83] The programme promised dramatic increases in growth for all sectors of the economy, including a fivefold increase in oil production by 1980 and an increase in natural gas production by a factor of fifteen in the same period.[84]

Although such growth rates were not to persist, the Soviet Union experienced an astonishing economic upswing during this period, including in the energy sector. At the end of the 1950s, even agriculture surprised with excellent harvests. Moreover, the Soviet Union seemed to be able to keep up with the United States in the field of high technology: to the complete surprise of the West, the Soviet space programme succeeded in 1957 in launching the first unmanned satellite ('Sputnik') into space. Just four years later, it also sent the first human being, Iurii Gagarin, into orbit.[85] In addition to space travel, which under Khrushchev became the international prestige project par excellence,

[80] Kozlov quoted in Fursenko (ed.), *Prezidium TsK KPSS*, vol. 1, pp. 413–28, here p. 418.
[81] Slavkina, *Neftegazovyi faktor*, pp. 263–64.
[82] Goldman, *The Enigma of Soviet Petroleum*, p. 35.
[83] Quoted in Slavkina, *Neftegazovyi faktor*, p. 264. [84] Ibid.
[85] Cf. Asif A. Siddiqi, *Sputnik and the Soviet Space Challenge*, Gainesville: University Press of Florida, 2003.

the Soviet Union excelled in the fields of weapons production, military and civilian nuclear technology, and computer science. The Soviet Union relied on its own capacities but also benefitted from the transfer of knowledge and technology that had taken place during the Second World War and, in later years, from an exceptionally well-functioning espionage network abroad that gave Soviet engineers access to relevant information.[86]

But when it came to producing goods for everyday use or the mass production of certain industrial products, the Soviet Union struggled. The reasons for this were numerous, but the problem lay particularly in the cumbersome system of the planned economy and the requirements of Gosplan, which urged enterprises to fulfil annual growth targets. Individual enterprises and workers were rewarded not for the quality of their products but for the quantities they produced. Moreover, in a centralised planning economy, there was hardly any direct relations or exchange of information among economic entities, which made the precise allocation of resources for an increasingly complex economic system a major challenge. This repeatedly led to malfunctioning of the industry, including the pipeline sector, which at that time was crucial for the further development of the oil and gas industries. In a letter of 8 March 1962 addressed directly to the then-head of Gosplan, Vladimir Novikov, the director of the Ukrainian Scientific Research Pipeline Institute located in Dnepropetrovsk, Iakov Osada, complained that 'prospective plans for the development of the USSR pipe industry are drawn up without due regard for the needs of the national economy for steel and cast-iron pipes, which leads to economic losses'.[87] In the case of the gas sector, which increasingly envisaged the use of large 1,020 mm diameter pipelines, the author saw the core of such 'miscalculations' in the 'neglect' of this industry's actual need to produce this type of pipe. Due to bad investments and restructuring gone wrong, Osada lamented, the existing pipeline-welding unit at the Chelyabinsk tube factory was unable to produce the required large diameter pipelines, which then had to be purchased abroad.[88]

Regarding the Soviet Union's potential for trade, this also meant that its industrial goods and other manufactured products were often of such poor quality that although they could be exported to the 'Third World' or

[86] Michael J. Sulick, *American Spies: Espionage against the US from the Cold War to the Present*, Washington, DC: Georgetown University Press, 2013, especially chapter 5 'Soviet Science and Technology Espionage, pp. 53–70.
[87] GARF, f. 5446, op. 96, d. 33, ll. 9–12, here l. 9.
[88] GARF, f. 5446, op. 96, d. 33, l. 9.

the countries of socialist Eastern Europe, they found little market in the capitalist West. To be sure, the Soviet Union did make efforts to sell its manufactured goods in the West, but this often worked poorly, if only because this trade was mostly carried out in the form of compensation transactions. Since neither the Soviet Union nor the other socialist states had large foreign currency reserves, the exchange of goods was the most common form of trade, especially among socialist states. Trade outside the socialist camp was more complicated, as can be seen, for example, from the agreement that the Soviet Union concluded with the United Kingdom in June 1959 for a period of five years. In this agreement, which was one of the first concluded by Moscow with a capitalist Western state, both sides listed the goods that were to be exchanged and were not subject to export restrictions. It was agreed 'that the facilities to be granted for the exchange of consumer goods by one party will be approximately of the same value as the facilities to be granted by the other party'.[89] The British side offered 'motor vehicles; textile manufacturers, including cotton textiles, ready-made clothing, knitwear and hosiery; medicines; photographic materials; sports goods; musical instruments; toys; cured herrings and white fish'. The Soviet list included 'motor cars; cameras; watches; matches; musical instruments; toys; handicrafts; tinned crab; vodka; wines and brandies'. Representatives of the two governments were to meet at least once a year, the agreement stipulated, to review and, if necessary, adjust the contractual arrangements.[90]

Basically, this agreement was a declaration of intent that provided for a complex form of barter transactions. This kind of commodity exchange was not ideal from the Soviet point of view, if only because it meant that the Soviet Union could not generate the foreign currency it so urgently needed. In addition, barter relationships could be costly in practice because they had to be constantly renegotiated and commodity values recalculated. The lists and commodity values, once fixed, also allowed little flexibility to react quickly to new needs and market changes. If, for example, the management of a Soviet factory approached the foreign trade department with a request to purchase abroad a certain machine that it needed for production, this was only possible if sufficient foreign

[89] While the United Kingdom was one of the first countries in Western Europe to draw up such an agreement with the Soviet Union, the pioneering role was played by West Germany, whose trade and economic treaty with the USSR had come into force a year earlier. Many other treaties were to follow. The 1959 treaty between the Soviet Union and the United Kingdom is included in Anita L. P. Burdett (ed.), *Oil Resources in Eastern Europe and the Caucasus*, vol. 7, 1960–1966, Cambridge: Cambridge University Press, 2012, pp. 90–93; quote from ibid., p. 92.

[90] Ibid.

currency was available or the purchase of such a machine was contractually provided for in the relevant exchange agreement. Moreover, barter trade with Western countries often functioned only inadequately because the buyers on the Western side repeatedly complained about the poor quality of Soviet products and sometimes sent the goods back.

In order to buy the necessary equipment for the rapidly developing chemical industry or the oil and gas sector, the question of financing imports was controversially debated among Soviet planners and within the country's leadership. It was initially the Soviet Union's huge gold reserves that were mainly used to buy modern technology, including large quantities of steel pipes. According to a Gosplan calculation of December 1958, '[in] order to meet the demand of the national economy for steel pipes' the country needed '70 tonnes [of pure gold] in 1959 and 80 tonnes in 1960', which had to be converted into foreign exchange roubles in order to buy the necessary quantities of steel pipes from the capitalist West.[91] However, and not least because the Soviet leadership realised the limitations of its gold reserves for the modernisation of the country's economy, the increase of exports of other raw material was considered, including the coveted oil. As Gosplan's director Novikov suggested during a meeting of the Presidium of the CC of the CPSU on 3 December 1961, 'it is better to sell foreign exchange goods (which is more profitable) than gold'.[92]

Of these 'foreign exchange goods', oil was a commodity the Soviet Union knew it had in large quantities and which was in high demand on the world market. In view of the enormous import requirements of Soviet industry, the Ministry of Foreign Trade proposed in a report of 10 August 1961, to be considered for the preparation of the next Seven-Year Plan, to raise the export of petroleum and petroleum products 3.7 times by 1965 over 1958 levels and to increase the export of coal by 182 per cent. A proportionally higher share of the additional quantity of oil was to flow to the Western European capitalist states. By 1965, the latter were to obtain 38 million tonnes of crude oil and petroleum products, while the socialist states were to receive 28 million tonnes.[93]

It was precisely oil, however, that was missing from the Soviet–British trade agreement, because in April 1959, just a few months before the agreement was signed, the British government had decided to impose an almost complete embargo on the import of oil from the Soviet Union. The reason given for this was the possible political implications of the

[91] RGAE, f. 4372, op. 77, d. 123, l. 78.
[92] Novikov quoted in Fursenko (ed.), *Prezidium TsK KPSS*, vol. 1, pp. 545–47, here p. 546.
[93] The report is contained in RGAE, f. 4372, op. 79, d. 734, ll. 52–58, here ll. 57–58.

excessive dependence that the import of 'red oil' might occasion in the liberal societies of the West. Other Western European states had fewer reservations. Not only did they import relatively cheap crude oil and petroleum products from the Soviet Union in ever-greater quantities, but they also went out of their way to provide the Soviet Union with loans, materials, and equipment for the expansion of its energy industry. In any case, by this time 'red oil' had once again become a contentious issue in international politics.

'Oil Offensive', NATO Sanctions, and Khrushchev's Failed Export Strategy

Towards the end of the 1950s, the state-owned Soviet oil export company Soiuznefteeksport began flooding the European market with ever-greater quantities of cheap oil. Thus began the Soviet 'oil offensive', as it was sometimes called in the West.[94] By 1960, the Soviet Union produced more oil than Venezuela and had moved into second place in the world behind the United States.[95] Exports also soared: While the Soviet Union had shipped a modest 3.7 million tonnes of oil abroad in 1955, the following years saw a major increase in oil volumes flowing westwards; by 1968 the Soviet Union was exporting 85.8 million tonnes, about half of which went to Western Europe.[96]

Although the quantities were steadily increasing, they remained too small to have any real relevance in the energy mix of individual Western European countries. Moreover, in view of the global oversupply of oil, the European countries could easily have switched to other providers in the event of difficulties with the Soviet Union. For its part, the returns that the Soviet Union generated from selling oil to the West were still relatively modest due to the low world market prices at the time. Hence, it would be inaccurate to speak of any great mutual dependence in Soviet–Western European energy relations. Nevertheless, from the late 1950s onwards, oil increasingly became part of the Western political discourse on an alleged Soviet threat.

When the British government imposed a formal embargo on the import of Soviet oil into Britain in 1959, it justified the move on the grounds that Moscow was using its oil as a means of gaining not only access to

[94] For example, Harold Lubell, *The Soviet Oil Offensive and Inter-Bloc Economic Competition*, Santa Monica, CA: RAND Corporation, 1961.
[95] Jensen-Eriksen, 'The Cold War in Energy Markets', pp. 196–97.
[96] Robert E. Ebel, *Communist Trade in Oil and Gas: An Evaluation of the Future Export Capabilities of the Soviet Bloc*, New York: Praeger, 1970, p. 39.

international markets but also political influence. However, internal British reports from the time show that the government was primarily concerned with protecting the economic interests of domestic energy companies and keeping at bay an unwelcome competitor in the British market that offered its products at much lower prices than Western firms.[97]

Similar ambivalences can be seen in the anti-Soviet arguments of international oil companies. Standard Oil of New Jersey's annual report for 1960, for example, stated that Soviet oil 'is becoming increasingly significant in free world markets after a virtual absence of more than twenty years'. It continued, 'with its production increasing, the Soviet Union is able to trade or barter oil for strategic industrial goods to meet the needs of its growing economy as well as to serve its political purposes'. In doing so, Standard Oil of New Jersey lamented, the Soviet Union was not guided by market cost considerations in setting prices for its oil exports, concluding, 'though the Soviet oil offensive is related to economic needs, the aim undoubtedly is also to weaken western alliances and disturb normal patterns of trade and investment'.[98] Standard Oil of New Jersey's underlying goal was clear: to use political arguments to convince Western governments, especially the US government, of the need to take action against trade in Soviet oil.

With the hardening of East–West relations in the early 1960s, these views increasingly found their way into the thinking of Western governments and organisations. The American National Petroleum Council, which had been founded at Truman's recommendation as early as 1946 and represented the interests of the US oil and gas industry, wrote in an influential report released in October 1962:

> In considering the problem of Soviet oil, it should be emphasized that, as a result of an absolute state monopoly over its foreign trade, the Soviet bloc is in a unique position to use trade for political purposes. Politics and trade cannot be considered apart when dealing with the communists. The ultimate goal of the Soviet Bloc is to extend its political control, destroy freedom and communize the world, and it uses its monopoly of foreign trade to further these objectives. This, in short, is the problem the Free World faces when trading with the Soviet bloc.[99]

[97] This is clear from discussions within the British government about the benefits of the embargo in the mid-1960s: Anita L. P. Burdett (ed.), *Oil Resources in Eastern Europe and the Caucasus*, vol. 8, 1967–1978, Cambridge: Cambridge University Press, 2012, especially part 1.2.; for further reading, see Niklas Jensen-Eriksen, '"Red Oil" and Western Reactions: The Case of Britain', in Perović (ed.), *Cold War Energy*, pp. 105–30.

[98] Standard Oil Company of New Jersey, *1960 Annual Report*, New York, 1961, pp. 3–4.

[99] National Petroleum Council, *Impact of Oil Exports from the Soviet Bloc: A Report of the National Petroleum Council's Committee and Working Subcommittee on the Impact of Oil Exports from the Soviet Bloc*, vol. I, Washington, DC: n.p., 1962, p. xiii. See also Bruce

It was certainly correct that Soviet trade organisations were in a relatively strong position vis-à-vis privately owned energy companies often competing among each other for prices and market access. At the same time, however, it seemed that even the US State Department basically knew that Soviet oil posed no real threat to European security at that time. Nevertheless, because it was not in Washington's interest for the Soviet Union to accumulate foreign currency through the sale of oil or for its trade organisations to gain market share in Europe, US strategy deliberately aimed to politicise Soviet oil exports, emphasising the security aspect. An internal discussion of the global oil situation held at the end of 1961 among the members of the Interdepartmental Committee of Under Secretaries on Foreign Economic Policy within the US State Department reveals that

> the average person in Italy gets his oil cheaper because Italy is importing Soviet oil. Industrialists in Europe can produce at less cost because of Soviet oil. Our argument has to be the danger of Soviet oil.[100]

The increasing opening of Western European markets to cheap Soviet oil led some to see it as a sinister plot orchestrated in Moscow to destabilise NATO.[101] Subsequently, in 1961, the issue of Soviet oil even made its way onto the agenda of the Western defense alliance. In addition to the United States, which did not buy oil from the Soviet Union, Great Britain, because of its existing embargo, had little hesitation in supporting an internal NATO recommendation that, in view of possible political implications, urged its members 'on their own responsibility to exercise caution and restraint in determining the level of their oil imports from the Soviet bloc'.[102]

As a result of growing East–West tensions stemming from the crises over Berlin in the summer of 1961 and the Cuban missile crisis in October 1962, measures became more concrete. Any export that, in Washington's view, contributed to the 'military or economic potential' of the Soviet Union or Communist-dominated countries that would 'prove detrimental to the national security of the United States' was to

W. Jentleson, 'From Consensus to Conflict: The Domestic Political Economy of East–West Energy Trade Policy', *International Organization*, 38, 4 (1984), pp. 625–60, here pp. 642–43.

[100] 'Summary Minutes of Meeting of the Interdepartmental Committee of Under Secretaries on Foreign Economic Policy', Washington, DC, 13 December 1961, in US Department of State (ed.), *Foreign Relations of the United States 1961–1963*, vol. IX, Foreign Economic Policy, Washington, DC: United States Government Printing Office, 1995, p. 774.

[101] Goldman, *The Enigma of Soviet Petroleum*, p. 69.

[102] Burdett (ed.), *Oil Resources in Eastern Europe and the Caucasus*, vol. 8, p. 283.

be embargoed.[103] As a result, the United States exerted significant pressure on its allies to go along with its policy and tighten multilateral export controls.[104] At Washington's urging, the NATO Council passed a resolution in November 1962 aimed at tightening the Western sanctions regime to prevent even already-agreed deliveries of large-diameter steel tubes to the Soviet Union. The main target was the Druzhba oil pipeline project, which was under construction at the time.[105] During this period, some Western media actively participated in the campaign against Soviet oil. On its front page on 3 June 1962, the *Chicago Daily Tribune*, for example, bluntly described the planned Druzhba oil pipeline as a 'Cold War weapon' and portrayed this infrastructure project as part of a Soviet 'attack' on Western Europe.[106]

Given that the West German government adhered strictly to the sanctions, the shortfall of large-diameter steel tubes ordered in West Germany had a serious effect on the Soviet Union. According to an internal report prepared by the State Committee for Iron and Nonferrous Metals Industry dated 22 January 1963, the Soviet Union needed between 673,000 and 700,000 tonnes of electrically welded steel pipes with a diameter of 1,020 mm for the construction of planned natural gas and oil pipelines in the year 1963 alone. According to the report, slightly more than half of these large diameter pipes were to be produced in three Soviet plants, while the rest, about 325,000 tonnes, had to be imported from abroad. It was anticipated that about 230,000 tonnes were to be delivered from the Federal Republic of Germany (FRG) and another 95,000 tonnes would have to be imported from Italy, Sweden, and Japan.[107] It was thus clear that the loss of West German steel pipes would pose a massive problem for Soviet energy transportation plans, not only with regard to the Druzhba oil pipeline but also Soviet domestic pipelines like the 'Bukhara-Ural' gas pipeline, a 4,500 km long pipeline project that required more than three times as much steel pipe as Druzhba.[108]

[103] 'Memorandum from Secretary of Commerce Hodges to the National Security Council', Washington, DC, 16 July 1962, in US Department of State (ed.), *Foreign Relations of the United States 1961–1963*, vol. IX, pp. 689–96, here p. 691.

[104] 'Current Economic Development: US–UK Hold East-West Talks', Washington, DC, 27 February 1962, in ibid., pp. 671–74; on the pipe embargo p. 674.

[105] Wörmann, *Osthandel als Problem der Atlantischen Allianz*, p. 31; on internal British discussions of Soviet energy in the early 1960s, see Jensen-Eriksen, '"Red Oil" and Western Reactions'.

[106] 'Soviet Pipe Line Threatens Oil Flood in West', *Chicago Daily Tribune*, 3 June 1962, p. 1.

[107] GARF, f. 5446, op. 97, d. 461, ll. 1–2.

[108] This emerges from a report sent by the director of Glavgaz, Kortunov, to the head of Gosplan, Novikov, on 12 April 1961, contained in RGAE, f. 4372, op. 63, d. 431, ll. 316–18.

In direct talks with their German counterparts, Soviet representatives made no secret of their anger at West Germany's breach of contract. Soviet Foreign Trade Minister Nikolai Patolichev was particularly indignant. As he explained to the West German ambassador in Moscow in February 1962, the Soviet Union had counted on these deliveries and had therefore decided not to expand its own tube production capacity. Moreover, Patolichev made clear that the fact that German companies were forced by their government to halt supplies of pipes put him personally in a difficult position, since it was he who had convinced the Soviet government that 'the German market, including the pipe market, is a good and reliable one'. If the Germans did indeed not deliver, 'he would have to tell his government that the West German tube market no longer existed for the Soviet Union and to recommend that their own tube capacity be expanded accordingly'. Patolichev told his counterpart that he considered this 'unfortunate' as it was 'disadvantageous for the Soviet Union to have to produce everything itself; it was a big country and therefore bought a lot of what it needed from abroad'.[109]

Even though Soviet production was ramped up to replace the shortfall in imports, the Soviet planning authorities were well aware of the problem of the poor quality of the tubes produced in the country's production facilities when they stated in the aforementioned report of 22 January 1963 that 'the State Committee for Iron and Nonferrous Metals Industry … together with Glavgaz had dealt with questions of the quality of steel sheets and pipes [supplied] by [Soviet enterprises] for the construction of high-pressure gas and oil pipelines'. The report's authors noted 'that the quality of the pipes produced by these plants [was] inferior to those supplied by foreign companies … due to the low quality of the steel sheets used for pipe production, which have low and unstable mechanical properties'.[110] Not for the first time, a Soviet report pointed out the quality problem in the Soviet metal industry and highlighted the urgent need to raise 'the culture of steel sheet production'.[111]

According to Italian historian Roberto Cantoni, NATO sources from this period do not give a consistent picture regarding the effectiveness of the sanctions. Although the sanctions had the effect of delaying the completion of the pipeline by a whole year, the Soviet Union, together with other CMEA states, still managed to complete the project by the

[109] Report by Ambassador Groepper to Federal Minister Schröder, Moscow, 2 February 1963, in *Akten zur Auswärtigen Politik der Bundesrepublik Deutschland (1963)*, edited by the Institut für Zeitgeschichte, Munich: Oldenbourg, 1994, pp. 240–44, here pp. 241–42.

[110] GARF, f. 5446, op. 97, d. 461, l. 6.

[111] GARF, f. 5446, op. 97, d. 461, l. 7.

end of 1964.[112] In addition to the Soviet Union now cranking up its own production of steel pipes, companies from non-NATO states, namely Sweden but also Japan, stepped into the breach to at least partially compensate for the loss of West German steel pipe supplies.[113] At Soviet request, Sweden in particular was to increase exports of large diameter steel tubes; in February 1963, the Soviets ordered some 200,000 tonnes of such pipes to be delivered in the period 1965–67.[114] Moreover, because the NATO Council's decision was recommendatory and thus not legally binding, NATO countries such as the United Kingdom and Italy tended to largely continue to honour their treaty obligations to the Soviet Union, much to the annoyance of West Germany.[115] In fact, the big losers were the West German steel factories such as Mannesmann, Hoesch, and Phoenix-Rheinrohr, which had been supplying steel pipes to the Soviet Union since the late 1950s and lost huge orders because of the boycott. The value of the previously agreed deliveries of some 163,000 tonnes of West German steel pipes to the Soviet Union in 1962/1963 was around 28 million US dollars at the time.[116]

Socialist propaganda heavily publicised the completion of the pipeline in its media; the GDR printed special stamps showing the course of the 'oil pipeline of friendship' on a map. Even though the realisation of this prestigious project was celebrated in the Socialist press and was cited as evidence of the superiority of the socialist economic system, the Western embargo brought to the fore the Soviet Union's massive energy transportation problem, which, although not publicly addressed, remained a matter of heated internal debate throughout the Khrushchev years and beyond. Khrushchev understood that in order to boost his petrochemical project and accelerate the development of the oil and gas industry, the Soviet Union would have to acquire technical equipment from abroad,

[112] Roberto Cantoni, 'What's in a Pipe? NATO's Confrontation on the 1962 Large-Diameter Pipe Embargo', 2016, especially p. 25, https://hal.archives-ouvertes.fr/hal-01291854/document (last accessed 8 July 2021); see also Roberto Cantoni, 'Debates at NATO and the EEC in Response to the Soviet "Oil Offensive" in the Early 1960s', in Perović (ed.), *Cold War Energy*, pp. 131–61.

[113] Angela Stent, *From Embargo to Ostpolitik: The Political Economy of West German-Soviet Relations, 1955–1980*, Cambridge: Cambridge University Press, 1981, p. 115.

[114] RGAE, f. 4372, op. 81, d. 259, ll. 12–14.

[115] Markus Engels and Petra Schwartz, 'Alliierte Restriktionen für die Aussenwirtschaftspolitik der Bundesrepublik Deutschland: Das Röhrenembargo von 1962/63 und das Erdgas-Röhren-Geschäft von 1982', in Helga Haftendorn and Henning Riecke (eds.), *Die volle Macht des souveränen Staates: Die alliierten Vorbehaltsrechte als Rahmenbedingungen westdeutscher Aussenpolitik 1949–1990*, Baden-Baden: Nomos, 1996, pp. 227–42, here pp. 231, 239.

[116] Ibid., p. 228.

and that trade in gold, oil, and other raw materials was essential, at least in the short term, to procure the necessary goods or, better still, to acquire licences to produce these goods in the Soviet Union. At a meeting of the CC of the CPSU in March 1963, Khrushchev even bluntly called for the theft of licenses, declaring, 'what we can't steal, we will have to buy. That's what the whole world is doing'. He referred to the example of the Japanese, claiming that they had 'paved their way to success with theft and purchases, mainly with theft, because the most cunning thieves of patents are the Japanese'.[117] Thus, in Khrushchev's perspective, the Soviet Union was to succeed in only a short time in manufacturing these goods in its own production plants according to Western plans and, if deemed beneficial, exporting these goods to capitalist foreign countries.

Khrushchev had recurrently announced that trade with the capitalist countries of the West was to take place only in those areas that were advantageous to the Soviet Union, that is, mostly high-quality technical goods. However, he explicitly criticised the continued purchase of industrial items such as steel pipes, as he was convinced that the Soviet Union could produce these products in its own factories. Thus, contrary to other opinions, such as those expressed by Glavgaz director Kortunov,[118] Khrushchev demanded that the Soviet steelworks manufacture these pipes themselves, arguing that the purchase of steel plates and pipes was typical of industrially backward countries that did not have their own metallurgy and machinery. He also feared that by buying large quantities of pipelines abroad, funds would be forfeited for importing other technical equipment necessary for his petrochemical project, to which he gave the highest priority. The Soviet leader, therefore, fought hard against those elements within Gosplan and government structures who advocated annual plans with a metal deficit and favoured the purchase of metal or semi-finished products from abroad, arguing that otherwise the plan could not be fulfilled.[119] Khrushchev's priority was clear: if the available means were scarce, he would rather postpone other projects – such as the further development of the gas industry – than

[117] RGANI, f. 52, op. 1, d. 257, ll. 60–61, quoted in Nekrasov, 'Decision-Making in the Soviet Energy Sector in Post-Stalinist Times', p. 180.

[118] Regarding the 'difficult situation' of the Soviet gas industry and the construction of the Druzhba oil pipeline, see, e.g., the report by Aleksei Kortunov, then head of Glavgaz, to Vladimir Novikov, Chairman of Gosplan, dated 12 April 1961, contained in RGAE, f. 4372, op. 63, d. 431, ll. 316–18.

[119] V. L. Nekrasov, *Dilemma Khrushcheva': Reformy Gosplana SSSR, neftekhemicheskii proekt i vyzovy kholodnoi voiny (vtoraia polovina 1950-kh–pervaia polovina 1960-kh-godov)*, Moscow: Institut vseobshchei istorii RAN, 2019, pp. 108–9.

compromise on his petrochemical project. He was therefore incensed when he learned in mid-1963 that Glavgaz director Kortunov, together with Gosplan, tried to go ahead with ordering more steel pipes for gas transportation projects inside the country in order the construct the pipeline from Bukhara in the Uzbek SSR towards the Urals, a major gas transportation venture that clearly did not figure high on Khrushchev's economic agenda at this time.[120]

Khrushchev also made his position quite plain regarding the nature of Soviet exports: under no circumstances should the Soviet Union become a mere provider of raw materials to the Western capitalists. Instead, the country was to establish itself as a 'global export power for consumer and processed goods', as Dunja Krempin similarly notes in her comprehensive study on the history of the Soviet gas industry.[121] When it became increasingly clear in 1962–63 that this would not succeed and that raw materials were comprising an ever-greater share of the Soviet export structure, Khrushchev sought vehemently to counter this tendency in his last years in office. In Khrushchev's opinion, crude oil should be used primarily for the needs of the Soviet petrochemical industry and then exported in processed form. Khrushchev expressed himself on this point numerous times, for example, in a memorandum to the Presidium of the CC of the CPSU on 29 March 1963:

> We and our country, which has huge reserves of gas and oil, must use this raw material, and make it the source of our country's wealth. We even have the potential, with the raw materials of gas and oil, to become a major exporter of mineral fertilisers and other chemical products to many countries in Europe, not to mention the Asian countries. Accordingly, we could even become competitors of the West.[122]

Although the Soviet Union continued to build up a chemical industry at this time, its products failed to become competitive with those manufactured in the West. Consequently, it was to be to a large extent Soviet crude oil and later natural gas that prevailed on the international market – a development that Khrushchev continued to lament on various occasions. Thus, the issue of oil was put on the agenda on of the meeting of the Presidium of the CC of the CPSU on 1 August 1963. Summarising the content of these discussions during a meeting of the Council of Ministers the next day, Khrushchev noted that

[120] Ibid., p. 106. [121] Krempin, *Die sibirische Wucht*, p. 419.
[122] Nikita Sergeevich Khrushchev, *Dva tsveta vremeni: Dokumenty iz lichnogo fonda N. S. Khrushcheva*, vol. 2, Moscow: Mezhdunarodnyi fond 'Demokratiia', 2009, pp. 719–21.

> [we] are still primitive in the way we exploit oil; we mainly sell our crude oil abroad, even though we know that it would be more profitable to sell petroleum products; but we are unable to do so. We need to set a new course to process as much petroleum as possible and trade in petroleum products, not crude oil.[123]

To the public's surprise, Khrushchev was overthrown on 14 October 1964 and stripped of his two posts as prime minister and general secretary of the party. By decision of the CC of the CPSU, Aleksei Kosygin was appointed the new prime minister, while Leonid Brezhnev would head the party and rule the country for the next eighteen years. Khrushchev's ouster was the result of growing resentment of a man whose reform efforts, while certainly pointing in the right direction, had become increasingly unpredictable: he had, for instance, led the world to the brink of a nuclear confrontation with the United States over the stationing of Soviet nuclear missiles in Cuba in October 1962. Under Khrushchev, the Soviet Union experienced an economic boom, especially in the second half of the 1950s. But Khrushchev was ultimately unable to keep his extravagant promises to raise living standards. By the early 1960s, if not before, it was clear that the Soviet Union would not be able to 'catch up and overtake' the United States regarding per capita gross domestic product in the foreseeable future.

As a reformer, Khrushchev achieved more than is generally acknowledged. His downfall was his increasingly erratic behaviour, which ultimately made him unacceptable to those around him. Khrushchev's ouster was not an expression of a desire to return to the Stalin era. Those who had engineered his ouster, however, wanted more stability for Soviet politics. During the long Brezhnev era, the Soviet Union was to improve relations cautiously but steadily with the Western world and to demonstrate that the Soviet Union was a predictable actor in world politics and international trade.

Looking back at Khrushchev's idea of establishing trade relations with the West, the Soviet Union's export structure was not to change in the way he advocated. His vision of the Soviet Union as a global manufacturing power was not to be realised. Instead, the Soviet Union would sell oil and natural gas in ever-greater quantities. Moreover, the price hikes of the 1970s would allow the country to generate unprecedented foreign currency revenues from the trade in raw materials, thus setting the stage for the Soviet Union's rise as an energy power of international significance. However, well until the late 1960s, it was still far from clear

[123] RGANI, f. 52, op. 1, d. 338, l. 94; Nekrasov, 'Decision-Making in the Soviet Energy Sector in Post-Stalinist Times', pp. 182, 197 (n. 91).

what precise course the Soviet Union would take in its energy export policy towards the capitalist West.

The Soviet Energy Debate in the Late 1960s

In addition to overall increasing oil production and exports, the commissioning of the Druzhba oil pipeline also had an impact on energy relations with individual Western European countries, because Soviet crude oil could now be transported westwards more quickly, more cheaply, and in larger quantities. Nevertheless, concerns about overdependence on the Soviet Union in terms of energy imports were hardly justifiable. For instance, while the FRG almost doubled its oil imports from the Soviet Union between 1965 and 1967 from 3.1 to 5.6 million tonnes,[124] Soviet crude oil still represented less than 10 per cent of West German oil consumption. Even in the case of Italy, which at that time imported the highest volume of oil from the Soviet Union, this share did not exceed 20 per cent.[125]

By the time NATO formally lifted the pipe embargo in November 1966, the discussion in the West no longer revolved around the possible dangers that 'red oil' might pose for Western Europe. Instead, Western observers were increasingly concerned that the Soviet Union might itself run short of oil soon due to declining growth rates, rising domestic demand, and its existing international supply obligations. Western experts thus doubted that the Soviet Union would be able to maintain its exports to the West in the coming years, much less increase them significantly.[126]

The actual state of the Soviet energy industry at that time could not be determined with certainty due to the lack or whitewashing of statistical data. The fact that Nikolai Baibakov, Stalin's former oil minister and head of Gosplan since 1965, was in Iran in April 1967 to negotiate the

[124] Burdett (ed.), *Oil Resources in Eastern Europe and the Caucasus*, vol. 8, p. 116.

[125] In 1966, the share in West Germany was 7.5 per cent, that in Italy 19 per cent; see Burdett (ed.), *Oil Resources in Eastern Europe and the Caucasus*, vol. 8, p. 59. For further information on the energy situation in Italy, see Pier Angelo Toninelli, 'Energy Supply and Economic Development in Italy: The Role of State Owned Companies', in Alain Beltran (ed.), *A Comparative History of National Oil Companies*, Brussels: Peter Lang, 2010, pp. 125–42.

[126] This emerges from secret American and British position papers; see Burdett (ed.), *Oil Resources in Eastern Europe and the Caucasus*, vol. 8; 'National Intelligence Estimate', Washington, DC, 14 November 1970, in US Department of State (ed.), *Foreign Relations of the United States 1969–1976*, vol. XXXVI, Energy Crisis, 1969–1974, Washington, DC: United States Government Printing Office, 1995, pp. 136–51, especially pp. 142–46.

import of Iranian oil and gas in return for Soviet economic aid and technology was interpreted by the British Foreign Office as an indication that the Soviet Union was preparing for a coming oil shortage in its own country.[127] In general, there was a widespread sense in Westminster, and even more so in Washington, that the Soviet Union might be tempted to become more involved in the oil-rich states of the Persian Gulf in order to solve its energy problems. US intelligence reports from the period repeatedly suggest that, in the event of a renewed outbreak of the Arab–Israeli conflict, such as the region had last experienced in June 1967, the Soviet Union might be tempted to provide assistance to the Arabs in return for greater influence over the Arab oil sector.[128]

A November 1970 American intelligence report saw the Soviet Union as 'self-sufficient in oil' and envisioned that it would 'remain so at least through 1975 and probably through 1980', yet predicted that 'the level of Soviet exports both to Eastern Europe and to non-Communist countries will depend to a growing degree … on Soviet ability to procure supplemental supplies of oil from the Middle East for reexport'.[129] The report's authors argued that this was due to the fact that Soviet oil fields were being depleted faster than expected, in part because 'poor extractive practices' had made it impossible to produce large quantities of reserves. The report acknowledged that the share of Soviet oil produced in recently discovered deposits in Central Asia and Western Siberia was increasing. However, its authors had doubts that this would offset declining growth in oil production in the future as the new production sites were 'far from centers of consumption in the western part of the USSR'. The report noted that due to 'extremes of climate, difficult terrain, reluctance of skilled specialists to work under such conditions, and shortage of suitable technology and equipment', exploitation of these reserves was 'difficult and costly, and the rate of increase in total production of oil is slowing down'.[130]

[127] Burdett (ed.), *Oil Resources in Eastern Europe and the Caucasus*, vol. 8, p. 80.

[128] For example, the report 'Prospects for US Access to World Oil Over the Next 15 Years or So', contained in 'Memorandum Prepared in the Central Intelligence Agency', Washington, DC, 28 August 1969, in US Department of State (ed.), *Foreign Relations of the United States 1969–1976*, vol. XXXVI, pp. 25–35, especially p. 26. The assumption that the Soviet Union might be tempted to expand into the Middle East to secure oil imports was also discussed in Western publications at the time. Cf. Robert Hunter, *The Soviet Dilemma in the Middle East: Part II; Oil and the Persian Gulf*, The Adelphi Papers 60, London: Institute for Strategic Studies, 1969, p. 5.

[129] 'National Intelligence Estimate, NIE 20/30-70', Washington, DC, 14 November 1970, in US Department of State (ed.), *Foreign Relations of the United States 1969–1976*, vol. XXXVI, pp. 136–51, here p. 143.

[130] Ibid., pp. 143–44.

In general, the Americans and the British, who did not import Soviet oil, had a different view of the global energy situation than, say, the West Germans, Italians, and French. Westminster and Washington saw the main threat to Western energy security in the fact that their globally operating energy companies could lose direct access to oil sources due to nationalisation tendencies in the oil-producing countries of North Africa and the Middle East. As the CIA noted in a 1969 report, the 'Seven Sisters' controlled 75 per cent of the global oil trade in 1968, whereas in 1952 the share had been well over 90 per cent.[131] Moreover, Western oil companies faced mounting pressure in various regions across the globe due to the Soviets' ability to offer their oil at discounted prices to nations such as Cuba, Ceylon, India, Guinea, and Ghana. This resulted in restricted market access and even the ousting of Western oil companies from these regions.[132] In return for aid and weapons, countries such as Algeria, Egypt, and Syria chose to sell their oil to the Soviet Union. The Soviet Union then used this oil for re-export or to free up more of its own oil for export.[133] From this perspective, the Soviet Union appeared as an adversary and potential disruptive factor of Western global oil interests.

As we learn from internal Soviet debates, the Soviet planners were well aware of the challenges facing the further development of their energy industry. In the second half of the 1960s, further huge gas fields were discovered in the north of Tyumen, including some of the world's largest at the time (Urengoi, Yamburg, and Medvezhe), with the potential to radically alter the Soviet Union's energy balance, freeing up additional oil for export and even gas for shipment to the lucrative Western European market. However, the question of when and whether the new Siberian gas fields should be developed, and to what extent the gas should be used for export, was a topic of controversial discussion at the time. While Kortunov, as head of the gas ministry that emerged from Glavgaz in 1965,[134] was generally more in favour of expanding the gas industry and supported international gas trade, others, including the new director of Gosplan, Baibakov, were more sceptical; they doubted that developing the distant Siberian gas fields and exporting gas to far-away European countries outside the socialist camp made economic sense given the lack of infrastructure and price competition from other emerging

[131] 'Memorandum Prepared in the Central Intelligence Agency', p. 26.
[132] Goldman, *The Enigma of Soviet Petroleum*, p. 71. [133] Ibid., pp. 76–77.
[134] The Ministry of Gas (Mingazprom) was created in 1965 as a successor to Glavgaz, which was established in 1956. The creation of a separate ministry for the gas industry meant an elevation of the status of the gas industry, putting it on an equal footing with the oil industry; see Högselius, *Red Gas*, p. 40.

international gas exporters such as Algeria and the Netherlands. Moreover, the Soviet planners understood that exporting gas was not like exporting oil. Oil was the Soviet Union's preferred export commodity because it could be traded flexibly, being transported by pipeline, tanker, and rail to buyers in Europe and beyond, and export volumes could be adjusted at short notice depending on demand and price. On the other hand, gas trade involved long-term contractual commitments between seller and buyer. Due to high initial investment costs resulting from developing new fields and building transportation infrastructure from scratch, it was important for the exporter to have the certainty that the recipient of gas would accept it over the period stipulated and at the agreed volumes and price conditions.[135]

An insight into the Soviet Union's internal deliberations is provided by a report dated 10 January 1967 and commissioned by Vladimir Kirillin, Deputy Chairman of the Council of Ministers and also Chairman of the State Committee for Science and Technology. The report, entitled 'Preliminary Considerations on the Percpective of the Development of Economic Relations with Western States in the Area of Energy', prepared by L. Vaag and A. Basistov and forwarded by V. Puzanov, was based on materials from various state commissions and 'exchanges of views' with representatives from the Academy of Science, Gosplan, the Ministry of Foreign Trade, and others.[136] The document was prepared at a time when the Soviet Union had decided in principle to begin initial negotiations on possible gas supplies with Western European countries such as Italy, Austria, France, Finland, and Sweden (but not yet with West Germany).[137]

The prospect of connecting Western Europe to the Soviet gas system was boosted by an agreement between the Soviet Union and Czechoslovakia on the construction of the Bratstvo ('brotherhood') gas pipeline for the export of gas through the Ukrainian SSR. The gas was to come from the western part of Ukraine, whose historically important gas fields were to supply Czechoslovakia until Siberian gas became available.[138] The agreement on the Bratstvo project was concluded in 1964, and the pipeline opened in 1967. The intention was to expand this pipeline to supply other CMEA states and eventually also Western European countries. Because of its geographical proximity, the most likely candidate was Austria, which in September 1968 became the first Western European country to receive Soviet gas via an extension of the

[135] Ibid., pp. 36–38.
[136] The report is contained in RGAE, f. 9480, op. 9, d. 324, ll. 2–13, here l. 2.
[137] Högselius, *Red Gas*, p. 9. [138] Ibid., p. 90.

Bratstvo pipeline. In 1966–67, however, negotiations were most advanced with Italy, the country that not only imported more Soviet oil than any other Western European nation at the time but was also eager to import Soviet gas and wanted to become the hub for future gas imports from the East to other European countries and to France in the first place.[139]

The authors of the January 1967 report, however, essentially argued against the export of gas to distant European countries. They began their argument by referring to the international situation. According to the report's authors, energy trade was still largely underdeveloped, with the construction of high-voltage power lines and the development of pipeline systems for the transportation of oil and gas mainly taking place within individual countries, rather than across national borders. In terms of international trade, energy sources such as coal, oil, and other energy minerals, as well as processed products, continued to be transported mainly by rail and sea but not via pipelines.[140] Regarding the expansion of Soviet energy exports to distant capitalist countries in Western Europe, the authors presented several arguments against the construction of transnational infrastructure, underlining the challenge of finding the optimal 'fuel and energy balance' for the Soviet Union itself. In the case of oil, the authors of the report pointed to the difficulty of coordinating the whole system of energy production, transportation, processing, and distribution in an economically rational and efficient way; in order to avoid poor planning and misallocation of investment, they argued for a more 'global' view that went beyond specific local perspectives and interests.[141]

If the authors considered this challenge enough in relation to the Soviet Union and, more broadly, to the socialist countries of Eastern Europe dependent on Soviet energy imports, they clearly saw enormous risks in involving the capitalist countries of Western Europe in such complex equations. The authors emphasised that it was difficult to assess the cost-effectiveness of exports because international markets tended to be subject to forces beyond the control of the Soviet Union. For example, the fact that the Netherlands was rapidly developing its newly discovered natural gas fields could 'fundamentally change the direction of imports and exports of electrical energy and fuels in the countries of Western Europe', as new large volumes of gas might ultimately affect not only the price of gas but energy prices in general.[142] According to the authors, this undermined long-term planning reliability, as the Soviet Union

[139] Ibid., pp. 35, 38–40, 59. [140] RGAE, f. 9480, op. 9, d. 324, l. 3.
[141] RGAE, f. 9480, op. 9, d. 324, l. 4. [142] RGAE, f. 9480, op. 9, d. 324, l. 5.

needed to have certainty that the high initial investment costs of building transportation infrastructure for gas, oil, and electricity transmission would be recouped over the years. Moreover, because relations with states of the capitalist West were far from 'politically stable', the authors saw a risk of major losses in case of supply interruptions for 'political motives'.[143] In the atmosphere of the Cold War, it was not only Western countries that were initially reluctant to engage economically with their Soviet counterpart out of security concerns but also vice versa. The authors considered the 'political factor' as 'one of the main reasons why the development of high-voltage transmission lines and [the building] of oil and gas pipelines between countries was postponed in favor of developing these modes of transportation inside countries'.[144]

Referring to the ongoing negotiations with Italy, France, and a number of 'other capitalist countries in Europe', the writers of the report thus took a critical view of all the export options under discussion at the time. These included the laying of a pipeline from gas fields in the Ukrainian SSR to Italy, the construction of a high-voltage power line for the transmission of electricity from Ukraine through Lombardy in northern Italy to France, and the construction of a pipeline to carry oil from Tatarstan and Bashkortostan in the Volga region to Italy and on to France.[145]

Relying on Gosplan's conservative cost estimates, the report's authors argued that it was important to consider the impact of exports on the Soviet Union's own energy balance. Since the European part of the Soviet Union was also suffering from an energy deficit, the costs of additional production and transportation of energy from the eastern regions of the country to the European part of the Soviet Union had to be included in the calculation as well. In the case of gas, the authors thus maintained that it was simply not profitable for the Soviet Union to export this commodity since the price on the European market was around ten exchange roubles per 1,000 m^3. According to the authors' calculations, 'a loss would not occur if the price of gas was traded for no less than 16.3 exchange roubles (18.1 U.S. dollars) for 1,000 m^3', which they doubted importers would agree to.[146]

In fact, it was the disagreement over price that complicated the Soviet–Italian negotiations on the gas pipeline project at that time, while Austria, through its company ÖMV (Österreichische Mineralölverwaltung Aktiengesellschaft), would eventually accept the Soviet Union's offer of 15.13 US dollars for 1,000 m^3, which was close to Gosplan's estimates

[143] RGAE, f. 9480, op. 9, d. 324, l. 5.
[144] RGAE, f. 9480, op. 9, d. 324, l. 5.
[145] RGAE, f. 9480, op. 9, d. 324, l. 6.
[146] RGAE, f. 9480, op. 9, d. 324, l. 8.

referred to in the aforementioned report.[147] For the Soviet Union, it was crucial to secure a sound deal, since the case of Austria was to serve as a baseline for treaty negotiations with other Western European states. This concerned not only the price of gas and the exact quantities supplied over time but the entire model of the economic deal, which in the Austrian case also included deliveries of steel pipes to the Soviet Union and a credit agreement between the Foreign Trade Bank of the USSR and the Austrian Control Bank.[148] Although the agreed gas supplies were modest, the Austrian case helped to broker further major gas contracts, which the Soviet Union signed with Italy's ENI (Ente Nazionale Idrocarburi) at the end of 1969 (after a less significant agreement had already been concluded in August 1967)[149] and with Germany's Ruhrgas in February 1970.[150] Negotiations with France took a little longer, but in August 1971, Gaz de France signed a contract to import Soviet gas over a twenty-year period, and the first Soviet gas arrived in 1976.[151]

The Soviet Union was negotiating with a number of Western European companies at the time, and by the mid-1970s five countries, West Germany, Italy, Austria, France, and Finland, were to receive Soviet gas in this initial phase of East–West natural gas trade. Of all the countries, it was the FRG that was subsequently to become the main buyer of Soviet natural gas, even though negotiations with West German companies did not begin until the summer of 1969. As will be shown in Chapter 4, by the end of the 1960s, the parameters for trade had changed considerably: political détente between the superpowers continued, relations between the Soviet Union and West Germany also improved steadily, and the world price of oil kept rising, making it increasingly profitable for the Soviet Union to sell its energy on the capitalist market.

147 Högselius, *Red Gas*, p. 62. 148 Ibid., p. 63.

149 Elisabetta Bini, 'A Challenge to Cold War Energy Politics? The US and Italy's Relations with the Soviet Union, 1958–1969', in Perović (ed.), *Cold War Energy*, pp. 201–30, here p. 220–22.

150 Dunja Krempin, 'Rise of Western Siberia and the Soviet-West German Energy Relationship During the 1970s', in Perović (ed.), *Cold War Energy*, pp. 253–81, here p. 260; see also Chapter 4 in this book.

151 Alain Beltran and Jean-Pierre Williot, 'Gaz de France and Soviet Natural Gas: Balancing Technological Constraints with Political Considerations, 1950s to 1980s', in Perović (ed.), *Cold War Energy*, pp. 230–52, here p. 238.

4 Path to Dependence

The autumn of 1973 witnessed three events that were significant for East–West energy relations. The first sent shock waves around the world: in October 1973, in response to Western support for Israel in the Yom Kippur War, the Arab members of OPEC cut production and imposed an embargo on the United States, the Netherlands, and other states supporting Israel. This drove up the price of oil massively, causing supply shortages in several Western countries and triggering the first global energy crisis of the modern era. The problem of excessive reliance on oil imports from the Arab world was brought home to Western consumer societies for the first time.

The second event made fewer headlines but was also of great, if initially rather symbolic, importance for energy relations between the West and the Soviet Union: in the same month, Soviet natural gas reached the FRG for the first time via an extension of the Eastern European pipeline system. This was the result of the conclusion of the first major Soviet–West German natural gas deals, which were facilitated by the East–West détente policy that had begun in the late 1960s but also by the efforts of Western European countries to diversify their energy imports away from North Africa and the Persian Gulf.

The third event did not register as an event in the West, nor even for most people in the Soviet Union, because hardly anyone was aware of it: in the winter of 1973–74, to meet its international supply obligations, the Soviet Union unceremoniously diverted natural gas intended for the Ukrainian SSR for export to the West. As a result, factories in Ukraine had to shut down and homes could not be heated. Citizens of the Soviet Union, the country with the world's largest proven fossil energy reserves, were left freezing. Although the Soviet Union managed to increase its oil and gas production, it still was to experience its own kind of energy crisis in the early 1970s.

Movements in the global energy system, the opportunities created by détente for East–West trade, and the energy challenges faced by the countries of the West, but also by the Soviet Union, created the historical conditions that allowed for increasing economic interdependence between the Soviet Union and Western Europe during the 1970s. By the 1960s, the Soviet Union had become a major supplier of oil and oil products to Europe. During the 1970s, natural gas was added, which the Soviet Union was producing in ever-increasing quantities. However, the Soviet Union could only meet its growing domestic energy needs and its international supply commitments if it succeeded in developing the large deposits in the northern part of Western Siberia. To achieve this costly and technically challenging goal, Moscow actively sought to intensify relations with Western companies. Although cooperation with American and Japanese companies to develop Siberian resources had collapsed by the mid-1970s due to political disagreements, Moscow found willing partners in Western Europe – first and foremost in West Germany. Western European banks provided the Soviet Union with the loans it needed to buy steel sheets, pipes, and other energy technology to build its expanding gas pipeline system; in return, the Soviet Union paid with natural gas deliveries. The oil trade may have brought the Soviet Union its greatest financial rewards, but it was the building of a physical gas transportation infrastructure that bound East and West closely together. A milestone was the decision in the early 1980s to construct a major export pipeline to transport natural gas directly from the Western Siberian fields in the northern part of Tyumen to Western Europe.

With oil prices rising steadily in the 1970s, the prospect of good business was a major incentive for the Soviet side to move closer to the capitalist states of the West. This path was not straightforward, however. In addition to economic considerations, the factors driving the Soviet leadership to agree to the massive expansion of its gas transportation corridor towards Western Europe were the increasingly tense relationship with the United States and the events in connection with the Iranian revolution of 1978–79. This chapter examines these different and intertwined strands of history in order to arrive at a comprehensive understanding of the growing energy interdependence between Western Europe and the Soviet Union during the Brezhnev era.

The Global Oil Crisis, East–West Trade, and Siberian Energy

The first half of the 1970s was marked by major shifts in the global oil market. Following the Second World War, the centre of gravity of global oil production had moved away from the Western Hemisphere to the Persian Gulf. This region, which comprised only about 5 per cent of global oil production in 1940, accounted for over 40 per cent of the total in 1973.[1] By that time, 80 per cent of the oil traded on the world market came from the non-Western OPEC states; OPEC was responsible for about half of world oil production, with Saudi Arabia and Iran alone producing a quarter of the total.[2] Not only were the United States, Western Europe, and Japan obtaining more and more oil from non-Western parts of the world, but oil became the single most important energy source. With unprecedented global economic growth and rising energy consumption, the global output of oil increased markedly: on a per capita basis, this meant that the amount of oil available in 1950 corresponded to an average of 1.5 barrels of oil per person; by 1973, this volume had risen to 5.3 barrels – even as the world's population doubled during this period.[3]

In the 1970s, the United States was still producing more crude oil than any other country. But America's national consumption had increased so much that already by the 1950s the country was hardly exporting any oil at all but importing more and more. For Western Europe, this dramatically changed the geography of oil imports: whereas in 1946 the United States, together with Mexico and Venezuela, had been responsible for 77 per cent of Western Europe's oil imports, just five years later the region was drawing four-fifths of its oil from the Persian Gulf states.[4] The fact that the United States was producing at its limit also meant that it was hardly in a position to absorb supply shortfalls using its own production reserves. As recoverable reserves declined, the United States relinquished its long-standing position as a swing producer, a compensatory producer capable of rapidly increasing its own production to offset global supply shortfalls. As spare production capacity plays a crucial role in determining the price of oil, the United States thus gradually lost its traditional influence on global oil price formation.[5]

Western Europe and the United States' increasing dependence on oil imports did not pose a problem as long as the Western international oil companies were able to control global production. This began to change in the late 1960s and became increasingly challenging in the early 1970s, when the OPEC countries succeeded in negotiating a higher share of the revenues from the sale of their oil with Western energy companies. Also, nationalisation efforts intensified in many OPEC countries: whereas state-owned companies controlled only about 10 per cent of the global

[1] Bukold, *Öl im 21. Jahrhundert*, p. 20.
[2] Euclid A. Rose, 'OPEC's Dominance of the Global Oil Market: The Rise of the World's Dependency on Oil', *Middle East Journal*, 58, 3 (2004), pp. 424–43, here p. 432.
[3] Ibid., p. 426. [4] Bukold, *Öl im 21. Jahrhundert*, pp. 21–22.
[5] Yergin, *The Prize*, p. 728.

oil industry in 1970, a decade later this share had risen to 70 per cent.[6] Thus, the global oil market had already undergone changes before the energy crisis. Yet it was not until the events of 1973–74 and the associated steep rise in prices that Western consumer societies were made all too aware of the impact these shifts had had on the balance of power in the international energy system.

The immediate trigger for the price rise was the Israeli–Arab war, which began on 6 October 1973, on the Jewish holiday of Yom Kippur, when Egypt and Syria launched a surprise attack on Israel. The war ended two and a half weeks later with the ceasefire agreement of 24 October 1973. During the war, the Arab states within OPEC showed solidarity with Egypt and Syria by cutting production and placing an embargo on oil shipments to the United States, the Netherlands, and other countries that supported Israel with weapons and military equipment. On 16 October 1973, the price of oil had climbed from three to five dollars and nearly twelve dollars a barrel by the end of the year. This marked the first successful use of the 'oil weapon' by non-Western oil-producing states against Western consumer nations. Previous attempts during the Suez Crisis in 1956 and the Six-Day War in 1967 had not been successful. Unlike in the past, the global oil market was already enormously tight by the time the war broke out in October 1973; as a result, diminished oil volumes available on the market and rising prices quickly made themselves felt in the consumer states. The price increase and the supply shortage were to contribute to the Western industrialised countries falling into recession in subsequent years.

Although the shifts in the power structure of the oil market had been apparent from the beginning of the 1970s, expressed in steadily rising prices, contemporaries experienced the events of 1973–74 as a 'shock'. Empty motorways and long queues in front of petrol stations were the images with which these events were to be associated in the West. The oil crisis marked the beginning of discussions within Western societies about energy, prosperity, and dependencies.[7] In the aftermath of the crisis, which only began to ease after the Arab states ended their embargo in the spring of 1974, Washington called on the European allies to coordinate better among themselves on energy issues. The result was the creation of the International Energy Agency (IEA), an association of Western consumer states intended to act as a kind of counterweight to OPEC. Among other things, the IEA obliged its members to build up

[6] David S. Painter, 'Oil and Geopolitics: The Oil Crises of the 1970s and the Cold War', *Historical Social Research*, 39, 4 (2014), pp. 186–208, here pp. 195–96.

[7] On the oil crisis of 1973–74 and its effects, see Venn, *The Oil Crisis*.

sufficient reserves to be able to absorb future shortfalls over a period of several months. At the same time, it stepped up conservation and energy efficiency efforts and began exploring ways to substitute other energy sources for oil.[8] Above all, however, the oil crisis of 1973–74 spurred the search for suppliers outside OPEC. Here the Soviet Union offered itself to the Western countries not only as an alternative oil supplier but also as the supplier of an alternative to oil. The Soviet Union had plenty of oil, but it also became the world's largest producer of natural gas during this period. Even the big Western energy corporations, once viewing the Soviet Union as a nuisance or even a threat to their global interests, began to see it as a potential energy partner.

In this context, the Yom Kippur War came at the worst possible moment for Moscow. It threatened to destroy in one fell swoop the process of rapprochement between East and West that had been so painstakingly begun in the late 1960s and continued even after Soviet-led Warsaw Pact forces entered Prague in August 1968 to crush the Czechoslovak reform movement. In fact, the Soviet Union found itself facing a dilemma. To maintain its credibility as a bulwark against imperialism and colonialism, Moscow officially sided with the Arab states, especially since Egypt and Syria were among the most important customers for Soviet military technology and weapons.[9] Thus, not a few in the West suspected Moscow of having a long hand behind the Arab oil embargo.

However, Moscow had no interest in escalation. Contrary to American assumptions at the time, the Soviet Union was not planning any military intervention to come to the aid of its Arab allies in their war against Israel.[10] Significantly, the Soviet media held back on anti-American propaganda and did not make the war the focus of their coverage. One day after the outbreak of hostilities, on 7 October 1973, *Pravda* reported extensively on its front page on Japanese Prime Minister Tanaka's visit to the Soviet Union and his talks with Soviet representatives. Apart from a small note, the conflict in the Middle East was relegated to the international section of *Pravda* on page 5.[11] As early as the beginning of

[8] Bukold, *Öl im 21. Jahrhundert*, pp. 37–38; on the history of the IEA, see Richard Scott, *The History of the International Energy Agency*, vol. 1, The First 20 Years: Origins and Structure, Paris: IEA, 2004; Richard Scott, *The History of the International Energy Agency*, vol. 2, Major Policies and Actions, Paris: IEA, 2004.

[9] Robbin F. Laird, 'Soviet Arms Trade with the Noncommunist Third World', *Proceedings of the Academy of Political Science*, 35, 3 (1984), The Soviet Union in the 1980s, pp. 196–213.

[10] Galia Golan, 'The Soviet Union and the Yom Kippur War, *Israel Affairs*, 6, 1 (1999), pp. 127–52, especially pp. 144–48.

[11] Iu. Glukhov, 'Napadenie Izrailia na Egipet i Siriiu', *Pravda*, 280, 7 October 1973, p. 5.

November 1973, after military operations in the Middle East had ended, the Soviet government signalled a willingness to resume diplomatic relations with Israel and to work toward a post-war settlement within the framework of the United Nations.[12]

The Yom Kippur War and the Arab oil boycott not only put the fragile détente between Washington and Moscow to the test but also strained Soviet–Western European relations. These had likewise improved significantly from the late 1960s onwards, as reflected in a marked upswing in trade and extensive economic cooperation. After a long downward slide, Soviet–West German economic relations had also picked up speed; the trade volume curve showed a steep upward trend from the early 1970s onwards. In part, this was because after the pipeline embargo imposed by NATO had been lifted in the autumn of 1966, export restrictions on steel pipes ceased to apply. It also had to do with the fact that bilateral relations had been fundamentally normalised within the framework of Bonn's new *Ostpolitik* under its Foreign Minister (1966–69) and Chancellor (1969–74) Willy Brandt, head of West Germany's Social Democratic Party.[13] This policy, which was guided by the idea that trade would ultimately promote change and rapprochement, was to be associated above all with Brandt, but it originated with the Social Democrat Egon Bahr, who was a close ally of Brandt and later served as Secretary of State in Brandt's Federal Chancellery. Already in a speech given in 1963, Bahr had coined the famous concept of 'change through rapprochement' (*Wandel durch Annäherung*), which was to become the guiding principle of German policy towards the GDR and socialist Eastern Europe in general. This idea was also morally motivated – through trade, change was to be made possible in the countries of the socialist 'Eastern bloc' and autocratic, dictatorial, and tyrannical regimes in general. It was hoped that by exchanging goods, one's own values would also be exported en passant and would ensure a change towards democracy in the medium or long term.[14]

The Soviet Union was less interested in change than it was in trade – and Soviet natural gas in particular opened up new market opportunities. Most of the gas that the Soviet Union produced was intended to supply

[12] *The Diary of Anatoly S. Chernyaev 1973: Translated by Anna Melyakova; Edited by Svetlana Savranskaya*, Washington, DC: The National Security Archive, 2013, p. 69 (entry dated 4 November 1973), https://nsarchive2.gwu.edu/NSAEBB/NSAEBB430/Chernyaev 1973 final PDF version.pdf (last accessed 15 July 2021).

[13] Krempin, 'Rise of Western Siberia and the Soviet-West German Energy Relationship During the 1970s', pp. 257–62.

[14] For further reading, see Benedikt Schoenborn, *Reconciliation Road: Willy Brandt, Ostpolitik and the Quest for European Peace*, New York: Berghahn, 2020.

domestic industries and households, with a view to freeing up more oil for export. After the Second World War, Poland obtained small amounts of natural gas from Ukrainian fields. In 1967, Czechoslovakia began receiving Soviet gas through the Bratstvo pipeline, and the following year, the first Soviet gas reached Austria. Until then, the gas consumed in Western Europe stemmed mainly from its own production. Italy and France were the leading gas producers in Western Europe; in the FRG, 70 per cent of gas in the early 1970s came from the country's own production.[15] Following the discovery of a gigantic gas field near Groningen in 1959, the Netherlands became the only European country able to fully supply itself with gas while also exporting substantial volumes to other Western European countries. However, the quantities of natural gas consumed by Western Europeans at that time were still very modest. It was not until the 1970s, when rising oil prices and geopolitical instability in the Middle East led to increased demand for gas, that Europe's own production became insufficient, and the Western Europeans began to look for new suppliers. In addition to Libya, Algeria, and the gas that would later be produced in the North Sea, the Soviet Union emerged as a viable option.[16]

After protracted negotiations, the Soviet Union concluded its first 'gas-for-pipes' deal with the FRG on 1 February 1970. In terms of its overall value, the agreement was huge by the standards of the time. The Soviet Union undertook to supply West Germany with almost three billion cubic metres of gas per year for twenty years.[17] In return, the Soviets received an initial loan of 1.2 billion German marks, financed by a consortium of West German banks, to buy steel pipes made in West Germany. It was agreed that the Mannesmann company, in cooperation with Thyssen and Krupp, would supply the large-diameter pipes for pipeline construction; in exchange, the German Ruhrgas group would be supplied with gas from the Soviet Union. The contract stipulated that the loan was to be paid off in the first few years through gas deliveries, after which the Soviet side was to receive hard West German currency for its gas.[18]

Only in retrospect did it become clear that this agreement was to initiate the resumption of those close economic ties between Germany and Russia that had existed until the invasion of the Soviet Union by the

[15] Högselius, *Red Gas*, p. 169. [16] Gustafson, *The Bridge*, pp. 107–39.

[17] The natural gas pipe deal of 1 February 1970 provided for West Germany to receive 53 billion cubic metres of natural gas over a period of twenty years (or 2.6 billion m^3 of gas per year): 'Röhren-Kredit: Salto am Trapez', *Der Spiegel*, 7, 9 February 1970, p. 34.

[18] Dietmar Bleidick, *Die Ruhrgas 1926 bis 2013: Aufstieg und Ende eines Marktführers*, Berlin, Boston: De Gruyter Oldenbourg, 2018, p. 306.

German Reich in 1941. The basis for the conclusion of this agreement was the complementary economic interests of the Soviet Union and the FRG, but it ultimately came to fruition thanks to individual German and Soviet representatives, who, in numerous rounds of talks, had built up the trust necessary for finalising such a far-reaching deal. Mistrust on the Soviet side originally ran particularly deep, as Moscow remembered all too well that it was the FRG that had broken the contract on supplying steel pipes for the construction of the Druzhba pipeline in 1962. In fact, when the Soviet Union began to negotiate the possibility of exporting its gas to Western European states in the second half of the 1960s, countries such as Austria, Italy, and France were initially on its list – but not West Germany.[19] Concrete negotiations between West German business circles (including Ruhrgas and Thyssen-Röhrenwerke AG) and the Soviet Union (including representatives of Soiuznefteeksport) on Soviet gas supplies in exchange for the delivery of German steel pipes started in earnest only in the summer of 1969.[20]

A central role in the Soviet–West German negotiations was played by Soviet Foreign Trade Minister Patolichev, who vigorously advocated the expansion of trade relations with Western countries.[21] While Ruhrgas chairman Herbert Schelberger figured prominently in the negotiations, celebrated on the German side at the time was the Bavarian Economics Minister Otto Schedl of the Christian Social Union in Bavaria, who had made a decisive contribution to the conclusion of the agreement: he had successfully lobbied for the 'red gas' to be transported first to Bavaria (Waidhaus) via an extension of the Eastern European network through Czechoslovakia, from whence the gas could be distributed further.[22]

The political impact of this agreement was significant, as the economic rapprochement strengthened the efforts to achieve détente in relations between East and West.[23] Shortly after the signing of the first Soviet–West German 'gas-for-pipes' deal, Brandt became the first German Chancellor to visit the GDR on 19 March 1970. In August 1970, Bahr

[19] Susanne Schattenberg, 'Pipeline Construction as "Soft Power" in Foreign Policy: Why the Soviet Union Started to Sell Gas to West Germany, 1966–1970', *Journal of Modern European History* (2022), pp. 1–20, here p. 7, doi:10.1177/16118944221130222.

[20] *Akten zur Auswärtigen Politik der Bundesrepublik Deutschland (1969)*, edited by the Institut für Zeitgeschichte, Munich: Oldenbourg, 2000, pp. 857–58 (including n. 1 and n. 3).

[21] V. L. Mal'kevich, I. L. Mitrofanov, and A. S. Ivanov, *Vneshniaia torgovlia SSSR pri N. S. Patolicheve, 1958–1985 gg.*, Moscow: O-vo sokhraneniia literaturnogo naslediia, 2010, p. 80.

[22] While Per Högselius in *Red Gas* gives credit to Otto Schedl, Jochen Bleidick in his book on the history of Ruhrgas emphasis the role of Ruhrgas chairman Herbert Schelberger; see Schattenberg, 'Pipeline Construction as "Soft Power" in Foreign Policy', pp. 3–4.

[23] Bleidick, *Die Ruhrgas*, pp. 287–88; Gustafson, *The Bridge*, pp. 70f.

negotiated the so-called Moscow Treaty with his Soviet counterpart, Foreign Minister Andrei Gromyko, in a marathon of talks that lasted several months, and which served as a model for subsequent treaties with Poland (1970) and Czechoslovakia (1973). The signatories assured each other that they would renounce all violence and recognise the inviolability of the existing European post-war borders, including the Oder-Neisse line and the border with the GDR.

Clearly, political rapprochement and ever closer economic ties went hand in hand – a fact that contemporaries on both sides of the Iron Curtain were also fully aware of.[24] When Brezhnev met with West German business and industry representatives during his first state visit to the FRG on 18–22 May 1973, he proclaimed that now that both sides had overcome 'the burden of the past' due to important political decisions, 'namely the signing of the 1970 [Moscow] Treaty', it was urgent to look for a 'new approach to economic and trade relations based on increased trust'. According to Brezhnev, the aim had to be to conclude 'major joint projects' and 'agreements on cooperation should not be made for two or three years, but for 40 to 50 years'.[25] Foreign Trade Minister Patolichev, who took part in these talks, went further, exclaiming:

> This is not the first time I have met with representatives of FRG business circles, and I know all those present very well. The most important deal ever concluded between the USSR and the FRG was the agreement on natural gas and pipelines. We should not stop there. We must go further.[26]

In fact, the successful conclusion of the agreement of 1 February 1970 in parallel with political rapprochement created the conditions for the signing of further energy treaties in the years that followed. Already on 6 July 1972, the FRG and the Soviet Union signed a new agreement on the increase of gas supplies, again to the tune of more than one billion German marks and again for a term of twenty years.[27] The first Soviet gas was to reach West Germany via an extension of the existing pipeline infrastructure as early as 1 October 1973; in the second half of the 1970s,

[24] Werner D. Lippert, *The Economic Diplomacy of Ostpolitik: Origins of NATO's Energy Dilemma*, New York: Berghahn, 2011, p. xv.

[25] Brezhnev made this statement in Bonn on 19 May 1973. The full record of Brezhnev's conversation is contained in I. V. Kazarina and M. Iu. Prozumenshchikov (eds.), *Novyi mir v Evrope: SSSR, FRG i Moskovskii dogovor 1970 goda po dokumentam TsK KPSS; Sbornik dokumentov*, Moscow: Kuchkovo Pole, 2020, pp. 657–64, here p. 658.

[26] Ibid., p. 663.

[27] *Akten zur Auswärtigen Politik der Bundesrepublik Deutschland (1980)*, edited by the Institut für Zeitgeschichte, Munich: Oldenbourg, 2011, p. 1048 (n. 32).

Italy and France were also to receive gas from the Soviet Union.[28] On 29 October 1974, the FRG and the Soviet Union signed a third contract, which provided for pipe deliveries to the Soviet Union worth 1.5 billion German marks in return for natural gas.[29] By the mid-1970s, the FRG had become the Soviet Union's most important trading partner, accounting for around 20 per cent of the total value of Soviet exports, with oil and gas the primary goods supplied by the Soviet Union to West Germany.[30]

In this phase of East–West cooperation, Western newspapers reported almost daily on new business deals. In the automotive sector, this was pioneered by the Italian carmaker Fiat; with its help, the Togliatti plant in Volgograd was constructed in 1968. This cooperation was in line with the Soviet government's intention, announced in 1966, to substantially increase automobile production during the 8th Five-Year Plan (1966–1970).[31] Along similar lines, dozens of companies from the FRG were involved in the construction of the world's largest truck production plant, established on the Kama River. In the chemical industry, it was mainly companies from Italy, France, and the United States with which the Soviet Union negotiated agreements worth millions. Within the framework of an Italian–Soviet agreement, the Italian oil company ENI agreed to construct six petrochemical factories with a total value of almost one billion US dollars in return for being supplied with Soviet crude oil, natural gas, and petrochemical products. In addition to such major projects, hundreds of smaller cooperative agreements were concluded during this period, covering everything from machinery and industrial equipment to computer technology, food processing, the manufacture of medicines, prefabricated houses and typewriters, and the import of certain raw materials and foodstuffs.[32]

[28] Jonathan P. Stern, 'Soviet Natural Gas in the World Economy', in Robert G. Jensen, Theodore Shabad, and Artur W. Wright (eds,), *Soviet Natural Resources in the World Economy*, Chicago, London: The University of Chicago Press, 1983, pp. 363–84, here p. 373

[29] *Akten zur Auswärtigen Politik der Bundesrepublik Deutschland (1980)*, p. 1048 (n. 32); Falk Illing, *Energiepolitik in Deutschland: Die energiepolitischen Massnahmen der Bundesregierung 1949–2013*, Baden-Baden: Nomos, 2012, p. 150.

[30] Heinrich Machowski, 'Soviet–West German Economic Relations: The Soviet Perspective', in Angela E. Stent (ed.), *Economic Relations with the Soviet Union: American and West-German Perspectives*, Boulder, London: Westview Press, 1985, pp. 49–67, here p. 53.

[31] D. M. Bloch, 'The Soviet Automobile Industry: Recent Developments in the Production of Passenger Cars, *New Zealand Slavonic Journal*, 7 (1971), pp. 14–31, especially pp. 17–19; on production figures, see Siegelbaum, *Cars for Comrades*, p. 239.

[32] W. Spohn, 'The Soviet Union's Technological Dependence on the World Market: Report and Commentary on an Empirical Study by A. C. Sutton (1)', *PROKLA: Zeitschrift für Kritische Sozialwissenschaft*, 5, 19/20/21 (1975), pp. 225–59, here pp. 225–26.

However, the Soviet Union did not only import technology and high-quality products from the West. At the beginning of the 1970s, the country repeatedly had to purchase large quantities of wheat from the United States and Canada in order to compensate for shortfalls in its own production.[33] Already in 1963, the Soviet Union under Khrushchev was forced for the first time to buy 12 million tonnes of wheat abroad. At the time, this cost the Soviet state a third of its gold reserves.[34] By the 1970s and 1980s, it would be the oil and natural gas yields that were increasingly used for foreign grain purchases when the Soviet agricultural economy produced too little due to crop failures or mismanagement. The volumes grew over time: whereas the Soviet Union bought 13.2 per cent of its grain abroad in 1973, this figure had risen to 23.9 per cent by 1975 and reached 41.4 per cent by 1981.[35] In a 1993 interview, Nikolai Baibakov, Gosplan director from 1955 to 1957 and then again from 1965 to 1985, cited substantial sums that the Soviet Union allegedly used from oil and gas sales to buy grain abroad in order to feed the cattle in the collective farms and to put bread on the table of Soviet citizens: a total of 5 billion US dollars from 1971 to 1975, 15 billion US dollars between 1976 and 1980, and as much as 35 billion US dollars in the first half of the 1980s.[36] These figures are largely consistent with US government estimates at the time.[37]

Thus, the energy sector increasingly became the heart of the Soviet economy – and it was here that the country was particularly in need of investment and cooperation. Production was stagnating both in the old fields of the Caucasus and in the Volga-Urals region, which was already approaching its production peak in the first half of the 1970s. If the country wanted to meet rising domestic demand while remaining a factor in the international raw materials trade, then it would be necessary to expand into the northern part of Western Siberia, where new large oil and natural gas fields had been discovered in the second half of the

[33] United States Department of Agriculture, 'U.S.S.R. Wheat Imports by Year', www.indexmundi.com/agriculture/?country=su&commodity=wheat&graph=imports (last accessed 15 July 2021); figures on Soviet grain imports from 1970 to 1985, based on Soviet statistics, can be found in Yegor Gaidar, *Collapse of an Empire: Lessons for Modern Russia*, Washington, DC: Brookings Institution Press, 2007, p. 98.

[34] Yegor Gaidar, *The Soviet Collapse: Grain and Oil*, American Enterprise Institute for Public Policy Research, April 2007, Washington, DC: AEI, 2007, p. 2.

[35] R. G. Pichoia, *Sovetskii Soiuz: Istoriia vlasti 1945–1991*, Moscow: RAGS, 1998, p. 370.

[36] Baibakov's interview was published in the Russian newspaper *Segodnia* on 10 November 1993 (p. 10); the relevant passages are referred to in Philipp Hanson, *The Rise and Fall of the Soviet Economy: An Economic History of the USSR from 1945*, London: Longman 2003, p. 163.

[37] Ibid.

1960s. Moscow was under no illusions about the fact that, due to Siberia's geographical remoteness and climatic conditions, developing Western Siberian oil and gas would be enormously difficult and expensive and could hardly be carried out in a useful time frame without assistance from abroad.

Soviet geologists had speculated as early as the late 1920s that the vast Siberian space might contain large deposits of oil, gas, and other valuable resources. But given the enormous distance from consumer centres and the inhospitable climatic conditions, systematic exploration of Siberia had long not been a priority for the Soviet leadership. In a context of scarce finances, emphasis was put on the then-promising production centres in the Caucasus. This only changed during the Second World War, when the Soviet leadership attached greater importance to oil and recognised the need to establish new production centres outside the Caucasus region. Thus, in addition to the Volga-Urals region, Siberia also came more into focus. Although the existence of oil and gas deposits in the southern part of the Tyumen region of Western Siberia was confirmed in the 1950s, it was not until a decade later that the Soviet leadership granted permission to carry out geological exploration work in the vast central and northern parts of this region. The corresponding government decrees 'On Measures to Intensify Geological Exploration of Oil and Natural Gas in Western Siberia' (1963) and 'On the Organisation of Preparatory Measures for the Industrial Exploitation of Localised Oil and Natural Gas Deposits' (1964) boosted Western Siberia's industrial development; about a dozen other government decrees were to follow.[38]

As a result, new fields were discovered, and the Western Siberian region would see increasing production volumes in the years to come. But this did not solve the economic and social problems that Soviet planners faced.[39] One of the biggest challenges was finding qualified personnel willing to work in the harsh Siberian conditions. Although the oil industry can generally be considered as not being as labour intensive as other industries like coal,[40] the initial development of oil (and later also gas) fields in the vast Siberian swamps required huge

[38] G. Iu. Koleva, 'Strategiia razvitiia zapadno-sibirskogo neftegazogo kompleksa (1960–1980-e gg.)', *Vestnik Tomskogo gosudarstvennogo universiteta*, 1 (2007), pp. 95–102, here p. 97; Krempin, *Die sibirische Wucht*, pp. 123–29.

[39] On the production figures, see M. V. Slavkina, *Triumf i tragediia: Razvitie neftegazogo kompleksa SSSR v 1960–1980-e gody*, Moscow: Nauka, 2002, p. 69.

[40] Timothy Mitchell, *Carbon Democracy: Political Power in the Age of Oil*, London: Verso, 2011.

amounts of qualified labour.[41] The party leadership thus committed thousands of members of the Communist youth organisation, the Komsomol, to work in Siberia,[42] it drew on large numbers of workers from regions that had experience with oil, such as Ukraine, Azerbaijan, Tatarstan, and Bashkortostan,[43] and also used a significant number of camp prisoners.[44] In order to make work in Siberia more attractive to well-trained specialists, the Tyumen Oblast Party Committee proposed paying them higher wages.[45] The region's party leadership also suggested that student groups were to be required to help build infrastructure, including schools, housing, and parts of the railroad, to be completed by the anniversary of the 'Great October Revolution' in 1967.[46] Some of the proposals made by the party were later implemented – among various benefits, workers in the oil and gas fields of Western Siberia were paid significantly higher wages than those in other parts of the country. Despite all these measures, however, the labour issue remained a problem and was regularly raised at scientific meetings and party conferences.[47]

Another challenge regarding the energy development of Western Siberia was technological. Soviet planners understood their 'energy problem' was of a completely different nature than the one faced by the United States and Western Europe. From the mid-1960s, when further

[41] Alexander Etkind, Yevhenii Poliakov, and Bohdan Shumylovych, 'Ukrainian Labor and Siberian Oil in the Late Soviet Empire', *Journal of Soviet and Post-Soviet Politics and Society*, 6, 2 (2020), pp. 241–80, here pp. 254–55.

[42] Cf. the speech of Soviet Gas Minister Aleksei Kortunov at the 12th Conference of the Tyumen Regional Komsomol Organisation in January 1966, in D. A. Smorodinskov (ed.), *Neft' i gaz Tiumeni v dokumentakh*, vol. 2, 1966–1970, Sverdlovsk: Sredne-Ural'skoe knizhnoe izdatel'stvo, 1973, pp. 20–21.

[43] Cf. Etkind, Poliakov, and Shumylovych, 'Ukrainian Labor and Siberian Oil in the Late Soviet Empire', pp. 241–80.

[44] It is not clear to what extent the Soviet Union used prisoners for oil and gas exploration work and pipeline construction in the 1960s and 1970s. In August 1982, the German news magazine *Der Spiegel* spoke of 100,000 prisoners and an unspecified number of workers from the German Democratic Republic: 'Dreckige Lüge', *Der Spiegel*, 33, 16 August 1982, pp. 94–96, here p. 94. See also the CIA report on the use of prisoners in pipeline construction in the early 1980s: Central Intelligence Agency, *Alleged Use of Forced Labor on Siberian Pipeline*, Memorandum for Richard Burt, Assistant Secretary of State, Washington, DC, 20 August 1982, www.foia.cia.gov/sites/default/files/document_conversions/89801/DOC_0000102966.pdf (last accessed 16 August 2021).

[45] Smorodinskov (ed.), *Neft' i gaz Tiumeni v dokumentakh*, p. 88.

[46] Ibid., pp. 83–84, 114.

[47] Smorodinskov (ed.), *Neft' i gaz Tiumeni v dokumentakh*, pp. 180–87; elaborating on the problem of labour recruitment in Western Siberia, see Krempin, *Die sibirische Wucht*, pp. 311–21; Dunja Krempin, 'Heroic "Black Gold"? Working for Oil and Gas in the Western Siberian Oil and Gas Complex of the 1960–1970s', in Touraj Atabaki, Elisabetta Bini, and Kaveh Ehsani (eds.), *Working for Oil: Comparative Social Histories of Labor in the Global Oil Industry*, Cham: Palgrave Macmillan, 2018, pp. 285–310.

large oil and gas deposits were discovered in the northern part of Tyumen, the question was never whether there were enough natural resources in the ground but how to exploit and transport these through the tundra and taiga to the industrialised zones in the distant European part of the country. The transportation question was all the more challenging because Soviet industry was still unable to produce enough of the high-quality large-diameter steel pipes needed for the construction of a huge transportation infrastructure, as the then Soviet deputy minister for gas, Iuli Bokserman, also acknowledged.[48]

Faced with a shortage of high-quality steel plates to build pipelines and thus solve the transportation problem, Gosplan, in cooperation with other ministries and institutions, developed a plan to build oversized gas pipelines with a diameter of 2–2.5 metres, that is, more than double the usual large pipelines with a diameter of 1,020–1,220 mm.[49] In a detailed report dated 14 October 1967 and addressed to Prime Minister Kosygin, its authors (Gosplan director Nikolai Baibakov, chairman of the Ministry of Gas (Mingazprom) Aleksei Kortunov, and Aleksandr Sidorenko, head of the Institut of Geology of the Academy of Science of the USSR) suggested that given that the 'main proven reserves of natural gas (more than 70 per cent) are in the eastern part of the country, while the fuel resources of the European part are limited', the most efficient way to transfer Western Siberian gas to 'the regions of the Center, North-West and West' is via 'superpower gas pipelines':[50]

> If we try to transport hundreds of billions of cubic metres of gas per year through pipelines with the maximum developed diameters, i.e. 1,020–1,220 mm, this would require an impossibly large amount of metal [for us] to produce in the coming years .... The most efficient way of transporting gas over long distances and a new technical solution to this problem, not only in our country but also worldwide, is the construction of high-capacity gas transportation lines with pipes up to 2.5 metres in diameter. In this case, the transportation capacity of the gas pipeline is eight to ten times higher than with pipes of a diameter of 1,020 mm, as the specific investment, operating costs, and metal consumption are greatly reduced.[51]

According to Gosplan, the construction of such large diameter pipes would not only ensure that sufficient gas was transported from the new Western Siberian fields to the European part of the Soviet Union but would create conditions to export natural gas 'to socialist camp countries

48 Krempin, *Die sibirische Wucht*, p. 180.
49 Reports and information of this plan were compiled in the summer and autumn of 1967 under the lead of Gosplan and are contained in RGAE, f. 4372, op. 66, d. 1767.
50 The report is contained in RGAE, f. 4372, op. 66, d. 1767, ll. 144–50, here ll. 144–45.
51 RGAE, f. 4372, op. 66, d. 1767, l. 145.

and some other countries, which would contribute to solving the issue of receiving pipes and equipment on credit'.[52] Even if Soviet factories were able to produce enough of these pipes in the future, the authors of the report were realistic enough to understand that 'in order to gain time', the country would need to import large diameter pipes and obtain these by 'supplying gas to Western Europe'.[53]

While Kosygin approved of the proposal and asked Gosplan to develop it further in cooperation with the relevant ministries, including the Ministry of Gas, the Ministry of Steel Industry, and the Ministry of Heavy Machinery,[54] the plan to build pipelines with a diameter of 2.5 metres was technically too difficult to ever be realised. Instead, the Soviet Union continued to expand cooperation with Western companies and imported ever larger amounts of steel pipes and other equipment necessary for building-up its gas industry and transportation network. Moreover, to strengthen relationships and acquire technological knowledge, the Soviet Union would repeatedly distinguish itself as a host of energy conferences, as it did in June 1971 when it succeeded in organising the 8th World Petroleum Congress. Around 5,000 participants from all over the world, most of them from the United States, France, West Germany, Great Britain, Japan, Iran, and Hungary, met for this congress, which lasted several days and was held under the official motto 'Oil for the benefit of mankind' in the newly built Rossiia hotel in Moscow.[55]

The Soviet side was ready to do business with anyone, and the most attractive area of cooperation at the time, from Moscow's point of view, was the development of Western Siberian gas. Soviet representatives conveyed the same message to all potential suitors, whether they be Americans, Germans, Japanese, French, or Canadians: Siberia was up for grabs, and anyone could take what they wanted if only the Soviet Union was provided with the credits to buy the necessary equipment. 'You have seen Siberia and its tremendous possibilities – help yourself!', Prime Minister Kosygin is said to have shouted to a German business delegation led by the influential entrepreneur Otto Wolff von

52 RGAE, f. 4372, op. 66, d. 1767, l. 145–46.
53 RGAE, f. 4372, op. 66, d. 1767, l. 147.
54 See the decree signed by Kosygin on 25 October 1967 'On Measures to Develop Major Gas Fields in the Northern Parts of the Tyumen Region and the Construction of Large-Scale Gas Pipelines to Supply Gas to the European Part', contained in RGAE, f. 4372, op. 66, d. 1767, l. 2.
55 Alexander Anatolyev, 'The Oil Summit of 1971', *Oil of Russia*, 3 (2011), www.oilru.com/or/48/1031/ (last accessed 6 June 2013).

Amerongen at the Moscow airport when the group returned from a trip to Siberia in January 1971.[56]

Unlike in the 1920s, however, Moscow did not seek simply to expand trade and economic-technical cooperation with Western companies but to conclude long-term cooperation projects. What the Soviet representatives touted to their Western counterparts at almost every available opportunity was nothing less than a comprehensive energy partnership lasting forty to fifty years. In talks with West German businessmen during his trip to the FRG in May 1973, Brezhnev made it clear that he considered the twenty-year gas contract 'too short a period' in view of the long-term opportunities offered by Siberia's vast natural resource potential.[57]

In the early 1970s, the Soviet focus was by no means only on the Western Europeans; it was especially on the Americans, with whom Moscow was determined to do business as part of its policy of rapprochement. In the spirit of establishing a 'lasting peace', the two most powerful states on earth were to expand their trade and economic relations in order to lend stability and sustainability to the détente between the superpowers, as Brezhnev repeatedly emphasised to US President Richard Nixon and representatives of the US government in personal talks at the beginning of the 1970s.[58] There was certainly sincerity behind this and not just economic calculation: Brezhnev had experienced the horrors of the Second World War himself and wanted to avoid a return to the dark times of the past at all costs.[59]

In this context, the Soviet-American 'North Star' natural gas project appeared particularly prominent. This project envisaged laying a pipeline some 4,000 km long from the Urengoi gas field in the northern part of Western Siberia, which had already been discovered in 1966 but had yet to be developed, to the vicinity of the Soviet port city of Murmansk north

[56] 'Sibirien: "Greifen Sie zu!"', *Der Spiegel*, 3, 14 January 1973, pp. 60–71, here p. 62.

[57] Cited from Brezhnev's record of conversation with FRG business and industry representatives in Bonn on 19 May 1973; see Kazarina and Prozumenshchikov (eds.), *Novyi mir v Evrope*, p. 662.

[58] See the transcripts of a series of conversations at which trade issues and energy projects were discussed in the run-up to and during the Soviet–US summit in June 1973; contained in US Department of State (ed.), *Foreign Relations of the United States 1969–1976*, vol. XV, Soviet Union, June 1972–August 1974, Washington, DC: United States Government Printing Office, 2011, especially pp. 51–59 (Brezhnev–Peterson), 280–91 (Brezhnev–Shultz), 399–418 (Brezhnev–Kissinger), 420–32 (Brezhnev–Kissinger), 460–62 (letter from Brezhnev to Nixon), 486–96 (Brezhnev–Nixon), 496–506 (Brezhnev–Nixon), 507–14 (Brezhnev–Nixon).

[59] Such a reading is also advocated by Susanne Schattenberg in her biography of Brezhnev: Susanne Schattenberg, *Leonid Breschnew: Staatsmann und Schauspieler im Schatten Stalins; Eine Biographie*, Cologne, Weimar, Vienna: Böhlau, 2017.

of the Arctic Circle, where it would be liquefied and shipped by tanker to the East Coast of the United States. In essence, the Soviet Union sought a compensation deal such as it had previously concluded with Western European countries: the United States was to provide technology, equipment, and loans; the Soviet Union would contribute the workers and the natural gas with which the loans, including interest, were to be paid off over several years. On the American side, it was a consortium of companies consisting of Texas Eastern, Tenneco, and Brown & Root that conducted the negotiations with the Soviet Union.[60] If completed, it was estimated that North Star could supply up to 2.5 per cent of total US gas demand by 1980 and 11.5 per cent of the gas used in the region served by the project – an area from Main to Tennessee.[61] Moscow also sought to undertake a project on a similar scale in the eastern part of its country with Japanese and US firms during this period. This endeavour, sometimes referred to as the 'Yakutia Project', was primarily concerned with the development of East Siberian natural gas, which was to be transported via a pipeline to Magadan on the Pacific and then liquefied and shipped by tanker to Japan and the West Coast of the United States.[62]

In contrast to the Soviet–West German agreements, the North Star project did not envisage transporting the Siberian gas to the European part of the country and feeding it into the existing pipeline system. Instead, the gas was to be brought directly to an Arctic port by constructing a new pipeline. Once there, it would be liquefied and shipped by tanker. The deal was estimated to be worth around 4 billion US dollars at the time,[63] which meant that it was not 'small potatoes', as US Secretary of Commerce Maurice Stans explained to Nixon in mid-November 1971.[64] The planned delivery volume was about 25 billion cubic metres

60 The only comprehensive overview of the North Star project to date is from 1975: Joseph T. Kosnik, *Natural Gas Imports from the Soviet Union: Financing the North Star Joint Venture Project*, New York: Praeger, 1975.

61 Klinghoffer, *The Soviet Union & International Oil Politics*, p. 268.

62 A detailed description of the two gas projects can be found in 'Memorandum from the President's Special Consultant for Energy (DiBona) to the President's Assistant for National Security Affairs (Kissinger)', Washington, DC, 19 March 1973, in US Department of State (ed.), *Foreign Relations of the United States 1969–1976*, vol. XXXVI, pp. 441–43; cf. on the American–Soviet and Soviet–Japanese energy projects also J. H. Chesshire and Miss C. Huggett, 'Primary Energy Production in the Soviet Union: Problems and Prospects', *Energy Policy*, 3, 3 (1975), pp. 223–44, here pp. 238–39.

63 Jentleson, 'From Consensus to Conflict', p. 645.

64 'Conversation among President Nixon, Secretary of Commerce Stans, Secretary of State Rogers, and the President's Deputy Assistant for National Security Affairs (Haig)', Washington, DC, 15 November 1971, in US Department of State (ed.), *Foreign Relations of the United States 1969–1976*, vol. XIV, Soviet Union, October 1971–May

of gas per year, approximately ten times more than the volume agreed with the West Germans in 1970. Later internal American estimates put the costs of the North Star project far higher, at up to 8–10 billion US dollars.[65]

Given the problems facing the Soviet economy at the time, it seemed clear that the Soviet Union was more dependent on cooperation with the West than vice versa. The United States, in particular, had gas reserves of its own that it could tap into as needed. Yet even though it was primarily Moscow that was pushing for closer economic cooperation, Soviet representatives did not want to appear too desperate in negotiations with their Western counterparts. Thus, during the Moscow summit talks between the United States and the Soviet Union in May 1972, Kosygin declared that the Soviet Union could easily do without US cooperation because it already had concluded large deals with the Western Europeans and all the socialist states; therefore it had 'almost more potential buyers' of gas than it actually needed.[66] Speaking to the Western Europeans, however, the Soviet negotiators took a different tack, describing deals with the United States as if they were already a fait accompli. In a clear effort to achieve the most advantageous terms possible, Brezhnev boasted to Chancellor Brandt during his first official visit to West Germany in May 1973 that he had offered the Americans a 'trillion cubic metres of gas; if the United States imported '250 to 300 billion cubic metres a year, that would be for 40 to 50 years'. He thus unequivocally urged his West German interlocutors to explore similar long-term options as soon as possible if they did not want to be left empty-handed.[67]

Western government and business circles were certainly interested in trading with the Soviet Union but were still somewhat restrained. When

1972, Washington, DC: United States Government Printing Office, 2006, pp. 37–46, here pp. 39–40.

65 A memorandum dated 12 December 1972 by Helmut Sonnenfeldt, a staff member of the US National Security Council, estimated the costs at 5–6 billion US dollars: US Department of State (ed.), *Foreign Relations of the United States 1969–1976*, vol. XXXVI, pp. 239–41, here p. 239; Governor John Connally, who participated in the talks between Brezhnev and Nixon at the June 1973 Soviet–US summit, put the cost at 8–10 billion US dollars: ibid., pp. 507–14, here p. 513.

66 Quote from Kosygin during the Moscow Summit Talks, 24 May 1972, in Edward C. Keefer (ed.), *Soviet-American Relations: The Détente Years, 1969–1972*, Washington, DC: United States Government Printing Office, 2007, p. 874.

67 Quote from Brezhnev on 20 May 1973 during talks with Chancellor Brandt in Bonn: *Akten zur Auswärtigen Politik der Bundesrepublik Deutschland (1973)*, edited by the Institut für Zeitgeschichte, Munich: Oldenbourg, 2004, pp. 758–65, here pp. 760–61; cf. also Otto Wolf von Amerongen, *Der Weg nach Osten: Vierzig Jahre Brückenbau für die deutsche Wirtschaft*, Munich: Droemer Knauer, 1992, p. 127.

Nixon discussed the natural gas project with his advisers for the first time in November 1971, he kept a low profile because it quickly became clear to him that trade was 'infinitely more important' for the Soviet Union than for the United States and that Washington should not give up this position lightly.[68] US Secretary of State William Rogers even saw trade with the Soviet Union as 'something of a weapon' that the United States could yield against Moscow.[69] For the Western Europeans, meanwhile, the challenge was that the projects the Soviets had in mind were too large – and thus too financially risky – to be borne by only one party. Moreover, any commitment of this magnitude required political backing. In the case of the United States, the world's most powerful economy, such an expansion of trade meant lifting restrictions on trade with communist states and expanding lending through the US Export-Import bank. Most notably, it implied granting the Soviet Union Most-Favoured-Nation (MFN) status. Without MFN, high tariffs would make Siberian LNG imports to the United States uncompetitive.[70] Both measures, however, required the approval of the US Congress, where great resistance was to be expected from the anti-communist and neo-conservative circles around the influential Democratic Senator Henry M. Jackson.[71]

Against this background, and in stark contrast to their Soviet counterparts, the US delegation at the Moscow summit in May 1972 was initially rather cautious on trade and economic issues.[72] A year later, to secure the policy of détente, Nixon expressed greater openness to the idea of closer economic cooperation with Moscow. In April 1973, two months before Brezhnev visited the United States, Nixon urged members of his cabinet to consider not only the economic benefits of a rapprochement between the United States and the Soviet Union but also the effect that the construction of 'this big pipeline they are talking about' could have on

68 'Conversation among President Nixon, Secretary of Commerce Stans, Secretary of State Rogers, and the President's Deputy Assistant for National Security Affairs (Haig)', Washington, DC, 15 November 1971, in US Department of State (ed.), *Foreign Relations of the United States 1969–1976*, vol. XIV, pp. 37–46, here p. 38.

69 Ibid., p. 39.

70 Jentleson, 'From Consensus to Conflict', p. 647.

71 'Memorandum from the President's Special Consultant for Energy', Washington, DC, 19 March 1973, in US Department of State (ed.), *Foreign Relations of the United States 1969–1976*, vol. XXXVI, p. 441. For further information on the role and views of Henry Jackson, see Robert G. Kaufman, *Henry M. Jackson: A Life in Politics*, Seattle: University of Washington Press, 2000, especially pp. 242–60.

72 The project was discussed several times during the Moscow Summit Talks, which lasted from 23–25 May 1972; see Keefer (ed.), *Soviet-American Relations*, pp. 851–52, 873–74, 880–82, 918–19.

'the whole relationship with the Soviet Union'.[73] At the same time, he wanted to present the gas deal as a tool in his domestic political fight against opposition in Congress, saying, 'Look, we need them on gas and so forth'.[74] In so doing, he went against people such as Charles DiBona, the president's special adviser on energy,[75] and Walter Levy, the renowned US oil analyst and foreign policy adviser,[76] both of whom urged restraint. Levy was sceptical of the gas project with the Soviet Union because he considered it too expensive and too risky. He favoured other possibilities, such as cooperation with the Soviet Union in the oil-rich states of the Middle East, namely Iraq, an opinion he once expressed to Henry Kissinger, the president's National Security Advisor.[77]

The US government under Nixon, however, stuck to its position and, despite resistance in Congress and sceptical voices in its own cabinet, was prepared to support its energy companies in the matter of the gas agreement with the Soviet Union. Thanks in particular to the commitment of US Treasury Secretary George Shultz, the American consortium of companies succeeded in concluding a preliminary agreement with the Soviet Foreign Trade Ministry on this matter in June 1973.[78] A month later, Occidental Petroleum signed a five-year contract with the Soviet government covering the exploration, production, and utilisation of natural gas and crude oil but also providing for cooperation in fertiliser production and the chemical sector, metal processing and refining, and other areas.[79] Japanese companies also became active, exploring the possibility of cooperative projects in the fields of Yakutian natural gas, coal mining, and the production of oil and gas on Sakhalin.[80] Both North Star and the Yakutia Project represent energy visions of the time, which will be explained in more detail below.

[73] 'Conversation between President Nixon and Members of the Cabinet', Washington, DC, 20 April 1973, in US Department of State (ed.), *Foreign Relations of the United States 1969–1976*, vol. XXXVI, p. 446.

[74] Ibid.

[75] 'Memorandum from the President's Special Consultant for Energy', Washington, DC, 19 March 1973, in ibid., pp. 441–43.

[76] 'Memorandum of Conversation', Washington, DC, 8 August 1973, in ibid., pp. 502–9.

[77] Ibid. [78] Högselius, *Red Gas*, p. 133.

[79] 'Memorandum from Secretary of Commerce Peterson to the President's Assistant for National Security Affairs (Kissinger) and the Executive Director of the Council for International Economic Policy (Flanigan)', Washington, DC, 19 August 1972, in US Department of State (ed.), *Foreign Relations of the United States 1969–1976*, vol. XV, pp. 75–79, here p. 76 (n. 3).

[80] Jeronim Perović and Dunja Krempin, '"The Key Is in Our Hands": Soviet Energy Strategy during Détente and the Global Oil Crises of the 1970s', *Historical Social Research*, 39, 4 (2014), pp. 113–44, here p. 128.

Energy Visions under Brezhnev

In the first half of the 1970s, the internal Soviet debate on the shape of the economic relationship with the West was always more than just a controversy between 'isolationists' and 'Westerners', as is sometimes suggested in Western Cold War literature.[81] By this time, the Soviet Union was already intertwined with the world economy through numerous trade and economic agreements – and Brezhnev, in talks with Western representatives, left no doubt that he was interested in further big deals. 'Our plans are certainly not aimed at autarky', he told West German television on 21 May 1973 during his visit to the FRG.[82]

In the wake of increasing economic globalisation, the Soviet Union was confronted with complex challenges that it sought to understand and to which it had to find the right answers. Different views were expressed in controversial discussions within the party leadership and also reflected in struggles for direction among the various ministries, within the Gosplan departments, and between the central authorities in Moscow and the country's oil- and gas-producing regions. Renowned research institutions of the Academy of Sciences, such as the Institute for World Economy and International Relations (IMEMO), also participated in the discussions and presented their views in relevant policy papers. Determining future economic priorities was no small task, as new focuses always implied shifts in the allocation of resources to the various sectors of the economy.

Overall, the oil and gas sectors were now given significantly more weight as a result of the global price increase. The Soviet leadership was increasingly aware of how much money could be made from commodity exports. Whereas in 1970 the Soviet Union earned about 1 billion US dollars from the sale of oil and oil products in the Western dollar zone, this amount tripled by 1974 and reached a peak of about 15 billion US dollars annually in the first half of the 1980s.[83] The development of Western Siberian raw materials was the way not only to secure the Soviet Union's energy needs in the long term but also to obtain the coveted Western currency. The formula seemed simple: 'Gas there – hard currency here', as Brezhnev once put it at an internal party meeting on

[81] Marshall I. Goldman, 'Will the Soviet Union Be an Autarky in 1984?', *International Security*, 3, 4 (1979), pp. 18–36.

[82] L. I. Brezhnev, *O vneshnei politike KPSS i Sovetskogo gosudarstva: Rechi i stat'i*, Moscow: Politizdat, 1973, p. 507, quoted in V. P. Gruzinov, *The USSR's Management of Foreign Trade: Edited with a Foreword by Edward A. Hewett*, White Plains, NY: M. E. Sharp, 1979, p. 18.

[83] Slavkina, *Neftegazovyi faktor*, p. 322.

5 February 1971. The Soviet General Secretary recognised in Siberian oil and gas the potential to change 'our entire existence':

> These are significant economic indicators. They will change our possibilities, our relationship with the whole of Europe – not only with the socialist countries, where we supply gas and oil, but also with France, Germany, and Italy. The key is in our hands.[84]

However, the path to exploiting Siberia's vast resource potential remained arduous, particularly because of the lack of consensus within the Politburo on the feasibility of large-scale international cooperation projects. Brezhnev's willingness to establish long-term structural dependencies on the West not only undermined the principle that the Soviet Union and its allies should seek to strive towards a self-sufficient economy separate from the capitalist West but also challenged the notion of an imminent demise of capitalism. For, according to critics within Brezhnev's Politburo, Moscow was supporting the ideological enemy in its efforts to avoid revolution by supplying energy. Nikolai Podgornyi, member of the Politburo and the nominal head of state of the Soviet Union, made comments along these lines at a Politburo meeting in April 1972, when its members were discussing the upcoming visit of the US president:

> It is inappropriate for us to get involved in these deals, with gas and oil pipelines. As if we are planning to sell off the whole of Siberia; plus, it makes us look technologically helpless. Can't we do the same things ourselves, without foreign capital?![85]

This kind of criticism, however, met with little sympathy from pragmatists like Baibakov, the Gosplan chairman. At the same meeting, he countered with the argument that while the Soviet Union was technically capable of laying the pipelines itself, it had 'no metal for pipes, nor for machines or other equipment'. Under these circumstances, the process of developing difficult fields would take 'at least 30 years' if the Soviet Union were to forgo foreign support.[86] Baibakov had long been sceptical about the comprehensive development of Western Siberian energy. Not only did the investment costs seem too high, but he also felt that in the low-price environment of the 1960s, Siberian raw materials, with their

[84] *General'nyi sekretar' L. I. Brezhnev 1964–1982: Spetsial'noe izdanie*, Moscow: Vestnik Arkhiva Prezidenta, 2006, p. 103.

[85] *The Diary of Anatoly S. Chernyaev 1972: Translated by Anna Melyakova; Edited by Svetlana Savranskaya*, Washington, DC: The National Security Archive, 2012, p. 11 (entry dated 8 April 1972), https://nsarchive2.gwu.edu/NSAEBB/NSAEBB379/ (last accessed 16 July 2021).

[86] Ibid., p. 12.

predicted high production costs, would have a difficult time on the world market compared to cheap Arab oil.

The opposition of such influential people as Baibakov contributed to delaying the energy development of Western Siberia for many years.[87] However, in the face of looming production bottlenecks, scarce foreign currency, and higher world market prices for oil, the Gosplan leader had changed his mind by the early 1970s. From then on, together with other like-minded people – including, in addition to Gas Minister Kortunov, Prime Minister Kosygin, Foreign Trade Minister Patolichev, and Foreign Minister Gromyko – he advocated the development of Western Siberian raw materials and the expansion of trade and economic cooperation with the West in order to achieve this goal. The Soviet Union desperately needed foreign currency, if only to pay for the grain it repeatedly had to buy abroad to offset the ravages of crop failures. Baibakov bluntly told the party comrades present at the April 1972 Politburo meeting that the only goods the Soviet Union could offer that interested the West were oil and gas.[88]

The export of oil and gas seemed all the more lucrative as oil prices had once again risen massively in the wake of the 1973–74 oil crisis and the Soviet dollar coffers continued to fill up.[89] However, the global oil crisis also embarrassed the Soviet Union vis-à-vis its Western European customers, as it was now difficult to conceal the fact that the country itself was struggling with supply bottlenecks. The oil shock came at a time when not only the Europeans, the Americans, and the Japanese, but also the Soviets, were consuming an increasing amount of oil. Western observers saw one sign of Soviet supply problems in the fact that the Soviet Union repeatedly defaulted on its oil delivery obligations to such Western European countries as France, Italy, and the FRG.[90] Moscow also proved unable to increase oil exports to Western Europe during the Arab embargo, despite repeated requests from Western governments. For example, in a letter to Brezhnev on 7 November 1973, in view of the Arab 'policy of blackmail', Chancellor Brandt asked the Soviet Secretary General 'whether and to what extent the Soviet Union would be willing

[87] Gustafson, *The Bridge*, pp. 39, 48–52; Högselius, *Red Gas*, p. 41.
[88] *The Diary of Anatoly S. Chernyaev 1972*, p. 11.
[89] Judith Thornthon, 'Resource Valuation and the Efficiency of Soviet Resource Production and Use', in Jensen, Shabad, and Wright (eds.), *Soviet Natural Resources in the World Economy*, pp. 597–613, here p. 600.
[90] See, for example, the reports of the British Embassy in Bonn (dated 19 December 1973) and Moscow (dated 8 January 1974) on the situation of Soviet oil supplies to Eastern and Western Europe in Burdett (ed.), *Oil Resources in Eastern Europe and the Caucasus*, vol. 8, pp. 427, 432–35.

or able to make short-term or medium-term deliveries [of oil]'.[91] Moscow, however, was unable to comply with this request immediately. In February 1974, an internal British government paper stated that the oil crisis had led not only to an 'extensive rethinking of energy policies in the developed Western countries' but also to an 'embarrassment to the Soviet Union', which, 'despite the expansion of its oil industry over the past decade', had proven incapable 'to become a substantial contributor to world supplies'.[92]

The Soviet Union's struggle with production and supply shortages was something Moscow tried to deny in public. Kosygin, for instance, announced in a public speech in Moscow on 12 June 1974 that 'such upheavals [as observed in the West] are not a feature of our Socialist planned economy'.[93] The Soviet Union had indeed managed to increase its production of raw materials: between 1960 and 1970, Soviet oil production more than doubled, from around 150 million tonnes per year to over 300 million tonnes, and was to continue rising thereafter, surpassing 600 million tonnes of oil per year in the early 1980s.[94] However, with the rapid expansion of energy-intensive industries and the commencement of mass production of automobiles, which absorbed an ever-larger share of oil production, the Soviet hunger for hydrocarbons also increased. This meant that virtually all of the additional oil that the Soviet Union produced between 1974 and 1978 was needed to satisfy the demand of an extremely wasteful domestic industry.[95] In order to free up more oil for export to the lucrative Western market, the Soviet Union either had to take steps to use existing energy more efficiently or it had to boost raw material production. Ultimately, the Soviet leadership opted not for an austerity programme but to expand its energy base by turning its attention to Tyumen and natural gas.

The Soviet government knew about the great challenges of the energy development of Western Siberia, which made it even more important to

[91] 'Federal Chancellor Brandt to the General Secretary of the CC of the CPSU, Brezhnev', 7 November 1973, in *Akten zur Auswärtigen Politik der Bundesrepublik Deutschland (1973)*, pp. 1780–81, here p. 1781.

[92] The report entitled 'Soviet Oil Production Problems' is contained in Burdett (ed.), *Oil Resources in Eastern Europe and the Caucasus*, vol. 8, pp. 445–50, here p. 445.

[93] Kosygin's speech is contained in English translation in *Daily Report, Soviet Union*, FBIS-SOV-74-115, US Foreign Broadcast Information Service/NTIS, 13 June 1974.

[94] Gaidar, *Collapse of an Empire*, p. 101 (based on Soviet statistics).

[95] In general, on the lack of efficiency and the problems of the Soviet planned economy model in the 1970s, see Alec Nove, 'USSR: Economic Policy and Methods after 1970', in Alec Nove, Hans-Hermann Höhmann, and Gertraud Seidenstecher (eds.), *The East European Economies in the 1970s*, London: Butterworths, 1982, pp. 17–44; for detail on the growing role of oil in the Soviet economy, see Slavkina, *Neftegazovyi faktor*, pp. 183–226.

win the cooperation of Western companies. Moreover, because the opening-up policy favoured by Brezhnev was subject to internal criticism, the government had to be able to demonstrate rapid success. How delicate this course was, however, became apparent during the hot phase of the Yom Kippur War and also in the course of the global energy crisis triggered by the Arab oil boycott: while the Soviet Union officially showed solidarity with the Arabs and Soviet newspapers such as *Pravda* portrayed their embargo policy as a legitimate 'uprising' against the 'greed-driven' capitalist companies, Moscow was reticent to take the same tack in direct communication with Western governments and instead used largely de-ideologised language.[96]

To avoid jeopardising the possibility of expanding cooperation with Western companies, the Soviet Union even tried to use the oil crisis for an actual charm offensive: in a programme intended for American listeners, Radio Moscow on 16 November 1973 called for cooperation between the Soviet Union and the West on the grounds that only in this way could 'the energy crisis ... be overcome'.[97] Two weeks earlier, a prominent member of the Soviet Academy of Sciences had announced on the same radio programme that the day was approaching when 'cold Siberia will light and heat New York', an unequivocal attempt to advertise the Soviet-American North Star project.[98] Soviet official representatives likewise took every available opportunity to promote economic cooperation: in a speech during a United Nations conference on resource problems and economic development in April 1974, for instance, Foreign Minister Gromyko offered the West long-term energy cooperation based on Soviet oil and gas exports without 'artificial barriers' in trade relations.[99]

It was during this period that Soviet planners set out to conduct a comprehensive assessment of their country's energy situation. With an eye to the preparation of the upcoming Five-Year Plan for 1976–1980, Vladimir Dolgikh, a senior member of the CPSU's Central Committee and a Secretary of that same institution, commissioned a study to analyse 'the position [of the Soviet Union] with regard to the use of oil and natural gas resources and the development of the oil and gas industry

96 Perović and Krempin, 'The Key Is in Our Hands', pp. 128–32.

97 Radio Moscow, 16 November 1973, in Burdett (ed.), *Oil Resources in Eastern Europe and the Caucasus*, vol. 8, pp. 407–8.

98 Radio Moscow, 4 November 1973, in ibid., p. 408.

99 'Na VI spetsial'noi sessii General'noi Assemblei OON: Vystuplenie A. A. Gromyko', *Pravda*, 102, 12 April 1974, p. 4.

under present conditions'.[100] This analysis, addressed to Brezhnev and dated 29 August 1974, may be considered an important document of its time – for the study provides a rare insight into how, in the mid-1970s, in the context of global supply fears and high world market prices for oil, the development prospects of the Soviet oil and gas industry were being considered at the highest level of the party's leadership.[101]

Significantly, the roughly ten-page analysis took as its point of departure not the situation in the Soviet energy sector but developments in the international energy market. The study's authors assumed that the energy crisis would worsen given that global reserves would become scarcer and geopolitical conflicts over raw materials would increase.[102] As a result, Western governments and companies were expected to push ahead with their search for new reserves, namely in the Middle East, and to seek to secure energy through long-term agreements and the expansion of their regional influence. 'Taking into account the worsening energy problems in the world', the Soviet Union was encouraged to define its energy policy and relations with the countries of the socialist area as well as with the capitalist states.[103] The study thus placed the Soviet energy sector within a larger global context and saw the shaping of energy policy as being dependent on movements in the international market environment.

The authors behind the Dolgikh study seemed to be convinced that the Soviet Union, based on its huge reserves, was in a position to massively increase oil and natural gas production in order to cover its own projected rising demand, supply the socialist states and simultaneously meet the capitalist countries' growing hunger for oil and natural gas. However, they also acknowledged that this would require a rapid increase in production, which could only be achieved through a huge investment programme. Due to the remoteness of the newly discovered production areas in the tundra, thousands of kilometres from the densely populated industrial centres in the European part of the country, the development of these resources posed significant challenges. Not only would substantial investment be required to set up new production facilities, but thousands of kilometres of pipelines would also need to be built to facilitate transport. New houses for workers and their families would have to be created, as well as airfields and roads. Refineries would have

100 The report dates from 29 August 1974 and is titled 'On Certain Questions in the Use of Oil and Natural Gas Resources and the Development of the Oil and Gas Industry under Present Conditions', contained in RGANI, f. 80, op. 1, d. 322, ll. 78–89, here l. 78.

101 Brezhnev forwarded the document to Georgii Tsukanov: RGANI, f. 80, op. 1, d. 322, l. 78.

102 RGANI, f. 80, op. 1, d. 322, l. 80.

103 RGANI, f. 80, op. 1, d. 322, l. 80.

to be constructed to process the raw materials, and industries would have to be set up to supply the oil and gas industry with the necessary equipment, including high-quality, large-diameter steel pipes that could withstand the high pressures caused by the Artic's extreme temperatures. Regarding gas production, the study's authors saw the most important future task as being the development of the deposits in the northern part of the Tyumen region:

> Our natural gas reserves are sufficient to increase gas production many times over …. However, it should be noted that over 60 per cent of our gas reserves are in the north of the Tyumen Oblast. In the European part of the USSR the gas fields, on the basis of which this industry began to develop, are exhausted, production is declining in many [fields] …. In order to increase gas production [in the north of the Tyumen Oblast] to [the planned] 180 billion cubic metres in 1980, it will be necessary to build [a system of] large-diameter gas pipelines over 30,000 km long with 16.5 million tonnes of pipe and about 200 compressor stations. This will require a total of over 18 billion roubles in investment, of which 13 billion roubles will have to be spent on gas transportation alone.[104]

It is clear from this passage that the transportation of gas over long distances was considered the most difficult and most expensive challenge. At the same time, the proposals for how to tackle this problem were 'not yet fully developed'. According to the study's authors, the State Committee for Science and Technology and the Academy of Sciences of the USSR were to get involved in looking for the optimal solution, drawing on 'international experience'.[105] The sticking point was the production of steel sheets for pipeline construction, which the Soviet Union was still unable to manufacture in sufficient quantities and, above all, in the desired quality. In fact, Soviet pipes were often of such poor quality that serious accidents were a regular occurrence. We learn from another report, commissioned by the CPSU's Central Committee Secretariat, and prepared on 6 July 1976, that in 1975 alone, the oil pipeline network suffered 150 serious accidents, while the gas pipelines were affected by 60 major accidents. The former had caused the spilling of about 1.5 million tonnes of oil, not to mention great financial losses and other 'material and moral damages'.[106]

Thus, in building up an energy transport system, the Soviet Union could not avoid importing steel pipes, which at that time it obtained mainly from the FRG and Japan.[107] To reduce these import dependencies in the future, the Dolgikh study proposed the construction of

[104] RGANI, f. 80, op. 1, d. 322, ll. 85–86. [105] RGANI, f. 80, op. 1, d. 322, l. 86.
[106] RGANI [Hoover Archive], f. 89, p. 26, d. 20, ll. 1–5, here ll. 1–2.
[107] Machowski, 'Soviet–West German Economic Relations', p. 53.

factories in the Soviet Union over the next ten years that would be capable of producing the equipment needed for the oil and gas industry. In order to ensure that these plants would supply the products in the necessary 'quality and reliability', the industrial equipment required was to be purchased abroad and paid for with '20–30 million tonnes of crude oil and petroleum products in freely convertible currency'.[108] The authors thus seemed to point to a deficiency inherent in the structure of the oil and gas industry when arguing that in order to increase oil and gas production to new levels, a key task was to strengthen and develop 'related industries to provide the oil and gas industry and geological organisations with equipment, mechanisation and automation, pipes and various chemicals'.[109]

What the authors seemed to be suggesting here, at least implicitly, was to create, as in the defense industry, a more vertically integrated structure whose production units were linked in such a way that their respective needs could be coordinated. For in a system that was fundamentally hierarchically organised, horizontal cooperation was the greatest challenge. Individual ministries and economic departments fought for themselves in the allocation of resources, and cooperation among the enterprises involved in the complicated production processes was also often insufficiently coordinated. There were no institutionalised exchanges of information between companies, and in practice, the energy sector was organised mainly through informal channels by party leaders in the centre and the various regions.[110] However, quality deficiencies or production gaps could often be compensated only, if at all, by short-term purchases of goods from abroad.[111]

The Dolgikh study also advocated intensifying cooperation with foreign companies in order to implement technically demanding energy projects, for example, in the increasingly important offshore sector. Especially the Caspian Sea basin, where the production of offshore oil had begun already in the 1950s, was to become a 'laboratory' in which new methods of extracting raw materials from the seabed were to be tested 'to perfection'; these methods could then be employed in other marine regions of the country. In the ice-covered shelf zones of the northern seas, cooperative ventures were to be contemplated with 'Japanese, American, and companies from other countries' to carry out 'experimental explorations and other work'. In particular, 'work with the

[108] RGANI, f. 80, op. 1, d. 322, ll. 86–87. [109] RGANI, f. 80, op. 1, d. 322, l. 82.

[110] Thane Gustafson, *Wheel of Fortune: The Battle for Oil and Power in Russia*, Cambridge, MA: Harvard University Press, 2012, pp. 32–33.

[111] Cf. also the remarks in Churilov, *Moia istoriia sovetskoi nefti*, pp. 25f.

participation of foreign enterprises on the territory of Sakhalin Island', to which the party leadership had already agreed in principle, was to be accelerated.[112]

The authors of the Dolgikh study also adopted a clear position on exports, stating that 'trade in oil, oil products, and natural gas' must take greater account of price developments:

> Under the current conditions of world prices for oil and oil products, one should be extremely cautious when concluding export transactions in the future, especially considering the fact that oil prices are changing dramatically. Under these conditions, one should refrain from concluding long-term contracts that provide for fixed prices for the entire period of their validity.[113]

Here the authors expressed subtle criticism of the Soviet Union's long-term supply agreements with the socialist states of Eastern Europe. At that time, these agreements were still based on a calculation model from 1958, which determined the price of oil in each case based on the last five years. In view of the sharp rise in world market prices in the wake of the global energy crisis of 1973–74, this meant that the Soviet Union was selling its raw materials to Eastern Europe at prices well below the world market price.[114] According to Western estimates at the time, the CMEA states in 1974 paid less than a third of the international market price for Soviet crude oil.[115] Moreover, these long-term commitments meant that large export volumes were tied up and could not be sold at significantly higher prices in the much more lucrative Western market. As Khrushchev had done, the authors of the Dolgikh study also criticised the Soviet Union's heavy dependence on the export of crude oil and called for an increase in the export of processed petroleum products.[116]

The study saw the greatest potential in the export of natural gas. They thus advocated 'building liquefaction plants and bringing gas to the world market in liquefied form' because 'in many countries, liquefaction of natural gas and long-distance transport in liquefied form are becoming standard practices'.[117] Apparently, the authors of the Dolgikh study supported the idea that gas in liquefied form was able to react more flexibly to changes in markets and prices, avoiding structural dependencies arising from physical pipeline connections. Indeed, nowhere does the document mention the idea of building gas export pipelines to

[112] RGANI, f. 80, op. 1, d. 322, l. 83. [113] RGANI, f. 80, op. 1, d. 322, l. 87.
[114] Suvi Kansikas, 'Calculating the Burden of Empire: Soviet Oil, East–West Trade, and the End of the Socialist Bloc', in Perović (ed.), *Cold War Energy*, pp. 345–69.
[115] Raimund Dietz, *Die Energiewirtschaft in Osteuropa und der UdSSR*, Vienna: Springer Verlag, 1984, p. 77.
[116] RGANI, f. 80, op. 1, d. 322, l. 87. [117] RGANI, f. 80, op. 1, d. 322, l. 88.

Western Europe, nor are there any references to large-scale, long-term energy partnerships between the Soviet Union and Western European companies. Rather, the potential for cooperation with the United States and Japan is explicitly emphasised several times, reflecting the desire at the time for closer ties with companies from these two countries and the appeal of gas liquefaction. The emphasis on working with US companies in particular was in line with the prevailing spirit of détente, which Brezhnev felt should be underpinned by a closer economic partnership between the two superpowers. However, as subsequent developments would show, many things turned out differently than envisaged in this document.

Energy Crisis and Its Consequences for the 'Eastern Bloc'

Under Brezhnev, the Soviet Union stood at the pinnacle of its power on the global stage. Militarily, the Moscow-controlled Warsaw Pact had achieved parity with NATO. Communism and Moscow's position of power within the 'Eastern bloc' seemed unchallenged after the violent suppression of the Prague Spring in 1968. The Soviet Union was active in some seventy states of the 'Third World': it ran economic and technical assistance programmes, provided billions of dollars' worth of military aid to dozens of states, and maintained military bases from Cuba to Syria to Angola.[118] Militarily and politically, therefore, the Soviet Union was a global superpower on par with the United States. However, economically and in terms of the standard of living for its population, the Soviet Union still lagged behind most Western capitalist states. Apart from the military-industrial sector and a few areas of cutting-edge technology, there was hardly anything left of the euphoria of 'catching up and overtaking' that had characterised the second half of the 1950s. Consequently, the Soviet Union's cooperation efforts in the 1970s can be seen as an attempt to prevent falling too far behind the economic progress of the West.

By the mid-1970s, the Soviet leaders and planners had embraced the idea of being part of a larger world market. However, determining the appropriate response to these global processes remained uncertain. Disillusionment had also settled in regarding the Soviet Union's economic performance and its attractiveness as an economic partner for its Eastern European socialist allies. To be sure, the Soviet leadership was never to abandon its Eastern European allies entirely since maintaining

[118] Petr Cherkasov, 'The Twilight of the Brezhnev Era', *Russian Politics and Law*, 43, 6 (2005), pp. 76–95, here p. 85.

and strengthening the bloc's internal cohesion was always Moscow's top priority. In confidential discussions with the leaders of the Eastern European Communist parties, however, Brezhnev increasingly pointed out the major problems facing his country, including the challenge of tapping into Siberian energy, and indicated to the Eastern European comrades that the Soviet Union could not continue to subsidise their economies to the extent that it had in the past. At a March 1975 meeting in Budapest with several leaders of Eastern European communist parties, including János Kádár of Hungary, Edward Gierek of Poland, and Erich Honecker of East Germany, Brezhnev made his position abundantly clear:

> Today I came here, figuratively speaking, with empty pockets .... Naturally, we are not refusing to continue to develop our cooperation. [But we] have to state honestly that we are faced with a number of difficult problems [in the Soviet Union]. Among them are the further improvement of the agriculture, increase of production of oil, [natural] gas and lumber, construction of the Baikal-Amur railroad, obligations to fraternal countries, and further improvement of the living standards of the population .... In order to transport [natural] gas from Tyumen to the European part [of the Soviet Union], to deliver it to Bratislava or Budapest, we need huge financial and material resources. We do not have enough pipes of our own, so we have to use currency to purchase them abroad. In short, there are many problems [and] we have thought seriously about how to make our economy more profitable.[119]

That year, Moscow replaced the model of fixed prices for oil supplied to the socialist countries of Eastern Europe with a new price-regulation formula based on the average world market price of the previous year. Although this enabled the Soviet Union to at least stabilise oil exports to Western Europe after the 1973–74 energy crisis, it came at the expense of its socialist allies in Eastern Europe.[120] According to estimates in a NATO Economic Committee report of 1976, Moscow had cut its oil exports to the CMEA countries by more than a third by the mid-1970s.[121] The latter were also now paying significantly more for Soviet

[119] Brezhnev quoted in 'Record of Conversation of Brezhnev with Leaders of Fraternal Parties of Socialist Countries, 18 March 1975', *History and Public Policy Program Digital Archive*, Library of Congress, Manuscript Division, Dmitrii Antonovich Volkogonov papers, 1887–1995, mm97083838, Reel 16, Container 24; Translated by Svetlana Savranskaya for the National Security Archive, https://digitalarchive.wilsoncenter.org/document/121171 (last accessed 8 November 2021).

[120] Michael De Groot, 'The Soviet Union, CMEA, and the Energy Crisis of the 1970s', *Journal of Cold War Studies*, 22, 4 (2020), pp. 4–30, here p. 16.

[121] This figure comes from a NATO Economic Committee working paper dated 20 July 1976 and entitled 'The Energy Situation in Comecon Countries in 1976' contained in US Department of State (ed.), *Foreign Relations of the United States, 1969–1976*, vol. XXXVI, pp. 621–66, here p. 624.

raw materials. In the case of East Germany, for example, the agreement for 1971–75 still provided for an oil price of 14 roubles per tonne, but under the modified price formula, the country was now paying 35 roubles per tonne. The price of gas (which has traditionally been linked to the price of oil) also rose: the GDR was now to pay 31 roubles per 1,000 cubic metres of gas instead of the original 14.25 roubles. Although the Soviet Union offered deferred payments and the prospect of low-interest loans to help the Eastern Europeans bear the increased costs, these higher oil and natural gas prices can be seen as a turning point for trade within the CMEA.[122]

Moscow also repeatedly called on its Eastern European allies to look for other importers for their oil. Even before the outbreak of the global oil crisis, Poland, which to that point had imported almost all its oil from the Soviet Union, began negotiations on oil imports with Algeria, Iraq, and Iran; immediately after the Arab embargo and in anticipation of possible cuts in Soviet oil supplies, a Polish delegation held talks in Tripoli in order to secure additional sources of imports.[123] Presumably also on Moscow's instructions, Poland negotiated an agreement with BP in 1971 to supply three million tonnes of oil over a ten-year period. Romania and Czechoslovakia reached barter agreements for Iranian oil in return for machinery and industrial equipment; Hungary, East Germany, and Czechoslovakia concluded similar agreements with Iraq.[124] Hungary and Czechoslovakia joined the Adria Oil Pipeline project, which was initiated already in the mid-1960s by non-aligned Yugoslavia. The pipeline was designed to transport Arab oil from the Adriatic port of Omišalj (in today's Croatia) to Yugoslav refineries and was to connect to the Hungarian and Czechoslovak pipeline systems via a northern branch, while the eastern branch was to be linked to the Romanian system. After several setbacks, the pipeline was put into operation in a scaled-down version in 1989; it now runs through Croatian and Hungarian territory and is connected to the Druzhba pipeline system via an extension.[125] Another consequence of the oil crisis was the Moscow-supported effort to increase the share of Eastern Europe's electricity that was generated by nuclear power plants. By 1978, a total of twenty-eight

122 De Groot, 'The Soviet Union, CMEA, and the Energy Crisis of the 1970s', p. 16.

123 'National Intelligence Estimate', Washington, DC, 5 December 1973, in US Department of State (ed.), *Foreign Relations of the United States 1969–1976*, vol. XXXVI, p. 741.

124 John A. Berry, 'Oil and Soviet Policy in the Middle East', *Middle East Journal*, 26, 2 (1972), pp. 149–60, here p. 153.

125 Cf. Ljubica Spaskovska, '"Crude" Alliance – Economic Decolonisation and Oil Power in the Non-Aligned World', *Contemporary European History*, 30, 4 (2021), pp. 528–43.

nuclear power plants had been built in the CMEA area, of which twenty-one were located in the Soviet Union.[126]

Given that Moscow increasingly resented its oil being committed to the bloc states, Soviet behaviour indicated that Moscow was less and less inclined to supply the Eastern European economies unconditionally with cheap Soviet commodities. Not only would Eastern Europe have to pay higher prices for Soviet oil and gas from the mid-1970s, but energy trade within the socialist camp, which had previously been based almost exclusively on barter and calculated in non-convertible transfer roubles,[127] would also increasingly be conducted in hard currency, which Moscow demanded for those oil deliveries that went beyond the original supply agreements.[128]

Despite the new price calculation formula of 1975, however, Moscow continued to negotiate prices and quantities with each Eastern European country individually, and political considerations always played a role in these negotiations. This was to become apparent with later political crises. Thus, in the face of the large strikes and workers' protests in Poland in 1980/81, the Soviet Union felt compelled to supply the country with raw materials and food in the hope of calming the population and helping the beleaguered Polish regime. The Soviet leadership asked nothing from the Poles in return; instead, it demanded solidarity from the other socialist states when the Kremlin decided to reduce the volume of oil and oil product supplies to them, selling some of the oil thus freed up on the world market to generate more foreign exchange that could be made available to the Polish regime. With hard Western currency, 'the Poles can buy what they need', Baibakov suggested at a meeting of the Soviet Politburo on 29 October 1980.[129] At the same time, the Soviet Union also significantly reduced the price at which they sold their oil to Poland, selling this commodity well below the international market price. 'We supply Poland with 13 million tonnes of oil at 90 roubles per tonne. If we consider that the world price stands at 170 roubles, then we don't get 80 roubles for each tonne from the Poles. We could sell all this oil for hard currency and the revenues would be enormous', as grudgingly stated by

[126] De Groot, 'The Soviet Union, CMEA, and the Energy Crisis of the 1970s', p. 27.

[127] The transfer ruble was an accounting currency introduced within CMEA in 1963 and used for the determination of the price of goods. Trade among CMEA countries was calculated in transfer rubles.

[128] Balmaceda, 'Der Weg in die Abhängigkeit', p. 168.

[129] The document is included in *Soviet Deliberations during the Polish Crisis, 1980–1981: Edited, Translated, Annotated, and Introduced by Mark Kramer*, Cold War International History Project, Special Working Paper 1, Washington, DC: Woodrow Wilson International Center for Scholars, April 1999, pp. 44–54, here p. 52.

Ivan Arkhipov, Deputy Chairman of the Soviet Union's Council of Ministers, during a session of the Politburo on 26 March 1981.[130]

Not only the people in the socialist states of Eastern Europe but also the citizens of the Soviet Union felt the effects of the country's 'energy crisis'. To appear as reliable a trading partner as possible, the Soviet leadership was determined to supply its clientele in Western Europe with the contractually agreed quantities of gas even during harsh winters. This meant that Moscow was prepared to supply gas that was not always actually available. In particular, the people in Ukraine suffered as a result. The situation was especially dramatic in the severe winter of 1973–74 when the gas supply to power stations, municipal facilities, households, and individual branches of industry in the Ukrainian SSR was curtailed or even cut off completely so that Western Europeans, who knew nothing of the situation in the East, could continue to heat their homes.[131] The inhabitants of the affected Ukrainian regions repeatedly complained in letters to Brezhnev and Kosygin about the dire situation in the winter months.[132] The Soviet media were careful not to report publicly on such serious difficulties, even if, in the late 1970s, they repeatedly informed their readers about the challenges facing energy production, particularly with regard to the development of energy resources in Western Siberia.[133]

The End of Détente and the Start of the Siberian Campaign

Soviet representatives had been lobbying in the West since the early 1970s to persuade companies from the United States, Europe, and Japan to participate in energy projects in Siberia. However, no large-scale economic partnership between the two superpowers was to materialise. Nixon's policy of détente faced strong opposition in the US Congress from the outset, and the passage of the Trade Act of 1974, which came into force in January 1975 under his successor Gerald Ford, dealt a severe blow to cooperation efforts.[134] The new Trade Act contained the Jackson-Vanik and Stevenson Amendments. The first amendment made MFN status conditional on greater freedom of Soviet Jews to emigrate, while the second prevented the granting of large loans or financial guarantees without final congressional approval. This also

[130] RGANI [Hoover Archive], f. 89, p. 42, d. 38, ll. 1–3, here l. 3.
[131] Högselius, *Red Gas*, pp. 159–62. [132] Gustafson, *The Bridge*, pp. 154–56.
[133] For example, S. Vtorushin and A. Murzin, 'Izkat' novye klady', *Pravda*, 222, 10 August 1977, p. 2.
[134] Hanns-Dieter Jacobsen, *Die Ost-West-Wirtschaftsbeziehungen als deutsch-amerikanisches Problem*, Baden-Baden: Nomos, 1986, pp. 142–47.

meant that obtaining direct credits or credit guarantees from the US Export-Import Bank was not possible, which was crucial given the significant amount of funds required to undertake the energy projects in Siberia.[135] Moscow rebuffed the demand for Jewish emigration, seeing it as an interference in its internal affairs, and in response to these resolutions, the Soviet Union in January 1975 rejected the entire trade agreement concluded in October 1972 with the United States.[136] To be sure, neither North Star nor the Yakutia Project were immediately abandoned. US firms attempted to implement the North Star deal with European assistance and to carry out the Yakutia Project with a combination of US commercial bank loans and Japanese Export-Import Bank loans. However, these efforts did not bear fruit, and by 1976, neither venture was being pursued further.[137]

The termination of these projects put a severe damper on the plan to develop Siberian gas resources with the help of foreign loans and technology. It also brought the idea of selling Siberian gas in liquid form on world markets to a virtual standstill. Against this background, many in the West doubted whether the Soviet Union would be able to maintain its exports at a high level in the coming years, let alone increase them significantly. It was true that the Soviet Union had experienced a bottleneck in oil supplies in the 1970s. But that the country would have to import significant amounts of oil in the near future, as the CIA predicted in two reports published in April 1977, proved to be a gross misjudgement.[138] For it was precisely in this period – perhaps also as a reaction to the pessimistic Western reports – that the Soviet leadership launched a large-scale mobilisation campaign to develop the gas deposits located in the north of Western Siberia. Unlike previous initiatives, this was to be done in a comprehensive manner, focusing not only on the extraction of fossil resources but also on the development of a number of industrial and infrastructure complexes. This comprehensive development of

[135] Goldman, *The Enigma of Soviet Petroleum*, pp. 79–80.

[136] Stern, 'Soviet Natural Gas in the World Economy', p. 376; John C. Campbell, 'Soviet–American Relations: Détente and Dispute', *Current History*, 69, 409 (1975), pp. 113–16, 146–47, 149–51, here p. 150.

[137] Stern, 'Soviet Natural Gas in the World Economy', p. 376.

[138] The study entitled 'The International Energy Situation: Outlook to 1985' was published on 18 April 1977; 'Prospects for Soviet Oil Production' on 25 April 1977; in the months that followed, the CIA published several other studies on the energy situation in the Soviet Union. Cf. *The Soviet Oil Situation: An Evaluation of CIA Analyses of Soviet Oil Production; Staff Report of the Senate Select Committee on the Intelligence United States Senate*, Washington, DC: United States Government Printing Office, 1978, p. 1. For a thorough discussion of the CIA's 1977 assessments, see Goldman, *The Enigma of Soviet Petroleum*.

Siberia, the practical implementation of which proved at times to be rather chaotic and ill-planned,[139] was to be given a similarly high priority in Soviet economic policy as the construction of the Baikal-Amur Mainline (BAM). As with Western Siberia's gas development project, the BAM undertaking was not intended solely as an infrastructure project for the transport of Siberian raw materials but was conceived as an element of a larger plan for the development and settlement of the Soviet Union's vast eastern regions.[140]

The Soviet leadership announced the start of its Siberian campaign at the 25th Party Congress in February 1976. Yet it was not until early 1978 that Soviet propaganda launched a major media offensive. Brezhnev himself publicly advocated this project, even though he had little personal interest in the country's oil and gas industry, as people like Kosygin and Baibakov were the driving forces behind it.[141] In March and April 1978, the Soviet General Secretary undertook a three-week train trip through Siberia. On this journey, which had been carefully orchestrated by the Soviet media, he visited industrial and military cities and gave speeches to workers, party delegates, soldiers, and members of youth organisations.[142] The trip marked the beginning of a large-scale public mobilisation campaign promoting the comprehensive industrial development of Siberia. The slogan 'Siberian Might' served as the headline for an article in the Soviet weekly *Literaturnaia Gazeta* on 1 May 1978 that detailed plans for the development of Western Siberia.[143] Other newspapers, such as *Pravda*, followed suit, regularly publishing articles reporting on progress in the industrial development of this vast region.[144]

The Soviet government had made the Siberian branch of the Academy of Sciences the leading organisation responsible for the coordination of

[139] Cf. the excellent study by Fiona Hill and Clifford G. Gaddy, *The Siberian Curse: How Communist Planners Left Russia Out in the Cold*, Washington, DC: Brookings Institution Press, 2003.

[140] Christopher J. Ward, *Brezhnev's Folly: The Building of BAM and Late Soviet Socialism*, Pittsburgh: University of Pittsburgh Press, 2009, pp. 6–11; for further reading, see Johannes Grützmacher, *Die Baikal-Amur-Magistrale: Vom stalinistischen Lager zum Mobilisierungsprojekt unter Brežnev*, Munich: Oldenbourg, 2012.

[141] Churilov, *Moia istoriia sovetskoi nefti*, p. 74.

[142] Johanna Roos, *Sibirien zwischen Ökonomie und Politik: Zur Erschliessung der Energieträger Erdöl und Erdgas*, Cologne: Verlag Wissenschaft und Politik, 1984, pp. 45–46.

[143] 'Sibirskii Razmakh', *Literaturnaia gazeta*, 1 May 1978, p. 10.

[144] For example, on the industrial complex in the Krasnoyarsk Oblast, see 'Khotia effekt podshchytan', *Pravda*, 134, 14 May 1978, p. 3; on the development of the Tyumen Oblast, see 'Mera zrelosti', *Pravda*, 137, 17 May 1978, p. 3. These and other articles were published under the rubric entitled: 'The Eastern Regions – a Complex Development' (*Vostochnym raionam – kompleksnoe razvitie*). On the Siberian campaign of 1978 in detail, see Krempin, *Die sibirische Wucht*, pp. 353–62.

the various scientific bodies involved in the complex development of Siberia, which was conducted under the programme title 'Siberia'.[145] The Siberian branch was responsible for the overall scientific supervision, the implementation of scientific solutions in industrial branches, and the training of specialised cadres. Siberia was to become the new 'continent of discoveries' and was presented as a 'future-oriented region' full of opportunities for innovative scientists and enthusiastic workers.[146] Accompanying the campaign were Soviet newspapers and numerous posters calling for people to join in this great Soviet endeavour. To attract workers, the *gazovik* was now elevated to hero status alongside the Siberian oil worker. Films such as 'Risk Strategy' (*Strategiia riska*, 1978), about the life of the famous Soviet geologist Farman Salmanov, glorified Siberian workers, a myth that was to be further cultivated through the publication of numerous memoirs of labourers in the gas and oil industries.[147]

The Soviet leaders knew that their country's economy was not in the best of shape. Brezhnev, in letters to the party and the people, complained astonishingly openly about economic inefficiency, unmotivated workers, problems in various branches of industry, and the excessively slow development of the Western Siberian oil and gas sectors.[148] The Soviet Union needed to expand trade to increase its foreign exchange reserves. Soviet representatives were thus actively seeking closer cooperation with Western European companies in the energy sector, recognising the limitations of their previous efforts with American and Japanese firms. This commitment to strengthening ties was demonstrated by Brezhnev's second state visit to West Germany in May 1978.

The specific form of the Soviet–Western European energy partnership, however, remained undetermined. Before the construction of a direct natural gas connection between Western Siberia and Europe in the form of an export pipeline was considered, the idea of a triangular relationship with Iran was at the forefront of discussions. At the time, Iran was not only one of the world's major oil producers but also had vast and largely

145 A. A. Trofimuk, *O rabote sibirskogo otdeleniia AN SSSR po kooperatsii nauchnykh issledovanii v regione i ispol'sovaniiu ikh resultatov v narodnom khoziastve strany: Osnovnye napravleniia organisatsionnoe soprovozhdenie i effektivnost' rabot po program 'Sibir'*, Novosibirsk: IEOPP SO AN SSSR, 1988.

146 Nikolaj Bajbakov, *Sache des Lebens: Aufzeichnungen eines Erdölarbeiters*, Berlin: Dietz Verlag, 1985, p. 393.

147 For example, Iu. G. Erv'e, *Sibirskie gorizonty*, Sverdlovsk: Sredne-Ural'skoe knizhnoe izdatel'stvo, 1968; V. Bakhilov, *Doroga k nefte*, Sverdlovsk: Sredne-Ural'skoe knizhnoe izdatel'stvo, 1975.

148 'Liebe Genossen, besinnt euch!', *Der Spiegel*, 18, 1 May 1978, pp. 116–30, here pp. 124–26.

untapped natural gas reserves. In the 1970s, Europe therefore fully expected Iran to become one of its major gas suppliers, alongside the Soviet Union, the Netherlands, Algeria, and Libya. But these expectations were not to be fulfilled.

The Iranian Factor

Iran was an important power in the Middle East with hegemonic ambitions, and the Iranian leadership under Shah Reza Pahlavi maintained good relations with the West and the Soviet Union alike. For Washington, Iran was, along with Israel, its most important regional ally. Between 1970 and 1978, the United States supplied Iran with military technology and equipment worth around 20 billion US dollars. In addition, thousands of Western military advisers and specialists were active in Iran.[149] In the 1970s, Iran was one of the most important exporters of oil globally. Before the revolution in early 1979, Iranian oil accounted for around 7 per cent of the total volume traded on the world market.[150]

It was characteristic of the country's internal political structure that Iran produced its oil almost exclusively for export. Because of this export orientation, the Iranian oil industry existed largely detached from other industries. This also meant that oil was used by the Iranian regime to modernise the country only to a limited extent. The Shah's leadership in Iran, although not widely supported by the population, chose to allocate the revenue generated from the oil industry towards the military and armaments, rather than investing in the development of the predominantly Shiite nation. While a narrow class was able to enrich itself through oil exports, the majority of the population hardly felt the benefits of their country's wealth, and many lived in poverty. This laid the groundwork for the social unrest that would shake the country from 1978 onwards, paving the way for the Islamic revolution and the seizure of power by the Shiite cleric Ayatollah Khomeini in early 1979.[151]

The Soviet Union, which shared a border of more than 2,000 km with Iran, was interested in cooperating with its southern neighbour due to

[149] James A. Bill, *The Eagle and the Lion: The Tragedy of Iranian–American Relations*, New Haven, London: Yale University Press, 1988, pp. 200–204.

[150] Samantha Gross, '1979 and the World's Second Oil Shock', in Suzanne Maloney (ed.), *The Iranian Revolution at 40*, Washington, DC: Brookings Institution Press, 2020, pp. 115–20, here p. 115.

[151] For further reading, see Shaul Bakhash, *The Reign of the Ayatollahs: Iran and the Islamic Revolution*, London: I. B. Tauris, 1985; Darioush Bayandor, *The Shah, the Islamic Revolution and the United States*, Cham: Palgrave Macmillan, 2019.

both security and economic considerations. Like the United States, Moscow sent its engineers to Iran to support the country's industrial development.[152] In addition, with the Soviet Union increasingly facing a supply bottleneck regarding its production of raw materials from the late 1960s onwards, Moscow sought to intensify cooperation with the Iranian oil and natural gas sectors in particular. During this period, the Soviet Union was cooperating in the energy sector with various other countries rich in oil and natural gas (namely Afghanistan, Iraq, Syria, and Algeria), providing Soviet technology, goods, and loans in exchange for raw materials.[153] The Soviet Union also sent its oil and gas specialists to Angola, Egypt, Nigeria, India, and Yemen. The volume of foreign activities increased during this period to such an extent that in 1967 the Soviet Ministry of Oil Industry established Sarubezhneft, a separate organisational unit within the Ministry responsible for work abroad.[154]

Iran had long been an important factor in the international oil market, but it was only in the 1960s that the country started to develop its natural gas reserves and look for possible markets in which to sell its gas profitably. As early as 1966, the Soviet Union and Iran negotiated an agreement under which Iranian gas would be transported northwards to the Soviet Union via the Azerbaijani SSR through the construction of a new pipeline. This pipeline was completed in October 1970. Some of the Iranian gas was consumed in the Soviet Caucasus and the rest transported further into southern and central Russia. At that time, the Soviet Union was the only country importing Iranian gas. After the oil shock of 1973–74, the Europeans also began to take a greater interest in Iranian gas, which they recognised not only as a welcome alternative to Arab oil but an important supplement to petroleum. The only question was how to transport Iranian gas to Europe.[155]

Several approaches were considered. The first possibility was building a pipeline through Turkey towards Europe. The second option was liquefying Iranian gas and shipping it to Europe. However, it was the third option – triangle trade between Western Europe, the Soviet Union, and Iran – that won early favour. This variant was of interest to the Europeans because it meant that existing pipeline systems could be used rather than needing to build an entire transport infrastructure from scratch.[156] A so-called switch agreement was envisaged, according to

[152] For further reading, see Aryeh Y. Yodfat, *The Soviet Union and Revolutionary Iran*, London: Croom Helm, 1984.
[153] Guan-Fu, 'Soviet Aid to the Third World', p. 87.
[154] RBK TEK 360, 'My pomogaem: Kak sovetskie i rossiiskie neftianiki rabotali za granitsei', http://tek360.rbc.ru/articles/110/ (last accessed 24 October 2021).
[155] Högselius, *Red Gas*, p. 172. [156] Bleidick, *Die Ruhrgas*, p. 337.

which Iran was to supply gas on the order of 12 billion cubic metres to the Soviet Union, mostly for consumption in the Caucasus.[157] To this end, the National Iranian Gas Company was to build a second pipeline to the Soviet Union that would run along the existing pipeline route. The plan was to open this pipeline by 1980. For its part, the Soviet Union was to release the same volume from its own production to the Western European market, with the FRG serving as a hub for further sales of the gas to other countries. On the Western European side, a consortium of businesses led by the German energy giant Ruhrgas was involved. In addition to Ruhrgas, which had a 50 per cent stake in the consortium, companies from France, Italy, and Austria were also to participate.[158]

After long and complicated negotiations, in April 1975 Iran (National Iranian Gas Company), the Soviet Union (Soiuzgazeksport), and the FRG (Ruhrgas) signed a preliminary memorandum that formed the basis of the contract finally concluded in Tehran on 30 November 1975. Other contracting parties were France (Gaz de France) and Austria (ÖMV); the Italian company ENI had by this point dropped out of the project.[159] The contract negotiations continued thereafter, and there were repeated changes and adjustments to this complex undertaking.[160] At the time, the Soviet–Iranian–European triangular deal was seen as a perfect demonstration of the fact that cooperation between states with different political, economic, and social systems and ideological views was possible in principle.

This triangular agreement did not mean that the Soviet Union did not have to increase its own gas production and expand its energy transportation system. With this new deal, they were committing themselves to exporting to Western Europe. Although the Soviet Union acted as a transit country for Iranian gas, this was mainly for domestic consumption. The gas that was actually to be piped to Europe was, according to the agreement, to come from Soviet production and be transported westwards via Soviet pipelines. Under the terms of the trilateral agreement, the Soviet Gas Ministry committed itself to providing an

157 Data on the volume of supplies vary. The figure of 12 billion cubic metres was quoted by the Soviet Vice-Minister Osipov in a conversation with the Swiss Federal Councillor Willi Ritschard at a meeting at the Soviet Foreign Trade Ministry on 16 May 1975. The transcript of the conversation is contained in 'Notiz über die Unterredung zwischen Herrn Bundesrat Willi Ritschard und Herrn Vizeminister Ossipov im Sowjetischen Aussenhandelsministerium am 16.5.1975, 10.30 bis 11.30 h', in https://dodis.ch/38788 (last accessed on 18 July 2021).

158 Ibid.

159 Bleidick, *Die Ruhrgas*, pp. 340–41.

160 Högselius, *Red Gas*, pp. 172–79; Bleidick, *Die Ruhrgas*, pp. 334–49.

additional 11 billion cubic metres of gas annually for export to Western Europe, which represented a 47 per cent increase in gas exports.[161]

From the Soviet perspective, importing Iranian gas appeared to be a favourable solution, offering some relief from the challenges and uncertainties associated with the large-scale and complex development of Western Siberia. The agreement with Iran alleviated the Soviet Union's domestic energy situation by supplementing it with additional gas supplies. Mitigating the risks was important because there were still voices among Soviet planners and in the Politburo who expressed considerable doubt that future export revenues would really justify the large investments in increasing production in the northern part of Western Siberia and in developing the export infrastructure. There was simply no clarity on the Soviet side as to whether the whole endeavour would pay off in the end. Precise cost-benefit calculations were difficult to make in view of such high investments and major risks. Moreover, in the 1970s there were strong voices arguing that it would be more economical to use the raw materials where they were produced. In other words, Western Siberian gas should not be transported over thousands of kilometres and consumed somewhere far away; instead, the gas should first be used to build up a domestic regional (Siberian) industry, and only when this was done should further distribution be considered.

The Soviet–Iranian gas pipeline was nearing completion when Iran abruptly withdrew from the deal following the outbreak of the revolution in early 1979. The new Islamic leadership under Ayatollah Khomeini not only stopped gas exports to the Soviet Union but also curbed oil exports. This led to another steep increase in world market prices and triggered the second global 'oil shock'. What initially looked like a bitter setback for Western European–Soviet energy plans was to become the most important external impetus for the establishment of an energy corridor between Siberia and Europe. For in the wake of this crisis, Moscow and its Western European trading partners decided to replace Iranian gas with Siberian gas and transport it to Western Europe via the building of a new export pipeline. Although the idea of creating a direct gas link between the fields of northern Siberia and Western Europe had been discussed in West German–Soviet trade talks since 1977–78, it was not until the Iranian revolution that this idea was prioritised and negotiated at the highest political level.[162]

[161] Högselius, *Red Gas*, p. 177.

[162] *Akten zur Auswärtigen Politik der Bundesrepublik Deutschland (1981)*, edited by the Institut für Zeitgeschichte, Munich: Oldenbourg, 2012, pp. 74–75, here n. 10.

Given that European–Iranian–Soviet triangle trade ultimately failed just as the American–Soviet gas partnership and the cooperation efforts between the Soviet Union and Japan had, this project barely found its way into the history books.[163] Yet a history of Soviet–Western European energy relations would be incomplete if it did not discuss the Iranian factor, as without it the idea of the first direct gas export pipeline between Western Siberia and Western Europe would likely not have been seriously considered at the time.

'The Largest Pipeline in the World' and US Sanctions

Compared to the upheavals that Western Europe experienced in 1973–74 with suppliers from the Arab world and in 1978–79 with Iran, Soviet energy deliveries were considered reliable and calculable. This was yet another reason why countries such as West Germany were interested in expanding energy relations. While the FRG was able to compensate for the shortfalls in oil supplies caused by the Iranian revolution by increasing imports from Libya, then ruled by Muammar al-Gaddafi,[164] the Soviet Union was to fill the gap in gas imports. Thus, at the talks between the leaders of the FRG and the Soviet Union, which took place in Moscow in July 1980, energy figured high on the agenda. Brezhnev and Kosygin picked up where they had left off in the discussions with the Americans in the early 1970s, except that this time they were negotiating a natural gas connection to Western Europe, not to the United States. Kosygin indicated that supplies would last for at least thirty-five years. The aim was thus a long-term partnership and not a 'stimulus pipeline', as Brezhnev and Kosygin made clear in talks with German Chancellor Helmut Schmidt:

> (BREZHNEV:) … The wishes of many companies and banks from the FRG are aimed at realising additional large deliveries of gas from the [Soviet Union]. The reality is this: We have large reserves of natural gas at our disposal, especially in Western Siberia, and we would be ready to increase supplies to the Federal Republic of Germany and other Western countries. For this purpose, a gas pipeline would have to be built from the northern areas of Tyumen to the western border of the Soviet Union. If we build such a pipeline, it will have to be a large one. 40 billion m^3 of natural gas a year are

[163] The history of the Iranian–Soviet–Western European triangular deal was first described in detail by Per Högselius: Högselius, *Red Gas*, especially pp. 172–77.

[164] Frank Bösch, 'Wie Europa von russischer Energie abhängig wurde', Bundeszentrale für politische Bildung, 25 November 2022, www.bpb.de/themen/wirtschaft/europa-wirtschaft/515221/wie-europa-von-russischer-energie-abhaengig-wurde/#footnote-reference-2 (last accessed 23 January 2023).

expected to flow through it, and we have included the project in our plans for the coming years. If there is interest, we want to agree on cooperation in its implementation.

(KOSYGIN:) … The natural gas pipeline presents us with major technical and geological problems. As for the reserves of natural gas, they are abundant. We are not building a stimulus pipeline. It should be in operation for 30 to 35 years. That's how long the supply will last. It will be the largest pipeline in the world.[165]

The pipeline project, which would ultimately be financed with loans from West Germany, France, Italy, and Great Britain, and the details of which were still being negotiated as late as 1983, took the familiar form of a 'gas-for-pipes' agreement. In return for Soviet natural resources, Western companies supplied large-diameter (1,450 mm) pipes, as well as compressor stations and other technical equipment. The import of steel pipes of high quality was important because despite repeated directives from the party leadership, the Soviet Union's own factories were still failing to produce steel in the quality and quantity necessary for the construction of large-diameter pipes.[166] West Germany was of particular importance, as Mannesmann was one of the few companies capable of producing high-quality large-diameter pipes. These pipes could not only withstand the extreme cold of Siberia but also withstand higher pressures (up to 125 atmospheres) than those produced in Soviet factories. This difference meant that a Mannesmann pipe could carry up to a third more gas through an existing pipeline of the same diameter.[167] The Soviet Union did, however, provide tens of thousands of workers to construct the routes, manufacture large amounts of additional pipelines in its factories, and supply some of the turbines and compressor stations.[168] Ultimately, the pipeline was to carry Western Siberian gas from Urengoi some 4,450 km to the town of Uzhgorod on the western border of the Ukrainian SSR and then on through Czechoslovakia and Austria to West Germany, France, and Italy.

The Soviet Union had previously undertaken similar large international pipeline projects with Western participation. The 2,750 km

[165] Quotations from the German–Soviet government talks in Moscow on 1 July 1980 are contained in *Akten zur Auswärtigen Politik der Bundesrepublik Deutschland (1980)*, pp. 1035–50, here pp. 1045, 1047.

[166] RGANI [Hoover Archive], f. 89, p. 26, d. 20, ll. 1–5.

[167] Charles William Carter, 'The Evolution of US Policy toward West German–Soviet Trade Relations 1969–89', *The International History Review* 34, 2 (2012), pp. 221–44, here pp. 230, 238.

[168] Steve Mufson, 'Anatomy of Continuing Pipeline Controversy: U.S. Is in Sharp Fight with European Allies', *Wall Street Journal*, 31 August 1982, p. 29.

Soiuz gas pipeline, which had been built as a CMEA project in cooperation between the Soviet Union, Bulgaria, the GDR, Poland, Czechoslovakia, and Hungary in 1975–78, had also benefitted from Western European loans.[169] However, the Siberian project negotiated at the beginning of the 1980s was a multi-billion-dollar undertaking that would become the largest East–West trade agreement made during the Cold War and was treated at the time as the 'deal of the century'.[170] Interest on the part of Western Europe was enormous: As Soviet Deputy Gas Minister Stepan Dereev explained to a Swiss delegation keen on obtaining gas supplies at a meeting in Moscow in September 1981, 'the USSR plans to sell a maximum of 40 billion m^3 per year through the [new] Urengoi pipeline, while there were requests from Western Europe for up to 70 billion m^3 per year'.[171] In fact, not all interested parties succeeded in securing Soviet gas. The Swiss, who had been negotiating in vain for the purchase of Soviet gas since 1968,[172] never managed to secure a direct deal with Soiuzgazeksport, the Soviet company in charge of foreign gas trade, but were to import this commodity for the first time in October 1988 through a contractual agreement between Swissgas and Ruhrgas.[173]

Unlike the North Star project, the Soviet Union did not initially emphasise this venture as an element of world peace. But the project unexpectedly became politically explosive when opposition to it arose within the US government. In talks with the German government, the

[169] On the construction of the Soiuz pipeline, see Flade, *Energy Infrastructures in the Eastern Bloc*, pp. 106–34.

[170] Ksenia Demidova, 'The Deal of the Century: The Reagan Administration and the Soviet Pipeline', in Kiran Klaus Patel and Kenneth Weisbrode (eds.), *European Integration and the Atlantic Community in the 1980s*, Cambridge: Cambridge University Press, 2013, pp. 59–82.

[171] The minutes of the conversation of 23 September 1981 are contained in the Swiss Federal Archives, Schweizerisches Bundesarchiv (BAR), E7115(A), 1991/189, Bd. 123, DSCN 3163/3164: 24.9.81, 'Aktennotiz, Besuch beim Gasministerium der UdSSR', compiled by E. Thurnheer and J. M. Judin (Swiss Embassy in Moscow), Moscow, 24 September 1981, p. 1.

[172] BAR, E7110(-), 1986/24, Bd. 107, DSCN 2025–2035: 25.6.75, 'Aktennotiz über die Besprechungen zum Thema Erdgasbeschaffung aus der Sowjetunion anlässlich der 3. Session der Gemischten sowjetisch-schweizerischen Kommission für wirtschaftlich-technische, wirtschaftliche und industrielle Zusammenarbeit vom 3.-5.6.1975 in Moskau', compiled by J.-P. Lauper (Swissgas), Zurich, 25 June 1975, p. 1.

[173] The contract stipulated that Soiuzgazeksport delivered the quantities of natural gas destined for Switzerland (some 360 million m^3 per year) to Waidhaus on the Czechoslovak–West German border. There the gas was taken over by Ruhrgas. Ruhrgas, as a contractual partner of Swissgas, delivered these quantities further on to Switzerland: BAR, E7115(A), 1999/338, Bd. 107 DSCN3820/3821/3822/3823: 9.5.89, 'Besuch von Herrn Staatssekretär Blankart in Moskau, 5.-8. Juni 1989; Handel Schweiz/UdSSR', Berne, 9 May 1989, p. 3.

United States had never made it a secret that they were worried about West Germany's growing dependence on Soviet energy. In reference to Finland's accommodating approach in its relations vis-à-vis Moscow after the end of the Second World War, Washington even spoke of the danger of the FRG's 'Finlandisation' should the country obtain more oil and gas from the Soviet Union. The United States thus repeatedly tried to convince the government in Bonn to turn away from this project by offering West Germany more American coal as a substitute for Soviet natural gas.[174]

The situation escalated at the end of 1981, when US President Ronald Reagan, in reaction to the imposition of martial law in Poland, ordered a complete embargo on the supply of steel pipes and pipeline technology to the Soviet Union. In fact, the embargo list covered all material supplies the gas pipeline system needed for construction.[175] In June 1982, Washington expanded the embargo by imposing sanctions on European companies that held US licenses. Almost twenty years after the NATO pipeline embargo of 1962, the Americans once again sought to prevent the Soviet–European energy rapprochement by tightening the sanctions' regime against the Soviet Union. This time, however, the Western European allies, including Japan, did not go along with the US decision, all the more so because the embargo not only threatened to restrict the general East–West trade in technical goods but also posed the problem of the extraterritorial application of law by asking non-American companies to cancel existing contracts with the Soviet Union.[176] The British government was particularly outraged by the Americans' behaviour and issued a directive forbidding its companies to comply with the sanctions imposed by Washington. Earlier, the governments of Italy, France, and the FRG had announced their opposition to the US demands and called on their companies to continue their cooperation with the Soviet Union.[177]

The rebellion of the Western Europeans testified to their growing self-confidence vis-à-vis American policy guidelines. Washington's action was also unprecedented in that Western European companies were not only to be forced to break already signed agreements with the Soviet Union, but the Americans presumed to interfere with the national sovereignty of their allies through the extraterritorial application of US

[174] Krempin, *Die sibirische Wucht*, pp. 392–93. [175] Bleidick, *Die Ruhrgas*, p. 319.

[176] Cf. Tyler Esno, 'Reagan's Economic War on the Soviet Union', *Diplomatic History*, 42, 2 (2018), pp. 281–304; Christian Th. Müller, 'Der Erdgas-Röhren-Konflikt 1981/82', in Greiner, Müller, and Weber (eds.), *Ökonomie im Kalten Krieg*, pp. 501–20.

[177] Illing, *Energiepolitik in Deutschland*, p. 151; Rita Dallas, 'Britain Orders Firms to Defy Pipeline Ban', *The Washington Post*, 3 August 1982, p. A6.

law.[178] The fact that West Germany did not follow suit this time was of particular importance and, apart from the political signal it sent, also had tangible economic reasons. For the Mannesmann company alone, the sale of large-diameter pipes to the Soviet Union accounted for around 60 per cent of total production at the time securing some 2,500 jobs. The new major contract for the construction of the pipeline from Siberia to Western Europe would have created at least 1,000 additional jobs. For other Western European companies involved in the project, the billion-dollar deal also meant thousands of jobs and enormous turnover. At a time when Western European economies were in recession and facing high unemployment rates, abandoning the Siberian pipeline deal was simply not feasible domestically.[179]

Even within the American administration, there was no unanimity on the embargo issue. Secretary of State Alexander Haig, for example, was expressly opposed to an overly restrictive approach because he recognised that the Western Europeans would not support such a move. US Secretary of Defense Caspar Weinberger, on the other hand, represented the faction within the American administration that advocated a hard line and ultimately prevailed.[180] The main concern of the hawks around Weinberger was that the Soviet Union would finance its military with hard currency earned from a gas deal. Moreover, the pipeline was a thorn in the Reagan administration's side because, in the American reading, the expansion of economic relations increased the scope for Soviet political influence in the affairs of Western Europe. Although Washington had already tightened its embargo policy after the Soviet invasion of Afghanistan, the immediate cause for the expansion of sanctions under Reagan were events in Poland in December 1981: when the Polish communist regime declared martial law in response to the mass protests led by the independent trade union 'Solidarity' (Solidarność), Washington suspected the long hand of the Kremlin and sought to punish the Soviet Union. Moreover, the imposition of sanctions was intended to send a warning signal to Moscow about a possible military intervention.[181]

178 Antony Blinken, *Ally versus Ally: America, Europe and the Siberian Pipeline Crisis*, New York: Praeger, 1987, pp. 112–15.

179 Ibid, pp. 32–33.

180 See, for example, the transcript of the National Security Council meeting on 6 July 1981, at which export controls on the oil and gas business with the Soviet Union were discussed: 'National Security Council Meeting', 6 July 1981, The Cabinet Room, Washington, DC, www.thereaganfiles.com/19810706-nsc-16.pdf (last accessed 18 July 2021).

181 David S. Painter, 'From Linkage to Economic Warfare: Energy, Soviet–American Relations, and the End of the Cold War', in Perović (ed.), *Cold War Energy*, pp. 283–318, here pp. 290–97.

Since numerous Western European companies, supported by their governments, continued to cooperate with the Soviet Union despite American threats and the Soviets also did everything in their power to push ahead with the construction of the pipeline, the sanctions created considerable uncertainty but were ultimately ineffective.[182] Western Europeans were particularly angered by the American action because Washington, for domestic political reasons, refused to extend the embargo to cover grain, which the Soviet Union was buying in large quantities from American farmers at the time. This further undermined the Americans' credibility in the eyes of the Europeans. When it became clear to the Reagan administration that its sanctions would not only fail to prevent the construction of the pipeline, but that this decision would also create a rift between Western Europe and the United States, Washington reversed its decision in November 1982 and lifted the embargo.[183]

The transatlantic row was about much more than economic interests. It expressed two different attitudes on the question of how to deal with the Soviet Union in the Cold War. Unlike in the past, the aim of US sanctions policy was to bring the Soviet Union, which Reagan considered nothing less than an 'evil empire', to its knees. Not balancing or containment but war by other means was the underlying objective of these coercive economic measures. Reagan thus deviated from a policy that until then had been based on the maxim that peace among the superpowers was possible as long as neither side challenged the vital interests of the other. Against this background, Reagan's actions met with criticism not only in American business circles but also in renowned US media such as the *New York Times* or the *Washington Post*.[184] For example, in a *New York Times* article of 12 September 1982 entitled 'The Case against Sanctions', George W. Ball, Undersecretary of State in the Kennedy administration and later US ambassador to the United Nations, sharply criticised what he saw as a highly dangerous policy on the part of the US government.[185]

The US–Western European pipeline row provided an opportunity for Soviet propaganda to condemn Washington's actions in the strongest possible terms. The party newspaper *Pravda* informed its readers with relish about the American–Western European dispute speaking of the

[182] Bleidick, *Die Ruhrgas*, p. 319. [183] For further reading, see Blinken, *Ally versus Ally*.

[184] A compilation of American public reactions is provided in John P. Hardt, *Soviet Pipeline*, Congressional Research Service, Washington, DC: The Library of Congress [1982].

[185] George W. Ball, 'The Case against Sanctions', *New York Times Magazine*, 12 September 1982, p. 63 (section 6).

'boomerang' of American sanctions for transatlantic relations and the fact that states like France, the FRG, Italy, and even Japan would resist the 'diktat' from Washington.[186] *Pravda* cartoonists resorted to the familiar hate imagery from the darkest days of the Cold War, depicting the United States as a grim 'Uncle Sam' who, armed with a morning star and scissors, was trying in vain to cut a steel pipe.[187] The gas pipeline became a matter of prestige of the first order and henceforth was painted by Soviet propaganda as an international project that would withstand American aggression. 'Urengoi Gas for the Whole World!' was the pathos-laden title of an article in *Pravda* on 24 September 1982 that reported on the status of the pipeline project.[188] Curiously, the word 'world' in Russian is *mir*, which has a double meaning and also translates as 'peace'. In this way, the Soviet Union tried to contrast the American embargo and Washington's alleged warmongering with its pipeline as a civilian economic and peace project.

On 11 September 1983, *Pravda* reported on its front page that the pipeline had been completed.[189] On 13 January 1984, gas from the Urengoi field reached Western Europe for the first time.[190] With this pipeline, the Soviet Union doubled its gas export volume and finally rose to become an energy superpower of international importance and Europe's preeminent supplier of raw materials. The so called Urengoi-Pomary-Uzhgorod gas export pipeline – an important addition to the existing gas transportation system through Ukraine – was not the first pipeline to carry Soviet gas to Western Europe. It was, however, the first one designed to exclusively serve the capitalist market of Western Europe, since the earlier export pipelines had all been extensions of Eastern European pipelines already in place. Moreover, the Urengoi gas export pipeline was only one of six new pipeline strings with a total length of 20,000 km, all of which had been built in the first half of the 1980s and connected Western Siberia with the rest of the Soviet Union.[191] Thus did the Soviet Union achieve the 'gasification' of the country announced in February 1981 at the 26th Party Congress, when

186 'Bumerang sanktsii', *Pravda*, 187, 6 July 1982, p. 5; 'Otvergaiut diktat SShA', *Pravda*, 203, 22 July 1982, p. 5.
187 *Pravda*, 190, 9 July 1982, p. 5.
188 'Gaz Urengoia – miru!', *Pravda*, 267, 24 September 1982, p. 4. On this also see Högselius, *Red Gas*, p. 197; Thane Gustafson, *The Soviet Gas Campaign: Politics and Policy in Soviet Decisionmaking*, Santa Monica, CA: RAND Corporation, 1983, p. 86.
189 'S vydaiushchimsia dostizheniem!', *Pravda*, 254, 11 September 1983, p. 1.
190 'Zhivye golosa istorii: God 1984-i, Gazprom komplektatsiia', *Press-tsentr, novosti*, 14 January 2019, https://komplektatsiya.gazprom.ru/press/news/2019/01/319/ (last accessed 18 August 2021).
191 Högselius, *Red Gas*, p. 197.

natural gas was officially declared the country's most important raw material.[192] In the first half of the 1980s, the total share of gas in the Soviet Union's energy production rose from 28.4 to 35.5 per cent; this was to increase further in subsequent years.[193] The consequences of the gasification that began in the late Soviet period were enduring: gas was to remain an important energy source in many countries that emerged from the break-up of the Soviet Union. In the case of Russia, it accounted for 54 per cent of the national energy mix in 2020.[194]

Soviet industry was in deep crisis at the beginning of the 1980s. But the development of the natural gas industry in northern Tyumen, which was realised thanks to large-scale international cooperation projects with Western companies, was a success story – as even the American press had to acknowledge at the time.[195] In fact, the Soviet leadership seemed to see in the development of the Western Siberian raw materials the Soviet Union's salvation from its pressing economic problems. Not only was sufficient energy once again available to the Soviet Union to meet its own needs for the foreseeable future, but by expanding its raw materials base, Moscow was also able to free up more gas – and above all additional oil – for export to Western Europe, enabling it to purchase larger quantities of Western consumer goods, technology, and grain.[196] In addition, the Soviet Union increasingly relied on the civilian use of nuclear energy, which further increased the available energy sources and freed up more oil and gas for export. In 1981, 6.5 per cent and by 1990 as much as 12 per cent of all electricity was produced by nuclear energy, while hydropower was responsible for about 14 per cent of Soviet electricity generation in the 1980s.[197]

Due to increased production and an expansion of its transborder pipeline network, Soviet net energy exports rose by 270 per cent between 1970 and 1988.[198] With Soviet oil and gas now accounting for 20 to 30 per cent of total consumption, the dependence of individual larger

192 Krempin, *Die sibirische Wucht*, p. 391.
193 *Narodnoe khoziaistvo SSSR v 1985 g.: Statisticheskii ezhegodnik*, Moscow: Finansy i statistika, 1986, p. 157.
194 Enerdata, 'Russia Energy Information', www.enerdata.net/estore/energy-market/russia/ (last accessed 7 August 2021).
195 Mufson, 'Anatomy of Continuing Pipeline Controversy'.
196 Thanks to the development of gas in Western Siberia, the export share of oil produced in the Soviet Union rose from 25.3 per cent in 1964 to 35.5 per cent in 1989. See the relevant compilation in Sergei Ermolaev, 'Formirovanie i razvitie neftegazovoi zavisimosti Sovetskogo Soiuza', Working Paper, Moscow: Carnegie Moscow Center, 2017, p. 43.
197 B. A. Semenov, 'Nuclear Power in the Soviet Union', *IAEA Bulletin*, 25, 2 (1983), pp. 47–59, here p. 47; Gestwa, *Die Stalinschen Grossbauten des Kommunismus*, p. 74.
198 Gustafson, *Crisis Amid Plenty*, p. 55.

Western European economies on the Soviet Union grew significantly, but so did the Soviet Union's dependence on Europe. According to US energy historian Thane Gustafson, in the early 1980s around 80 per cent of Soviet hard currency earnings came from oil and gas exports (with crude oil and oil products accounting for the bulk of these earnings).[199] The global rise in the price of oil brought about a lasting change to the Soviet export structure; according to official Soviet statistics, at the end of the 1960s 'fuels and electrical energy' accounted for only about 15 per cent of total foreign trade turnover, but this share rose year by year to exceed 50 per cent in the early 1980s.[200]

The Soviet Union had finally become dependent on oil and gas. Just how problematic this would turn out to be became clear in the mid-1980s, when world oil prices collapsed accelerating the downturn of the Soviet economy. Indeed, the Soviet experience was to show how close curse and blessing can lie in the case of resource abundance.

[199] Ibid., p. 56.

[200] Gosudarstvennyi komitet SSSR po statistike, *Narodnoe khoziastvo SSSR za 70 let: Iubileinyi statisticheskii ezhegondik*, Moscow: Finansy i statistika, 1987, see the chapter 'Vneshniaia torgovlia', http://istmat.info/node/9321 (last accessed 25 May 2021).

5 Crisis, Collapse, and Resurgence

Never in its history was the Soviet Union more integrated into world trade and more dependent on raw material exports than in the first half of the 1980s. With oil as the country's main export commodity, the collapse of world oil prices in the mid-1980s was thus to place an additional heavy burden on the Soviet economy. The Soviet Union did not disintegrate because oil prices were low. However, the significant decline in oil prices during that time greatly intensified the existing systemic economic crisis that the country had been grappling with for a considerable period. The Soviet leadership under General Secretary Mikhail Gorbachev, in office since March 1985, tried to overcome economic problems through comprehensive reforms. Gorbachev's 'perestroika' (restructuring) was accompanied by the policy of 'glasnost' (transparency). This meant that criticism of the system could now be voiced publicly. With this measure, Gorbachev sought to win society over for his reforms and to strengthen his position vis-à-vis conservative circles in the state and the party apparatus. But his policies also created scope for political forces to turn against him, against the party, against communist ideology, and thus against everything that held the country together. His greatest adversary was the radical reformer Boris Yeltsin, who was elected Russia's first president in June 1991 and called for greater autonomy for Russia from the Soviet Union.

In December 1991, the Soviet Union formally ceased to exist. The break-up into fifteen independent states meant not only the dissolution of the political space but also an unravelling of the close economic ties that had previously existed among the Soviet republics. The transformation from a planned to a market economy was marked by profound economic and social upheavals in Russia and some of the other former Soviet republics. In Russia, the oil sector was severely affected, being largely privatised and passing into the hands of new super-rich, the so-called oligarchs. The 1990s in Russia witnessed the selling-out of the state, which had hardly any funds left to guarantee such essential services as the payment of pensions, public security, or the maintenance of infrastructure. The Chechen secessionist movement, along with pressure for autonomy in other regions of the country, even called Russia's territorial unity into question.

Quite unexpectedly for many observers at the time, Yeltsin's successor, the then largely unknown Vladimir Putin, succeeded in stabilising the political situation and restoring the state's control over central sectors of the economy in only a short time. The Russian army's renewed invasion of Chechnia put an end to that republic's drive for independence. The Kremlin set about either eliminating notable oligarchs altogether or making them subservient to the state. The most prominent victim of this policy was Mikhail Khodorkovskii, who had turned the oil company Yukos into one of Russia's most successful international enterprises. The Russian government tightened the laws on the participation of international companies in the exploitation of strategically important oil and gas fields, even driving out some of the foreign companies that had invested heavily in the Russian energy sector. When the price of oil rose sharply in the early 2000s, profits from exports picked up. Thus, the Russian state again had sufficient tax revenues to strengthen state institutions, increase spending for the armed forces and the security apparatus, and provide essential public services.

This chapter spans a wide arc: it traces developments in the energy sector starting with the systemic crisis under Gorbachev, through Russia's difficult beginnings after the collapse of the Soviet Union, to the consolidation and re-emergence of Russia as a great power under Putin. In this turbulent phase of Russian history, it becomes clear once again how closely the fate of the country was interwoven with the situation in the energy sector.

Oil Price Collapse and System Failure

In 1986, the price of oil collapsed by about two-thirds.[1] The world market was oversaturated, in large part because Saudi Arabia had ramped up production and flooded the market with oil. According to the so-called Reagan Victory School, which attributes the collapse of the Soviet Union to Reagan's policies, the Saudi government had entered into a secret agreement with Washington to bring down the oil price by increasing the volume of oil on the market and thus harm the Soviet

[1] Gail E. Tverberg, 'Oil Prices And The Fall Of The Soviet Union', *OilPrice.com*, 11 August 2011, https://oilprice.com/Energy/Oil-Prices/Oil-Prices-And-The-Fall-Of-The-Soviet-Union.html (last accessed 18 July 2021).

Union economically.[2] Such American–Saudi collusion must be doubted, however, as no historical documents have yet surfaced to confirm it.[3] In any case, it was not only the increase in Saudi production that led to the price collapse but also the fact that more suppliers from the non-OPEC region were putting oil on the international market. These included Norway, which had begun oil and gas production in the early 1980s.[4]

According to Russian economist Yegor Gaidar, who became prime minister under Yeltsin in 1992 and was one of the most important reformers in the Russian government at the time, the Soviet state was losing around 20 billion US dollars in revenue annually in the second half of the 1980s as a result of the collapse in the price of oil.[5] Discussions within the inner circle of the Politburo show that the country's party leadership recognised this development as a threat to economic stability. According to the diaries of Anatolii Cherniaev, Gorbachev's foreign policy advisor, the Soviet party leader addressed his comrades in dramatic terms at a Politburo meeting on 8 October 1987 regarding the collapse in oil prices:

> All members of the Central Committee, each and every one, are responsible not only for their seat but also for their country. You must know that last year we lost 12 billion roubles' [about 17.9 billion U.S. dollars at contemporary exchange rates][6] worth of hard currency because of oil. This year another six billion and from vodka another nine billion [roubles]. We must all bear this in mind, all members of the Central Committee. When the situation becomes precarious.[7]

When Gorbachev spoke of vodka, he problematised the loss of tax revenue from the sale of alcohol. To limit the widespread and health-damaging consumption of alcohol in the Soviet Union, the freshly minted General Secretary issued a decree in May 1985, that is, shortly after taking office, that provided for an increase in the prices of alcoholic

[2] The most prominent representative of this view is the conservative American journalist Peter Schweizer, see *Victory: The Reagan Administration's Secret Strategy that Hastened the Collapse of the Soviet Union*, New York: Atlantic Monthly Press, 1994; Peter Schweizer, *Reagan's War: The Epic Story of His Forty-Year Struggle and Final Triumph Over Communism*, New York: Doubleday, 2002, here pp. 238–41.

[3] For a critical discussion of Schweizer's theses, see Painter, 'From Linkage to Economic Warfare', pp. 284–85, 302–304.

[4] Bukold, *Öl im 21. Jahrhundert*, p. 43; Marshall, *Petrostate*, p. 51.

[5] Gaidar, *The Soviet Collapse*, pp. 4–5; Gaidar, *Collapse of Empire*, p. 135.

[6] The exchange rate at the time was 1 ruble = 1.4925 US dollars; see https://en.wikipedia.org/wiki/Soviet_ruble#Historical_official_exchange_rates (last accesse 6 November 2021).

[7] *Dnevniki A. S. Cherniaeva: Sovetskaia politika 1972–1991 gg. – vzgliad iznutri; 1987 god*, [The National Security Archive, Washington, DC], p. 52; https://nsarchive.gwu.edu/rus/text_files/Chernyaev/1987.pdf (last accessed 18 July 2021).

beverages and severely restricted sales overall. This led to a significant reduction in the legal sale and consumption of alcohol. Even though the decree resulted in a decline in alcohol-related acute deaths and an increase in life expectancy, especially among men, the measure was extremely unpopular with the Soviet population. Moreover, it meant a loss of important tax revenues for the state. By October 1988, the Soviet leadership found itself forced to cancel the anti-alcohol campaign. The state's failed fight against alcohol and for the health of its citizens was emblematic of the crisis in which Soviet state and society found themselves in the second half of the 1980s.[8]

The fact that the collapse in oil prices caused so much concern among the country's political leaders is an indication that the Soviet Union was much more closely integrated into the world economy at that time than official Soviet statistics would suggest. According to Soviet data, exports to and imports from the West accounted for about 4 per cent of gross domestic product in the late Soviet period, if the trade figures were converted at the official exchange rate.[9] Western research, which has often relied on these figures, has thus for a long time tended to largely neglect the importance of the world market to the Soviet economy.[10] However, trade may have been far more significant: if the value of foreign goods is calculated using domestic prices for foreign trade items rather than the foreign prices converted to roubles based on the official rouble exchange rate used by Soviet trade statistics, then calculations such as those by economists Vladimir G. Treml and Barry L. Kostinsky show that the share of foreign trade to national income may have been far higher. According to Treml and Kostinsky, who conducted their research already in the early 1980s, international trade (exports and imports combined) accounted for about 25 per cent of gross domestic product in 1978, a share that would only increase in subsequent years.[11] Depending on the method of calculation, other studies arrive at different

[8] Jay Bhattacharya, Christina Gathmann, and Grant Miller, 'The Gorbachev Anti-Alcohol Campaign and Russia's Mortality Crisis', *American Economic Journal: Applied Economics*, 5, 2 (2013), pp. 232–60.

[9] Hanson, *The Rise and Fall of the Soviet Economy*, p. 159.

[10] Carsten Goehrke, for example, believes that the world market played 'no central role' for the Soviet economy: Goehrke, *Russland*, p. 138.

[11] Vladimir G. Treml and Barry L. Kostinsky, *Domestic Value of Soviet Foreign Trade: Exports and Imports in the 1972 Input-Output Table*, Foreign Economic Report 20, Washington, DC: United States Department of Commerce, Bureau of the Census, 1982, p. 14; also Vladimir G. Treml, 'Soviet Dependence on Foreign Trade', Paper presented at Colloquium on 'External Economic Relations of CMEA Countries: Their Significance and Impact in a Global Perspective', Brussels, NATO, Economics Directorate, 6–8 April 1983, p. 35.

figures,[12] but a consensus seems to have emerged in recent research that the Soviet Union was far more involved in and dependent on the world market than originally assumed. According to US economic historian Oscar Sanchez-Sibony, the Soviet economy in the late 1970s and early 1980s was about as integrated into world trade as the Japanese one; the country was therefore equally vulnerable to oil price fluctuations and global economic crises.[13]

With an export structure that was dominated by oil, petroleum products, natural gas, and other fuels and raw materials, it was hardly surprising that the country should experience the oil price collapse in the mid-1980s in a tangible way. Nevertheless, it would be wrong to try to establish a causal link between low oil prices and the collapse of the Soviet Union. Gaidar aptly describes this connection in his book *Collapse of an Empire* when he explains that 'developments in the oil market' were not the reason but the 'pretext' for the collapse of the Soviet Union.[14] In other words, the lower returns from oil did not trigger the collapse of the Soviet Union but revealed flaws in an economic system that was increasingly subsidised by export revenues and was already in profound crisis. The unexpected windfall generated by Siberian oil in the 1970s and early 1980s had allowed the Soviet leaders to postpone and then bury economic reforms; but now, with a steep decline in prices, the 'law of diminishing returns' applied even to a socialist state.[15] The low oil prices did not directly cause the Soviet Union's disintegration; rather, low oil prices are to be seen as a stimulus for Gorbachev's reform efforts; also, it should be borne in mind that shortly before the Soviet Union fell apart, the country was again generating significantly more foreign exchange revenues in the Western dollar zone due to the rise in world market prices for oil from 1989–90.[16]

Already Khrushchev had been aware that the model of the planned economy, as conceived in the 1920s, was no longer able to meet the increasingly complex requirements of the Soviet national economy. He identified the powerful centralised institutions such as the Gosplan and the cumbersome ministries as bureaucratic 'monsters' that needed to be tamed.[17] The basic idea of his reforms was to get Soviet society

[12] Cf. Hanson, *The Rise and Fall of the Soviet Economy*, p. 159.
[13] Sanchez-Sibony, *Red Globalization*, especially pp. 4–6.
[14] Gaidar, *Collapse of an Empire*, p. 249. [15] Etkind, *Nature's Evil*, p. 262.
[16] In 1989, the Soviet Union is said to have earned 14.66 billion US dollars from oil sales in the Western 'dollar zone', only about 7 per cent less than in 1985: Slavkina, *Neftegazovyi faktor*, p. 322.
[17] Nekrasov, 'Decision-Making in the Soviet Energy Sector in Post-Stalinist Times', pp. 173, 181.

more involved in local planning and administrative processes through the creation of over 100 regional 'economic councils' (Sovnarkhozy). This was primarily intended to improve the flow of information between factories and the bureaucracy, ultimately raising the country's national economic output.[18] However, Khrushchev's attempts to soften the planning structure with its powerful ministries by territorialising the administrative structure were immediately reversed after he was deposed.[19]

Although the Soviet Union under Brezhnev returned to the former organisational model, even the new General Secretary, at least at the beginning of his term, recognised overcoming bureaucratic hurdles and the constant distribution struggles as among the greatest challenges to the country's economic development. Brezhnev once complained during a public appearance before representatives of local state and party committees and enterprises in 1965 that any five-year plan would have to specify where investments should be concentrated in order to implement big ideas: 'If we give 20 kopecks to everyone, no idea can be realised.'[20] At the same time, Prime Minister Kosygin initiated reform measures aimed at increasing the efficiency and productivity of enterprises by, among other things, granting them larger autonomy in internal organisational matters of their companies and in setting prices and wages for employees. Between 1965 and 1970, the Soviet economy saw higher growth figures than in the previous period, but because economic growth weakened again from the beginning of the 1970s, Kosygin's reforms came under criticism, were revised, and partly reversed.[21]

Drawing on past experience, Gorbachev and his team of reformers recognised that economic growth could not be achieved by 'perfecting' the centrally planned economy, as Kosygin had attempted in 1965. They understood the need for fundamental change, involving not only decentralisation but also the introduction of elements of a market economy. Gorbachev's policy of opening to the West was also to be seen in this context. The creation of favourable international conditions was a prerequisite for pushing ahead with domestic reforms and diverting resources from the military-industrial sector to civilian economic

[18] Frey, *Arktischer Heizraum*, p. 226.
[19] Cf. on Khrushchev's 'Sovnarkhozy Reforms', see Nataliya Kibita, *Soviet Economic Management under Khrushchev: The Sovnarkhoz Reform*, London, New York: Routdledge, 2013.
[20] *General'nyi sekretar' L. I. Brezhnev 1964–1982*, p. 43.
[21] Aappo Kähönen, 'Optimal Planning, Optimal Economy, Optimal Life? The Kosygin Reforms, 1965–72', in Miklóssy and Ilic (eds.), *Competition in Socialist Society*, pp. 23–40; for an overview of Soviet GDP growth figures for 1950–1990, see Hanson, *The Rise and Fall of the Soviet Economy*, p. 249.

projects. The disarmament negotiations with Washington, the reduction of military expenditures, the cutback of billions in aid to countries of the 'Third World', and the withdrawal of the Soviet army from Afghanistan, which was completed in 1989, were components of these efforts. Since Gorbachev's reforms met with resistance in the ranks of conservative party forces and the powerful military apparatus, he sought to mobilise society behind these comprehensive transformation efforts. Under the slogan of glasnost, a concept he first presented in a keynote speech at the 27th Party Congress on 25 February 1986, reforms were to be discussed more openly in society. This eventually led to a relaxation of the Soviet government's strict controls on freedom of speech and the press.[22]

In the economic sphere, Gorbachev introduced increasingly radical measures to reform the system. The 'Law on Cooperatives', adopted in 1988, legalised private enterprises for the first time since the early 1920s and granted them the right to operate as independent market units in the areas of services, production, and foreign trade. In effect, this softened the state's monopoly on foreign trade for the first time in almost seventy years. However, Gorbachev did not see his reforms as a departure from Marxism-Leninism, nor did he strive for a complete transformation of the existing command economy into a market economy. Rather, the Soviet General Secretary saw himself in the tradition of Lenin: Gorbachev adhered in principle to the model of the state-controlled planned economy but allowed private property and free trade to a modest extent, a situation akin to the New Economic Policy phase of the 1920s.

The spaces created by Gorbachev were perceived by some as an opportunity for new business activities. For many citizens, however, the reform period had negative connotations. They witnessed the disintegration of a system that was less and less able to provide the populace with sufficient food, basic goods, and services. When the state had ample funds, the shortcomings caused by the deficits of the cumbersome planned economy could be made up for. But when, in the mid-1980s, the returns from the export of oil also collapsed, the state increasingly lacked the means even to provide sufficient basic foodstuffs for its citizens. This failure soon became apparent to all: long queues formed in front of half-empty grocery stores every day in Soviet cities, as well as in the other countries of socialist Eastern Europe. When the situation did not stabilise despite Gorbachev's measures, the Soviet government was forced to take a step that would have been unthinkable just a few years

[22] Gorbachev's speech at the 27th Party Congress can be found in: *XXVII s"ezd Kommunisticheskoi partii Sovetskogo Soiuza, 25 fevr. – 6 marta 1986 g.: Stenograficheskii otchet*, in 3 vols, vol. 2, Moscow: Politizdat, 1986, pp. 297–302.

earlier: in March 1991, the government decided to free up prices on a number of basic foodstuffs. Daily essentials thus went from being scarce to being unaffordable for many people.[23]

As socialism rapidly approached bankruptcy, the party's prestige diminished – and with it the credibility of the communist ideology on which the Soviet system was based. The superiority of the socialist model of development over the capitalist system, which had until recently been propounded, appeared to an increasing number of people to be a blatant lie.

Cracks in the 'Eastern Bloc' and the Soviet Demise

Until the collapse of the oil price in the mid-1980s, commodity exports had not only provided the Soviet Union with foreign exchange to cushion the effects of the internal crisis but had also formed the glue that held together the socialist camp.[24] In the second half of the 1980s, the situation worsened as not only the world price of oil remained at a relatively low level but also the growth rates of Soviet oil fields declined. The monthly production rates in the Soviet oil fields had been showing a downward trend from the autumn of 1983, for the first time since the Second World War. Aware of the enormous importance of the raw materials sector for the Soviet economy, Gorbachev travelled to Tyumen, the country's oil and gas capital, in September 1985, just six months after taking office, to address the sector's problems in a discussion with local representatives that was unprecedentedly open for the time. In the usual authoritarian manner of Soviet officials, he had several local administrators and managers dismissed and demanded immediate measures to increase production.[25]

Oil production thus rose again in January 1986 and would grow at record pace for another two and a half years. But the upturn was short-lived. Production declined sharply at the end of 1988, showing that mere exhortations and changes in local management had not been enough to bring about lasting structural improvements.[26] As is evident

[23] Gaidar, *Collapse of an Empire*, pp. 211–13.
[24] On this, see Lorenz Lüthi, 'Drifting Apart: Soviet Energy and the Cohesion of the Communist Bloc in the 1970s and 1980s', in Perović (ed.), *Cold War Energy*, pp. 371–99.
[25] Robert Gillette, 'Huge Oil Field Dying: Soviet Methods Cited', *Los Angeles Times*, 29 September 1985, www.latimes.com/archives/la-xpm-1985-09-29-mn-19049-story.html (last accessed 26 September 2021).
[26] Marshall I. Goldman, 'Gorbachev the Economist', *Foreign Affairs*, 69, 2 (1990), pp. 28–44, here p. 31.

from an extensive report by the Soviet Union's Ministry of the Oil Industry dated 24 May 1989, the situation was dire.[27] The author of the report, Oil Minister Vassilii Dinkov, complained in particular of 'repeated shortfalls in the delivery of equipment and materials directly related to oil production', which 'significantly impedes operations'.[28] While the Soviet Union produced a staggering 624.3 million tonnes of oil in 1988, production plummeted by nearly 20 per cent, to 515.8 million tonnes by 1991 due to outdated technology, continued mismanagement, and the use of harmful extraction methods.[29]

As production fell, the Soviet Union was not only in danger of being unable to meet its supply commitments to Western European countries. Moscow also faced the problem of being unable to provide sufficient raw materials to its allies in the socialist states of Eastern Europe. Interstate trade, which within CMEA was still largely based on the exchange of goods, risked collapsing completely. As a result, the former close economic and trade relations between the Soviet Union and the individual states of the crumbling 'Eastern bloc' gradually began to dissolve, without, however, a model for a new type of relationship having been found, as the authors of an internal memorandum compiled in February 1989 by the International Department of the CC of the CPSU lamented.[30]

The collapse of oil production also called into question the deeply rooted notion of a linear growth model. At its core, Soviet industrial policy expected a steady increase in production volumes, based on the assumption that the country's resource wealth was virtually inexhaustible. Thus, the success of economic policy was measured solely in terms of ever-increasing growth. A statistical forecast of 30 May 1973 prepared under the direction of Gosplan director Baibakov on the projected development of the energy sector may serve as a representative example of such ideas and, at the same time, as an illustration of Gosplan's completely unrealistic planning and forecasts. He prepared this paper on behalf of Georgii Tsukanov, a high-ranking member of the CC of the CPSU and one of Brezhnev's closest confidants. In the document, Baibakov projected that by 1990 the Soviet Union would be able to increase oil production to a

[27] The report titled 'On Measures to Meet the 1989 Oil Production Target', dated 24 May 1989 and signed by the Minister of the Oil Industry Vassilii Dinkov, is contained in GARF, f. 5446, op. 150, d. 1575, ll. 113–18.

[28] GARF, f. 5446, op. 150, d. 1575, l. 116.

[29] Gaidar, *Collapse of an Empire*, p. 163.

[30] 'Memorandum from the International Department of the Central Committee of the CPSU to Alexander Yakovlev', February 1989, History and Public Policy Program Digital Archive, Archive of the Gorbachev Foundation, Moscow; on file at the National Security Archive, donated by Professor Jacques Levesque; Translated by Svetlana Savranskaya and Gary Goldberg, https://digitalarchive.wilsoncenter.org/document/112485 (last accessed 8 November 2021).

staggering 820–40 million tonnes, twice the 1972 level. He predicted similarly exaggerated rates of increase for natural gas. Had these numbers been accurate, the Soviet Union would not only have had sufficient energy for its own development for the foreseeable future but would also have been in a position to supply the socialist states of Eastern Europe as well as capitalist customers in Western Europe with steadily increasing oil and gas volumes.[31]

Accordingly, it is hardly surprising that the members of the Soviet state and party leadership had no answer ready when, after the collapse in oil prices, production also fell. The only solution they saw was to do once again everything they could to increase production to at least alleviate the symptoms of the crisis. A sense of the atmosphere at the time can be gleaned from an excerpt from the transcript of a meeting on 17 September 1990 at which senior Soviet officials discussed the precarious supply situation of their Eastern European allies, many of whom were already undergoing profound transitions to democracy and liberal market reforms and thus moving their countries away from the Soviet Union. The participants were Nikolai Ryzhkov, Chairman of the Council of Ministers; his two deputies, Stepan Sitarian and Lev Riabov; and Iurii Masliukov, who had succeeded Baibakov as head of Gosplan in 1985:[32]

[RYZHKOV:] What will we do with 547 [million] tons [of oil], how will the country live?

[RIABOV:] For domestic consumption, there will be 467 million tons .... Exports are falling.

[RYZHKOV:] But still, what needs to be done to get 580, as we had discussed at first?

[RIABOV:] Those are very difficult numbers. We need to increase drilling and introduce 25–26 thousand new wells ....

[SITARIAN:] How much money is needed [to achieve this] ...?

[RIABOV:] Approximately 800 million rubles in convertible currency.

[SITARIAN:] And how much will you give? ...

[RYZHKOV:] Your [Riabov's] task is to find a way to get out of the situation ....

[RIABOV:] ... I hold meetings of the government commission twice a month, and I have constant shorter meetings too. There are no resources. None....

[RYZHKOV:] Leonid Ivanovich [Riabov], please ....

[SITARIAN:] The general situation is such that if export is 60 million [tons of oil], then we put the relationship with other countries in an extremely difficult position. That is, if today 34 million tons goes to hard currency [i.e., to the capitalist West], that leaves 26 million for all the Eastern European

31 RGANI, f. 80, op. 1, d. 322, ll. 18–46.

32 The passages of the conversation printed in Gaidar's book are contained in the Russian language in the original in GARF, f. 5446, op. 162, d. 379, ll. 131–37, 143–49; in the English translation in Gaidar, *Collapse of an Empire*, pp. 163–64.

countries plus Finland, India, Cuba, and so on .... The point is that we cannot fail to deliver oil to certain countries .... If we give Poland zero, then Poland will not sell us anything ....

[MASLIUKOV:] We understand that the only source of hard currency is of course oil ... [and therefore we must] take the most determined measures to achieve additional oil production .... I have the presentiment that if we do not make all of the necessary decisions now, then ... [t]hings can end most critically in the socialist countries. This will lead us to a real crash, and not just for us, but for our entire system.

When Masliukov underlined that the 'most determined measures' should be taken in the oil industry, he meant in practice an even more merciless exploitation of the existing resources. Since there was no time to drill new wells on a large scale and the financial means for importing Western technology were largely lacking, Soviet petroleum engineers often saw no option but to increase the pressure in the reservoirs by injecting water, thereby forcing more oil out of the wells. This method is generally used in oil production. However, to meet the oftentimes implausible planning targets, Soviet engineers frequently pumped more water into the oil fields than would have been beneficial for optimal exploitation. In the short term, this boosted oil production, but in the medium to long term, it reduced recoverable reserves. This was because if the oil-bearing rock was watered down too much, the Soviet engineers ran the risk that only water would gush out of the wells.[33] In other words, the fields were partially destroyed and production eventually collapsed even further.[34] Between 1989 and 1990, production in the Russian Soviet Socialist Republic (RSFSR) alone fell by more than 36 per cent, and between 1990 and 1991 the production slump was as much as 54 per cent.[35] In an April 1991 study, a high-profile state commission concluded that the situation in the oil fields was beyond repair. To return oil production in the Soviet Union to at least the level of 1989, an investment amounting to half the state budget would be necessary.[36]

Soviet planners were accustomed to generating foreign exchange by supplying raw materials to the West. This allowed them to compensate for shortages in their own economy. Since this model no longer worked profitably in the low-price environment of the second half of the 1980s, the Soviet Union increasingly turned to borrowing in the West to finance industrial projects, as well as to repay the interest on its growing international debt. Unlike other CMEA countries – namely Poland,

[33] 'Zu stark gewässert', *Der Spiegel*, 37, 9 September 1990, pp. 129–30.
[34] Gustafson, *Wheel of Fortune*, pp. 39–40. [35] Gaidar, *Collapse of an Empire*, p. 163.
[36] Gustafson, *Wheel of Fortune*, p. 48.

Romania, the GDR, and Hungary – the Soviet Union had historically not had a serious debt problem thanks to the hard currency generated by its export of raw materials.[37] This changed only at the end of the 1980s, as the Soviet Union faced a decline in foreign exchange earnings from commodity exports. Simultaneously, the new policy of détente between East and West opened up avenues for obtaining Western loans, providing the Soviet Union with opportunities to address its economic challenges.

The FRG proved to be one of the Soviet Union's most important financial backers at this time. After the momentous event following the fall of the Berlin Wall, a new era began with the prospect of German reunification on the horizon. Recognising that Moscow would be open to support the unity of Germany, the West German government under Helmuth Kohl showed greater flexibility on credit issues. In June 1990, it agreed to guarantee a loan of 5 billion German marks to the Soviet Union, which was granted by a consortium of West German banks.[38] Bonn thus accommodated, at least to some extent, the request of the Soviet leadership, which had approached the West German government in early May of that year with a request for a loan totalling 20 billion German marks, to be paid out over a period of five to seven years.[39] In view of the Soviet Union's enormous economic problems, even this sum seemed to Western observers at the time to be no more than a drop in the ocean. According to an American expert estimate, the Soviet Union would have needed about 140 billion US dollars at that time to reorganise its economy.[40]

As a further measure against the crisis, Moscow envisaged the expansion and deepening of cooperation with Western companies. From the point of view of Western businesses, the energy sector was particularly appealing because cooperation seemed relatively simple here: as always, Western companies were to provide technology and equipment, secured by the granting of loans, and the Soviet side was to supply raw materials in return. At the same time, Western observers and government agencies understood the Soviet energy industry was struggling with major problems. For example, an internal report of the FRG's Ministry of Economics on 7 November 1990 stated that Soviet oil production was suffering from a sharp drop in output because of technical problems and

[37] Carl H. McMillan, 'Multinationals from the Second World: Growth of Foreign Investment by Soviet and East European Enterprises', London: Macmillan Press, 1987, p. 20.

[38] *Akten zur Auswärtigen Politik der Bundesrepublik Deutschland (1990)*, edited by the Institut für Zeitgeschichte, Berlin, Boston: De Gruyter Oldenbourg, 2021, p. 810 (n. 10).

[39] Ibid., p. 640. [40] Ibid., p. 810.

'financial bottlenecks'. Therefore, 'the Soviets today are more open to cooperation with Western oil companies' than in earlier years. Whereas previously they had only been interested in individual 'supplies and services', they were now seeking 'joint ventures' in order to 'quickly stabilise and increase their declining oil production'.[41]

But as long as the planned economy officially prevailed, cooperation often turned out to be extremely laborious in practice. A report in the German news magazine *Der Spiegel* on 9 September 1990 vividly illustrates this problem using the example of a German–Soviet cooperation project for the recovery of associated natural gas:

> The owner of a Cologne engineering company wanted to help the Soviets to turn the now senselessly flared gas into money. A recovery plant for 120,000 tonnes of gas a year was to be delivered. The financing of the project was already secured: a German trader was ready to buy the products that were to be extracted from the gas. But nothing came of the fine plan. Moscow banned the deal on the grounds that the refinery had not met its previous production target. If the plant did not supply enough products for domestic needs, it was not allowed to export. [German refinery specialist Arno] Koernig tried in vain to make it clear to the plan fetishists in Moscow that the products intended for export were only to be made from gas that had been burned so far. The Muscovites remained stubborn: they would rather have gas worth many millions of marks a year burned than deviate even a whit from their plan figures.[42]

The problem with the reforms initiated by Gorbachev was that the introduction of market economy elements called for flexibility in a system that was not prepared for it. Gorbachev was convinced that it would be enough to allow criticism of the system so that mistakes could be publicly identified and corrected. However, instead of triggering the hoped-for social dynamism and bringing about an upturn in the economy, his reforms created new insecurity and increased the incentives for business activities in the grey area of legality. As a result, not only did his actions antagonise the conservative currents within the state and party apparatus, but his half-finished reform steps also failed to win over the democratically oriented forces to his cause. What Gorbachev could not have foreseen was that his policy of glasnost would not merely expose the shortcomings of the system. Rather, the system itself, the communist ideology on which that system was based, and the Communist Party that embodied that system were increasingly questioned. While his reforms certainly triggered a social dynamic, this unfolded to his disadvantage. The forces that Gorbachev summoned got out of control and ultimately led to the destruction of the whole.

[41] Ibid., p. 1571. [42] 'Zu stark gewässert', pp. 129–30.

Like Gorbachev, many observers in the West at the time completely misjudged the enormous power of nationalism, which offered itself as a kind of substitute ideology for communism. The decisive factor in the disintegration of the Soviet Union was ultimately not the secessionist aspirations of individual republics on the fringes of the Soviet Union, however, but the fact that even the Russian leadership under Yeltsin opposed the Soviet leadership and demanded greater autonomy. As in the Baltic states, Georgia, Ukraine, and Armenia, the Russian leadership under Boris Yeltsin fostered a sense of resentment towards the Soviet centre. Elected in June 1991 as Russia's president, Yeltsin portrayed his republic as a victim and demanded greater political and economic autonomy, including full control over all natural resources within Russian territory. Through his charismatic approach, Yeltsin skilfully turned sections of the political elite and the Russian population against the Soviet state and party leadership.

In this struggle between different ideas and claims, Gorbachev increasingly found himself in a quandary. When Gorbachev, who in addition to his function as General Secretary had also held the office of President since March 1990, wanted to accommodate the Union republics with a treaty on the transformation of the Soviet Union into a loose federation of sovereign states, a group of reactionary forces allied themselves against him. On 19 August 1991, a coup d'état took place. A self-styled 'State Committee on the State of Emergency', which included several high-ranking ministers and generals, had tanks rolled out into the streets of Moscow and briefly took power in the country. Gorbachev, who was at his dacha in the Crimea at the time, was placed under house arrest. For Yeltsin, on the other hand, this event was to prove fortuitous: he seized the opportunity and took to the streets of Moscow alongside tens of thousands of Russians to protest the coup plotters' seizure of power. Parts of the Soviet army joined him.[43]

The attempted coup, which failed after only three days, was the final nail in the coffin of the Soviet Union. In its wake, several Soviet republics that had previously declared themselves sovereign proclaimed complete independence. Gorbachev returned from exile disempowered, while Yeltsin became a popular hero and in November 1991 decreed the banning of the Communist Party on Russian soil. In the end, it was not Gorbachev who announced the formal dissolution of the Soviet Union but the leaderships of Belarus, Ukraine, and Russia. On 7 December 1991, the three statesmen met in a dacha near Viskuli in the Belorussian

[43] Cf. Ignaz Lozo, *Der Putsch gegen Gorbatschow und das Ende der Sowjetunion*, Cologne, Weimar, Vienna: Böhlau, 2014.

Belovezh Forest to proclaim the end of the Soviet Union on the following day and launch the Commonwealth of Independent States (CIS) as a loose confederation of former Soviet republics. Gorbachev was president of a state that no longer existed. He, therefore, had no choice but to appear before the television cameras on 25 December 1991 and announce his resignation.

The 'Wild 1990s': Privatisation and Oligarchs

With the disintegration of the Soviet Union, not only was a huge territorial empire destroyed but also a unified economic and political space. Trade and customs barriers were erected at the borders of the former republics and people could travel from one country to another only with passports. However, in many cases, it was to take years before relations were put on a new footing and clear rules were introduced for trade and economic exchanges. Even long after the collapse of the Soviet Union, states often conducted their trade in goods not on a monetary basis but in the form of barter. Energy trade between Russia and Turkmenistan, for example, was based primarily on a non-monetary basis until the mid-2000s. The Russian state-owned gas company Gazprom bought Turkmen gas, which at that time still relied exclusively on the Russian pipeline system for exports, and paid for it with Russian goods and investments in the Turkmen energy industry.[44] Russian–Ukrainian gas trade functioned in a similar way, consisting of a mix of monetary and commodity exchanges and often involving obscure intermediaries in addition to the two state-owned companies, Gazprom and Naftohas (Ukraine).[45]

The disintegration of the single economic space was compounded by a profound crisis in many of the post-Soviet states. In Russia, oil production collapsed by about 40 per cent between 1989 and 1997 and remained at a low level until the end of the 1990s. The world oil price also hovered at minimal levels, reaching a bottom of 12 US dollars per barrel in 1998.[46] Not a single Russian oil company was able to maintain, let alone increase, production in the 1990s.[47] Often, the new owners of

[44] Indra Overland, 'Natural Gas and Russia–Turkmenistan Relations', *Russian Analytical Digest*, 56 (2009), pp. 9–13.
[45] Jeronim Perović, 'Farce ums Gas: Russland, die Ukraine und die EU-Energiepolitik,' *Osteuropa*, 59, 1 (2009), pp. 19–35.
[46] Peter Rutland, 'The Political Economy of Energy in Russia', in Slawomir Raszewski (ed.), *The International Political Economy of Oil and Gas*, New York: Palgrave Macmillan, 2018, pp. 23–39, here p. 28; for production figures, see chart no. 13 in *Russian Analytical Digest*, 217 (2011), p. 33.
[47] Marshall, *Petrostate*, p. 56.

the privatised companies were busy secreting their short-term profits in foreign accounts instead of investing them in their companies. In parallel with the outflow of billions of dollars abroad during the 1990s, millions of well-educated Russians who did not believe in a future at home emigrated to the United States and Western Europe. Because Russia was suffering from hyperinflation and was also unable to establish a functioning tax system, the Russian state lacked the money to pay for such essential services as social welfare, security, education, and the maintenance of public infrastructure.

The economic downturn bottomed out in August 1998, when inflation spiralled out of control in the wake of the so-called rouble crisis and the Russian government was effectively forced to declare state bankruptcy.[48] Symbolic of the economic malaise was the street scene in Moscow and other Russian cities, which in the 1990s was marked by poverty and decline. Outside metro stations, pensioners lined up in long rows to offer their few possessions for sale. Alcoholism, disease, and violence contributed to a drastic drop in life expectancy, which fell below 60 years for men. Such a low life expectancy was unprecedented for a developed industrial nation at the end of the twentieth century.[49]

The once-powerful state, which had controlled all national property in the Soviet era, withdrew further and further in the 1990s to give market forces a free hand. According to the neoliberal economic theory that Russian reformers were relying on at the time for their transformation plans, the market, not the state, was supposed to correct the system's flaws.[50] But the withdrawal of the state turned out to be disorderly and improvised. Within a very short space of time, a huge gap opened up between those who were able to benefit from liberalisation and enrich themselves and the mass of people who were unable to cope with the changes and were plunged into social hardship virtually overnight. Members of this small group of the newly rich succeeded, in often highly dubious transactions, in grabbing lucrative state sinecures, including large parts of the oil industry.[51]

[48] Hansjörg Herr, 'Die Finanzkrise in Russland im Gefolge der Asienkrise', *Aus Politik und Zeitgeschichte*, B37–38 (2000), www.bpb.de/apuz/25451/die-finanzkrise-in-russland-im-gefolge-der-asienkrise (last accessed 20 July 2021).

[49] Mark G. Field, 'The Health and Demographic Crisis in Post-Soviet Russia', in Mark G. Field and Judyth L. Twigg (eds.), *Russia's Torn Safety Nets: Health and Social Welfare During the Transition*, New York: St. Martin's Press, 2000, pp. 11–42.

[50] Peter Rutland, 'Neoliberalism and the Russian Transition', *Review of International Political Economy*, 20, 2 (2013), pp. 332–62.

[51] Cf. Klaus Heller, *Russlands wilde Jahre: Der neue Kapitalismus in der Ära Jelzin*, Paderborn: Schöningh, 2016, especially pp. 175–295 (chapters VII–X).

This was possible because the old order, based on a planned economy and state ownership, was abolished without a new system having been introduced, let alone tested. The reformers' primary goal was to dismantle the former system as completely and quickly as possible in order to render impossible the return of communism and the planned economy. Privatisation was thus not only conceived as an economic development model but also understood as a political measure in the reformers' struggle against the old communist elite, which had retreated but was far from defeated. The fact that privatisation and the market economy plunged the country into chaos and impoverished many people was accepted by the reformers as collateral damage of what they considered their noble goals. Representatives of Western governments, think tanks, and organisations such as the World Bank and the IMF encouraged the Russian reformers in their efforts to subject the country's economy to 'shock therapy' along the lines of Poland and other east-central European states.[52]

The poorly thought-out nature of the reforms was particularly evident in the case of taxation. In the Soviet Union, the tax had been deducted from employees' wages before they were paid, with the result that many were not even aware that they were paying money to the state. Similarly, state-owned enterprises automatically paid a corporate tax. This changed abruptly after privatisation. People were now sent tax forms on which they had to fill in their earnings and pay taxes to the state. The tax rate was also relatively high, amounting to about 30 per cent of income in the 1990s. However, given the predicament in which many found themselves, hardly anyone paid taxes, and because the state lacked the bureaucratic capacity to effectively collect them due to scarce financial resources, the shortfalls were significant.[53] Because of the complexity of the tax system in the 1990s and the unreliability of economic data, no one knew exactly how much tax was lost, but estimates put the shortfall in 1996 alone at about 150 trillion roubles (about 28 billion US dollars at the time). The loss was compounded by the fact that large industrial enterprises often did not pay their taxes at all or not in full. The country's largest company, Gazprom, is said to have owed the state 15 trillion roubles in 1996 – 10 per cent of the shortfall in tax revenues at the

[52] R. G. Gidadhubli and Arun Mohanty, 'Continuing Debate over "Shock Therapy"', *Economic and Political Weekly*, 37, 50 (2002), pp. 4998–5002.

[53] On the problem of tax evasion in 1990s, see Daniel Treisman, 'Russia's Taxing Problem', *Foreign Policy*, 112 (1998), pp. 55–66; James Alm, Jorge Martinez-Vazquez, and Benno Torgler, 'Russian Tax Morale in the 1990s', *Proceedings: Annual Conference on Taxation and Minutes of the Annual Meeting of the National Tax Association*, 98 (2005), pp. 287–92.

time.[54] In 2000, of Russia's seventy million taxpayers, only three million paid their taxes.[55]

The dismantling of the Soviet-style command economy in the 1990s, without a viable alternative, also precipitated economic collapse. When the centralised distribution system was dissolved, there was initially no functioning market and thus no substitute for the old order. This meant that factory managers, who had previously approached the central government planning authority with a list of the things they needed to procure, now had no idea where to get their raw materials or equipment from. This was particularly difficult if a factory had sourced certain production parts from other Soviet republics, but the collapse of the Soviet Union had broken up these relationships. Consequently, many plants had to stop production temporarily or shut down completely; workers went without pay or were laid off.

Privatisation did not come out of the blue. The beginnings of free trade, combined with the right to private property, were already permitted in the late 1980s. On the basis of the 'Law on Cooperatives' passed under Gorbachev, tens of thousands of small businesses such as restaurants, laundries, and discos were set up in the form of cooperatives. These operated alongside the shadow economy that had long existed in the Soviet Union. A large proportion of these cooperatives were established within state companies, in what was essentially a covert form of privatisation. Russia thus already had some experience of a market economy when the country was hit by the first major wave of privatisation in June 1992.[56] With the aim of involving as many people as possible in democratisation 'from below' in as short a time as possible, the reformers within the Russian government, led by Anatolii Chubais, came up with the idea of issuing each citizen with a 10,000-ruble share voucher. With this voucher, people had several options. They could exchange it for shares in their own company, becoming shareholders. They could participate in auctions where shares in companies were sold. They could invest in voucher investment funds. Finally, they were free to sell their voucher to third parties. Because many were in need of money at the time, the latter option was particularly popular. However, the massive oversupply of vouchers, coupled with the rapid collapse of the Russian rouble, meant that the value of individual notes soon fell far below their

[54] 'Russia's Tax Crisis', *New York Times*, 17 October 1996, p. 26 (Section A).

[55] Marshall, *Petrostate*, p. 57.

[56] Roland Götz, 'Vom privatatisierten Staat zum verstaatlichen Markt? Eigentum in der Sowjetunion und in Russland, *Osteuropa*, 63, 5/6 (2013), pp. 315–32, here pp. 317–18.

face value.[57] Until the autumn of 1992, the sale of a voucher could still buy a medium-priced men's suit, but by the end of 1993, the market value of a voucher was approaching that of three to four bottles of vodka.[58]

The purpose of this privatisation campaign through vouchers, which at first did not comprise certain strategic segments of the economy including large parts of the mineral resource sector, the timber industry, pipelines, or public transportation, was not merely to transfer state property into the hands of private individuals as quickly and comprehensively as possible. Rather, the aim was to consolidate the democratisation project and the transition from a planned to a market economy by giving each citizen a stake in its persistence. This corresponded to the declared political goal of the reformers to make it impossible for the still-powerful Communist Party, which had officially been allowed to operate again as a political party by decision of the Russian Constitutional Court in November 1992, to ever return to power.

According to statistics, about 25 million Russian citizens invested their vouchers in check investment funds, and about 40 million in shares of various companies. One-third of all vouchers were resold. In 1992, a total of 46,800 state-owned enterprises were privatised; in 1993, this number rose to 88,600, and in 1994 to 112,600. Within two years, most of the objects of the so-called small privatisation had been taken out of state hands, including more than 85,000 restaurants, clothing stores, and cafes.[59] Given these numbers, the reformers considered privatisation a success, even though millions of people sank into poverty and therefore could not see any benefit to themselves in these reforms. Moreover, even after privatisation, many enterprises were on the verge of bankruptcy; although they were now in private hands, they often lacked the investment necessary to keep them going. When privatisation vouchers flowed into economically ailing companies, there were no dividends for investors. Many voucher investment funds also went bust and were liquidated. Voucher privatisation may have prevented a return to the old system, but

[57] Anders Åslund, *Russia's Capitalist Revolution: Why Market Reform Succeeded and Democracy Failed*, Washington, DC: Peterson Institute for International Economics, 2007, especially pp. 107–10; Heller, *Russlands wilde Jahre*, pp. 197–225.

[58] '[Privatisierung:] Wörterbuch der Wilden 1990er', *dekoder*, www.dekoder.org/de/article/1990er-bilder-alltag (last accessed 19 May 2023).

[59] Dar'ia Stanislavets, 'Privatizatsii v Rossii 20 let: Istoriia s prodolzheniem', *Praim*, 9 June 2012, https://1prime.ru/Financial_market/20120609/757520789.html (last accessed 6 August 2021).

its social consequences offended many Russians' sense of justice, as even Chubais was later forced to admit.[60]

It was during this first wave of privatisation that, in parallel with mass impoverishment, a few became wealthy because they bought up voucher notes in large numbers, sometimes hundreds of thousands of them, and then became owners of former state enterprises. The means to do so had been acquired by this group of future billionaires, known as 'oligarchs', in the late Soviet period. In terms of their biographies, the Russian oligarchs can be divided into two broad categories. The first type included oligarchs who came from the shadow economy and the semi-criminal milieu. They made money in the late 1980s through partly corrupt or even criminal machinations, using the new freedoms available under Gorbachev for various trading activities. At that time, good business could be done especially with the import of Western goods, which were lacking in the Soviet Union. Mikhail Chernoi, who together with his brother Lev was to gain control of large parts of the Russian aluminium industry in the 1990s, exported metals and coal on a private basis and imported cheap cars, which were in short supply in the Soviet Union. Boris Berezovskii, who would be one of Yeltsin's key supporters in his 1996 presidential campaign, also became rich in the late 1980s, mainly from trading cars. Mikhail Khodorkovskii, who was to become immensely wealthy through his oil company Yukos, amassed a fortune in the late Soviet period by importing computers from abroad, among other things.[61]

The second group consisted of state officials or heads of companies who took advantage of privatisation to acquire the factories they managed or over which they presided as state officials through insider knowledge and connections. Often, the new owners were less concerned with innovation and growth than with making profits as quickly as possible, for instance, by exporting raw materials abroad, after which they would let their company go bankrupt. However, there are also several examples where the directors put their heart and soul into the companies and did a lot to get them going again. This was the case, for example, with the oil company Lukoil, which emerged from the Soviet oil industry. Based on a presidential decree passed in November 1992, Lukoil was founded as a private company in April 1993 by the former deputy chairman of the Soviet oil and gas industry, Vagit Alekperov. Because of his good

[60] Ewa Dabrowska, 'Voucher-Privatisierung, *dekoder*, 14 August 2018, www.dekoder.org/de/gnose/voucher-privatisierung-wirtschaftsreform#fuss4 (last accessed 21 July 2021).

[61] For further reading, see David E. Hoffmann, *The Oligarchs: Wealth and Power in the New Russia*, New York: Public Affairs, 2001.

relations with the Kremlin, Alekperov remained head of what is still the largest private oil company in Russia when other oligarchs were expropriated after Putin took office.[62]

Voucher privatisation, which was a key part of the transfer of state assets into private hands in the early 1990s, represented only the first major wave of privatisation in Russia. The second wave occurred in the mid-1990s, when the state, faced with a precarious financial situation, felt compelled to cede further state-owned enterprises to private parties. The model applied – the 'loans-for-shares' scheme – was even more controversial than voucher privatisation because a number of energy companies, the most valuable assets of the former Soviet economy, were also now being sold off.

Oil prices were still low, the tax system was not working, and the state thus still had only limited access to the revenues of Russian companies. To generate tax revenue, the companies needed to become profitable again. The idea of this programme, devised by then Deputy Prime Minister Vladimir Potanin, was that the new banks set up by the oligarchs would provide loans to the state. In return, the state agreed to pledge some of its large enterprises, which had not yet been privatised or had only been partially privatised, to the oligarchs' banks or to cede them shares in these companies. The plan was for the state to reacquire these shares with future tax revenues. In the event that the state could not muster the funds for repurchasing, the pledged shares were to be auctioned off at open bids.[63]

Even to observers at the time, it was no great surprise when it soon became apparent that this would not work and that the state would eventually be forced to auction off some of its most valuable assets. What was disturbing, however, was that the auctions were not conducted transparently. Indeed, the companies were often transferred into the possession of those banks that had pledged the share packages to the state. This is exactly how Khodorkovskii, who at the time was the owner of the private bank Menatep, came into possession of the oil company Yukos; Yukos was then Russia's second largest oil company, having originally emerged already in May 1993 from various state-owned Soviet companies, most importantly the Western Siberian Yuganskneftegaz oil and gas company. When the state's shares of this company were auctioned off in December 1995, Khodorkovskii paid just

62 Peter Maass, 'The Triumph of the Quiet Tycoon', *New York Times*, 1 August 2004, p. 24 (Section 6).

63 On this subject in detail, see Chrystia Freeland, *Sale of the Century: Russia's Wild Ride from Communism to Capitalism*, New York: Crown Business, 2000.

310 million US dollars for a firm that was probably worth at least 5 billion US dollars at the time. Berezovskii bought Sibneft, another oil giant estimated to be worth around 3 billion US dollars, for a mere 100 million US dollars.[64] With the sale of its oil companies, the Russian state hawked its true gems at prices that were far too low. For the oil industry, this meant that in just a few years the share of state-owned companies in Russian oil production plummeted from more than 80 per cent in the mid-1990s to just 13 per cent in 2003.[65] By the time the privatisation of the oil industry was completed, just three companies were still state-owned: Rosneft, which belonged to the Russian central state, as well as Tatneft and Bashneft, which were owned by the regional administrations of the Republic of Tatarstan and the Republic of Bashkortostan, respectively.[66]

The oil industry was thus largely privatised until the early 2000s. By contrast, the state never completely relinquished control over the gas industry. Unlike the Ministry of Oil, which began to privatise production – and in some cases also local transport systems and refineries – in the early 1990s and divided the industry into many individual companies, the Ministry of the Gas Industry transformed itself as early as 1989 into the Gazprom company under the leadership of Viktor Chernomyrdin. It was largely thanks to Chernomyrdin's personal commitment that Gazprom was not broken up after the collapse of the Soviet Union. Even reform minister Gaidar recognised how important it was to preserve the unity of the company under state control. After all, large parts of Russian industry depended on gas supplies, and millions of households were heated by gas. State control ensured that businesses and people alike had access to cheap energy even in uncertain times.[67] Although the company was transformed into a joint-stock company, the state held just under 40 per cent of the stock from the outset and later increased this to a majority stake.[68]

Even though Gazprom was by far the country's most important gas producer during the 1990s and 2000s, and in 2020 still remained responsible for around 66 per cent of natural gas production in Russia and for

[64] Marshall I. Goldman, 'Putin and the Oligarchs', *Foreign Affairs*, 83, 6 (2004), pp. 33–44, here p. 35.
[65] On the share of state-owned companies in Russia's oil and gas Production, see Figure 1 in *Russian Analytical Digest*, 113 (2012), p. 7.
[66] Heiko Pleines, 'Der Staat als Eigentümer', *Russland-Analysen*, 217 (2011), pp. 29–30, here p. 30; on ownership in the Russian oil and gas industry, see the tables and graphs in ibid., pp. 30–31.
[67] Gustafson, *The Bridge*, pp. 247–53.
[68] Kevin Rosner, *Gazprom and the Russian State*, London: GMB, 2005, especially pp. 9–18.

11 per cent of the gas produced worldwide,[69] it was never the company's goal to completely monopolise production. Independent gas producers were also able to establish themselves during the Yeltsin era, notably the company Novatek, which became Russia's second-largest gas producer and made a name for itself primarily in gas production in northern Siberia (on the Yamal peninsula) and in the production and export of natural gas in liquefied form.[70] Crucially, however, Gazprom retained control of the entire pipeline network. This made perfect sense given the great importance of gas to the energy supply of the entire country.[71] But control of the pipelines also gave the company a monopoly on exports and an important means of exerting pressure on the other gas producers, who were only allowed to supply the domestic market or export gas in liquid form. The situation was similar in the oil industry: although production was largely privatised, most parts of the transport system, including the export pipelines, remained in the hands of the Russian state through Transneft, the state-owned company that emerged from the Soviet company Glavtransneft in 1993.[72] Russia ships most of its oil by tanker, but it is through state-controlled pipelines that the raw material is transported to the country's maritime ports.

Although the Russian oligarchs had appropriated the oil companies using often dubious methods and acquired them far below their market value, they managed to revive production in just a few years. They thus played their part in saving the industry from ruin. Russia benefitted from the fact that, after the end of the Cold War, the West lifted its boycott on the transfer of high technology; with regard to oil drilling, for example, techniques could thus be used that opened up new possibilities for production. Numerous Russian companies joined forces with foreign firms and introduced modern management methods. The 1990s were an era of foreign investment and joint ventures: while forty-two joint ventures between foreign and Russian companies in the oil industry had been registered by 1993, a year later there were already seventy – accounting for almost 15 per cent of total Russian oil output.[73]

However, the largest foreign direct investments in the oil and gas industry took place in the years that followed. To develop the deposits

[69] Gazprom, 'Gas and Oil Production', www.gazprom.com/about/production/extraction/ (last accessed 22 September 2021).
[70] James Henderson, *Non-Gazprom Gas Producers in Russia*, Oxford: The Oxford Institute for Energy Studies, 2010.
[71] Gustafson, *Wheel of Fortune*, pp. 58–59.
[72] Moser, *Oil and the Economy of Russia*, p. 97.
[73] James Watson, 'Foreign Investment in Russia: The Case of the Oil Industry', *Europe-Asia Studies*, 48, 3 (1996), pp. 429–55, here p. 433.

on the Sakhalin Peninsula, a number of foreign companies participated in the major Sakhalin projects (Sakhalin-1 and Sakhalin-2), which were completed in the mid-1990s, under 'production sharing agreements' (PSAs). BP also increased its involvement in Russia when it merged its Russian operations with Tyumen Oil Company in 2003 to form TNK-BP, making it Russia's third-largest oil company at the time. Germany's BASF entered Russian gas production through a joint venture with Gazprom. In addition, ConocoPhillips (US) and E.ON Ruhrgas (Germany) bought into the Russian oil and gas industry through portfolio investments: ConocoPhillips acquired 20 per cent of Lukoil's share capital, while E.ON Ruhrgas acquired 6 per cent of Gazprom's shares. By the mid-2000s, Russian oil and gas production accounted for about one-third of total foreign investment, with oil refining absorbing another 7 per cent.[74] Russia's oil and gas industry recovered at a rapid pace, and technology, investment, and organisational know-how from abroad played a significant role.[75]

'Return of the State' under Putin

The 1990s featured a gigantic distribution struggle for state sinecures. This was fought not only between the state and the oligarchs but also among the oligarchs. The oligarchs tried to secure their business empires primarily through close ties to politics. However, they also expanded their position of power by reaching into other areas, for example, by trying to secure control over the media. Thus, Vladimir Gusinskii, founder and owner of Most Bank, created a media empire (Media-Most) that included the first private Russian television station, NTV, which distinguished itself with balanced but also very critical reporting on the politics of the Russian government and especially on the Chechen war. Berezovskii likewise expanded his influence in the media landscape by buying the largest state television station to compete with his arch-rival, Gusinskii. Still other oligarchs set about becoming politically

[74] Heiko Pleines, 'Developing Russia's Oil and Gas Industry', in Jeronim Perović, Robert W. Orttung, and Andreas Wenger (eds.), *Russian Energy Power and Foreign Relations: Implications for Conflict and Cooperation*, London, New York: Routledge, 2009, pp. 71–86, here pp. 72–73.

[75] On the situation in the Russian oil industry in general, see Li-Chen Sim, *The Rise and Fall of Privatization in the Russian Oil Industry*, Basingstoke, New York: Palgrave Macmillan, 2008; Stephen Fortescue, *Russia's Oil Barons and Metal Magnates: Oligarchs and the State in Transition*, Basingstoke, New York: Palgrave Macmillan, 2006; Gustafson, *Wheel of Fortune*; for a discussion of the performance of Russian oil companies and the importance of foreign ownership and investment, see Moser, *Oil and the Economy of Russia*, pp. 114–24.

active. The most prominent example is Khodorkovskii, who in the early 2000s had risen to become Russia's richest man, with an estimated fortune of around 15 billion US dollars. He used his money to support political parties critical of the Kremlin and even toyed with the idea of running for president.

Power not only shifted horizontally in the 1990s, from the state towards the oligarchs, but also moved vertically, from the central state authority to the individual autonomous republics and territories of Russia (the then 89 'subjects of the federation'). Small 'principalities', often based on corrupt power structures, emerged across the country. The regions formed states within the state and, like the Republic of Tatarstan, sometimes even pursued their own interests internationally.[76] In addition, the republics of Tatarstan and Bashkortostan, located in the Volga-Urals region, controlled the oil in their territories through their companies, Tatneft and Bashneft. Other republics, most notably Chechnia, attempted to break away from Russia altogether. The Russian state waged an extremely costly and unpopular war against the Chechen separatists in the 1990s – and, defeated, had to withdraw its army in 1996 in what amounted to an unprecedented humiliation.[77]

The Yeltsin period marked the temporary capitulation of a state that found itself unable to plan and act strategically due to a lack of financial resources and a highly inefficient bureaucratic apparatus. The Russian central state had lost control not only of strategic sectors of the economy but also of parts of the political sphere. This state did not represent a consolidated entity but looked like a conglomerate of individual departments, ministries, and individuals, each pursuing their own interests, and all the while under the influence of powerful economic groupings and oligarchs. In the 1990s, therefore, not a few believed that not only was the Russian central state in shambles but Russia itself was threatened with disintegration.

It was at this juncture that Putin entered the scene. Only a year after his appointment to head Russia's domestic intelligence agency, the FSB, Yeltsin was promoting him to prime minister in August 1999. Later that year, he became the country's acting president. In March 2000, Putin was elected president of Russia. More quickly than many expected, the

[76] Stephan DeSpiegeleire, 'Gullivers Fäden: Die russischen Regionen und die Aussen- und Sicherheitspolitik der Russischen Föderation', in Hans-Joachim Spanger (ed.), *Russland und der Westen*, Frankfurt am Main: Campus Verlag, 1998, pp. 150–76, here p. 161.

[77] On regionalisation trends in the 1990s, see Jeronim Perović, *Die Regionen Russlands als neue politische Kraft: Chancen und Gefahren des Regionalismus für Russland*, Bern: Peter Lang, 2001; on the First Chechen War 1994–1996, see Anatol Lieven, *Chechnya: Tombstone of Russian Power*, New Haven, London: Yale University Press, 1998.

then largely unknown former intelligence chief was able to restore state control over key sectors of the economy, including the oil industry, and either eliminate individual oligarchs altogether or bring them into line. With equally surprising speed, the state was able to restore the 'power vertical' and the pendulum moved away from the individual subjects of the federation back to the federal centre. Not only did Putin, as one of his first acts as prime minister, have the Russian military invade Chechnia again in autumn 1999 to end its quest for independence with brute military force, but he also severely curtailed the power of regional presidents and governors by having them re-appointed directly by Moscow from 2004 onwards and curtailing the rights and competences of Russia's regions.[78]

Privatisation, which had been approved by Yeltsin and implemented by his reformers, had been intended to be so radical as to make a return to the former communist system impossible. But Chubais and his comrades-in-arms were sorely mistaken if they believed that privatisation would prevent the resurgence of the centralist state. The Russian state had retreated under Yeltsin and was in a kind of slumber when Putin took office; control of economic and, to some extent, political life had been left to other forces. But even in the largely privatised oil sector, the state still had important leverage: all the mineral resources that lay beneath the earth's surface legally belonged to the state. In the same way, through Gazprom and Transneft, the state effectively controlled companies' access to the pipeline transportation system. It was the state that issued extraction licenses to the companies, and the companies had to have their plans for developing and regulating reserves approved by state authorities.[79] Similarly, even if many private security services had been established in Russia in the 1990s, it was the state that had the constitutional monopoly on the use of force and could, if necessary, employ its security forces also against real and perceived tax evaders.

The state thus had various means at its disposal to exert pressure on companies and their owners: it could refuse to grant a licence to a particular company or withdraw it if, for example, the company did not pay its taxes in full or if the state authorities interpreted this to be the case. The state could also thwart companies' plans if it did not agree with their development strategies. And it was the state that allocated export

[78] Matthes Buhbe and Gabriele Gorzka (eds.), *Russland heute: Rezentralisierung des Staates unter Putin*, Wiesbaden: Verlag für Sozialwissenschaften, 2007.

[79] Andreas Heinrich and Heiko Pleines, *Tax Burden and Tax Behaviour of Russian Economic Sectors: Part II; Taxation of the Russian Oil and Gas Industry*, Arbeitspapiere und Materialien/Forschungsstelle Osteuropa an der Universität Bremen 28, Bremen: Forschungsstelle Osteuropa an der Universität Bremen, 2001, especially pp. 9–10, 20.

quotas to companies in the transportation system controlled through state-owned enterprises. This meant that the state had an influence on the quantities of oil and gas that individual companies could transport via pipeline and, in the case of oil, sell abroad. Private companies had therefore enjoyed a great deal of leeway in the 1990s only because the state granted them this freedom. After Putin took office, the state simply went back to making use of the possibilities that were legally open to it – even if in the years that followed, the state under Putin was increasingly using this right in an arbitrary manner to accumulate power and eliminate unwelcome opponents.

The rapid strengthening of the state also reflected sensitivities in Russian society: in the view of many Russians, a strong central power was necessary for the restoration of law and order. Putin was more convinced of this than anyone and emphasised it repeatedly and unequivocally. Deep insights into his thinking and his programme for Russia could be gleaned as early as his memorable speech on 30 December 1999 on the occasion of the turn of the millennium ('Russia on the Threshold of the Millennium'):

> Etatism [*gosudarstvennichestvo*]. Russia will not soon, if ever, become a second edition of, say, the US or England, where liberal values have a deep historical tradition. In our country, the state, its institutions, and structures have always played an exceptionally important role in the life of the country and the people. For Russians, a strong state is not an anomaly or something to be fought against, but rather a source and guarantor of order, the initiator and main driving force of any change.[80]

In view of the decentralisation tendencies at the time and against the background of Chechen secessionist aspirations, there was a well-founded fear in Russia of a territorial disintegration. According to Putin, only a 'powerful' Russia was capable of prospering and successfully mastering internal challenges and external threats, as he emphasised in his State of the Nation Address on 16 May 2003:

> Our entire historical experience shows that a country like Russia can live and develop within its existing borders only if it is a strong nation. All of the periods during which Russia has been weakened, whether politically or economically, have always and inexorably brought to the fore the threat of the country's collapse.[81]

[80] Author's translation from Vladimir Putin, 'Rossiia na rubezhe tysiacheletii', *Nezavisimaia gazeta*, 30 December 1999, www.ng.ru/politics/1999-12-30/4_millenium.html (last accessed 21 July 2021).

[81] Vladimir Putin, 'Annual Address to the Federal Assembly of the Russian Federation', 16 May 2003, Moscow, Kremlin, http://en.kremlin.ru/events/president/transcripts/21998 (last accessed 21 July 2021). In the Russian original, Putin talks of a 'strong state' [*sil'noi derzhavoi*].

As a consequence, the former FSB director not only put an end to Chechen independence and aspirations for regional autonomy but also sought to regain control over the central sectors of the Russian economy. In his relations with the oligarchs, he did not immediately go for confrontation but rather offered them cooperation, provided they behaved loyally to the state, paid their taxes on time, and refrained from pursuing policies that conflicted with the interests of the central government.

As early as February 2000, shortly after taking office as acting president, Putin made it clear to the oligarchs at a meeting that they could no longer count on special treatment, however rich they were. Instead, he said, he would treat them in the same way as he would 'the owner of a small bakery or a shoe repair shop'.[82] Later that year, on 28 July, Putin invited the most powerful business representatives to the Kremlin and again explained to them how he envisioned the future relationship between politics and business.[83] For his part, he promised not to reverse privatisation. In exchange, he cautioned, the business leaders present should avoid acting like a new 'elite' and trying to influence the state apparatus.[84] In other words, the oligarchs should stay out of politics.[85]

Some of the oligarchs accepted this deal and continued to do business. New oligarchs could become powerful under Putin if they played by the rules. Some of the most prominent oligarchs at the time, however, could hardly hope to find a compromise with Putin. Berezovskii, for example, supported Putin even before he became prime minister because he believed it would enable him to manipulate him more easily thereafter. When Putin became president, however, irreconcilable differences between the two quickly emerged, and only a few months after Putin's election as president, Berezovskii went into exile. He settled in London, where he was found dead in his bathroom in 2013 under still-unexplained circumstances. Gusinskii, who had also initially supported Putin financially, emigrated to Israel in 2001 following a short stint in a Russian prison. Just like Berezovskii, Gusinskii had exposed himself too much through his media activities to be able to subordinate himself to the Kremlin now.[86]

82 Putin quoted in Goldman, 'Putin and the Oligarchs', p. 36.
83 'Vladimir Putin vstretilsia s rukovoditeliami riada krupneishikh kompanii i kommercheskikh bankov Rossii', 28 July 2000, Moscow, Kremlin, http://kremlin.ru/events/president/news/38471 (last accessed 21 July 2021).
84 Ibid.; Evgenii Fedunenko, 'Kak Vladimir Putin vstrechalsia s krupnym bisnesom: Istoriia voprosa', *Kommersant'*, 24 December 2015, https://www.kommersant.ru/doc/2884721 (last accessed 21 July 2021).
85 Goldman, *Petrostate*, pp. 102–4.
86 On Berezovskii and Gusinskii, see William Tompson, 'Putin and the "Oligarchs": A Two-sided Commitment Problem', in Alex Pravda (ed.), *Leading Russia: Putin in*

For Khodorkovskii, the end came later. At first, it looked as if continued existence under Putin would be possible. But Khodorkovskii had gone too far from the Kremlin's point of view. He was publicly critical of Putin and his political course and repeatedly denounced state corruption. He also challenged the state in terms of economic policy: at the time, Yukos was on the verge of achieving an even more prominent position in the oil sector through a merger with Sibneft, which ran completely counter to the Kremlin's efforts to regain state control over oil production. The Russian leadership was also annoyed by Khodorkovskii's intentions to build a private oil pipeline to China, as this would have effectively undermined the state's export monopoly. In addition, the oligarch had developed plans to sell shares in his company to the American oil company Chevron. This was likewise highly inconvenient for the Russian state at a time when it was seeking to reassert control over a strategically important sector. The final straw, however, was the oligarch's political activities: he began to support opposition parties and developed political ambitions of his own. On the pretext of tax evasion, Khodorkovskii and the vice-chairman of Yukos, Platon Lebedev, were finally arrested in October 2003, convicted by the courts, and exiled to a penal camp in Siberia. In 2013, Putin pardoned Khodorkovskii, who initially lived in exile in Switzerland near Rapperswil. In 2015, the family moved on to London. Lebedev was released from prison in 2014.[87]

The Khodorkovskii case was politically motivated and significant for Russia's domestic politics, as the televised trial of the Yukos leadership took on the character of a public spectacle. Everyone was supposed to hear the accusations against him. The clear message was meant to be chilling: no one, not even Russia's richest man, was above the law. Putin seemed to have followed through on what he had told the oligarchs three and a half years earlier: that he would treat them the same as the owners of a bakery or a shoe repair shop. Faced with increasing demands for tax refunds, Yukos was finally declared bankrupt by court order. The company was broken up and its most profitable core, Yuganskneftegaz, was sold for a song to the state oil company Rosneft, making the latter Russia's most powerful oil company in one fell swoop.[88]

Perspective; Essays in Honour of Archie Brown, Oxford: Oxford University Press, 2005, pp. 179–203.

87 On Khodorkovskii and the 'Yukos Affair', see Marshall I. Goldman, 'The Yukos Affair', *Current History*, 103, 675 (2004), pp. 319–23; Richard Sakwa, *Putin and the Oligarch: The Khodorkovsky – Yukos Affair*, London: I. B. Tauris, 2014; Gustafson, *Wheel of Fortune*, pp. 272–318.

88 Hans-Henning Schröder, 'Der Mineralölkonzern "Rosneft": Kommerzieller Erfolg und Einsatz politischer Machtmittel', *Russland-Analysen*, 348 (2018), pp. 9–13, here p. 10.

Many in Russia were aware that the Khodorkovskii trial was not strictly legal and that the court's verdict was largely arbitrary. If the trial had been based on purely legal grounds, many people who had acquired wealth in the 1990s would have faced retrospective prosecution. Instead, Putin used Khodorkovskii as an example to showcase the potential consequences for those who challenge the state and engage in political meddling. The move against Khodorkovskii was also strategic, as Putin recognised the widespread public support for the imprisonment of such an influential and wealthy tycoon. People in the West may have been outraged by the action against Khodorkovskii, but many in Russia felt a certain satisfaction that Khodorkovskii, who had enriched himself more than anyone else in the 1990s, was now getting his 'just' punishment, as opinion polls from the time confirm.[89] Polls also show that most Russians were against selling strategic sectors of the economy to foreign companies. The fact that the break-up of Yukos caused the planned deal with Chevron to fall through thus met with the public's approval as well.[90]

The Importance of Raw Materials in the New Russia

When Putin took office, Russia was in a state of deep political and economic crisis. Yet in addition to its seat on the UN Security Council and its nuclear weapons, the country still had its natural resources, namely oil and gas, which were to be used as efficiently and strategically as possible. From the Kremlin's point of view, however, the prerequisite for this was that the state brought the mineral sector back under its full control. The assumption that Putin had drawn up a master plan for the energy industry already in the mid-1990s while working as an aide to the mayor of St Petersburg, Anatolii Sobchak, is probably not correct. In his dissertation submitted to the St Petersburg State Mining University in June 1997, parts of which were plagiarised, he focused primarily on the regional development of St Petersburg, not on national energy and economic policy.[91] His emphasis began to shift to national concerns only

[89] Opinion polls conducted by the Gudkov Centre in November 2003 on the Yukos affair show that the majority were convinced that Putin was behind it and that this case was essentially a political reckoning; nevertheless, when asked what feelings this affair evoked in them, 33 per cent of respondents said that it had caused them 'joy and satisfaction', 19 per cent were astonished, and only 10 per cent were worried or even outraged; 38 per cent had no opinion: Lev Gudkov and Boris Dubin, 'Der Oligarch als Volksfeind: Der Nutzen des Falls Chodorkovskij für das Putin-Regime', *Osteuropa*, 55, 7 (2005), pp. 52–75.

[90] Pleines, 'Developing Russia's Oil and Gas Industry', p. 73.

[91] Harley Balzer, 'The Putin Thesis and Russian Energy Policy', *Post-Soviet Affairs*, 21, 3 (2005), pp. 210–25, especially p. 214; there is some confusion in the Western literature whether Putin's thesis is publicly accessible or not. Brookings scholars Igor Danchenko

in the late 1990s, when he was seconded to Moscow as FSB director in July 1998, becoming prime minister under Yeltsin a year later. In 1999, he published a journal article in which he dealt more specifically with economic issues and energy policy.[92]

Presumably, the ideas he expounds in this article were developed under the influence of Igor Sechin, a close confidant of Putin's from the Petersburg years who studied at the same university. Sechin accompanied Putin to Moscow, was appointed chairman of Rosneft in 2004, and was to become one of the Russian president's most important advisers. Sechin himself wrote his dissertation, published in 1998, on oil.[93] Both Sechin's dissertation and Putin's essay blamed the lack of state leadership for Russia's economic decline in the 1990s. What is striking in both works is that neither Putin nor Sechin opposed the free-market economy. They believed that relying on capitalism alone would not be enough to restore growth and prosperity. They recognised the need for a state that could intervene in the economy in a regulatory capacity. This intervention was seen as necessary to secure direct access to crucial tax revenues in the resource sector.[94]

As president, Putin largely set out to implement these ideas, gradually returning the Russian economy to a form of state capitalism. One of his first acts in office was to initiate a tax reform that would put more money in the state's coffers. Among other things, the government lowered the income tax to 13 per cent, a simplification of the tax system intended to have a positive effect on the tax morale of Russian citizens.[95] Corporate

and Clifford Gaddy seem to have been able to obtain a copy of the 218-page dissertation, which they downloaded from the Russian State Library in 2002; these authors also demonstrate that parts of Putin's dissertation were plagiarised: Igor Danchenko and Clifford Gaddy, 'The Mystery of Vladimir Putin's Dissertation', edited versions of presentations by the authors at a Brookings Institution, Foreign Policy Program panel, Washington, DC, 30 March 2006, www.brookings.edu/wp-content/uploads/2012/09/Putin-Dissertation-Event-remarks-with-slides.pdf (last accessed 13 July 2022).

[92] Harley, 'The Putin Thesis and Russian Energy Policy', p. 216.

[93] In 1998, Sechin defended his doctoral thesis at the St Petersburg State Mining University on the topic of 'Economic Evaluation of Investment Projects for the Transit of Oil and Petroleum Products'. In the same year, the University Publishing House published his book entitled 'Problems of the Development of the Export of Petroleum and Petroleum Products from the Russian Federation and the Formation of Regional Transit Projects'. Detailed information on Sechin's biography can be found in 'Sechin, Igor: Prezident NK "Rosneft"', *Lentapedia*, https://lenta.ru/lib/14160890/full.htm (last accessed 18 August 2021).

[94] Extensive quotes from Putin's article (which seems to be no longer accessible) can be found in Martha Brill Olcott, *The Energy Dimension in Russian Global Strategy: Vladimir Putin and the Geopolitics of Oil*, Houston, TX: The James A. Baker III Institute for Public Policy of the Rice University, 2004, especially pp. 3–10.

[95] Cf., on the tax reform, Ralf Wiegert, 'Die russische Steuerreform – neuer Schub für höheres Wachstum?', in Paul J. J. Welfens and Ralf Wiegert (eds.), *Transformationskrise*

taxation was also adjusted. Until then, it had been extremely difficult for the state to levy taxes on the annual profits reported by companies, as it was easy to conceal actual earnings or manipulate the figures. In the case of oil companies, the Russian government decided to base the tax more closely than before on the export price of oil, regardless of how much turnover the company made or the quality and performance of the production field. In addition to the tax on production, the government skimmed off percentage increases in margins above a certain price per barrel of oil. The higher the oil price, the higher the profits for the company, but proportionally much less than they had to pay to the state.[96] Whereas in 1999 Russian companies exported oil, natural gas, and petroleum products worth around 30 billion US dollars, this figure had risen to over 100 billion US dollars by 2004 due to rising world market prices and export volumes.[97] This resulted in Russian oil and gas companies, whether private or state-owned, paying about ten times as much in taxes to the Russian state in the mid-2000s than they did in 1999.[98]

For the Russian state budget, this meant an enormous influx of money. The oil and gas industry at that time employed only about 2 per cent of the Russian working population – less than, for example, the state railways. Yet in the mid-2000s, the sector was generating almost half of state revenues and was responsible – depending on the method of calculation – for around a quarter of gross domestic product.[99] For comparison, this was around three times the proportion that North Sea oil production comprised of UK GDP at the peak of production in the early 1980s.[100] In addition to the various taxes on energy companies, the

und neue Wirtschaftsreformen in Russland, Heidelberg: Physica-Verlag, 2002, pp. 97–118; Jakob Fruchtmann, 'Steuern durch Macht – Macht durch Steuern: Die russische Steuerpolitik unter Putin', *Osteuropa*, 52, 3 (2002), pp. 346–61.

96 Moser, *Oil and the Economy of Russia*, pp. 101–2; Roland Götz, *Russlands Ressourcen: Auswirkungen auf die inneren Verhältnisse und die Aussenpolitik*, SWP Diskussionspapier, FG 5, 2006/02, Berlin: Stiftung für Wissenschaft und Politik, 2006, p. 5.

97 Shinichiro Tabata, 'Price Differences, Taxes and the Stabilization Fund', in Michael Ellman (ed.), *Russia's Oil and Natural Gas: Bonanza or Curse?*, London: Anthem Press, 2006, pp. 35–54, here p. 36 (Table 3.1).

98 Clifford G. Gaddy and Barry W. Ickes, 'Resource Rents and the Russian Economy', *Eurasian Geography and Economics*, 46, 8 (2005), pp. 559–83, here p. 564.

99 Philip Hanson, 'The Sustainability of Russia's Energy Power: Implications for the Russian Economy', in Perović, Orttung, and Wenger (eds.), *Russian Energy Power and Foreign Relations*, pp. 23–50, here p. 27; Slavkina, *Neftegazovyi faktor*, pp. 382–83.

100 Peter Oppenheimer and Sergiy Maslichenko, 'Energy and the Economy: An Introduction', in Ellman (ed.), *Russia's Oil and Natural Gas*, pp. 15–32, here p. 18.

Russian government also benefitted from the dividends of those oil and gas companies in which the state held shares.[101]

Due to high oil prices, which began to rise just as Putin took office as president at the beginning of the 2000s and continued to climb after 2003 as a result of the Iraq war, the Kremlin now had the financial means to strengthen the state apparatus. Tax revenues from the oil sector made it possible not only to pay pensions and maintain and expand public infrastructure but also to increase the state budget for the military and the ever-larger security apparatus. In addition, thanks to revenues from commodity exports, the Russian state was able to pay off most of the international debts it had accumulated in the late Soviet period, transfer billions into a national wealth fund, and accumulate large gold and foreign currency reserves.[102]

The value of total oil and gas rents – defined in simple terms as revenue received from the sale of these resources minus the cost of production – was gigantic. According to calculations by US economists Clifford Gaddy and Barry Ickes, Russian oil and gas rents in 2008, when oil was trading at times for over 100 US dollars per barrel, totalled nearly 650 billion US dollars, 'an amount that was larger than Russia's entire GDP in any year prior to 2003'.[103] While estimates prior to Russia's invasion of Ukraine in 2022 suggest that the state sector accounted for only about a third of the economy – comparable to the United States – this does not fully capture the extent of the state's actual influence over the economy.[104] In Russia, a few large companies emerged to account for the lion's share of economic output. In 2020, Russia's 500 largest companies generated some 80 per cent of the country's domestic product. In this group of the largest companies, the oil and gas sector accounted for about 36 per cent of turnover and half of profits. The top twenty companies in this ranking, led by Gazprom, Rosneft, and Lukoil, generated half of the total revenue.[105]

[101] The tax system has been adjusted repeatedly since then. See Heli Simola and Laura Solanko, *Overview of Russia's Oil and Gas Sector*, BOFIT Policy Brief 5, Helsinki: Bank of Finland, BOFIT – Institute for Economies in Transition, 2017, pp. 30–31.

[102] Eduard Steiner, 'Putin hortet viele Milliarden Dollar aus den Ölverkäufen', *Welt*, 15 July 2018, www.welt.de/wirtschaft/article179355200/Nationaler-Wohlfahrtsfonds-Putin-hortet-viele-Milliarden-Dollar-aus-den-Oelverkaeufen.html (last accessed 7 August 2021).

[103] Clifford G. Gaddy and Barry W. Ickes, 'Russia's Dependence on Resources', in Michael V. Alexeev and Shlomo Weber (eds.), *The Oxford Handbook of the Russian Economy*, New York: Oxford University Press, 2013, pp. 309–49, here p. 315.

[104] Roland Götz, 'Das Ausmass des öffentlichen Sektors in Russland', *Russland-Analysen*, 366 (2019), pp. 2–8 (including tables and graphs).

[105] RBK, 'Reiting krupneishikh kompanii Rossii RBK 500: Osnovnye fakty', 15 October 2020, www.rbc.ru/economics/15/10/2020/5f86306e9a7947c85f43e19c (last accessed

Putin quickly realised that whoever controlled the natural resources sector controlled Russia. In this context, Putin's system was also at times referred to as 'Russia, Inc.': Russia as a colossal energy company headed by the president as its senior manager.[106] This is not a new phenomenon in Russian history. The well-known British economic historian Alec Nove once described the Soviet Union as the 'largest company in the world' and 'USSR, Inc.' because of its centralised organisational structure with an all-powerful party leadership.[107] The historical context has changed since Putin came to power. But at its core, Russia under Putin returned to a patrimonial system of running the country, with key positions in the administration, economy, and security apparatus filled by close confidants of the president.

For the state to regain full control of the central sectors of the economy, it was also necessary, from the Kremlin's point of view, to reduce the influence of foreign companies. Under Putin, the Kremlin corrected the privatisation 'mistakes' of the 1990s, when Russia ceded strategic assets to private Russian businessmen at bargain prices and sold some of its most lucrative oil fields to foreign companies. Notably, during Putin's second term as president (2004–8), the Russian leadership went about to partially reverse the share of foreign ownership in the energy sector. Russian law henceforth prohibited foreign majority stakes in those larger oil and gas fields deemed 'strategic'.[108]

In the case of Sakahlin-2, the only PSA in which no Russian company was originally involved, the state forced the foreign companies participating in this project to cede a majority share to Gazprom in 2006 on the pretext of complying with environmental regulations. Gazprom thus not only took control of this energy project, but also gained for the first time a foothold in the increasingly important liquefied natural gas industry.[109] Putin himself was more than convinced of the correctness of this course of action, describing the Sakhalin-2 PSA to a journalist from *The Times* on 4 June 2007 as a 'colonial agreement' that had 'absolutely nothing to do with Russia's national interests':

21 July 2021); on this, also see Jeronim Perović, 'Sucht nach Öl: Das "System Putin" und die Folgen der Wirtschaftskrise', *Russland-Analysen*, 313 (2016), pp. 2–7, here p. 3.

106 Clifford G. Gaddy and Andrew C. Kuchins, 'Putin's Plan', *The Washington Quarterly*, 31, 2 (2008), pp. 117–29, here p. 120f.

107 Alec Nove, *Das sowjetische Wirtschaftssystem*, Baden-Baden: Nomos, 1980, p. 24; cf. also Krempin, *Die sibirische Wucht*, p. 78.

108 Gustafson, *Wheel of Fortune*, pp. 433–35.

109 Nina Poussenkova, 'All Quiet on the Eastern Front …', *Russian Analytical Digest*, 33 (2008), pp. 13–18, here p. 15.

> I can only regret that in the early 1990s Russian officials allowed such incidents to take place, incidents for which they should have been put in prison. Implementing this treaty resulted in a situation in which, for a long period of time, Russia allowed its natural resources to be exploited and received nothing in return. Almost nothing at all.[110]

Another example of de facto expropriation was the Kovykta gas project in eastern Siberia, which was operated by RUSIA Petroleum and in which the British-Russian company TNK-BP had a 62.4 per cent stake. This majority stake held by a foreign company was a thorn in the Kremlin's side. At the end of June 2007, after months of intense pressure, TNK-BP agreed to sell its stake in RUSIA Petroleum for 700 to 900 million US dollars, an extremely modest amount given the huge potential of the field.[111] The deal never materialised in this form, and in June 2010 RUSIA Petroleum filed for bankruptcy. But TNK-BP ultimately failed to withstand the pressure and was fully acquired by Rosneft in 2013. Just three years later, Rosneft also absorbed Bashneft by dubious methods, enhancing its already dominant position as Russia's largest oil producer.[112]

The Kremlin was not interested in re-nationalising the entire oil and gas sectors or forcing out foreigners completely. Rather, powerful, state-controlled companies – so-called national champions – were to set the tone in both sectors. In the gas sector, such a company already existed in the form of Gazprom. In 2001, shortly after his inauguration as Russia's elected president, Putin had members of Gazprom's board of directors and supervisory board replaced with his confidants. He appointed his good acquaintance Aleksei Miller as chairman of Gazprom. Like Sechin, Miller was from St Petersburg, and from 1991 to 1996 he was a member of Putin's Foreign Relations Committee team in the St Petersburg mayor's office.[113] Until the mid-2000s, the state gradually bought up

[110] [Vladimir Putin], 'Interview with Newspaper Journalists from G8 Member Countries', 4 June 2007, http://en.kremlin.ru/events/president/transcripts/24313 (last accessed 8 September 2021).

[111] 'Gazprom Gets Kovykta Gas Field on the Cheap', *The St. Petersburg Times*, 26 June 2007; on this, also see Jeronim Perović and Robert W. Orttung, 'Russia's Role for Global Energy Security', in Andreas Wenger, Robert W. Orttung, and Jeronim Perović (eds.), *Energy and the Transformation of International Relations: Toward a New Producer-Consumer Framework*, The Oxford Institute for Energy Studies, Oxford: Oxford University Press, 2009, pp. 117–57, here p. 126.

[112] Roland Götz, 'Uljukajews Fall und Jewtuschenkows Niederlage: Rosnefts Expansion durch Annexion', *Russland-Analysen*, 348 (2018), pp. 2–4.

[113] Detailed information on Miller's biography can be found in 'Miller, Aleksei: Predsedatel' pravleniia, zamestitel' predsedatelia soveta direktorov OAO "Gazprom"', *Lentapedia*, https://lenta.ru/lib/14160384/ (last accessed 10 September 2021).

shares in Gazprom in order to increase its stake in the company to over 50 per cent.[114]

Gazprom subsequently became one of the world's leading energy companies, with a market capitalisation of 73.5 billion US dollars in 2020 according to Forbes, and developed activities far beyond its original core business of gas production and export.[115] Thanks to its acquisition of the private Russian oil company Sibneft (later Gazprom Neft), Gazprom in the mid-2000s also expanded into the oil business becoming one of Russia's major oil producers. The company entered oil and gas exploration and production in a number of countries, including Algeria, Bolivia, Iraq, Kazakhstan, Uzbekistan, Serbia, and Vietnam. Gazprom obtained licenses for exploration and production in the UK, Danish and Dutch sectors of the North Sea and established cooperation projects with German companies along the entire value chain, from gas production in Russia to delivery to end users in Germany. The company also acquired access to underground gas storage facilities in several European countries.[116]

The situation in the oil sector presented a more complex picture. Until 2003–4, private companies were responsible for almost 90 per cent of production. The turning point was the campaign against Khodorkovskii: the break-up of Yukos provided the opportunity to incorporate Yuganskneftegaz into Rosneft, making it Russia's biggest oil company and enabling it to gradually expand its market position through further takeovers. Thanks to these acquisitions, Rosneft managed to control around half of Russia's oil production by the mid-2000s, and, with its refineries, also acquired the largest capacity in the country for processing crude oil. The smaller private oil companies became therefore dependent on cooperation with state-owned companies for both refining and transport.

Like Gazprom, Rosneft also developed extensive international activities.[117] In January 2019, its concession agreement to operate an export crude oil pipeline in the Kurdish part of Iraq came into effect. Rosneft

[114] Jonas Grätz, *Russland als globaler Wirtschaftsakteur: Handlungsressourcen und Strategien der Öl- und Gaskonzerne*, Munich: Oldenbourg 2013, pp. 105, 108.

[115] As of 31 May 2021: Forbes, 'Gazprom', www.forbes.com/companies/gazprom/?sh=74efb61b7ec8 (last accessed 11 September 2021). A compilation of Gazprom's global activities (as of c. 2013), can be found in Grätz, *Russland als globaler Wirtschaftsakteur*, pp. 418–24.

[116] The data are taken from: Gazprom, 'Gazprom in Figures 2016–2020: Factbook', www.gazprom.com/f/posts/45/961659/gazprom-in-figures-2016-2020-en.pdf (last accessed 21 July 2021).

[117] For an overview of Rosneft's global activities (as of ca. 2013), see Grätz, *Russland als globaler Wirtschaftsakteur*, pp. 427–28.

acquired nearly half of the equity stake in Mumbai-based private oil company Nayara Energy, concluded a joint venture with Indonesia's state-owned oil and gas company Pertamina (PT Pertamina Rosneft Pengolahan dan Petrokimia), and signed a contract with Spain's Tecnicas Reunidas SA for oil refining and petrochemical complex projects on the island of Java, Indonesia. In Germany, Rosneft bought 30 per cent shares of Bayernoil, the largest refining company in Bavaria. In 2019, Rosneft Deutschland GmbH started direct marketing of petroleum products, which it supplied to customers in Germany, Poland, the Czech Republic, Austria, France, and Switzerland.[118] Due to their close relations with the Kremlin, both Rosneft and Gazprom were often favoured when new projects were awarded.

However, despite nationalisation and centralisation tendencies in the oil sector, large private companies such as Lukoil and Surgutneftegas as well as around 200 smaller companies continued to be active in Russian oil production. In addition, as of 2017, three foreign companies still remained involved in Russian oil and gas production under PSA agreements.[119] Of all the private oil companies, Lukoil was the largest and internationally most active.[120] With the acquisition of Getty Oil in 2000, Lukoil became the first Russian company ever to take over an American company, maintaining a network of around 2,000 gas stations in a dozen US states. Over the years, the company got engaged in projects in around thirty countries and acquired stakes in oil production in Kazakhstan, Uzbekistan, Azerbaijan, Iraq, the Republic of Congo, and Egypt. It was operating refineries not only in Russia but also in Ukraine, Bulgaria, Romania, Italy, and the Netherlands.[121]

Russia's first fifteen years since the collapse of the Soviet Union are comparable to the 1920s, when Bolshevik Russia opened up to foreign investment under the New Economic Policy and, thanks to Western support, oil production rebounded within a few years. Similar to what happened under Stalin from the late 1920s onwards, the state drove foreign companies out of the country once industry recovered and the economy started to grow. Unlike in the early Soviet era, however, foreign companies in the new Russia were allowed to participate in oil and gas projects with minority stakes, although the legal hurdles to market entry

[118] Information from Rosneft's website; see Rosneft, 'Rosneft at a Glance', www.rosneft.com/about/Rosneft_today/ (last accessed 7 July 2021).

[119] Simola and Solanko, *Overview of Russia's Oil and Gas Sector*, p. 5.

[120] For an overview of Lukoil's global activities (as of ca. 2013), see Grätz, *Russland als globaler Wirtschaftsakteur*, pp. 424–26.

[121] Information from Lukoil's website; see Lukoil, 'Geographic Reach', www.lukoil.com/Company/BusinessOperation/GeographicReach (last accessed 21 July 2021).

were raised under Putin.[122] Nor was it the Russian government's goal to reverse privatisation entirely. The Russian state was primarily concerned with control over national resources and access to the revenues generated by companies. Moreover, control of the extractive sector allowed the state to influence pricing in the domestic market. This left open the possibility for the Kremlin to subsidise the country's economy through the provision of discounted energy.

To be sure, the Russian state's approach to natural resources was no exception in the global context. Governments in other countries have also often been restrictive when it came to the involvement of private or foreign companies in strategically important sectors. With important exceptions such as the United States, production and reserves in most oil- and gas-rich countries are now concentrated in the hands of a few state-owned companies. The World Bank estimates that state-owned energy companies produced about 75 per cent of the world's oil and natural gas in 2011 and controlled about 90 per cent of the world's known reserves. According to the report, state-owned companies dominated production in some of the world's most oil- and gas-rich countries, including Saudi Arabia, Mexico, Venezuela, and Iran, and played a central role in the energy sectors of many emerging economies; in 2011, eighteen of the world's twenty-five largest oil and gas companies were state-owned.[123]

The impediment of foreign companies' access to the Russian raw materials sector was thus in line with a global trend. But Russia's efforts to regain control over key sectors of its industry under Putin also need to be understood in a wider historical context: deeply embedded in the collective memory are the events of the Russian Civil War, when the Bolsheviks lost control over large parts of the non-Russian-populated periphery and found themselves cut off from vital supplies of raw materials. In the process, they had to contend with anti-revolutionary forces at home and with foreign invasions. More than the Russian Civil War, however, it was Nazi Germany's attack on the Soviet Union in the Second World War and the Wehrmacht's attempt to cut the country off from Caucasian oil that fuelled fears of foreign covetousness. The consolidation of Soviet control over the parts of Eastern Europe occupied by the Red Army after the Second World War was seen as an attempt to create buffer zones that would protect Russia from such hostile attacks in the future. Scepticism towards foreign influence in strategic sectors of the economy thus reflected a tension familiar from Russian history: the claim

[122] Gustafson, *Wheel of Fortune*, pp. 434–35. [123] Ibid.

to be able to exist independently as a great power and the actual large dependence of the Russian economy on international markets for raw materials and on access to technology, knowledge, and investment from abroad.

In the Grip of Fossil Fuels

Tsar Alexander III is alleged to have said that Russia has only two allies: its army and its navy. Looking back on Putin's first two terms as president, one might similarly conclude that oil and gas were the Russian state's best friends during those critical eight years.[124] Indeed, the consolidation of the Russian state under Putin has been closely linked to its ability to regain control of the extractive sector, especially the oil industry.

However, the heavy reliance on oil, gas, and commodity trade has also had its drawbacks, as evidenced by the vulnerability of the Russian economy to fluctuations in international oil prices. When revenues from oil and gas exports fell sharply in the wake of low world market prices after 2014, the share of tax revenues from this sector in the Russian budget fell to below 40 per cent.[125] Russia was able to cushion the shock of the oil price collapse to some extent through a prudent fiscal policy and due to its large gold and foreign exchange reserves. However, the introduction of Western sanctions in 2014 and the low oil price put massive pressure on Russia's economic performance and forced the state to make some drastic cuts; even defence spending had to be temporarily reduced.[126] Russian citizens also felt the effects of this crisis, as demonstrated by the fact that real income fell by around 20 per cent between October 2014 and May 2016.[127] When the Russian government announced a sharp increase in the retirement age in 2018, citing 'financial necessity', nation-wide protests erupted, once again highlighting the danger of a prolonged period of low oil prices and how this situation can create social instability for a country heavily reliant on oil rents.[128]

124 Jeronim Perović, 'Russian Energy Power: Domestic and International Dimensions', in Perović, Orttung, and Wenger (eds.), *Russian Energy Power and Foreign Relations*, pp. 1–20, here p. 6.
125 Simola and Solanko, *Overview of Russia's Oil and Gas Sector*, pp. 30–31.
126 Jeronim Perović, *The Putin System*, CSS Analyses in Security Policy 225, Zurich: Center for Security Studies, ETH Zurich, 2018, here p. 2.
127 K. Pezoldt, T. A. Lukičeva, and I. V. Vorob'eva, 'Russlands Mittelschicht in der Krise: Kauf- und Konsumverhalten im Wandel', *Osteuropa*, 67, 5 (2017), pp. 143–52, here p. 143.
128 'Russia Pension Protests: Fresh Anti-Reform Rallies Held', *BBC News*, 2 September 2018, www.bbc.com/news/world-europe-45389797 (last accessed 28 May 2023).

At least rhetorically, the country's political leadership seems to be aware of the potential risks that this dependence involves. In public speeches and interviews, Putin has been repeatedly referring to the lack of diversity in the Russian economy as one of the major challenges for the future.[129] In reality, however, the Russian economy never made a serious effort to break away from its reliance on fossil fuel exports, especially as long as there was so much money to be made from selling oil and gas. The dilemma for Russia was that high world oil prices provided little incentive to change this system in the long term, while low prices had the potential to plunge the country into economic difficulties. It was thus no coincidence that the Soviet Union collapsed during a period of low oil prices – nor that Putin managed to stabilise the country when world oil prices had settled at high levels. Instead of overcoming this dilemma, the Putin regime hedged its bets and, rather than, for example, investing in the country's vast potential of renewable energies, including hydropower, wind, biomass, and solar energy,[130] the Kremlin leadership prioritised the funding of the internal security apparatus, cracked down on opposition figures, and did everything it could to continue to control key sectors of the economy through elites loyal to the state. For their part, the country's business elites, many of whom also hold state offices, sought to be closer to the centre of political power than before, because they were beneficiaries of the system and saw their survival tied to the regime's resilience.

At some point, the Russian state will have to look for ways to reduce the country's economic dependence on fossil fuels and commodity exports. So far, however, there has been little effort to decarbonise the industry, strengthen the non-fossil part of the energy sector, or promote sectors of the economy that are independent of the state, such as small and medium-sized enterprises (SMEs). Support for SMEs in particular would have greatly helped to diversify the Russian economy. In 2019, this sector contributed only 20 per cent to Russia's gross domestic product – far less than in the European Union, for example, where its share was around 56 per cent over the same period. To unleash the

[129] For example, on 15 June 2017, on the occasion of his annual television appearance 'Direct Wire': [Vladimir Putin], 'Priamaia liniia s Vladimirom Putinym, v efire telekanalov "Pervyi", "Rossiia 1", "Rossiia 24", radiostanitsii "Maiak", "Vesti FM" i "Radio Rossiia" vyshla 15-ia spetsial'naia programma "Priamaia liniia s Vladimirom Putinym"', 15 June 2017, http://kremlin.ru/events/president/news/54790 (last accessed 28 October 2017).

[130] Natural gas, oil, and coal accounted for nearly 90 per cent of Russia's total energy consumption in 2020. Consumption in 2020 was broken down into Gas (54 per cent), followed by oil (20 per cent), coal (15 per cent), nuclear (8 per cent), hydropower (2 per cent), and biomass (1 per cent). Data from Enerdata, 'Russia Energy Information'.

innovative potential of Russian society, it would have been necessary not only to increase legal certainty but also to reduce bureaucratic obstacles, fight corruption more resolutely, and provide loans for SMEs.[131]

But the real problem with effective diversification was that the system created under Putin over more than two decades left no room for a thriving private sector. If the top priority was to preserve a system that equated political power with control over the economy and, above all, oil and gas revenues, then it could not be assumed that the state had any interest in promoting a sector consisting of private SMEs, which by their very structure would be far more difficult to control than a few dozen large companies and oligarchs loyal to the state. In the 'Putin system', society was (and still is) the big factor of uncertainty – and the state always wanted to keep it under control as much as possible.[132]

From the point of view of a state living off the export of raw materials, the population is largely superfluous; to maintain social stability and prevent people from challenging the elite's claim to power, the government takes care of its citizens by providing essential services such as health care, education, or subsidised heating.[133] In this sense, Russia shows characteristics typical for a petrostate, where one of the basic normative principles of democracy, 'no taxation without representation', does not work; as long as revenues from the sale of oil and other commodities remain high, the state does not really depend on taxes from the population.[134] As in other contexts, this may give rise for governments feeling less accountable towards the population, leading to corruption, inequality, and ultimately a lack of trust between the state and society.

[131] Michael Martin Richter, 'Russische kleine und mittlere Unternehmen (KMUs) in der Corona-Krise – Ein Sterben auf Raten', *Russland-Analysen*, 404 (2021), pp. 10–13, here p. 10.

[132] Perović, *The Putin System*, p. 3.

[133] Alexander Etkind, 'Bevölkerung: überflüssig – Russland leidet an der von seinen abgehobenen Eliten verhängten "Öl-Krankheit"', *Neue Zürcher Zeitung*, 24 December 2019, www.nzz.ch/meinung/bevoelkerung-ueberfluessig-russland-leidet-an-der-oel-krankheit-ld.1529872?reduced=true (last accessed 27 September 2021).

[134] Etkind, *Nature's Evil*, pp. 266–67.

6 Energy, Geopolitics, and War

Energy is constitutive of a country's wealth, power, and progress. With energy serving as a fundamental pillar of modern economies, governments around the world have attached immense importance to the position and influence of their respective energy companies in the international market. Resource-poor nations strive to secure reliable and affordable access to energy, while resource-rich nations prioritise secure markets and transport routes. Given the strategic nature of energy, it is unsurprising that the global energy market has rarely been shaped solely by market forces. Geopolitical tensions, concerns over resource scarcity, and the strategic decisions of governments and powerful companies have significantly shaped the energy landscape. Russia, with its abundant reserves of oil, gas, and other natural resources, has been an integral part of this complex story from the beginning.

While political considerations have accompanied Russia's historical journey as an international energy power, economic rationales were the underlying driving force throughout most of the twentieth century and beyond. The Bolsheviks saw broadening the country's energy base as key to modernising and consolidating their socialist system. Trade in cheap oil and other commodities allowed the country to break out of its international isolation after the Russian Civil War and gain access to Western capital, technology, and know-how. The antagonism of the Cold War could not prevent the establishment of long-term energy cooperation projects that would profoundly change the nature of economic relations between the Soviet Union and Western Europe. This relationship was driven by the prospect of economic benefit but was also made possible by the assumption on both sides of the Iron Curtain that the closer the partnership, the lower the risk of disruption and confrontation.

This logic of Cold War energy interdependence, based on a combination of mutually beneficial economic and political interests, helped to build up stable trade relations between East and West. This did not mean, however, that Moscow would not use its economic power, including cutting off exports of oil and other raw materials, to assert its interests vis-à-vis countries not formally aligned with the Western capitalist camp. In the early stages of the Cold War, the most famous case was neutral Finland. Dissatisfied with the composition of the Finnish government, the Kremlin leadership imposed a short-term embargo on the export of oil in 1958 in a bid to force its neighbour to change the composition of its government. The Soviet Union offered oil, technology, and the expertise of its engineers to its socialist allies and to friendly governments around the world but stopped providing support when these states did not follow Moscow's directions – as in the case of Yugoslavia following the break between Stalin and Tito in 1948 or when relations with Mao's China deteriorated in the late 1950s.

From a European perspective, therefore, it is certainly true that throughout the Cold War and beyond – at least until the outbreak of the Russian–Ukrainian war in 2022 – Russia proved to be a dependable energy supplier. Apart from minor technical failures and accidents, there were no significant interruptions in energy flows between Russia and Western Europe. For some of Russia's neighbours and former socialist allies, however, Russia was anything but a reliable partner. Already in the last days of the Soviet Union, in the spring of 1990, the Kremlin leadership under Gorbachev decided to impose temporary economic sanctions on Lithuania, including a halt to oil and gas supplies, to prevent this Soviet republic from seceding from the union state.[1] This behaviour was to continue after the collapse of the Soviet Union. In his study of Russian energy policy, Robert Larsson identified some fifty-five instances between 1992 and 2006 where Russia had interrupted or threatened to interrupt oil or gas supplies to former Soviet republics.[2] In particular, Russia exerted its 'petro-power' against Belarus, Ukraine, Moldova, and Georgia, repeatedly using supply volumes and prices as part of a 'carrot and stick' policy.[3] In the mid-2000s, for example, Gazprom sold its gas to Belarus at significantly lower prices than it did to Ukraine because Minsk agreed in principle to sell the Russian company a share in its gas pipeline network, while Kyiv had expressly rejected such a move.[4]

[1] Jürgen Buch, 'Wie Moskau schon vor 32 Jahren Litauen das Gas abklemmte', *Der Spiegel*, 21 July 2022, www.spiegel.de/geschichte/energieblockade-gegen-litauen-1990-man-muss-klar-sagen-auf-welcher-seite-man-steht-a-a784c548-50b8-4aa3-a67c-e96309c1a854 (last accessed 22 July 2022).

[2] Robert L. Larsson, *Russia's Energy Policy: Security Dimensions and Russia's Reliability as an Energy Supplier*, Stockholm: Swedish Defence Research Agency, 2006, in particular p. 4 and p. 262f.

[3] Randall Newnham, 'Oil, Carrots, and Sticks: Russia's Energy Resources as a Foreign Policy Tool', *Journal of Eurasian Studies*, 2, 2 (2011), pp. 134–43.

[4] Simon Pirani, *Ukraine's Gas Sector*, Oxford: The Oxford Institute for Energy Studies, 2007, p. 9; on the different prices, see diagrams 3 and 4 in 'Gazprom's Foreign Policy', *Russian Analytical Digest*, 41(2008), p. 12.

The repeated Russian–Ukrainian gas crises gave European countries increasing cause for concern, as cuts in supplies also affected customers outside Ukraine. The first major Russian–Ukrainian gas row came in 2006. Of those that followed, the 2009 conflict was particularly momentous: when negotiations on setting the price of natural gas for the new year broke down, Gazprom stopped supplies to Ukraine for two weeks in the middle of winter. Since, at that time, Gazprom was still piping most of the gas it sent to Europe through Ukraine, the disruption led to supply shortages in some twenty European countries that imported Russian gas, triggering an energy crisis the likes of which Europe had not seen since the 1970s. The impact of the crisis was felt most acutely in the east-central and south-eastern European states, which were highly dependent on Russian gas imports and where the lack of gas meant that many people could no longer even heat their homes.[5]

Energy disputes between Russia and its post-Soviet neighbours have often been about much more than prices and volumes; they have been about fundamental issues of sovereignty, power, and dependency. Especially during the major gas row of 2009, the Ukrainian government interpreted Russia's behaviour as evidence that the Kremlin, through its state-controlled company Gazprom, would not hesitate to use energy as a 'weapon' to keep Ukraine and other neighbouring countries in Russia's sphere of influence. Gazprom's management, meanwhile, sought to present a different picture to the international public. In the Russian view, Gazprom was being held hostage by a notoriously unreliable neighbour who not only regularly failed to pay its debts to Gazprom but also illegally diverted natural gas destined for European customers for its own purposes; according to Russia's reading, Gazprom was thus forced to cut off gas supplies, including those destined for customers outside Ukraine.[6]

Within the EU, concerns about dependence on an increasingly authoritarian Russia predated 2009, but it was the experience of this major gas crisis that triggered a fundamental debate about the future handling of Russian raw materials imports. As a result, Brussels passed new laws prohibiting energy companies from monopolising production, transport, and distribution to the end consumer. Gazprom's position of power in the European energy market thus suffered a serious setback. At the same time, however, it was very clear that most European countries did not seriously consider moving away from Russian oil and gas. In fact, even following the Russian–Ukrainian conflict of 2014–15, when Gazprom once again – and this time permanently – halted gas supplies to

[5] Perović, 'Farce ums Gas', p. 19. [6] Ibid., p. 20f.

the Ukrainian market, Russian overall gas deliveries to Europe, including Turkey, continued to increase.[7] If Russian gas represented 29 per cent of total EU imports in 2014, this share, including imports by the United Kingdom, had surged to 37 per cent by 2019.[8]

Moreover, Gazprom continued to push for the construction of additional pipelines that would bypass Ukrainian territory in order to reduce its dependency on Ukraine as the main transport route for Russian gas destined for Europe. In December 2014, Putin cancelled the South Stream pipeline project through the Black Sea to Bulgaria due to new EU regulations on energy market unbundling, which were implemented after the 2009 Russian–Ukrainian gas dispute. In response, Gazprom partnered with the Turkish state energy company BOTAŞ to construct a second pipeline, called Turkish Stream, through the Black Sea to Turkey. This pipeline followed the path of the Blue Stream pipeline, which had been completed in 2010 to supply Turkey and other states in south-eastern Europe with gas. At the same time, Gazprom in June 2015 managed to sign a major agreement with several European companies on the construction of a second gas pipeline through the Baltic Sea to connect Russia directly to Germany (Nord Stream 2).

Both pipeline projects were subject to US sanctions but were nevertheless completed. The discussions surrounding Nord Stream 2 were particularly fierce – and strikingly similar to the disputes between Americans and Western Europeans over the construction of the Urengoi gas export pipeline in 1981–82. In particular, Germany, which was the main economic beneficiary of the project, tended to view this pipeline as an important symbolic bridge to Russia that needed to be nurtured in the context of increasing geopolitical tensions. If Russia was dependent on commodity revenues and on Europe as its main export destination for oil and gas, the argument went, Russia would continue to try to present itself as a reliable energy supplier that would also offer its pipeline gas at cheaper prices than its LNG competitors. Essentially, the argument for deepening cooperation with Russia followed the same logic as Germany's *Ostpolitik* of the late 1960s, namely that trade would eventually lead to change and rapprochement – even though Russia had by this time long since left the path of Western-style democracy.

7 If Gazprom's natural gas exports made to countries outside the former Soviet Union stood at 158.6 billion m^3 in 2015, this figure rose to around 200 billion in 2018 and 2019, and dropped to 174.9 billion in 2020. See Gazprom Export, 'Gas Supplies to Europe', https://gazpromexport.ru/en/statistics/ (last accessed 24 July 2022).

8 IEA, 'Share of Russia in European Union and United Kingdom Gas Demand, 2001–2021', 20 May 2022, www.iea.org/data-and-statistics/charts/share-of-russia-in-european-union-and-united-kingdom-gas-demand-2001-2021 (last accessed 24 July 2022).

By contrast, opponents – primarily the United States, Poland, and Ukraine – stressed that Nord Stream 2 ran counter to the EU's stated goal of greater import diversification.[9] Just as, during the pipeline dispute of 1981–82, Reagan had offered the Europeans more coal from the United States in place of Soviet gas, Washington offered American shale gas in liquid form as a substitute for Russian natural gas.[10] From the Ukrainian point of view, Nord Stream 2 was about much more: Kyiv claimed that with its two new gas links, Nord Stream 2 and Turkish Stream, Russia would for the first time have enough export capacity to be able to largely do without Ukraine for the transit of its gas to Europe. If Russia no longer depended on the Ukrainian transport corridor, Kyiv worried, Ukraine would lose its last bargaining chip against its powerful neighbour, making it vulnerable in future negotiations on economic cooperation and energy imports – and also weakening its position when it came to resolving the conflict in the Donbas or repelling new military threats by Russia.[11] Moreover, Ukraine feared that if it lost its status as a transit country for Russian gas, it would forfeit not only annual revenues of two to three billion US dollars but also its position and influence in the larger European energy market.[12]

In the wake of further US sanctions imposed at the end of 2019, work on the Nord Stream 2 pipeline was halted for about a year as individual companies stopped their participation in the project in response to US pressure. Particularly problematic was the fact that the Swiss service provider Allseas withdrew its lay vessels and suspended all activities related to the construction of the pipeline in line with US demands.[13] It was only after a Russian lay vessel stepped into the breach and the German government signalled that it would continue to support the

[9] Robert Stüwe, 'Unpacking the German Debate on Nord Stream 2', *Russian Analytical Digest*, 267 (2021), pp. 5–14.

[10] Todd Prince, 'U.S. Efforts to Derail Russian Pipelines to Europe Have Failed since the 1960s: Will Nord Stream 2 Be Any Different?', *Radio Free Europe/Radio Liberty*, 13 August 2019, www.rferl.org/a/us-efforts-stop-russia-pipelines-will-nord-stream-2-be-different/30107938.html (last accessed 3 October 2019).

[11] Marc Champion and Daryana Krasnolutska, 'Russia's New Pipeline Makes Ukraine Worry Less about Gas but More about War', *Bloomberg*, 24 September 2021, www.bloomberg.com/news/articles/2021-09-24/nord-stream-2-pipeline-news-ukraine-worries-less-about-gas-more-about-war (last accessed 22 October 2021).

[12] Jeronim Perović and Maria Shagina, *Nord Stream 2: It's Time to Change Perspective*, CSS Policy Perspectives, Vol. 9/6, Zurich: Center for Security Studies, ETH Zurich, 2021.

[13] Matthias Jauch, 'Allseas plant keine Fortsetzung der Pipeline-Verlegung', *Der Tagesspiegel*, 31 December 2019, www.tagesspiegel.de/politik/nach-us-sanktionen-wegen-nord-stream-2-allseas-plant-keine-fortsetzung-der-pipeline-verlegung/25375366.html (last accessed 10 September 2021).

project that work resumed in February 2021.[14] By this time, the Turkish Stream pipeline project, also subject to US sanctions, had been completed. In early summer 2021, when it became apparent that Nord Stream 2 was also nearing completion, Washington abandoned its opposition to the pipeline. According to US President Joe Biden, extending sanctions to the Gazprom-owned operating company Nord Stream 2 AG, based in Zug, Switzerland, would have been 'counterproductive' for America's relationship with Europe.[15] In July 2021, Washington and Berlin formally settled their differences in a joint statement in support of Ukraine, European energy security, and climate goals. In it, both sides asserted, among other things, that they were prepared to impose new sanctions on Moscow 'should Russia attempt to use energy as a weapon or commit further aggressive acts against Ukraine'.[16]

It was therefore hardly surprising that on 22 February 2022, in direct response to Russia's escalating move to formally recognise the independence of the Luhansk and Donetsk 'people's republics', which are part of Ukraine under international law, the German government decided to halt the certification process for the Nord Stream 2 pipeline, thereby preventing the pipeline from coming onstream.[17] Just two days later, Russia attacked Ukraine, prompting an unprecedented disruption of European–Russian political and economic relations, including in the energy sector. For the first time since Soviet gas arrived in Austria in 1968, Russia lowered or even cut off gas supplies to several European countries in retaliation for Western sanctions and support for Ukraine, raising the spectre of Europe's worst energy nightmare, as shortages were feared and prices soared. In fact, by displaying the same pattern of behaviour towards Europe that it has long shown towards its

[14] 'Nord Stream 2: Arbeiten wieder aufgenommen', *ZDF heute*, 6 February 2021, www.zdf.de/nachrichten/politik/nord-stream-pipeline-arbeiten-wiederaufnahme-100.html (last accessed 10 September 2021).

[15] 'Biden zu Nord Stream 2: "Sanktionen wären kontraproduktiv gewesen"', *ARD Tagesschau*, 26 May 2021, www.tagesschau.de/ausland/amerika/biden-nordstream-2-sanktionen-101.html (last accessed 11 September 2021).

[16] [Auswärtiges Amt der Bundesrepublik Deutschland], 'Gemeinsame Erklärung der USA und Deutschlands zur Unterstützung der Ukraine, der europäischen Energiesicherheit und unserer Klimaziele', *Pressemitteilung*, 21 July 2021, www.auswaertiges-amt.de/de/newsroom/gemeinsame-erklaerung-usa-und-deutschland/2472074 (last accessed 3 October 2021). Cf. also Maria Shagina and Kirsten Westphal, *Nord Stream 2 and the Energy Security Dilemma: Opportunities, Options and Obstacles for a Grand Bargain*, SWP Comment 46, Berlin: SWP, German Institute for International and Security Affairs, 2021.

[17] Oliver Maksan and René Höltschi, 'Deutschland stoppt Nord Stream 2 – doch beerdigt ist das Projekt noch nicht', *Neue Zürcher Zeitung*, 22 February 2022, www.nzz.ch/international/nord-stream-2-kanzler-scholz-stoppt-zertifizierungsverfahren-ld.1671116 (last accessed 24 July 2022).

post-Soviet neighbours, Russia has broken with its decades-long tradition of seeming to prioritise economics over politics when dealing with states outside of what Moscow considers its immediate sphere of influence.

To be sure, energy prices on the European market had already skyrocketed before Russia's military aggression against Ukraine. In late 2021, Europe's wholesale gas price was over five times higher than it had been at the beginning of that year. A barrel of oil was 50 per cent more expensive; the prices of coal and electricity had also increased significantly. The images of long queues of cars in front of British petrol stations revived memories of the energy crisis of 1973–74. Yet unlike in the 1970s, when it was the Arab members of OPEC that had driven up the price of oil through their embargo policy, in the autumn of 2021, it was Russia that was at the centre of the debate. Due to the high gas prices, the term 'blackmail' was widely used in Western media. Russia's state-company Gazprom was accused of not increasing gas supply to Europe despite rising demand and empty storage facilities as a means of exerting pressure to hasten the completion of Nord Stream 2.

Embargoes and supply disruptions have the potential to severely affect global markets. Yet a look at a hundred years of energy history shows that strategically important raw materials such as oil have always found their way back onto the market as long as there has been demand, enabling trade and relations between states with differing political, economic, and social systems. Due to its enormous wealth of oil, gas, and other natural resources, Russia is therefore likely to remain important for global energy. The question is to what extent, through which routes, and at what prices Russian natural resources will enter the market – and which countries will be among Russia's most important customers. Even though the trend towards a reorientation of Russian exports away from Europe and towards the Asia-Pacific and other world regions has been evident for some time and has intensified with the start of the Russian–Ukrainian war in 2022, it is difficult to imagine a complete and permanent decoupling of Russian energy from Europe as long as European industry and households continue to rely on fossil fuels.

For Russia, too, a comprehensive geographical reorientation of its energy exports away from Europe would be difficult to achieve, given existing infrastructure connections and the reliance of Russia's energy sector on Western investment and technology transfer. While redirecting oil flows may be feasible, as Russia exports most of its oil by tanker, gas is more of a problem. It would take many years to build the pipeline capacity to increase exports to China and other Asian countries to the level of the volumes supplied to the EU in 2021 (155 billion m^3).

Moreover, this would require not only an increase in Asian demand but also continued Russian access to capital and technology for maintaining its natural gas production (including from new LNG-production facilities) at a high level. This will be difficult due to Western sanctions and also because of the withdrawal of hundreds of Western firms from Russia since the outbreak of the Russian–Ukrainian war in February 2022. In the energy sector alone, more than 40 per cent of international companies have pulled out of or temporarily suspended their operations in Russia by the end of 2022, including such major companies as BP, Shell, and Exxon Mobil.[18]

The fact that the purchase of oil and gas from authoritarian Russia was causing unease in Europe even before Russia's attack on Ukraine was understandable in the context of Russia's increasingly aggressive behaviour and geopolitical uncertainty. Europe is therefore right to reduce its overdependence on Russian resources and diversify its gas and oil imports. Above all, Europe should seize the opportunity to promote non–fossil energy sources and accelerate decarbonisation. The 'energy bridge' between Europe and Russia has been severely damaged, symbolised by the destruction of three of the four strands of the Nord Stream pipeline system in September 2022. But the prospect of Russia now completely isolating itself from Europe and aligning even more closely with other authoritarian states such as China is not edifying. The idealistic notion of 'change through rapprochement' may have failed, but losing Russia altogether cannot be in Europe's long-term interest either.

[18] Cf. Perović, *Russia's Future as an Energy Power.*

Conclusion

Russia's abundant natural resources have not determined its history but have instead provided avenues for specific paths of development. The Bolsheviks of the early Soviet era considered oil to play a rather subordinate role in the industrialisation and modernisation of the country compared to, for example, coal. Lenin, however, recognised oil as a valuable commodity that could be used in the field of international diplomacy as well as an export product to earn hard currency and acquire Western technology. In the 1920s, the sale of crude oil and petroleum products did not yet generate the high returns that were to be achieved in the 1970s and early 1980s. But the 'black gold' from the Soviet Caucasus was in great demand on international markets. It lent itself to international trade and attracted Western companies to invest in the Soviet energy sector.

The triumph of Soviet oil, which the Soviet Union distributed through its trade organisations and state-owned enterprises in Europe and around the world, was brought to a halt only by the Great Depression and stagnating domestic production growth rates in the 1930s. During the Second World War, Soviet oil production plummeted by a third as Hitler's armies marched on Grozny and Baku, since Stalin had given orders to dismantle or outright destroy petroleum facilities to prevent them from falling into enemy hands. At the same time, this existential threat situation led to a sustained re-evaluation of oil in Soviet energy policy. Even as the war with Nazi Germany raged, the Soviet Union set about developing new oil fields in the Volga-Urals region. Thanks to these deposits, the country was able to sell ever-greater volumes of oil abroad in the 1950s. During the Cold War, Soviet crude oil and petroleum products and, later, natural gas became binding agents in the 'Eastern bloc' controlled by Moscow. With the development of the gigantic Western Siberian oil and gas fields in the 1960s and especially in the 1970s, the Soviet Union also had enough raw materials at its disposal to become Western Europe's most important energy supplier. The foreign exchange earnings generated in the Western dollar zone from the oil and gas business became an indispensable source of income for Moscow. Meanwhile, energy trade with the socialist 'fraternal states', which was mainly conducted through barter transactions, appeared to the Soviet Union to be less and less profitable.

The history of energy is closely linked to Russia's rise as a modern great power. At the same time, Russian energy history is part of global history. As the only major industrial nation of the twentieth century, Russia was largely able to supply itself with energy from its own raw material base. To exploit these resources, however, the country was dependent on foreign capital and cooperation with international companies. It was trade in raw materials and primary goods that gave Russia access to Western technology, credit, and knowledge that it needed for its industrial development. These international exchanges were accompanied by transnational contacts between politicians, trade officials, scientists, and representatives of the oil and gas industry. In this way, trust was built across the Iron Curtain, which in the case of Soviet–Western European relations from the late 1960s onwards was an important precondition for the conclusion of ever larger long-term gas trade agreements.

Most sectors of the Soviet economy were crisis-ridden in the 1970s and 1980s. However, the development of the Western Siberian gas deposits may be seen as perhaps the last great success story of late Soviet industrial economic development. Gas rose to become the most important component of the Soviet energy mix during this period. Moreover, gas could be profitably sold abroad through existing international cooperation agreements, and the large quantities of gas freed up more oil for export to the lucrative Western market. At the same time, however, Moscow's claim to be able to exist as a great power independently of and on an equal footing with the capitalist economies collided more than ever before with the reality of ever-increasing dependence on Western sales markets and foreign exchange earnings.

Until the early 1960s, the idea was still widespread within the party leadership that by expanding trade relations with the economically advanced Western countries, the Soviet Union would build up its own industrial capacities, thereby enabling the country to 'catch up and overtake' the West in the near future. According to Khrushchev, the Soviet Union was not to be reduced to the status of a commodities' supplier to the Western capitalists but was to become an exporter of manufactured goods that could compete on the world market. However, as the Soviet Union was unable to develop its energy sector independently of foreign credits and technology imports, its dependence on raw material exports increased over time. Although the volume of foreign trade grew and international economic arrangements became more sophisticated, the Soviet Union's participation in the global capitalist economy remained limited to its role as an exporter of raw materials, as it failed to become an industrialised economic superpower capable of producing and selling high-quality goods and manufactured products.

To be sure, the precise form that international economic cooperation was to take remained largely open even at the beginning of the 1970s. During the détente period between the two superpowers, Moscow initially favoured large energy deals with American and Japanese companies – not pipelines to Europe but multibillion-dollar projects for the liquefaction of Siberian natural gas to be shipped across the world's oceans dominated Soviet energy visions at the time. The fact that ever closer energy ties with Western European countries eventually prevailed was due both to the positive experience of concluding trade agreements between Soviet and Western European companies and to the continuing deterioration in relations between Moscow and Washington. The two global energy crises of the 1970s also served to accelerate the energy rapprochement between the Soviet Union and Western Europe. Governments in Europe, keen to reduce their heavy dependence on oil imports from the Persian Gulf, saw Soviet gas as a way of diversifying their imports and reducing the share of oil in their countries' energy mix.

In the case of the FRG, which became not only the main buyer but also the central hub for Soviet energy exports to other Western European countries, Moscow wanted to hedge against possible embargoes, such as the one imposed by NATO on the supply of steel pipes in 1962 and saw the creation of mutual dependencies as a way of mitigating such a threat in the future. The efforts of specific personalities on both the West German and Soviet sides to restore mutual trust played no small part in the trade negotiations that led to the conclusion of the major 'gas-for-pipes' deals in the early 1970s; while building trust was essential, however, it was even better to create structural conditions to minimise potential risks.

The Soviet Union relied on revenues from trade in commodities for the modernisation of its economy. Over time, however, export earnings were used to compensate for the shortcomings of an increasingly unbalanced economic system. In the late Soviet period, a substantial portion of the foreign exchange earnings generated from oil sales had to be spent on buying American grain. The Soviet agricultural sector, which was plagued by drought, mismanagement, and poor planning, was simply unable to produce enough grain for its own population. In an environment of high world market prices for oil in the 1970s and early 1980s, the Soviet Union thus propped up its command economy by expanding raw material exports to the West. It was only when oil prices collapsed in the mid-1980s that the party leadership under Gorbachev could no longer avoid introducing comprehensive reforms designed to save the planned economy and socialism. The attempt failed because the system collapsed under the pressure of the reforms and growing national discontent.

The new democratic beginnings after 1991 proved difficult for Russia. While a few took advantage of the freedoms of the liberalised market for shameless self-enrichment, millions were left behind in social hardship and poverty. Against the backdrop of the profound social, economic, and political crisis of the 1990s, it was easy for Yeltsin's successor to credibly claim that he had restored law and order in Russia and thus laid the foundations for growth and prosperity. In Putin's narrative, the 1990s have exclusively negative connotations. He thus concealed the fact that the upswing would not have been possible without the painful reforms of his predecessor. It was under Putin and with rising oil prices that the Russian economy was to recover in the 2000s. But the seeds of this recovery were sown with the changes of the 1990s, which enabled part of Russian society to demonstrate its innovative potential, irrespective of the price of oil. The oil industry, in particular, benefitted from the opening of the country to foreign capital and joint ventures with Western companies, as this contributed to the stabilisation and subsequent upswing of this sector.

The 1990s suggested that an alternative historical trajectory might have been possible for Russia. Under Putin, however, Russia embarked on a path essentially aimed at restoring state control over the strategically important mineral resources sector and thus securing access to the revenues from oil and gas exports. In the process, the state visibly reduced both the scope for private enterprise in the country and the influence of foreign companies. For a while, this path seemed to be quite profitable. The economy was growing; people's incomes were rising. Energy profits also paid for the modernisation of the Russian armed forces and the ever-expanding state security apparatus. But Russia ossified politically, and the economy lacked innovation. Under the authoritarian leadership established under Putin, Russian society was given less and less freedom to participate actively and confidently in shaping the country's future.

Russia's energy wealth has historically been a key pillar of state power and an essential foundation of the country's economy. But especially since Putin came to power, this wealth has also been the Achilles' heel of a system based on the redistribution of oil and gas revenues tightly controlled by a highly centralised state. This toxic link between energy and power has stifled social dynamism and made much-needed changes to the economic and political system extremely difficult.

Bibliography

Archives

Gosudarstvennyi Arkhiv Rossiiskoi Federatsii (GARF): f. 5446
Rossiiskii Gosudarstvennyi Arkhiv Ekonomiki (RGAE): f. 4372, f. 9480
Rossiiskii Gosudarstvennyi Arkhiv Noveishei Istorii (RGANI): f. 80, f. 52
Rossiiskii Gosudarstvennyi Arkhiv Noveishei Istorii (RGANI) [Hoover Archive]: f. 89
Rossiiskii Gosudarstvennyi Arkhiv Sotsial'no-Politicheskoi Istorii (RGASPI): f. 77
Schweizerisches Bundesarchiv (BAR)

Document Collections, Published Primary Sources, and Speeches

XXVII s''ezd Kommunisticheskoi partii Sovetskogo Soiuza, 25 fevr.–6 marta 1986 g.: Stenograficheskii otchet, in 3 vols., vol. 2, Moscow: Politizdat, 1986.

Akten zur Auswärtigen Politik der Bundesrepublik Deutschland (1963), edited by the Institut für Zeitgeschichte, Munich: Oldenbourg, 1994.

Akten zur Auswärtigen Politik der Bundesrepublik Deutschland (1969), edited by the Institut für Zeitgeschichte, Munich: Oldenbourg, 2000.

Akten zur Auswärtigen Politik der Bundesrepublik Deutschland (1973), edited by the Institut für Zeitgeschichte, Munich: Oldenbourg, 2004.

Akten zur Auswärtigen Politik der Bundesrepublik Deutschland (1980), edited by the Institut für Zeitgeschichte, Munich: Oldenbourg, 2011.

Akten zur Auswärtigen Politik der Bundesrepublik Deutschland (1981), edited by the Institut für Zeitgeschichte, Munich: Oldenbourg, 2012.

Akten zur Auswärtigen Politik der Bundesrepublik Deutschland (1990), edited by the Institut für Zeitgeschichte, Berlin, Boston: De Gruyter, Oldenbourg, 2021.

[Auswärtiges Amt der Bundesrepublik Deutschland], 'Gemeinsame Erklärung der USA und Deutschlands zur Unterstützung der Ukraine, der europäischen Energiesicherheit und unserer Klimaziele', *Pressemitteilung*, 21 July 2021, www.auswaertiges-amt.de/de/newsroom/gemeinsame-erklaerung-usa-und-deutschland/2472074 (last accessed 3 October 2021).

Brezhnev, L. I., *O vneshnei politike KPSS i Sovetskogo gosudarstva: Rechi i stat'i*, Moscow: Politizdat, 1973.

Burdett, Anita L. P. (ed.), *Oil Resources in Eastern Europe and the Caucasus*, vol. 7, 1960–1966, Cambridge: Cambridge University Press, 2012.

(ed.), *Oil Resources in Eastern Europe and the Caucasus*, vol. 8, 1967–1978, Cambridge: Cambridge University Press, 2012.

Central Intelligence Agency, 'Alleged Use of Forced Labor on Siberian Pipeline, Memorandum for Richard Burt, Assistant Secretary of State', Washington, DC, 20 August 1982, www.foia.cia.gov/sites/default/files/document_conversions/89801/DOC_0000102966.pdf (last accessed 16 August 2021).

'The Impeding Soviet Oil Crisis, Intelligence Memorandum', Washington, DC, 1977, www.cia.gov/readingroom/docs/DOC_0000498607.pdf (last accessed 10 July 2021).

Daily Report, Soviet Union, FBIS-SOV-74-115, US Foreign Broadcast Information Service/NTIS, 13 June 1974 [translation of speech by Aleksei Kosygin on 12 June 1974].

Dekrety Sovetskoi vlasti, vol. 11, October–November 1920, Moscow: Politizdat, 1983.

Fursenko, A. A. (ed.), *Prezidium TsK KPSS 1954–1964: Chernovye protokol'nye zapisi zasedanii; Stenogrammy; Postanovleniia*, in 3 vols., vol. 1, Chernovye protokol'nye zapisi zasedanii: Stenogrammy, Moscow: Politicheskaia entsiklopedia, 2003.

Prezidium TsK KPSS 1954–1964: Chernovye protokol'nye zapisi zasedanii; Stenogrammy; Postanovleniia, in 3 vols., vol. 1, Postanovleniia, Moscow: Politicheskaia entsiklopedia, 2015.

General'nyi sekretar' L. I. Brezhnev 1964–1982: Spetsial'noe izdanie, Moscow: Vestnik Arkhiva Prezidenta, 2006.

Hardt, John P., *Soviet Pipeline*, Congressional Research Service, Washington, DC: The Library of Congress [1982].

[Hitler, Adolf], 'Denkschrift Hitlers über die Aufgaben eines Vierjahresplans', *Vierteljahrshefte für Zeitgeschichte*, 3, 2 (1955), pp. 204–10.

Kazarina, I. V., and M. Iu. Prozumenshchikov (eds.), *Novyi mir v Evrope: SSSR, FRG i Moskovskii dogovor 1970 goda po dokumentam TsK KPSS; Sbornik dokumentov*, Moscow: Kuchkovo Pole, 2020.

Keefer, Edward C. (ed.), *Soviet-American Relations: The Détente Years, 1969–1972*, Washington, DC: United States Government Printing Office, 2007.

Khlevniuk, O. V. et al., *Zakliuchennye na stroikakh kommunizma: Gulag i ob''ekty energetiki v SSSR; Sobranie dokumentov i fotografii*, Moscow: ROSSPEN, 2008.

Khrushchev, Nikita Sergeevich, *Dva tsveta vremeni: Dokumenty iz lichnogo fonda N. S. Khrushcheva*, vol. 2, Moscow: Mezhdunarodnyi fond 'Demokratiia', 2009.

Khrushchev in America: Full Texts of the Speeches Made by N. S. Khrushchev Chairman of the Council of Ministers of the USSR on His Tour of the United States, September 15–27, 1959; Translated from the Book Published in the USSR Entitled 'Live in Peace and Friendship!', New York: Crosscurrents Press, 1960.

Lenin, V. I., *Collected Works*, vol. 31, Moscow: Progress, 1966.

Collected Works, vol. 32, Moscow: Progress, 1973.

Collected Works, vol. 33, Moscow: Progress, 1973.

The Immediate Tasks of the Soviet Government, Moscow: Foreign Languages Publishing House, 1951.

[Litvinov, M. M.], 'Die Sowjetunion auf der Weltwirtschaftskonferenz: Rede des Aussenkommissars der Sowjetunion, M. M. Litwinow, gehalten am 14. Juni 1933 auf der Londoner Weltwirtschaftskonferenz', *Sowjetwirtschaft und Aussenhandel: Halbmonatszeitschrift der Handelsvertretung der UdSSR in Deutschland*, 12, 11 (1933), pp. 2–8.

'Memorandum from the International Department of the Central Committee of the CPSU to Alexander Yakovlev', February 1989, *History and Public Policy Program Digital Archive*, Archive of the Gorbachev Foundation, Moscow; on file at the National Security Archive, donated by Professor Jacques Levesque; Translated by Svetlana Savranskaya and Gary Goldberg, https://digitalarchive.wilsoncenter.org/document/112485 (last accessed 8 November 2021).

'Na VI spetsial'noi sessii General'noi Assemblei OON: Vystuplenie A. A. Gromyko', *Pravda*, 102, 12 April 1974, p. 4.

Narodnyi komissariat po inostrannym delam [RSFSR], *Materialy Genueskoi Konferentsii (podgotovka, otchety zasedanii, raboty komissii, diplomaticheskaia perepiska i pr.)*, Moscow: n.p., 1922, pp. 78–82.

National Petroleum Council, *Impact of Oil Exports from the Soviet Bloc: A Report of the National Petroleum Council's Committee and Working Subcommittee on the Impact of Oil Exports from the Soviet Bloc*, vol. I, Washington, DC: n.p., 1962.

'National Security Council Meeting', 6 July 1981, The Cabinet Room, Washington, DC, https://www.thereaganfiles.com/19810706-nsc-16.pdf (last accessed 18 July 2021).

'Notes on the Conversation of Comrade N. S. Khrushchev with Comrade W. Ulbricht on 1 August 1961', *History and Public Policy Program Digital Archive*, f. 52, op. 1, d. 557; obtained and translated by Hope M. Harrison and included in CWIHP e-Dossier No. 23, https://digitalarchive.wilsoncenter.org/document/110206 (last accessed 6 November 2021).

'Notiz über die Unterredung zwischen Herrn Bundesrat Willi Ritschard und Herrn Vizeminister Ossipov im Sowjetischen Aussenhandelsministerium am 16.5.1975, 10.30 bis 11.30 h', in https://dodis.ch/38788 (last accessed on 18 July 2021).

'Ob organizatsii v vedenii Narodnogo komissariata vneshnei torgovli Vsesoiuznogo ob''edineniia po eksportu nefti i nefteproduktov ("Soiuznefteeksport")', Moscow, Kremlin, 26 February 1931', *Istoricheskie materialy* (Istmat), http://istmat.info/node/54632 (last accessed 30 April 2021).

Papers Relating to the Foreign Relations of the United States 1923, vol. II, Washington, DC: United States Government Printing Office, 1938.

Petroleum Industry Research Foundation, 'Special Report: The Role of Oil in the Soviet Economy', *Pirinc Reports on World Business*, 15 October 1956.

Procacci, Giuliano et al. (eds.), *The Cominform: Minutes of the Three Conferences 1947/1948/1949*, Milano: Feltrinelli Editore Milano, 1994.

Public Papers of the Presidents of the United States, *Jimmy Carter 1980–1981 (In Three Books): Book I – January 1 to May 23, 1980*, Washington, DC: United States Government Printing Office, 1981.

[Putin, Vladimir], 'Annual Address to the Federal Assembly of the Russian Federation', 16 May 2003, Moscow, Kremlin, http://en.kremlin.ru/events/president/transcripts/21998 (last accessed 21 July 2021).

'Interview with Newspaper Journalists from G8 Member Countries', 4 June 2007, http://en.kremlin.ru/events/president/transcripts/24313 (last accessed 8 September 2021).

'Priamaia liniia s Vladimirom Putinym, V efire telekanalov "Pervyi", "Rossiia 1", "Rossiia 24", radiostanitsii "Maiak", "Vesti FM" i "Radio Rossiia" vyshla 15-ia spetsial'naia programma "Priamaia liniia s Vladimirom Putinym"', 15 June 2017, http://kremlin.ru/events/president/news/54790 (last accessed 28 October 2017).

'Rossiia na rubezhe tysiacheletii', *Nezavisimaia gazeta*, 30 December 1999, www.ng.ru/politics/1999-12-30/4_millenium.html (last accessed 21 July 2021).

'Record of Conversation of Brezhnev with Leaders of Fraternal Parties of Socialist Countries, 18 March 1975', *History and Public Policy Program Digital Archive*, Library of Congress, Manuscript Division, Dmitrii Antonovich Volkogonov papers, 1887–1995, mm97083838, Reel 16, Container 24; Translated by Svetlana Savranskaya for the National Security Archive, https://digitalarchive.wilsoncenter.org/document/121171 (last accessed 8 November 2021).

Russia: The Official Report of the British Trades Union Delegation to Russia and Caucasia Nov. and Dec., 1924, London: Co-Operative Printing Society, 1925.

Smorodinskov, D. A. (ed.), *Neft' i gaz Tiumeni v dokumentakh*, vol. 2, 1966–1970, Sverdlovsk: Sredne-Ural'skoe knizhnoe izdatel'stvo, 1973.

Snopkov, Aleksander, Pavel Snopkov, and Aleksandr Shkliaruk, *Shest'sot plakatov*, Moscow: Kontakt-Kul'tura, 2004.

'Soviet Deliberations during the Polish Crisis, 1980–1981: Edited, Translated, Annotated, and Introduced by Mark Kramer', Cold War International History Project, Special Working Paper 1, Washington, DC: Woodrow Wilson International Center for Scholars, April 1999.

Stalin, I., Politika Sovetskoi vlasti po natsional'nomu voprosu v Rossii, *Pravda*, 226, 10 (October 1920), p. 2.

[Stalin, J. V.], 'Speech Delivered by Stalin at a Meeting of Voters of the Stalin Electoral District, Moscow, 9 February 1946', History and Public Policy Program Digital Archive, Gospolitizdat, Moscow, 1946, https://digitalarchive.wilsoncenter.org/document/116179 (last accessed 3 November 2021).

Works, vol. 7, Moscow: Foreign Languages Publishing House, 1954.

Works, vol. 10, Moscow: Foreign Languages Publishing House, 1954.

Standard Oil Company of New Jersey, *1960 Annual Report*, New York, 1961.

The Soviet Oil Situation: An Evaluation of CIA Analyses of Soviet Oil Production; Staff Report of the Senate Select Committee on the Intelligence United States Senate, Washington, DC: United States Government Printing Office, 1978.

US Department of State (ed.), *Foreign Relations of the United States 1946*, vol. VI, Eastern Europe, The Soviet Union, Washington, DC: United States Government Printing Office, 1969.

Foreign Relations of the United States 1958–1960, vol. X, Part 1, Eastern Europe Region; Soviet Union; Cyprus, Washington, DC: United States Government Printing Office, 1993.

Foreign Relations of the United States 1961–1963, vol. IX, Foreign Economic Policy, Washington, DC: United States Government Printing Office, 1995.

Foreign Relations of the United States 1969–1976, vol. XXXVI, Energy Crisis, 1969–1974, Washington, DC: United States Government Printing Office, 1995.

Foreign Relations of the United States 1969–1976, vol. XIV, Soviet Union, October 1971–May 1972, Washington, DC: United States Government Printing Office, 2006.

Foreign Relations of the United States 1969–1976, vol. XV, Soviet Union, June 1972–August 1974, Washington, DC: United States Government Printing Office, 2011.

'Visit to the United Kingdom of Bulganin and Khrushchev, 19–27 April 1956', *History and Public Policy Program Digital Archive*, FO 371/122836, Document obtained by James Vaughan, https://digitalarchive.wilsoncenter.org/document/123798 (last accessed 6 November 2021).

Memoires and Diaries

Amerongen, Otto Wolf von, *Der Weg nach Osten: Vierzig Jahre Brückenbau für die deutsche Wirtschaft*, Munich: Droemer Knauer, 1992.

Bajbakov, Nikolaj, *Sache des Lebens: Aufzeichnungen eines Erdölarbeiters*, Berlin: Dietz Verlag, 1985.

Bakhilov, V., *Doroga k nefte*, Sverdlovsk: Sredne-Ural'skoe knizhnoe izdatel'stvo, 1975.

Churilov, L. D., *Moia istoriia sovetskoi nefti (zapisksi poslednego ministra)*, Moscow: Izd-vo 'Neftianoe khoziaistvo', 2016.

Dnevniki A. S. Cherniaeva: Sovetskaia politika 1972–1991 gg. – vzgliad iznutri; 1987 god, [Washington, DC: The National Security Archive], https://nsarchive.gwu.edu/rus/text_files/Chernyaev/1987.pdf (last accessed 18 July 2021).

The Diary of Anatoly S. Chernyaev 1972: Translated by Anna Melyakova, edited by Svetlana Savranskaya, Washington, DC: The National Security Archive, 2012, www2.gwu.edu/~nsarchiv/NSAEBB/NSAEBB379/1972 as of May 24, 2012 FINAL.pdf (last accessed 16 July 2021).

The Diary of Anatoly S. Chernyaev 1973: Translated by Anna Melyakova, edited by Washington, DC: The National Security Archive, 2013, https://nsarchive2.gwu.edu/NSAEBB/NSAEBB430/Chernyaev 1973 final PDF version.pdf (last accessed 15 July 2021).

The Memoirs of Count Witte: Translated from the Original Russian Manuscript and Edited by Abraham Yarmolinsky, Garden City, NY, and Toronto: Doubleday, Page, and Company, 1921.

Soviet Statistics

'Foreign Trade Statistics', *Soviet and Eastern European Foreign Trade*, 3, 1 (1967), pp. 39–64.

Gosudarstvennyi komitet SSSR po statistike, *Narodnoe khoziastvo SSSR za 70 let: Iubileinyi statisticheskii ezhegondik*, Moscow: Finansy i statistika, 1987.
Ministerstvo vneshnei torgovli SSSR, *Vneshniaia torgovlia SSSR za 1918–1940 gg.: Statisticheskii obzor*, Moscow: Vneshtorgizdat, 1960.
Narodnoe khoziaistvo SSSR v 1985 g.: Statisticheskii ezhegodnik, Moscow: Finansy i statistika, 1986.

Newspaper Articles up to 1991

'Americans to Work Russian Oil Tract', *New York Times*, 24 September 1922, p. 9.
Ball, George W., 'The Case against Sanctions', *New York Times Magazine*, 12 September 1982, p. 63 (Section 6).
'Barnsdall Confirms Baku Oil Negotiations', *New York Times*, 29 March 1922, p. 30.
'Bumerang sanktsii', *Pravda*, 187, 6 July 1982, p. 5.
Dallas, Rita, 'Britain Orders Firms to Defy Pipeline Ban', *Washington Post*, 3 August 1982, p. A6.
'Dreckige Lüge', *Der Spiegel*, 33, 16 August 1982, pp. 94–96.
'Gaz Urengoia - miru!', *Pravda*, 267, 24 September 1982, p. 4.
Gillette, Robert, 'Huge Oil Field Dying: Soviet Methods Cited', *Los Angeles Times*, 29 September 1985, www.latimes.com/archives/la-xpm-1985-09-29-mn-19049-story.html (last accessed 26 September 2021).
Glukhov, Iu., 'Napadenie Izrailia na Egipet i Siriiu', *Pravda*, 280, 7 October 1973, p. 5.
'Khotia effekt podshchytan', *Pravda*, 134, 14 May 1978, p. 3.
'Liebe Genossen, besinnt euch!', *Der Spiegel*, 18, 1 May 1978, pp. 116–30.
'Mera zrelosti', *Pravda*, 137, 17 May 1978, p. 3.
Miletskii, Ia., 'Davaite torgovat'!', *Ogonek*, 18, 26 April 1959, pp. 24–25.
Mufson, Steve, 'Anatomy of Continuing Pipeline Controversy: U.S. Is in Sharp Fight with European Allies', *Wall Street Journal*, 31 August 1982, p. 29.
'Otvergaiut diktat SShA', *Pravda*, 22 July 1982, p. 5.
'Polozhenie na Kavkaze: (Beseda s tov. Stalinym)', *Pravda*, 269, 30 November 1920, p. 1.
'Röhren-Kredit: Salto am Trapez', *Der Spiegel*, 7, 9 February 1970, p. 34.
'Sending Engineers to Baku: Barnsdall Corporation Will Have no Backing from Washington', *New York Times*, 21 January 1923, p. 5.
Serebrovskii, [A.], 'Amerikantsi i burenie na bakinskikh promyslakh', *Pravda*, 212, 21 September 1922, p. 1.
'Sibirien: "Greifen Sie zu!"', *Der Spiegel*, 3, 14 January 1973, pp. 60–71.
'Sibirskii Razmakh', *Literaturnaia gazeta*, 1 May 1978, p. 10.
'Soviet Pipe Line Threatens Oil Flood in West', *Chicago Daily Tribune*, 3 June 1962, p. 1.
'S vydaiushchimsia dostizheniem!', *Pravda*, 254, 11 September 1983, p. 1.
Vtorushin, S., and A. Murzin, 'Izkat' novye klady', *Pravda*, 222, 10 August 1977, p. 2.
'"Zu stark gewässert"', *Der Spiegel*, 37, 9 September 1990, pp. 129–30.

Internet Resources

BP, 'Statistical Review of World Energy 2021', www.bp.com/content/dam/bp/business-sites/en/global/corporate/pdfs/energy-economics/statistical-review/bp-stats-review-2021-oil.pdf (last accessed 5 January 2022)

Dekoder, '[Privatisierung:] Wörterbuch der Wilden 1990er', www.dekoder.org/de/article/1990er-bilder-alltag (last accessed 19 May 2023).

Enerdata, 'Russia Energy Information', www.enerdata.net/estore/energy-market/russia/ (last accessed 7 August 2021).

Forbes, 'Gazprom', www.forbes.com/companies/gazprom/?sh=74efb61b7ec8 (last accessed 11 September 2021).

'Fortune Global 500', https://fortune.com/global500/ (last accessed 23 June 2021).

Gazprom, 'Gas and Oil Production', www.gazprom.com/about/production/extraction/ (last accessed 22 September 2021).

'Gazprom in Figures 2016–2020: Factbook', www.gazprom.com/f/posts/45/961659/gazprom-in-figures-2016-2020-en.pdf (last accessed 21 July 2021).

Gazprom Export, 'Gas Supplies to Europe', https://gazpromexport.ru/en/statis tics/ (last accessed 24 July 2022).

IEA, 'Share of Russia in European Union and United Kingdom Gas Demand, 2001–2021', 20 May 2022, www.iea.org/data-and-statistics/charts/share-of-russia-in-european-union-and-united-kingdom-gas-demand-2001-2021 (last accessed 24 July 2022).

Lukoil, 'Geographic Reach', www.lukoil.com/Company/BusinessOperation/GeographicReach (last accessed 21 July 2021).

'Oil Dependence and U.S. Foreign Policy 1850–2017', www.cfr.org/timeline/oil-dependence-and-us-foreign-policy (last accessed 16 August 2021).

Our World in Data, 'Primary Energy Consumption by Source, 2021', https://ourworldindata.org/grapher/primary-energy-source-bar?country=~OWID_WRL (last accessed 5 January 2022).

RBK, 'Reiting krupneishikh kompanii Rossii RBK 500: Osnovnye fakty,' 15 October 2020, www.rbc.ru/economics/15/10/2020/5f86306e9a7947c85f43e19c (last accessed 21 July 2021).

RBK TEK 360, 'My pomogaem: Kak sovetskie i rossiiskie neftianiki rabotali za granitsei', http://tek360.rbc.ru/articles/110/ (last accessed 24 October 2021).

Rosneft, 'Rosneft at a Glance', www.rosneft.com/about/Rosneft_today/ (last accessed 7 July 2021).

'Russian Oil Products Ltd', www.blisworth.org.uk/images/Canal/Arm/ROP.htm (last accessed 28 April 2021).

Sovietposters.com, [Neftianiki, bol'she nefti Rodine! Vypolnim piatiletku v 4 goda! Poster by P. Krivonogov, 1948], www.sovietposters.com/posters/oilmen-more-oil-to-the-motherland (last accessed 13 July 2021).

Statistica, 'Transport Volume of Crude Oil in Seaborne Trade Worldwide from 2010 to 2021', www.statista.com/statistics/264013/transport-volume-of-crude-oil-in-seaborne-trade/ (last accessed 5 January 2022).

US Department of Agriculture, 'U.S.S.R. Wheat Imports by Year', www.indexmundi.com/agriculture/?country=su&commodity=wheat&graph=imports (last accessed 15 July 2021).

US Energy Information Administration (EIA), 'Natural Gas Explained: Natural Gas Imports and Exports', www.eia.gov/energyexplained/natural-gas/imports-and-exports.php (last accessed 16 September 2021).

Secondary Literature

Alekperov, V. Iu., *Neft' Rossii: Proshloe, nastoiashee i budushchee*, Moscow: Kreativnaia ekonomika, 2011.

Alm, James, Jorge Martinez-Vazquez, and Benno Torgler, 'Russian Tax Morale in the 1990s', *Proceedings: Annual Conference on Taxation and Minutes of the Annual Meeting of the National Tax Association*, 98 (2005), pp. 287–92.

Anatolyev, Alexander, 'The Oil Summit of 1971', *Oil of Russia*, 3 (2011), www.oilru.com/or/48/1031/ (last accessed 6 June 2013).

Åsbrink, Brita, 'Emanuel Nobel Is Forced to Leave Everything and Flee', *The Nobel Brothers*, http://www.branobelhistory.com/themes/the-nobel-brothers/-emanuel-nobel-is-forced-to-leave-everything-and-flee/ (last accessed 16 August 2021).

Åslund, Anders, *Russia's Capitalist Revolution: Why Market Reform Succeeded and Democracy Failed*, Washington, DC: Peterson Institute for International Economics, 2007.

Asschenfeldt, Friedrich, and Max Trecker, '"Den Bolschewismus in der Wiege erdrosseln": Die Blockade der Entente gegen Sowjetrussland', *Osteuropa*, 71, 10/11 (2021), pp. 47–58.

Aust, Martin (ed.), *Globalisierung imperial und sozialistisch: Russland und die Sowjetunion in der Globalgeschichte 1851–1991*, Globalgeschichte 13, Frankfurt am Main: Campus Verlag, 2013.

Autio-Sarasmo, Sari, 'Khrushchev and the Challenge of Technological Progress', in Melanie Ilic and Jeremy Smith (eds.), *Khrushchev in the Kremlin: Policy and Government in the Soviet Union, 1953–1964*, London, New York: Routledge, 2011, pp. 133–49.

Baar, Lothar, Rainer Karlsch, and Werner Matschke, *Kriegsfolgen und Kriegslasten Deutschlands: Zerstörungen, Demontagen und Reparationen*, Studien zur Wirtschaftsgeschichte 1, Berlin: Humboldt-Universität, Institut für Wirtschaftsgeschichte, 1993.

Bakhash, Shaul, *The Reign of the Ayatollahs: Iran and the Islamic Revolution*, London: I. B. Tauris, 1985.

Bakhtizin, R. N., A. S. Vereshchagin, and M. Iu. Kiiko, *'Neftianoi faktor' v Rossiiskoi gosudarstvennoi politike: Dorevoliutsionnyi i sovetskii periody*, Ufa: Neftegazovoe delo, 2007.

Balmaceda, Margarita M., 'Der Weg in die Abhängigkeit: Ostmitteleuropa am Energietropf der UdSSR', *Osteuropa*, 54, 9/10 (2004), pp. 162–79.

Balzer, Harley, 'The Putin Thesis and Russian Energy Policy', *Post-Soviet Affairs*, 21, 3 (2005), pp. 210–25.

Baumgart, Winfried, 'Das "KaspiUnternehmen" – Grössenwahn Ludendorffs oder Routineplanung des Deutschen Generalstabs? Erster Teil: Ein kritischer Rückblick auf die deutsche militärische Intervention im Kaukasus am Ende des Ersten Weltkriegs', *Jahrbücher für Geschichte Osteuropas*, 18, 1 (1970), pp. 47–126.

Bayandor, Darioush, *The Shah, the Islamic Revolution and the United States*, Cham: Palgrave Macmillan, 2019.

Bayer, Waltraud, 'Der legitimierte Raub: Der Umgang mit Kunstschätzen in der Sowjetunion, 1917–1938', *Osteuropa*, 56, 1/2 (2006), pp. 55–70.

Bebel, August, *Die Frau und der Sozialismus*, Zurich-Hottingen: Verlag der Volksbuchhandlung, 1879.

Beltran, Alain, and Jean-Pierre Williot, 'Gaz de France and Soviet Natural Gas: Balancing Technological Constraints with Political Considerations, 1950s to 1980s', in Jeronim Perović (ed.), *Cold War Energy: A Transnational History of Soviet Oil and Gas*, Cham: Palgrave Macmillan, 2017, pp. 230–52.

Berry, John A., 'Oil and Soviet Policy in the Middle East', *Middle East Journal*, 26, 2 (1972), pp. 149–60.

Beyrau, Dietrich, 'Das bolschewistische Projekt als Utopie und soziale Praxis', in Wolfgang Hardtwig (ed.), *Utopie und politische Herrschaft im Europa der Zwischenkriegszeit*, Munich: Oldenburg, 2003, pp. 13–40.

'Behind the Scenes of Russia's Gas Strategy', *Enerdata Executive Brief*, July 2023, https://d1owejb4br3l12.cloudfront.net/publications/executive-briefing/russia-gas-strategy.pdf (last accessed 30 August 2023).

Bezugol'nyi, A. Iu., *Narody Kavkaza i Krasnaia Armiia, 1918–1945 gody*, Moscow: Veche, 2007.

Bhattacharya, Jay, Christina Gathmann, and Grant Miller, 'The Gorbachev Anti-Alcohol Campaign and Russia's Mortality Crisis', *American Economic Journal: Applied Economics*, 5, 2 (2013), pp. 232–60.

'Biden zu Nord Stream 2: "Sanktionen wären kontraproduktiv gewesen"', ARD Tagesschau, 26 May 2021, www.tagesschau.de/ausland/amerika/biden-nord stream-2-sanktionen-101.html (last accessed 11 September 2021).

Bill, James A., *The Eagle and the Lion: The Tragedy of Iranian–American Relations*, New Haven, CT, London: Yale University Press, 1988.

Bini, Elisabetta, 'A Challenge to Cold War Energy Politics? The US and Italy's Relations with the Soviet Union, 1958–1969', in Jeronim Perović (ed.), *Cold War Energy: A Transnational History of Soviet Oil and Gas*, Cham: Palgrave Macmillan, 2017, pp. 201–30.

Bini, Elisabetta, Giuliano Garavini, and Federico Romero (eds.), *Oil Shock: The 1973 Crisis and Its Economic Legacy*, London: I. B. Tauris, 2016.

Blasi, Walter, and Martin Malek, 'Eine "Klasse auf Rädern": Die Anfänge der Motorisierung in der Sowjetunion – vom Auto und Traktor zum Panzer', *Zeitschrift für Weltgeschichte*, 20, 1 (2020), pp. 191–224.

Bleidick, Dietmar, *Die Ruhrgas 1926 bis 2013: Aufstieg und Ende eines Marktführers*, Berlin, Boston: De Gruyter Oldenbourg, 2018.

Blinken, Antony, *Ally versus Ally: America, Europe and the Siberian Pipeline Crisis*, New York: Praeger, 1987.

Bloch, D. M., 'The Soviet Automobile Industry: Recent Developments in the Production of Passenger Cars', *New Zealand Slavonic Journal*, 7 (1971), pp. 14–31.

Bogolepov, A. A., 'Die Konzessionen in Sowjetrussland', *Zeitschrift für die gesamte Staatswissenschaft / Journal of Institutional and Theoretical Economics*, 91, 1 (1931), pp. 86–114.

Bordova, E. V. et al., *Gosudarstvennaia politika v neftegazovoi sfere v kontekste rossiiskoi modernizatsii*, Moscow: MAORI, 2014.

Borhi, László, 'The Merchants of the Kremlin: The Economic Roots of Soviet Expansion in Hungary', Cold War International History Project, Working Paper 28, Washington, DC: Woodrow Wilson International Center for Scholars, 2000.

Bösch, Frank, 'Wie Europa von russischer Energie abhängig wurde', Bundeszentrale für politische Bildung, 25 November 2022, www.bpb.de/themen/wirtschaft/europa-wirtschaft/515221/wie-europa-von-russischer-energie-abhaengig-wurde/#footnote-reference-2 (last accessed 23 January 2023).

Bowden, Julian, 'That's the Spirit! The Russian Oil Products Ltd. (ROP) and the British Oil Market, 1924–39', *Journal of European Economic History*, 17, 3 (1988), pp. 641–63.

[B. R.], 'Wirtschaftliche Unabhängigkeit und Autarkie', *Sowjetwirtschaft und Aussenhandel: Halbmonatszeitschrift der Handelsvertretung der UdSSR in Deutschland*, 12, 6 (1933), pp. 2–7.

Brinegar, Sara, 'The Oil Deal: Nariman Narimanov and the Sovietization of Azerbaijan', *Slavic Review*, 76, 2 (2017), pp. 372–94.

Brinegar, Sara G., 'Baku at All Costs: The Politics of Oil in the Soviet State', PhD dissertation, University of Wisconsin–Madison, 2014.

Buch, Jürgen, 'Wie Moskau schon vor 32 Jahren Litauen das Gas abklemmte', *Der Spiegel*, 21 July 2022, www.spiegel.de/geschichte/energieblockade-gegen-litauen-1990-man-muss-klar-sagen-auf-welcher-seite-man-steht-a-a784c548-50b8-4aa3-a67c-e96309c1a854 (last accessed 22 July 2022).

Buhbe, Matthes, and Gabriele Gorzka (eds.), *Russland heute: Rezentralisierung des Staates unter Putin*, Wiesbaden: Verlag für Sozialwissenschaften, 2007.

Bukold, Steffen, *Öl im 21. Jahrhundert*, vol. 1, Munich: Oldenbourg, 2009.

Butenina, Natalya V., 'Lend-Lease: The Oil Factor', *Oil of Russia*, 12, 1 (2005), www.oilru.com/or/22/360/ (last accessed 1 January 2013).

Campbell, John C., 'Soviet–American Relations: Détente and Dispute', *Current History*, 69, 409 (1975), pp. 113–16, 146–47, 149–51.

Cantoni, Roberto, 'Debates at NATO and the EEC in Response to the Soviet "Oil Offensive" in the Early 1960s', in Jeronim Perović (ed.), *Cold War Energy: A Transnational History of Soviet Oil and Gas*, Cham: Palgrave Macmillan, 2017, pp. 131–61.

'What's in a Pipe? NATO's Confrontation on the 1962 Large-Diameter Pipe Embargo', 2016, https://hal.archives-ouvertes.fr/hal-01291854/document (last accessed 8 July 2021).

Carter, Charles William, 'The Evolution of US Policy toward West German–Soviet Trade Relations 1969–89', *The International History Review* 34, 2 (2012), pp. 221–44.

Champion, Marc, and Daryana Krasnolutska, 'Russia's New Pipeline Makes Ukraine Worry Less About Gas But More About War', *Bloomberg*, 24 September 2021, https://www.bloomberg.com/news/articles/2021-09-24/nord-stream-2-pipeline-news-ukraine-worries-less-about-gas-more-about-war (last accessed 22 October 2021).

Cherkasov, Petr, 'The Twilight of the Brezhnev Era', *Russian Politics and Law*, 43, 6 (2005), pp. 76–95.

Chernow, Ron: *Titan: The Life of John D. Rockefeller, Sr.*, 2nd ed., New York: Vintage Books, 2004.

Chesshire, J. H., and Miss C. Huggett, 'Primary Energy Production in the Soviet Union: Problems and Prospects', *Energy Policy*, 3, 3 (1975), pp. 223–44.

'China's Russian Oil Imports Spike, Surpassing Saudi Supplies', *Radio Free Europe/Radio Liberty*, 20 June 2022, www.rferl.org/a/china-oil-russia-imports/31906255.html (last accessed 26 January 2023).

Churakov, D. O. (ed.), *Istoriia Rossii XX – nachala XXI veka*, vol. 2, 1941–2016: Uchebnik dlia akademicheskogo bakalavariata, 2nd rev. and expanded ed., Moscow: Izdatel'stvo Iurait, 2017.

Coleman, James L., 'The American Whale Oil Industry: A Look Back to the Future of the American Petroleum Industry?', *Nonrenewable Resources*, 4 (1995), pp. 273–88.

Considine, Jennifer I., and William A. Kerr, *The Russian Oil Economy*, Cheltenham: Edward Elgar, 2002.

Coopersmith, Jonathan, *The Electrification of Russia, 1880–1926*, Ithaca, NY: Cornell University Press, 1992.

Craig, J., F. Gerali, F. MacAulay, and R. Sorkhabi (eds.), *History of the European Oil and Gas Industry*, London: Geological Society of London, 2018.

Dabrowska, Ewa, 'Voucher-Privatisierung', *dekoder*, 14 August 2018, www.dekoder.org/de/gnose/voucher-privatisierung-wirtschaftsreform#fuss4 (last accessed 21 July 2021).

Dahl, Erik J., 'Naval Innovation: From Coal to Oil', *Joint Force Quarterly (JFQ)* (2000/2001), pp. 50–56.

Danchenko, Igor, and Clifford Gaddy, 'The Mystery of Vladimir Putin's Dissertation', edited versions of presentations by the authors at a Brookings Institution, Foreign Policy Program panel, Washington, DC, 30 March 2006, www.brookings.edu/wp-content/uploads/2012/09/Putin-Dissertation-Event-remarks-with-slides.pdf (last accessed 13 July 2022).

Dangerfield, Martin, 'Sozialistische Ökonomische Integration: Der Rat für Gegenseitige Wirtschaftshilfe (RGW)', in Bernd Greiner, Christian Th. Müller, and Claudia Weber (eds.), *Ökonomie im Kalten Krieg*, Studien zum Kalten Krieg 4, Hamburg: Hamburger Edition, 2010, pp. 348–69.

Davies, R. W., M. B. Tauger, and S. G. Wheatcroft, 'Stalin, Grain Stocks and the Famine of 1932–1933', *Slavic Review*, 54, 3 (1995), pp. 642–57.

De Groot, Michael, 'The Soviet Union, CMEA, and the Energy Crisis of the 1970s', *Journal of Cold War Studies*, 22, 4 (2020), pp. 4–30.

Demidova, Ksenia, 'The Deal of the Century: The Reagan Administration and the Soviet Pipeline', in Kiran Klaus Patel and Kenneth Weisbrode (eds.), *European Integration and the Atlantic Community in the 1980s*, Cambridge: Cambridge University Press, 2013, pp. 59–82.

'Der Reichtum natürlicher Energie in der UdSSR', *Sowjetwirtschaft und Aussenhandel: Halbmonatszeitschrift der Handelsvertretung der UdSSR in Deutschland*, 16, 21/22 (1937), pp. 7–10.

DeSpiegeleire, Stephan, 'Gullivers Fäden: Die russischen Regionen und die Aussen- und Sicherheitspolitik der Russischen Föderation', in Hans-

Joachim Spanger (ed.), *Russland und der Westen*, Frankfurt am Main: Campus Verlag, 1998, pp. 150–76.

Dietz, Raimund, *Die Energiewirtschaft in Osteuropa und der UdSSR*, Vienna: Springer Verlag, 1984.

Dohan, Michael R., 'The Economic Origins of Soviet Autarky 1927/28–1934', *Slavic Review*, 35, 4 (1976), pp. 603–35.

Dorn, Harold, 'Hugh Lincoln Cooper and the First Détente', *Technology and Culture*, 20, 2 (1979), pp. 322–47.

Ebel, Robert E., *Communist Trade in Oil and Gas: An Evaluation of the Future Export Capabilities of the Soviet Bloc*, New York: Praeger, 1970.

Egorova, Nataliia, 'Stalin's Oil Policy and the Iranian Crisis of 1945–1946', in Jeronim Perović (ed.), *Cold War Energy: A Transnational History of Soviet Oil and Gas*, Cham: Palgrave Macmillan, 2017, pp. 79–104.

Elizar'ev, V. N., 'Inostrannyi kapital v sakhalinkikh neftegazovykh proiektakh: Kak eto nachalos', *Aktual'nye problemy gumanitarnykh i estestvennykh nauk*, 2/1 (2016), pp. 74–77.

Engels, Markus, and Petra Schwartz, 'Alliierte Restriktionen für die Aussenwirtschaftspolitik der Bundesrepublik Deutschland: Das Röhrenembargo von 1962/63 und das Erdgas-Röhren-Geschäft von 1982', in Helga Haftendorn and Henning Riecke (eds.), *Die volle Macht des souveränen Staates: Die alliierten Vorbehaltsrechte als Rahmenbedingungen westdeutscher Aussenpolitik 1949–1990*, Baden-Baden: Nomos, 1996, pp. 227–42.

Engelstein, Laura, *Russia in Flames: War, Revolution, Civil War 1914–1921*, New York: Oxford University Press, 2018.

Ermolaev, Sergei, 'Formirovanie i razvitie neftegazovoi zavisimosti Sovetskogo Soiuza', Working Paper, Moscow: Carnegie Moscow Center, 2017.

Erv'e, Iu. G., *Sibirskie gorizonty*, Sverdlovsk: Sredne-Ural'skoe knizhnoe izdatel'stvo, 1968.

Esno, Tyler, 'Reagan's Economic War on the Soviet Union', *Diplomatic History*, 42, 2 (2018), pp. 281–304.

Etkind, Alexander, 'Bevölkerung: überflüssig – Russland leidet an der von seinen abgehobenen Eliten verhängten "Öl-Krankheit"', *Neue Zürcher Zeitung*, 24 December 2019, www.nzz.ch/meinung/bevoelkerung-ueberfluessig-russland-leidet-an-der-oel-krankheit-ld.1529872?reduced=true (last accessed 27 September 2021).

Nature's Evil: A Cultural History of Natural Resources, Cambridge: Polity Press, 2021.

Etkind, Alexander, Yevhenii Poliakov, and Bohdan Shumylovych, 'Ukrainian Labor and Siberian Oil in the Late Soviet Empire', *Journal of Soviet and post-Soviet politics and society*, 6, 2 (2020), pp. 241–80.

Evdoshenko, Iu. V., '"Barnsdal'skaia istoriia", ili neftianaia kontsessiia, kotoraia okazalas' nikomu ne nuzhno', *Ekonomicheskaia istoriia: Ezhegodnik 2014/15*, Moscow: Institut rossiiskoi istorii RAN, 2016, pp. 393–436.

Fedunenko, Evgenii, 'Kak Vladimir Putin vstrechalsia s krupnym bisnesom: Istoriia voprosa', *Kommersant'*, 24 December 2015, www.kommersant.ru/doc/2884721 (last accessed 21 July 2021).

Ferrier, R. W., *The History of The British Petroleum Company*, vol. 1, The Developing Years 1901–1932, Cambridge: Cambridge University Press, 1982.

Field, Mark G., 'The Health and Demographic Crisis in Post-Soviet Russia', in Mark G. Field and Judyth L. Twigg (eds.), *Russia's Torn Safety Nets: Health and Social Welfare during the Transition*, New York: St. Martin's Press, 2000, pp. 11–42.

Fischer, Louis, *Oil Imperialism: The International Struggle for Petroleum*, London: International, 1926.

Flade, Falk, 'Creating a Common Energy Space: The Building of the Druzhba Oil Pipeline', in Jeronim Perović (ed.), *Cold War Energy: A Transnational History of Soviet Oil and Gas*, Cham: Palgrave Macmillan, 2017, pp. 321–44.

Energy Infrastructures in the Eastern Bloc: Poland and the Construction of Transnational Electricity, Oil, and Gas Systems, Wiesbaden: Harrasowitz Verlag, 2017.

Flory, Harriette, 'The Arcos Raid and the Rupture of Anglo–Soviet Relations, 1927', *Journal of Contemporary History*, 12, 4 (1977), pp. 707–23.

Forsmann, Jana, *Testfall für die 'Grossen Drei': Die Besetzung Irans durch Briten, Sowjets und Amerikaner 1941–1946*, Cologne, Weimar, Vienna: Böhlau, 2009.

Fortescue, Stephen, *Russia's Oil Barons and Metal Magnates: Oligarchs and the State in Transition*, Basingstoke, New York: Palgrave Macmillan, 2006.

Freeland, Chrystia, *Sale of the Century: Russia's Wild Ride from Communism to Capitalism*, New York: Crown Business, 2000.

Frey, Felix, *Arktischer Heizraum: Das Energiesystem Kola zwischen regionaler Autarkie und gesamtwirtschaftlicher Verflechtung 1928–1974*, Osteuropa in Geschichte und Gegenwart 4, Vienna, Cologne, Weimar: Böhlau, 2019.

Friedensburg, Ferdinand, *Das Erdöl im Weltkrieg*, Stuttgart: Enke, 1939.

Fruchtmann, Jakob, 'Steuern durch Macht – Macht durch Steuern: Die russische Steuerpolitik unter Putin', *Osteuropa*, 52, 3 (2002), pp. 346–61.

Gaddis, John Lewis, *The Cold War: A New History*, New York: Penguin Press, 2005.

Gaddy, Clifford G., and Andrew C. Kuchins, 'Putin's Plan', *The Washington Quarterly*, 31, 2 (2008), pp. 117–29.

Gaddy, Clifford G., and Barry W. Ickes, 'Resource Rents and the Russian Economy', *Eurasian Geography and Economics*, 46, 8 (2005), pp. 559–83.

'Russia's Dependence on Resources', in Michael V. Alexeev and Shlomo Weber (eds.): *The Oxford Handbook of the Russian Economy*, New York: Oxford University Press, 2013, pp. 309–49.

Gaidar, Yegor, *Collapse of an Empire: Lessons for Modern Russia*, Washington, DC: Brookings Institution Press, 2007.

The Soviet Collapse: Grain and Oil, American Enterprise Institute for Public Policy Research, April 2007, Washington, DC: AEI, 2007, p. 2.

Garavini, Giuliano, *The Rise and Fall of OPEC in the Twentieth Century*, Oxford: Oxford University Press, 2019.

Gaworek, Norbert H., 'From Blockade to Trade: Allied Economic Warfare against Soviet Russia, June 1919 to January 1920', *Jahrbücher für Geschichte Osteuropas*, 23, 1 (1975), pp. 39–69.

'Gazprom Gets Kovykta Gas Field on the Cheap', *St. Petersburg Times*, 26 June 2007.

'Gazprom's Foreign Policy', *Russian Analytical Digest*, 41(2008).

Gestwa, Klaus, *Die Stalinschen Grossbauten des Kommunismus: Sowjetische Technik- und Umweltgeschichte, 1948–1967*, Munich: Oldenbourg, 2010.

'"Energetische Brücken" und "Klimafabriken": Das energetische Weltbild der Sowjetunion', *Osteuropa*, 54, 9/10 (2004), pp. 15–38.

Gibb, George Sweet, and Evelyn H. Knowlton, *History of Standard Oil Company New Jersey*, vol. 2, The Resurgent Years 1911–1927, New York: Harper, 1956.

Gibbs, David N., 'Reassessing Soviet Motives for Invading Afghanistan: A Declassified History', *Critical Asian Studies*, 38, 2 (2006), pp. 239–63.

Gibianskij, Leonid, 'Die Gründung des Rates für Gegenseitige Wirtschaftshilfe', in Walter M. Iber and Peter Ruggenthaler (eds.), *Stalins Wirtschaftspolitik an der sowjetischen Peripherie: Ein Überblick auf der Basis sowjetischer und osteuropäischer Quellen*, Innsbruck, Vienna, Bolzano: Studien Verlag, 2011, pp. 21–41.

Gidadhubli R. G., and Arun Mohanty, 'Continuing Debate over "Shock Therapy"', *Economic and Political Weekly*, 37, 50 (2002), pp. 4998–5002.

Gillette, Philip S., 'American Capital in the Contest for Soviet Oil, 1920–23', *Soviet Studies*, 24, 4 (1973), pp. 477–90.

Glässer, Wiebke, *Marktmacht und Politik: Das internationale Kartell der Ölgesellschaften 1960–1975*, Schriftenreihe zur Zeitschrift für Unternehmensgeschichte 32, Berlin, Boston: De Gruyter Oldenbourg, 2019.

Goehrke, Carsten, *Russland: Eine Strukturgeschichte*, Paderborn: Schöningh, 2010.

Gökay, Bülent, 'The Battle for Baku (May–September 1918): A Peculiar Episode in the History of the Caucasus', *Middle Eastern Studies*, 34, 1 (1998), pp. 30–50.

Golan, Galia, 'The Soviet Union and the Yom Kippur War, *Israel Affairs*, 6, 1 (1999), pp. 127–52.

Goldman, Marshall I., 'Gorbachev the Economist', *Foreign Affairs*, 69, 2 (1990), pp. 28–44.

Petrostate: Putin, Power and the New Russia, New York: Oxford University Press, 2010.

'Putin and the Oligarchs', *Foreign Affairs*, 83, 6 (2004), pp. 33–44

'Soviet Trade and Aid', *Challenge*, 12, 3 (1963), pp. 30–33.

The Enigma of Soviet Petroleum: Half-Full or Half-Empty?, London: George Allen & Unwin, 1980.

'The Yukos Affair', *Current History*, 103, 675 (2004), pp. 319–23.

'Will the Soviet Union be an Autarky in 1984?', *International Security*, 3, 4 (1979), pp. 18–36.

Gork'ii, M., L. Averbakh, and S. Firin (eds.), *Belomorsko-Baltiiskii Kanal imeni Stalina: Istoriia stroitel'stva, 1931–1934 gg.*, Moscow: OGIZ, 1934 [new edition 1998].

Götz, Roland, 'Das Ausmass des öffentlichen Sektors in Russland', *Russland-Analysen*, 366 (2019), pp. 2–8.

Russlands Ressourcen: Auswirkungen auf die inneren Verhältnisse und die Aussenpolitik, SWP Diskussionspapier, FG 5, 2006/02, Berlin: Stiftung für Wissenschaft und Politik, 2006.

'Uljukajews Fall und Jewtuschenkows Niederlage: Rosnefts Expansion durch Annexion', *Russland-Analysen*, 348 (2018), pp. 2–4.

'Vom privatatisierten Staat zum verstaatlichen Markt? Eigentum in der Sowjetunion und in Russland, *Osteuropa*, 63, 5/6 (2013), pp. 315–32.

Grätz, Jonas, *Russland als globaler Wirtschaftsakteur: Handlungsressourcen und Strategien der Öl- und Gaskonzerne*, Munich: Oldenbourg 2013.

Greiner, Bernd, Christian Th. Müller, and Claudia Weber (eds.), *Ökonomie im Kalten Krieg*, Studien zum Kalten Krieg 4, Hamburg: Hamburger Edition, 2010.

Gross, Samantha, '1979 and the World's Second Oil Shock', in Suzanne Maloney (ed.), *The Iranian Revolution at 40*, Washington, DC: Brookings Institution Press, 2020, pp. 115–20.

Grützmacher, Johannes, *Die Baikal-Amur-Magistrale: Vom stalinistischen Lager zum Mobilisierungsprojekt unter Brežnev*, Munich: Oldenbourg, 2012.

Gruzinov, V. P., *The USSR's Management of Foreign Trade: Edited with a Foreword by Edward A. Hewett*, White Plains, NY: M. E. Sharp, 1979.

Guan-Fu, Gu, 'Soviet Aid to the Third World: An Analysis of Its Strategy', *Soviet Studies*, 35, 1 (1983), pp. 71–89.

Gubkin, I. M., 'Die Naphtavorkommen in der Sowjetunion', *Die Volkswirtschaft der Union der Sozialistischen Sowjet-Republiken*, 11, 10 (1932), pp. 8–16.

Die Naturschätze der UdSSR und ihre Auswertung, Moscow: Verlagsgenossenschaft ausländischer Arbeiter in der UdSSR, 1932.

Gudkov, Lev, and Boris Dubin, 'Der Oligarch als Volksfeind: Der Nutzen des Falls Chodorkovskij für das Putin-Regime', *Osteuropa*, 55, 7 (2005), pp. 52–75.

Gustafson, Thane, *Crisis Amid Plenty: The Politics of Soviet Energy under Brezhnev and Gorbachev*, Princeton, NJ: Princeton University Press, 1989.

The Bridge: Natural Gas in a Redivided Europe, Cambridge, MA: Harvard University Press, 2020.

The Soviet Gas Campaign: Politics and Policy in Soviet Decisionmaking, Santa Monica, CA: RAND Corporation, 1983.

Wheel of Fortune: The Battle for Oil and Power in Russia, Cambridge, MA: Harvard University Press, 2012.

Hanson, Philipp, *The Rise and Fall of the Soviet Economy: An Economic History of the USSR from 1945*, London: Longman 2003.

'The Sustainability of Russia's Energy Power: Implications for the Russian Economy', in Jeronim Perović, Robert W. Orttung, and Andreas Wenger (eds.), *Russian Energy Power and Foreign Relations: Implications for Conflict and Cooperation*, London, New York: Routledge, 2009, pp. 23–50.

Harbutt, Fraser, 'American Challenge, Soviet Response: The Beginning of the Cold War, February–May, 1946', *Political Science Quarterly*, 96, 4 (1981/82), pp. 623–39.

Harrison, Mark, *Accounting for War: Soviet Production, Employment, and the Defence Burden, 1940–1945*, Cambridge: Cambridge University Press, 1996.

Haumann, Heiko, *Beginn der Planwirtschaft: Elektrifizierung, Wirtschaftsplanung und gesellschaftliche Entwicklung Sowjetrusslands 1917–21*, Dusseldorf: Bertelsmann, 1974.

Hayward, Joel, 'Too Little, Too Late: An Analysis of Hitler's Failure in August 1942 to Damage Soviet Oil Production', *The Journal of Military History*, 64, 3 (2000), pp. 769–94.

Heinrich, Andreas, and Heiko Pleines, *Tax Burden and Tax Behaviour of Russian Economic Sectors: Part II; Taxation of the Russian Oil and Gas Industry*, Arbeitspapiere und Materialien/Forschungsstelle Osteuropa an der Universität Bremen 28, Bremen: Forschungsstelle Osteuropa an der Universität Bremen, 2001.

Heller, Klaus, *Russlands wilde Jahre: Der neue Kapitalismus in der Ära Jelzin*, Paderborn: Schöningh, 2016.

Hempel, Rainer, 'Abraham Gesner: Father of the Petroleum Industry', *German Canadian Yearbook*, 17 (2002), pp. 129–38.

Henderson, James, *Non-Gazprom Gas Producers in Russia*, Oxford: The Oxford Institute for Energy Studies, 2010.

Henderson, James, and Arild Moe, *The Globalization of Russian Gas: Political and Commercial Catalysts*, Cheltenham: Edward Elgar, 2019.

Herr, Hansjörg, 'Die Finanzkrise in Russland im Gefolge der Asienkrise', *Aus Politik und Zeitgeschichte*, B37–38 (2000), www.bpb.de/apuz/25451/die-finanzkrise-in-russland-im-gefolge-der-asienkrise (last accessed 20 July 2021).

Heyman, Hans, 'Oil in Soviet–Western Relations in the Interwar Years', *The American Slavic and East European Review*, 7, 4 (1948), pp. 303–16.

Hildermeier, Manfred, *Geschichte Russlands*, 2nd ed., Munich: Beck, 2013.

Hill, Fiona, and Clifford G. Gaddy, *The Siberian Curse: How Communist Planners Left Russia Out in the Cold*. Washington, DC: Brookings Institution Press, 2003.

Hinnebusch, Raymond, 'The US Invasion of Iraq: Explanations and Implications, Critique', *Critical Middle Eastern Studies*, 16, 3 (2007), pp. 209–28.

Hoffmann, David E., *The Oligarchs: Wealth and Power in the New Russia*, New York: Public Affairs, 2001.

Hoffmann, Karl, 'Die russische Erdölfrage in der Politik', *Zeitschrift für Politik*, 19 (1930), pp. 657–75.

Högselius, Per, *Red Gas: Russia and the Origins of European Energy Dependence*, New York: Palgrave Macmillan, 2013.

et al., *Europe's Infrastructure Transition: Economy, War, Nature*, Basingstoke: Palgrave Macmillan, 2016.

Hunter, Robert, *The Soviet Dilemma in the Middle East: Part II; Oil and the Persian Gulf*, The Adelphi Papers 60, London: Institute for Strategic Studies, 1969.

Iber, Walter M., 'Erdöl statt Reparationen: Die sowjetische Mineralölverwaltung in Österreich 1945–1955', *Vierteljahrshefte für Zeitgeschichte*, 57, 4 (2009), pp. 571–605.

Igolkin, A. A., 'Import oborudovaniia kak faktor razvitiia neftianoi promyshlennosti v gody dovoennykh piatiletok', *Ekonomicheskii zhurnal*, 9 (2005), pp. 208–20 [online pp. 1–16], https://cyberleninka.ru/article/n/import-oborudovaniya-kak-faktor-razvitiya-neftyanoy-promyshlennosti-v-gody-dovoennyh-pyatiletok (last accessed 13 July 2021).

Neftianaia politika SSSR v 1928–1940-m godakh, Moscow: Institut rossiiskoi istorii RAN, 2005.

Neftianaia promyshlennost' SSSR (1928–1950-e gody), Moscow: Institut ekonomiki RAN, 2011.

Sovetskaia neftianaia politika v 1940-m–1950-m godakh, Moscow: Institut rossiiskoi istorii RAN, 2009.

'Sovetskii neftianoi eksport v gody predvoennykh piatiletok', *Neftianoe khoziastvo*, 9 (2006), pp. 139–41.

Illing, Falk, *Energiepolitik in Deutschland: Die energiepolitischen Massnahmen der Bundesregierung 1949–2013*, Baden-Baden: Nomos, 2012.

Jacobsen, Hanns-Dieter, *Die Ost-West-Wirtschaftsbeziehungen als deutsch-amerikanisches Problem*, Baden-Baden: Nomos, 1986.

Jaloustre, Pierre, 'The Oil Interests of the Rothschild of Paris: Between World Competition and the Russian Government (1883–1912)', unpublished paper, EBHA - 11th Annual Conference, Geneva, 13–15 September 2007.

Jauch, Matthias, 'Allseas plant keine Fortsetzung der Pipeline-Verlegung', *Der Tagesspiegel*, 31 December 2019, www.tagesspiegel.de/politik/nach-us-sanktionen-wegen-nord-stream-2-allseas-plant-keine-fortsetzung-der-pipeline-verlegung/25375366.html (last accessed 10 September 2021).

Jensen-Eriksen, Niklas, '"Red Oil" and Western Reactions: The Case of Britain', in Jeronim Perović (ed.), *Cold War Energy: A Transnational History of Soviet Oil and Gas*, Cham: Palgrave Macmillan, 2017, pp. 105–30.

'The Cold War in Energy Markets: British Efforts to Contain Soviet Oil Exports to Non-Communist Countries, 1950–1965', in Alain Beltran (ed.), *Le pétrole et la guerre: Oil and War*, Brussels: Peter Lang, 2012, pp. 191–207.

'The First Wave of the Soviet Oil Offensive: The Anglo-American Alliance and the Flow of "Red Oil" to Finland during the 1950s', *Business History*, 49, 3 (2007), pp. 348–66.

Jentleson, Bruce W., 'From Consensus to Conflict: The Domestic Political Economy of East–West Energy Trade Policy', *International Organization*, 38, 4 (1984), pp. 625–60.

Jones, Geoffrey, and Clive Trebilcock, 'Russian Industry and British Business, 1910–1930: Oil and Armaments', *Journal of European Economic History*, 11 (1982), pp. 61–103.

Kähönen, Aappo, 'Optimal Planning, Optimal Economy, Optimal Life? The Kosygin Reforms, 1965–72', in Katalin Miklóssy and Melanie Ilic (eds.), *Competition in Socialist Society*, London, New York: Routledge, 2014, pp. 23–40.

Kansikas, Suvi, 'Calculating the Burden of Empire: Soviet Oil, East-West Trade, and the End of the Socialist Bloc', in Jeronim Perović (ed.), *Cold War Energy: A Transnational History of Soviet Oil and Gas*, Cham: Palgrave Macmillan, 2017, pp. 345–69.

Kardaś, Szymon, *Great Ambitions: Russia Expands on the LNG Market*, OSW Commentary 394, Warsaw: Centre for Eastern Studies, 17 May 2021.

Kashurina, Anna, '1917–2017: Sto let vneshnei torgovli po-russki – II vypusk', *Proved*, 4 April 2017, http://провэд.рф/economics/fea/41508-1917-2017-sto-let-vneshney-topgovli-po-pusski-ii-vypusk.html (last accessed 13 July 2021).

Kaufman, Robert G., *Henry M. Jackson: A Life in Politics*, Seattle: University of Washington Press, 2000.

Kemp, John, 'Column: U.S. Gas Industry Increasingly Relies on LNG Exports', *Reuters*, 26 March 2021, www.reuters.com/article/us-column-global-gas-kemp-idUSKBN2BI2HV (last accessed 16 September 2021).

Khromov, Semen S., *Inostrannye kontsessii v SSSR: Istoricheskii ocherk; Dokumenty*, part I, Moscow: Institut rossiiskoi istorii RAN, 2006.

Leonid Krasin: Neizvestnye stranitsy biografii, 1920–1926 gg., Moscow: Institut rossiiskoi istorii RAN, 2001.

Kibita, Nataliya, *Soviet Economic Management Under Khrushchev: The Sovnarkhoz Reform*, London, New York: Routdledge, 2013.

Kireev, Maxim, 'Mega-Deal: Russland nimmt Gasleitung von Sibirien nach China in Betrieb', *MDR*, 2 December 2019, www.mdr.de/nachrichten/welt/osteuropa/ostblogger/russlands-globale-gasprojekte-nordstream-und-andere-pipelines100.html (last accessed 26 July 2021).

Klinghoffer, Arthur Jay, *The Soviet Union & International Oil Politics*, New York: Columbia University Press, 1977.

Kockel, Titus, *German Oil Policy 1928–1938*, Berlin: Akademie Verlag, 2015.

Koleva, G. Iu., 'Neft' vmesto uglia: Vliianie vengreskikh sobytii 1956 g. na izmeneiia v energeticheskoi politike SSSR', *Vestnik Tomskogo gosudarstvennogo universiteta*, 399 (2015), pp. 74–79.

'Strategiia razvitiia zapadno-sibirskogo neftegazogo kompleksa (1960–1980-e gg.)', *Vestnik Tomskogo gosudarstvennogo universiteta*, 1 (2007), pp. 95–102.

Kosnik, Joseph T., *Natural Gas Imports from the Soviet Union: Financing the North Star Joint Venture Project*, New York: Praeger, 1975.

Kostornichenko, V. N., 'Deiatel'nost' A. P. Serebrovskogo po modernizatsii otechestvennoi neftianoi promyshlennosti perioda NEPA: Privlechenie amerikanskogo kapitala', *Vestnik RUDN: Seriia 'Istoriia Rossii'*, 4 (2007), pp. 64–71.

Kosykh, E. S., 'Diskussii v RKP (b): Argumenty "za" i "protiv" inostrannykh kontsessii', *Universum: Obshchestvennye nauki; Elektron. nauchn. zhurn.*, 16, 6 (2015), http://7universum.com/ru/social/archive/item/2270 (last accessed 8 July 2021).

Krejci-Graf, K., *Erdöl: Naturgeschichte eines Rohstoffes*, 2nd rev. ed., Berlin, Göttingen, Heidelberg: Springer Verlag, 1955.

Krempin, Dunja, *Die sibirische Wucht: Der Aufstieg der Sowjetunion zur globalen Gasmacht, 1964–1982*, Osteuropa in Geschichte und Gegenwart 7, Vienna, Cologne, Weimar: Böhlau, 2020.

'Heroic "Black Gold"? Working for Oil and Gas in the Western Siberian Oil and Gas Complex of the 1960–1970s', in Touraj Atabaki, Elisabetta Bini, and Kaveh Ehsani (eds.), *Working for Oil: Comparative Social Histories of Labor in the Global Oil Industry*, Cham: Palgrave Macmillan, 2018, pp. 285–310.

'Rise of Western Siberia and the Soviet–West German Energy Relationship During the 1970s', in Jeronim Perović (ed.), *Cold War Energy: A Transnational History of Soviet Oil and Gas*, Cham: Palgrave Macmillan, 2017, pp. 253–81.

Krüger, Jochen, 'Entstalinisierung unter Chruschtschow', *dekoder*, 20 December 2018, www.dekoder.org/de/gnose/entstalinisierung-chruschtschow-geheimrede-tauwetter#fuss4 (last accessed 17 May 2021).

Laird, Robbin F., 'Soviet Arms Trade with the Noncommunist Third World', *Proceedings of the Academy of Political Science*, 35, 3 (1984), The Soviet Union in the 1980s, pp. 196–213.

Larsson, Robert L., *Russia's Energy Policy: Security Dimensions and Russia's Reliability as an Energy Supplier*, Stockholm: Swedish Defence Research Agency, 2006.

Lees, Lorraine M., *Keeping Tito Afloat: The United States, Yugoslavia, and the Cold War*, University Park: The Pennsylvania University Press, 1997.

Levin, M., and I. Sheveleva, 'Inostrannye kontsessii v 1920-kh godakh v SSSR: "Pochemu rasstalis'"?', *Voprosi ekonomiki*, 1 (2016), pp. 1–20.

Lieven, Anatol, *Chechnya: Tombstone of Russian Power*, New Haven, CT, London: Yale University Press, 1998.

Lippert, Werner D., *The Economic Diplomacy of Ostpolitik: Origins of NATO's Energy Dilemma*, New York: Berghahn, 2011.

Lozo, Ignaz, *Der Putsch gegen Gorbatschow und das Ende der Sowjetunion*, Cologne, Weimar, Vienna: Böhlau, 2014.

Lubell, Harold, *The Soviet Oil Offensive and Inter-Bloc Economic Competition*, Santa Monica, CA: RAND Corporation, 1961.

Lüthi, Lorenz, 'Drifting Apart: Soviet Energy and the Cohesion of the Communist Bloc in the 1970s and 1980s', in Jeronim Perović (ed.), *Cold War Energy: A Transnational History of Soviet Oil and Gas*, Cham: Palgrave Macmillan, 2017, pp. 371–99.

Maass, Peter, 'The Triumph of the Quiet Tycoon', *New York Times*, 1 August 2004, p. 24 (Section 6).

Machowski, Heinrich, 'Soviet–West German Economic Relations: The Soviet Perspective', in Angela E. Stent (ed.), *Economic Relations with the Soviet Union: American and West-German Perspectives*, Boulder, London: Westview Press, 1985, pp. 49–67.

Makarov, A. N., 'Die Anerkennung der Sowjetregierung durch die Vereinigten Staaten', *Zeitschrift für ausländisches Recht und Völkerrecht*, 4 (1934), pp. 1–24.

Maksan, Oliver, and René Höltschi, 'Deutschland stoppt Nord Stream 2 – doch beerdigt ist das Projekt noch nicht', *Neue Zürcher Zeitung*, 22 February 2022, www.nzz.ch/international/nord-stream-2-kanzler-scholz-stoppt-zertifizier ungsverfahren-ld.1671116 (last accessed 24 July 2022).

Mal'kevich, V. L., I. L. Mitrofanov, and A. S. Ivanov, *Vneshniaia torgovlia SSSR pri N. S. Patolicheve, 1958–1985 gg.*, Moscow: O-vo sokhraneniia literaturnogo naslediia, 2010.

Margolina, Sonja, 'Geographie und Herrschaft: Russland und das Öl – eine alte imperiale Strategie gelangt zu neuer Entfaltung', *Neue Zürcher Zeitung*, 13 July 2006, p. 25.

Matveichuk, Aleksandr, 'V tiskakh pervoi piatiletki', *Neft' Rossii*, 2 (2011), www .oilru.com/nr/214/5271/ (last accessed 7 July 2021)

Mautner, Wilhelm, 'Das russische Erdöl und die Petroleumpolitik', *Osteuropa*, 2, 5 (1927), pp. 241–60.

McFarland, Victor, *Oil Powers: A History of the U.S.-Saudi Alliance*, New York: Columbia University Press, 2020.

McMillan, Carl H., *Multinationals from the Second World: Growth of Foreign Investment by Soviet and East European Enterprises*, London: Macmillan Press, 1987.

McNabb, David E., *Oil and the Creation of Iraq: Policy Failures and the 1914–1918 War in Mesopotamia*, New York, London: Routledge, 2016.

'Miller, Aleksei: Predsedatel' pravleniia, zamestitel' predsedatelia soveta direktorov OAO "Gazprom"', *Lentapedia*, https://lenta.ru/lib/14160384/ (last accessed 10 September 2021).

Mitchell, Timothy, *Carbon Democracy: Political Power in the Age of Oil*, London: Verso, 2011.

More, Charles, *Black Gold: Britain and Oil in the Twentieth Century*, London: Bloomsbury, 2009.

Morgoliusov-Turkovskii, A. M., *Spravochnik po toplivu, osveditel'nym produktam i smazochnym materialam*, Moscow: Gosudarstvennoe tekhnicheskoe izdanie, 1926.

Moser, Nat, *Oil and the Economy of Russia: From the Late Tsarist to the Post-Soviet Period*, London, New York: Routledge, 2018.

Müller, Christian Th., 'Der Erdgas-Röhren-Konflikt 1981/82', in Bernd Greiner, Christian Th. Müller, and Claudia Weber (eds.), *Ökonomie im Kalten Krieg*, Studien zum Kalten Krieg 4, Hamburg: Hamburger Edition, 2010, pp. 501–20.

Jenseits der Materialschlacht: Der Erste Weltkrieg als Bewegungskrieg, Paderborn: Schöningh, 2018.

Müller, Clara, 'Zwischen Verhandlungsbereitschaft und Boykott: Grossbritannien und sowjetisches Erdöl 1920–1927', master's thesis, University of Zurich, 2019.

Munting, Roger, 'British Business and the Politics of Trade with the USSR during the New Economic Policy (NEP)', *Business History*, 48, 2 (2006), pp. 254–71.

Nekrasov, Viacheslav, 'Decision-Making in the Soviet Energy Sector in Post-Stalinist Times: The Failure of Khrushchev's Economic Modernization Strategy', in Jeronim Perović (ed.), *Cold War Energy: A Transnational History of Soviet Oil and Gas*, Cham: Palgrave Macmillan, 2017, pp. 165–99.

Nekrasov, V. L., *'Dilemma Khrushcheva': Reformy Gosplana SSSR, neftekhemicheskii proekt i vyzovy kholodnoi voiny (vtoraia polovina 1950-kh–pervaia polovina 1960-kh-godov)*, Moscow: Institut vseobshchei istorii RAN, 2019.

Neutatz, Dietmar, *Träume und Alpträume: Eine Geschichte Russlands im 20. Jahrhundert*, Munich: Beck, 2013.

Newnham, Randall, 'Oil, Carrots, and Sticks: Russia's Energy Resources as a Foreign Policy Tool', *Journal of Eurasian Studies*, 2, 2 (2011), pp. 134–43.

'Nord Stream 2: Arbeiten wieder aufgenommen', *ZDF heute*, 6 February 2021, www.zdf.de/nachrichten/politik/nord-stream-pipeline-arbeiten-wiederaufnahme-100.html (last accessed 10 September 2021).

Nove, Alec, *Das sowjetische Wirtschaftssystem*, Baden-Baden: Nomos, 1980.

'USSR: Economic Policy and Methods after 1970', in Alec Nove, Hans-Hermann Höhmann, and Gertraud Seidenstecher (eds.), *The East European Economies in the 1970s*, London: Butterworths, 1982, pp. 17–44.

Oblath, G., and P. Pete, 'Trade with the Soviet Union: The Finnish Case', *Acta Oeconomica*, 35, 1/2 (1985), pp. 165–94.

Olcott, Martha Brill, *The Energy Dimension in Russian Global Strategy: Vladimir Putin and the Geopolitics of Oil*, Houston, TX: The James A. Baker III Institute for Public Policy of the Rice University, 2004.

Oppenheimer, Peter, and Sergiy Maslichenko, 'Energy and the Economy: An Introduction', in Michael Ellman (ed.), *Russia's Oil and Natural Gas: Bonanza or Curse?*, London: Anthem Press, 2006, pp. 15–32.

Overland, Indra, 'Natural Gas and Russia–Turkmenistan Relations', *Russian Analytical Digest*, 56 (2009), pp. 9–13.

Owen, Edgar Wesley, *Trek of the Oil Finders: A History of Exploration for Petroleum*, Tulsa, OK: American Association of Petroleum Geologists, 1975.

Painter, David S., 'From Linkage to Economic Warfare: Energy, Soviet–American Relations, and the End of the Cold War', in Jeronim Perović (ed.), *Cold War Energy: A Transnational History of Soviet Oil and Gas*, Cham: Palgrave Macmillan, 2017, pp. 283–318.

'Oil and Geopolitics: The Oil Crises of the 1970s and the Cold War', *Historical Social Research*, 39, 4 (2014), pp. 186–208.

Parish, Scott D., and Mikhail M. Narinsky, *New Evidence on the Soviet Rejection of the Marshall Plan 1947: Two Reports*, Cold War International History Project, Working Paper 9, Washington, DC: Woodrow Wilson International Center for Scholars, 1994.

Patermann, Saskia, 'Das sind die grössten Öl- und Gaskonzerne der Welt', *Handelsblatt*, 23 February 2023, www.handelsblatt.com/unternehmen/energie/shell-total-bp-das-sind-die-groessten-oel-und-gaskonzerne-der-welt/25342258.html?utm_source=pocket-newtab-global-de-DE (last accessed 3 March 2023).

Perović, Jeronim, *Die Regionen Russlands als neue politische Kraft: Chancen und Gefahren des Regionalismus für Russland*, Bern: Peter Lang, 2001.

'Farce ums Gas: Russland, die Ukraine und die EU-Energiepolitik,' *Osteuropa*, 59, 1 (2009), pp. 19–35.

From Conquest to Deportation: The North Caucasus under Russian Rule, New York: Oxford University Press, 2018

'Russian Energy Power: Domestic and International Dimensions', in Jeronim Perović, Robert W. Orttung, and Andreas Wenger (eds.), *Russian Energy Power and Foreign Relations: Implications for Conflict and Cooperation*, London, New York: Routledge, 2009, pp. 1–20.

Russia's Future as an Energy Power, CSS Analyses in Security Policy 316, Zurich: Center for Security Studies, ETH Zurich, December 2022.

'Russlands Aufstieg zur Energiegrossmacht: Geschichte einer gesamteuropäischen Verflechtung', *Osteuropa*, 63, 7 (2013), pp. 5–28.

'Sucht nach Öl: Das "System Putin" und die Folgen der Wirtschaftskrise', *Russland-Analysen*, 313 (2016), pp. 2–7.

The Putin System, CSS Analyses in Security Policy 225, Zurich: Center for Security Studies, ETH Zurich, 2018.

'The Tito-Stalin Split: A Reassessment in Light of New Evidence', *Journal of Cold War Studies*, 9, 2 (2007), pp. 32–63.

Perović, Jeronim (ed.), *Cold War Energy: A Transnational History of Soviet Oil and Gas*, Cham: Palgrave Macmillan, 2017.

Perović, Jeronim, and Dunja Krempin, '"The Key Is in Our Hands": Soviet Energy Strategy during Détente and the Global Oil Crises of the 1970s', *Historical Social Research*, 39, 4 (2014), pp. 113–44.

Perović, Jeronim, and Maria Shagina, *Nord Stream 2: It's Time to Change Perspective*, CSS Policy Perspectives, Vol. 9/6, Zurich: Center for Security Studies, ETH Zurich, 2021.

Perović, Jeronim, and Robert W. Orttung, 'Russia's Role for Global Energy Security', in Andreas Wenger, Robert W. Orttung, and Jeronim Perović (eds.), *Energy and the Transformation of International Relations: Toward a New Producer-Consumer Framework*, The Oxford Institute for Energy Studies, Oxford: Oxford University Press, 2009, pp. 117–57.

Pezoldt, K., T. A. Lukičeva, and I. V. Vorob'eva, 'Russlands Mittelschicht in der Krise: Kauf- und Konsumverhalten im Wandel', *Osteuropa*, 67, 5 (2017), pp. 143–52.

Pichoia, R. G., *Sovetskii Soiuz: Istoriia vlasti 1945–1991*, Moscow: RAGS, 1998.

Pick, O., and A. Wiesman, 'Sputniks and Sausages: Soviet Drive for Consumer Goods', *The World Today*, 15, 12 (1959), pp. 472–81.

Pirani, Simon, *Ukraine's Gas Sector*, Oxford: The Oxford Institute for Energy Studies, 2007.

Pleines, Heiko, 'Der Staat als Eigentümer', *Russland-Analysen*, 217 (2011), pp. 29–30.

'Developing Russia's Oil and Gas Industry', in Jeronim Perović, Robert W. Orttung, and Andreas Wenger (eds.), *Russian Energy Power and Foreign Relations: Implications for Conflict and Cooperation*, London, New York: Routledge, 2009, pp. 71–86.

Poussenkova, Nina, 'All Quiet on the Eastern Front ...', *Russian Analytical Digest*, 33 (2008), pp. 13–18.

Prince, Todd, 'U.S. Efforts to Derail Russian Pipelines to Europe Have Failed since the 1960s: Will Nord Stream 2 Be Any Different?', *Radio Free Europe/Radio Liberty*, 13 August 2019, www.rferl.org/a/us-efforts-stop-russia-pipelines-will-nord-stream-2-be-different/30107938.html (last accessed 3 October 2019).

Radisch, Erik, *Der Rat für Gegenseitige Wirtschaftshilfe als Konsensimperium (1949–1971)*, Stuttgart: Franz Steiner Verlag, 2022.

Rainio-Niemi, Johanna, 'Neutrality as Compromises: Finland's Cold War Neutrality', in Mark Kramer, Aryo Makko, and Peter Ruggenthaler (eds.), *The Soviet Union and Cold War Neutrality and Nonalignment in Europe*, Lanham: Lexington Books, 2021, pp. 75–100.

Redwood, Boverton, 'The Future of Oil Fuel', *Journal of the Royal Society of Arts*, 62, 3188 (1913), pp. 103–16.

Rehschuh, Felix, *Aufstieg zur Energiemacht: Der sowjetische Weg ins Erdölzeitalter, 1930er bis 1950er Jahre*, Osteuropa in Geschichte und Gegenwart 1, Vienna, Cologne, Weimar: Böhlau, 2018.

Richter, Michael Martin, 'Russische kleine und mittlere Unternehmen (KMUs) in der Corona-Krise – Ein Sterben auf Raten', *Russland-Analysen*, 404 (2021), pp. 10–13.

Roberts, Glyn, *The Most Powerful Man in the World: The Life of Sir Henri Deterding*, New York: Covici Friede, 1938.

Rogers, Douglas, *The Depths of Russia: Oil, Power, and Culture after Socialism*, Ithaca, NY: Cornell University Press, 2015.

Roos, Johanna, *Sibirien zwischen Ökonomie und Politik: Zur Erschliessung der Energieträger Erdöl und Erdgas*, Cologne: Verlag Wissenschaft und Politik, 1984.

Rose, Euclid A., 'OPEC's Dominance of the Global Oil Market: The Rise of the World's Dependency on Oil', *Middle East Journal*, 58, 3 (2004), pp. 424–43.

Rosner, Kevin, *Gazprom and the Russian State*, London: GMB, 2005.

Ross, Michael L., *The Oil Curse: How Petroleum Wealth Shapes the Development of Nations*, Princeton, NJ: Princeton University Press, 2012.

Russell, Jeremy: *Energy as a Factor in Soviet Foreign Policy*, Lexington, MA, Farnborough 1976.

'Russia Pension Protests: Fresh Anti-Reform Rallies Held', *BBC News*, 2 September 2018, www.bbc.com/news/world-europe-45389797 (last accessed 28 May 2023).

'Russia's Tax Crisis', *New York Times*, 17 October 1996, p. 26 (Section A).

Rutland, Peter, 'Neoliberalism and the Russian Transition', *Review of International Political Economy*, 20, 2 (2013), pp. 332–62.

'The Political Economy of Energy in Russia', in Slawomir Raszewski (ed.), *The International Political Economy of Oil and Gas*, New York: Palgrave Macmillan, 2018, pp. 23–39.

Sakwa, Richard, *Putin and the Oligarch: The Khodorkovsky – Yukos Affair*, London: I. B. Tauris, 2014.

Salzmann, Stephanie, *Great Britain, Germany and the Soviet Union: Rapallo and After, 1922–1934*, Woodbridge: The Boydell Press, 2003.

Sanchez-Sibony, Oscar, *Red Globalization: The Political Economy of the Soviet Cold War from Stalin to Khrushchev*, Cambridge: Cambridge University Press, 2014.

Schattenberg, Susanne, *Leonid Breschnew: Staatsmann und Schauspieler im Schatten Stalins; Eine Biographie*, Cologne, Weimar, Vienna: Böhlau Verlag, 2017.

'Pipeline Construction as "Soft Power" in Foreign Policy: Why the Soviet Union Started to Sell Gas to West Germany, 1966–1970', *Journal of Modern European History* (2022), pp. 1–20, doi:10.1177/16118944221130222.

Scherrer, Jutta, '"To Catch Up and Overtake" the West: Soviet Discourse on Socialist Competition, in Katalin Miklóssy and Melanie Ilic (eds.), *Competition in Socialist Society*, London, New York: Routledge, 2014, pp. 10–22.

Schoenborn, Benedikt, *Reconciliation Road: Willy Brandt, Ostpolitik and the Quest for European Peace*, New York: Berghahn, 2020.

Schönfeld, Roland, 'The USA in the Economic Relations between East and West', *Soviet and Eastern European Foreign Trade*, 10, 1 (1974), pp. 3–18.

Schröder, Hans-Henning, 'Der Mineralölkonzern "Rosneft": Kommerzieller Erfolg und Einsatz politischer Machtmittel', *Russland-Analysen*, 348 (2018), pp. 9–13.

Schweizer, Peter, *Reagan's War: The Epic Story of His Forty-Year Struggle and Final Triumph Over Communism*, New York: Doubleday, 2002.

Victory: The Reagan Administration's Secret Strategy That Hastened the Collapse of the Soviet Union, New York: Atlantic Monthly Press, 1994.

Scott, Richard, *The History of the International Energy Agency*, vol. 1, The First 20 Years: Origins and Structure, Paris: IEA, 2004.

The History of the International Energy Agency, vol. 2, Major Policies and Actions, Paris: IEA, 2004.

'Sechin, Igor': Prezident NK "Rosneft"', *Lentapedia*, https://lenta.ru/lib/14160890/full.htm (last accessed 18 August 2021).

Semenov, B. A., 'Nuclear Power in the Soviet Union', *IAEA Bulletin*, 25, 2 (1983), pp. 47–59.

Semjonow, Juri, *Erdöl aus dem Osten: Die Geschichte der Erdöl- und Erdgasindustrie in der Sowjetunion*, Düsseldorf: Econ, 1973.

Sergeeva, Ts. Kh., 'Bor'ba za neft', teoreticheskie diskussii i stanovlenie sovetskoi modeli upravleniia neftianoi otrasl'iu 1910–1940-e gg.', *Vestnik Kazanskogo tekhnicheskogo universiteta*, 15, 5 (2012), pp. 154–62.

Shagina, Maria, and Kirsten Westphal, *Nord Stream 2 and the Energy Security Dilemma: Opportunities, Options and Obstacles for a Grand Bargain*, SWP Comment 46, Berlin: SWP, German Institute for International and Security Affairs, 2021.

Shalkus, G. A., 'Sozdanie i deiatel'nost' iaponskikh kontsessii na Severnom Sakhaline v 1925–1944 gg.', *Sibirskii torgovo-ekonomicheskii zhurnal*, 7 (2008), pp. 87–91.

Shilnikova, Irina V., 'Foreign Concessions in the USSR Textile Industry in the 1920s and early 1930s: The Public-Private Partnership Experience', *Russian Journal of Economics*, 7 (2021), pp. 160–84.

Shpotov, B. M., 'Ispol'yovanie opyta SShA v rekonstruktsii sovetskoi neftianoi promyshlennosti v 1920–30-e gg.', *Rossiiskii zhurnal' menedzhmenta*, 4, 1 (2006), pp. 163–78.

Sicotte, Jonathan, 'Alexandr Serebrovskii and the Modernization of the Soviet Oil Industry – 1924 to 1929', *The Soviet and Post-Soviet Review* (2021), pp. 1–30, https://doi.org/10.30965/18763324-BJA10032 (last accessed 16 August 2021).

Siddiqi, Asif A., *Sputnik and the Soviet Space Challenge*, Gainesville: University Press of Florida, 2003.

Siegel, Katherine, *Loans and Legitimacy: The Evolution of Soviet-American Relations 1919–1933*, Lexington: The University Press of Kentucky, 1996.

Siegelbaum, Lewis H., *Cars for Comrades: The Life of the Soviet Automobile*, Ithaca, NY: Cornell University Press, 2008.

(ed.), *The Socialist Car: Automobility in the Eastern Bloc*, Ithaca, NY: Cornell University Press, 2011.

Sim, Li-Chen, *The Rise and Fall of Privatization in the Russian Oil Industry*, Basingstoke, New York: Palgrave Macmillan, 2008.

Simola, Heli, and Laura Solanko, *Overview of Russia's Oil and Gas Sector*, BOFIT Policy Brief 5, Helsinki: Bank of Finland, BOFIT – Institute for Economies in Transition, 2017, pp. 30–31.

Sitariu, Mihaela, 'British-Romanian Relations during the Cold War', PhD thesis, Western University, London [Canada], 2013.

Slavkina, M. V., *Neftegazovyi faktor v otechestvennoi modernizatsii 1939–2008*, Moscow: Ves' mir, 2015.

Triumf i tragediia: Razvitie neftegazogo kompleksa SSSR v 1960–1980-e gody, Moscow: Nauka, 2002.

Sokolov, A. K., 'Sovetskii "Neftesindikat" na vnutrennem i mezhdunarodnom rynkakh v 1920-e gg.', in L. I. Borodkina (ed.), *Ekonomicheskaia istoriia: Obozrenie*, vol. 10, Moscow: n.p., 2005, pp. 101–31.

Spaskovska, Ljubica, '"Crude" Alliance – Economic Decolonisation and Oil Power in the Non-aligned World', *Contemporary European History*, 30, 4 (2021), pp. 528–43.

Spohn, W., 'The Soviet Union's Technological Dependence on the World Market: Report and Commentary on an Empirical Study by A. C. Sutton (1)', *PROKLA: Zeitschrift für Kritische Sozialwissenschaft*, 5, 19/20/21 (1975), pp. 225–59.

Stanislavets, Dar'ia, 'Privatizatsii v Rossii 20 let: Istoriia s prodolzheniem', *Praim*, 9 June 2012, https://1prime.ru/Financial_market/20120609/757520789.html (last accessed 6 August 2021).

Stark, Tamás, '"Malenki Robot" – Hungarian Forced Labourers in the Soviet Union (1944–1955)', *Minorities Research*, 7 (2005), pp. 155–67.

Steiner, André, *Von Plan zu Plan: Eine Wirtschaftsgeschichte der DDR*, Munich: Deutsche Verlags-Anstalt, 2004.

Steiner, Eduard, 'Putin hortet viele Milliarden Dollar aus den Ölverkäufen', *Welt*, 15 July 2018, www.welt.de/wirtschaft/article179355200/Nationaler-Wohlfahrtsfonds-Putin-hortet-viele-Milliarden-Dollar-aus-den-Oelverkaeufen.html (last accessed 7 August 2021).

Stent, Angela, *From Embargo to Ostpolitik: The Political Economy of West German-Soviet Relations, 1955–1980*, Cambridge: Cambridge University Press, 1981.

Stern, Jonathan P., 'Soviet Natural Gas in the World Economy', in Robert G. Jensen, Theodore Shabad, and Artur W. Wright (eds.), *Soviet Natural Resources in the World Economy*, Chicago, London: The University of Chicago Press, 1983, pp. 363–84.

Stüwe, Robert, 'Unpacking the German Debate on Nord Stream 2', *Russian Analytical Digest*, 267 (2021), pp. 5–14.

Sulick, Michael J., *American Spies: Espionage against the US from the Cold War to the Present*, Washington, DC: Georgetown University Press, 2013.

Sutton, Antony C., *Western Technology and Soviet Economic Development 1917 to 1930*, 2nd ed., Stanford, CA: Hoover Institution on War, Revolution and Peace, 1970.

Tabata, Shinichiro, 'Price Differences, Taxes and the Stabilization Fund', in Michael Ellman (ed.), *Russia's Oil and Natural Gas: Bonanza or Curse?*, London: Anthem Press, 2006, pp. 35–54.

Taubinger, László von, 'Die sowjetisch-rumänischen Gesellschaften', *Osteuropa*, 5, 2 (1956), pp. 145–49.

Technology & Soviet Energy Availability, Washington, DC: United States Government Printing Office, 1981.

Thornthon, Judith, 'Resource Valuation and the Efficiency of Soviet Resource Production and Use', in Robert Jensen, Theodore Shabad, and Arthur W. Wright (eds.), *Soviet Natural Resources in the World Economy*, Chicago, London: The University of Chicago Press, 1983, pp. 597–613.

Tolf, Robert W., *The Russian Rockefellers: The Saga of the Nobel Family and the Russian Oil Industry*, Stanford, CA: Hoover Institution Press, 1976.

Tompson, William, 'Putin and the "Oligarchs": A Two-sided Commitment Problem', in Alex Pravda (ed.), *Leading Russia: Putin in Perspective; Essays in Honour of Archie Brown*, Oxford: Oxford University Press, 2005, pp. 179–203.

Toninelli, Pier Angelo, 'Energy Supply and Economic Development in Italy: The Role of State Owned Companies', in Alain Beltran (ed.), *A Comparative History of National Oil Companies*, Brussels: Peter Lang, 2010, pp. 125–42.

Tordo, Silvana, Brandon S. Tracy, and Noora Arfaa, *National Oil Companies and Value Creation*, World Bank Working Paper 218, Washington, DC: The World Bank, 2011.

Trachtenberg, J., 'The Soviet Oil Offensive', *The Living Age* (September 1933), pp. 35–37.

Treisman, Daniel, 'Russia's Taxing Problem', *Foreign Policy*, 112 (1998), pp. 55–66.

Treml, Vladimir G., 'Soviet Dependence on Foreign Trade', Paper presented at Colloquium on 'External Economic Relations of CMEA Countries: Their Significance and Impact in a Global Perspective', Brussels, NATO, Economics Directorate, 6–8 April 1983.

Treml, Vladimir G., and Barry L. Kostinsky, *Domestic Value of Soviet Foreign Trade: Exports and Imports in the 1972 Input-Output Table*, Foreign Economic Report 20, Washington, DC: United States Department of Commerce, Bureau of the Census, 1982.

Trofimuk, A. A., *O rabote sibirskogo otdeleniia AN SSSR po kooperatsii nauchnykh issledovanii v regione i ispol'sovaniiu ikh resultatov v narodnom khoziastve strany: Osnovnye napravleniia organisatsionnoe soprovozhdenie i effektivnost' rabot po program 'Sibir'*, Novosibirsk: IEOPP SO AN SSSR, 1988.

Turner, Barry, *Suez 1956: The Inside Story of the First Oil War*, London: Hodder & Stoughton, 2006.

Tverberg, Gail E., 'Oil Prices and the Fall of the Soviet Union', *OilPrice.com*, 11 August 2011, https://oilprice.com/Energy/Oil-Prices/Oil-Prices-And-The-Fall-Of-The-Soviet-Union.html (last accessed 18 July 2021).

Vale, Michel, and Jochen Bethkenhagen, 'The Development of GDR Economic Relations with the USSR', *International Journal of Politics*, 12, 1/2 (1982), GDR Foreign Policy (Part II), pp. 232–60.

Venn, Fiona, *The Oil Crisis*, London: Routledge, 2002.

'Vladimir Putin vstretilsia s rukovoditeliami riada krupneishikh kompanii i kommercheskikh bankov Rossii', 28 July 2000, Moscow, Kremlin, http://kremlin.ru/events/president/news/38471 (last accessed 21 July 2021).

Ward, Christopher J., *Brezhnev's Folly: The Building of BAM and Late Soviet Socialism*, Pittsburgh: University of Pittsburgh Press, 2009.

Watson, James, 'Foreign Investment in Russia: The Case of the Oil Industry', *Europe-Asia Studies*, 48, 3 (1996), pp. 429–55.

Weber, Claudia, *Der Pakt: Stalin, Hitler und die Geschichte einer mörderischen Allianz 1939–1945*, Munich: Beck, 2019.

Wenzel, Siegfried, 'Die DDR-Wirtschaft im Spannungsfeld zwischen objektiven Bedingungen und Politik der SED', in Ludwig Elm, Dietmar Keller, and Reinhard Mocek (eds.), *Ansichten zur Geschichte der DDR*, vol. 6, Wirtschaft, Eggersdorf: Verlag Matthias Kirchner, 1996, pp. 89–164.

Westad, Odd Arne, *The Global Cold War*, Cambridge: Cambridge University Press, 2007.

White, Christine A., *British & American Commercial Relations with Soviet Russia, 1918–1924*, Chapel Hill: University of North Carolina Press,1992.

White, David, 'The Petroleum Resources of the World', *The Annals of the American Academy of Political and Social Science*, 89 (1920), pp. 111–34.

Wiegert, Ralf, 'Die russische Steuerreform – neuer Schub für höheres Wachstum?', in Paul J. J. Welfens and Ralf Wiegert (eds.), *Transformationskrise und neue Wirtschaftsreformen in Russland*, Heidelberg: Physica-Verlag, 2002, pp. 97–118.

Williams, Andrew J., *Trading with the Bolsheviks: The Politics of East–West Trade, 1920–39*, Manchester, New York: Manchester University Press,1992.

Wörmann, Claudia, *Osthandel als Problem der atlantischen Allianz: Erfahrungen aus dem Erdgas-Röhren-Geschäft mit der UdSSR*, Bonn: Europa Union Verlag, 1986.

Yergin, Daniel, *The Prize: The Epic Quest for Oil, Money, and Power*, New York: Free Press, 2009.

Yodfat, Aryeh Y., *The Soviet Union and Revolutionary Iran*, London: Croom Helm, 1984.

Zachmann, Karin, 'Past and Present Energy Societies', in Nina Möller and Karin Zachmann (eds.), *Past and Present Energy Societies: How Energy Connects Politics, Technologies and Cultures*, Bielefeld: transcript, 2012, pp. 7–41.

Zadorozhnyi, Aleksandr, '"Ne pripomniu lichnosti so stol' tragicheski razdvoennym soznaniem": Posle Stalina; Kak Nikita Khrushchev pytalsia izmenit' SSSR i shto iz etogo vyshlo', 17 April 2019, www.znak.com/2019-04-17/posle_stalina_kak_nikita_hruchev_pytalsya_izmenit_sssr_i_chto_iz_etogo_vyshlo (last accessed 17 May 2021).

Zagorul'ko, M. M., V. V. Bulatov, and V. N. Kostornichenko, *'Vikkers' v Rossii*, Volgograd: Izd-vo VolGU, 2012.

Zolotova, I. P., 'Opyt ispol'zovaniia kontsessii v narodnom khoziaistve Rossii', *Vestnik BNTU*, 4 (2010), pp. 75–80.

'Zhivye golosa istorii: God 1984-i, Gazprom komplektatsiia', *Press-tsentr, novosti*, 14 January 2019, https://komplektatsiya.gazprom.ru/press/news/2019/01/319/ (last accessed 18 August 2021).

Index